CONCENTRATE Q&A
COMPANY LAW

CONCENTRATE
Q&A
COMPANY LAW

Imogen Moore

Lecturer in Law
University of Reading

OXFORD
UNIVERSITY PRESS

OXFORD

UNIVERSITY PRESS

Great Clarendon Street, Oxford, OX2 6DP,
United Kingdom

Oxford University Press is a department of the University of Oxford.
It furthers the University's objective of excellence in research, scholarship,
and education by publishing worldwide. Oxford is a registered trade mark of
Oxford University Press in the UK and in certain other countries

Published in the United States of America by Oxford University Press
198 Madison Avenue, New York, NY 10016, United States of America

British Library Cataloguing in Publication Data
Data available

Library of Congress Control Number: 2016942461

ISBN 978–0–19–874522–8

Printed in Great Britain by
Bell & Bain Ltd., Glasgow

Contents

Editor's acknowledgements   vi

Preface   ix

Guide to the book   x

Guide to the Online Resource Centre   xi

Table of cases   xii

Table of legislation   xix

1 Exam Skills for Success in Company Law   1

2 Companies and Corporate Personality   4

3 The Corporate Constitution   29

4 Shares and Shareholders   50

5 Directors' Duties   70

6 Company Management and Governance   100

7 Minority Shareholder Remedies   121

8 Corporate Liability: Contracts, Torts, and Crimes   142

9 Share Capital   163

10 Loan Capital   184

11 Corporate Insolvency   200

12 Mixed Topic Questions   226

13 Skills for Success in Coursework Assessments   246

Index   249

Editor's acknowledgements

The brand-new Concentrate Q&A series from Oxford University Press has been developed alongside hundreds of students and lecturers from a range of universities across the UK.

I'd like to take this opportunity to thank all those law students who've filled in questionnaires, completed in-depth reviews of sample materials, attended focus groups, and provided us with the insight and feedback we needed to shape a series relevant for today's law students.

Also to the lecturers the length and breadth of the UK who have given so generously of their time by being heavily involved in our lengthy review process; their inside information gained from experience as teachers and examiners has been vital in the shaping of this new series.

You told us that you wanted a Q&A book that:

- gives you tips to help you understand exactly what the question is asking
- offers focused guidance on how to structure your answer and develop your arguments
- uses clear and simple diagrams to help you see how to structure your answers at a glance
- highlights key debates and extra points for you to add to your answers to get the highest marks
- flags common mistakes to avoid when answering questions
- offers detailed advice on coursework assignments as well as exams
- provides focused reading suggestions to help you develop in-depth knowledge for when you are looking for the highest marks
- is accompanied by a great range of online support

We listened and we have delivered.

We are confident that because they provide exactly what you told us you need, the Concentrate Q&As offer you better support and a greater chance for succeeding than any competing series.

We wish you all the best throughout your law course and in your exams and hope that these guides give you the confidence to tackle any question that you encounter, and give you the skills you need to excel during your studies and beyond.

Good luck
Carol Barber, Senior Publishing Editor

This is what you said:

'The content is exceptional; the best Q&A books that I've read'

Wendy Chinenye Akaigwe, law student, London Metropolitan University

'Since I started using the OUP Q&A guides my grades have dramatically improved'

Glen Sylvester, law student, Bournemouth University

'A sure-fire way to get a 1st class result'

Naomi M, law student, Coventry University

'100% would recommend. Makes you feel like you will pass with flying colours'

Elysia Marie Vaughan, law student, University of Hertfordshire

'Excellent. Very detailed which makes a change from the brief answers in other Q&A books . . . fantastic'

Frances Easton, law student, University of Birmingham

This is what your lecturers said:

'Much more substantial and less superficial than competitor Q&As. Some guides are rather too simplistic but the OUP guides are much better than the norm'

Dr Tony Harvey, Principal law lecturer, Liverpool John Moores University

'Cleverly and carefully put together. Every bit as good as one would expect from OUP, you really have cornered the market in the revision guides sector. I am also a huge fan of the OUP Concentrate series and I think that these books sit neatly alongside this'

Alice Blythe, law lecturer, University of Bolton

'I think Q&A guides are crucial and advise my students to buy early on'

Loretta Trickett, law lecturer, Nottingham Trent University

'Students often lack experience in writing full answers but seeing suggested answers like this provides them with confidence and structure. I will be recommending this book to my students not just for revision purposes but for the duration of the unit'

Nick Longworth, law lecturer, Manchester Metropolitan University

Preface

Concentrate Q&A Company Law is designed to assist your learning, understanding and revision of company law. It covers the core topics featured in most company law courses (including corporate personality, the constitution, shares and share capital, directors' duties, and shareholder remedies), and many related topics such as corporate governance and corporate insolvency. The text has been substantially rewritten and rearranged, and includes many new features to aid your study of the subject and help you develop your skills in answering company law questions. This edition incorporates recent legal developments both in the courts (including *Eclairs Group Ltd v JKX Oil & Gas* [2015] UKSC 71 in the Supreme Court) and statute (including changes made by **Small Business Enterprise and Employment Act 2015**).

While this book functions generally as an aid to study and revision (reminding you of the various topics you have studied and how they interrelate), it is written in particular with a view to final examinations in company law, showing you how issues might be effectively explained and analysed in the context of exam questions. With the time constraints of exams in mind the answers do not exceed 1,500 words. Separate chapters providing more general advice on approaching company law exams and coursework are also provided.

The answers in this book should not be viewed as 'model answers' that you could simply repeat in any exam—even if that were academically acceptable (it isn't!), the questions you face will of course be different from the ones here. Instead you should use the book to develop your understanding, and the skills you need to answer your exam questions. By working through the questions and answers (ideally attempting each question yourself before reading the answer provided), you can test your knowledge and understanding, and develop your skills in applying that to essays and problems.

This new *Concentrate Q&A Company Law* is the first without direct input from Stephen Judge, but I hope his influence lingers—not least in the breadth, depth, and clarity of coverage that I have attempted to maintain. Sincere thanks to him for passing on a text that has been a pleasure to develop. I must also thank the team at OUP who have shown such enthusiasm and appreciation of student needs in the development of this series; with particular thanks to Lucy Hyde for her apparently boundless patience and good cheer.

Teaching company law is stimulating, challenging, and (almost) always enjoyable. It would not be so had I not been blessed with so many wonderful colleagues and students. My company law colleagues provide invaluable support, encouragement, ideas, and fun—in recent years I must thank in particular Laura Bennett, Peter Bailey, Luke Price, and Onyeka Osuji, although with all due acknowledgement that any errors and idiosyncrasies in this text are entirely my own. My students—past and present—continue to provide inspiration, motivation, and a great deal of humour—thank you all. Finally (though not in importance)—my family: thank you for your continued love, support, and patience.

Whatever the stage you are at in your company law journey, I hope you find this book useful in your studies and wish you every success. This edition states the law as known to the author on 12 January 2016.

Imogen Moore
January 2016

Guide to the book

Every book in the Concentrate Q&A series contains the following features:

ARE YOU READY?

Are you ready to face the exam? This box at the start of each chapter identifies the key topics and cases that you need to have learned, revised, and understood before tackling the questions in each chapter.

DIAGRAM ANSWER PLANS

Not sure where to begin? Clear diagram answer plans at the start of each question help you see how to structure your answer at a glance, and take you through each point step-by-step.

KEY DEBATES

Demonstrating your knowledge of the crucial debates is a sure-fire way to impress examiners. These at-a-glance boxes help remind you of the key debates relevant to each topic, which you should discuss in your answers to get the highest marks.

SUGGESTED ANSWER

What makes a great answer great? Our authors show you the thought process behind their own answers, and how you can do the same in your exam. Key sentences are highlighted and advice is given on how to structure your answer well and develop your arguments.

QUESTION

Each question represents a typical essay or problem question so that you know exactly what to expect in your exam.

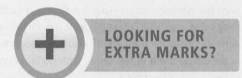

LOOKING FOR EXTRA MARKS?

Don't settle for a good answer—make it great! This feature gives you extra points to include in the exam if you want to gain more marks and make your answer stand out.

CAUTION!

Don't fall into any traps! This feature points out common mistakes that students make, and which you need to avoid when answering each question.

TAKING THINGS FURTHER

Really push yourself and impress your examiner by going beyond what is expected. Focused further reading suggestions allow you to develop in-depth knowledge of the subject for when you are looking for the highest marks.

Guide to the Online Resource Centre

Every book in the Concentrate Q&A series is supported by additional online materials to aid your study and revision: www.oxfordtextbooks.co.uk/orc/qanda

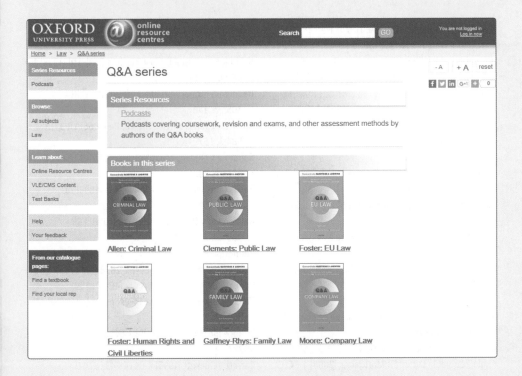

- ● Extra essay and problem questions.
- ● Bonus questions to help you practise and refine your technique. Questions are annotated, highlighting key terms and legal issues to help you plan your own answers. An indication of what your answers should cover is also provided.
- ● Online versions of the diagram answer plans.

- ● Video guidance on how to put an answer plan together.
- ● Flashcard glossaries of key terms.
- ● Audio advice on revision and exam technique from Nigel Foster.
- ● Audio advice on coursework technique.
- ● Audio advice on other assessment methods, for example MCQs, presentations, or mooting.

Table of cases

A and BC Chewing Gum Ltd, Re [1975] 1 All ER 1017; [1975] 1 WLR 579 . . . 47, 138

A Company, Re [1985] BCLC 333 . . . 19

A Company, Re (No 836 of 1995) [1996] BCLC 192 . . . 134, 139

ABC Coupler & Engineering Ltd, Re [1961] 1 WLR 243 . . . 209

Adams v Cape Industries plc [1990] Ch 433 . . . 19, 20, 21, 23, 25, 229, 230

Agnew v IRC; Re Brumark Investments Ltd [2001] 2 AC 710 . . . 184, 187, 188, 189

Airbase (UK) Ltd, Re [2008] EWHC 124 (Ch) . . . 213

Albazero, The [1977] AC 774 . . . 20

Alexander Ward and Co Ltd v Samyang Navigation Co Ltd [1975] 1 WLR 673 . . . 103

Allen v Gold Reefs of West Africa Ltd [1900] 1 Ch 656 . . . 32, 37, 42, 66, 102, 233

Allen v Hyatt (1914) 30 TLR 444 . . . 72

Aluminium Industrie Vaassen v Romalpa Aluminium [1976] 1 WLR 676 . . . 216

Andrews v Gas Meter Co [1897] 1 Ch 361 . . . 60

Anglo Petroleum Ltd v TFB Mortgages [2008] 1 BCLC 185 . . . 180

Antonio v Antonio [2010] EWHC 1199 . . . 44

Antonio Gramsci Shipping Corporation v Lembergs [2013] EWCA Civ 730 . . . 25, 26

Arab Bank plc v Mercantile Holdings Ltd [1994] 2 All ER 74 . . . 179

Armagh Shoes Ltd, Re [1984] BCLC 405 . . . 187

Arthur D Little Ltd (In Administration) v Ableco Finance LLC [2003] Ch 217 . . . 188, 191

Ashbury Railway Carriage and Iron Co Ltd v Riche (1875) LR 7 HL 653 . . . 148, 153

Astec (BSR) plc, Re [1998] 2 BCLC 556 . . . 130

Attorney General of Belize v Belize Telecom Ltd [2009] UKPC 10 . . . 37

Attorney-General's Reference (No 2 of 1982) [1984] QB 624 . . . 12

Attorney-General's Reference (No 2 of 1999) [2000] QB 796 . . . 159

Automatic Self-Cleansing Filter Syndicate Co Ltd v Cuninghame [1906] 2 Ch 34 . . . 102, 111

Aveling Barford Ltd v Perion [1989] BCLC 626 . . . 176

B. Liggett (Liverpool) Ltd v Barclays Bank Ltd [1928] 1 KB 48 . . . 155

Badgerhill Properties Ltd v Cottrell [1991] BCLC 805 . . . 146

Bahia and San Francisco Rly Co, Re (1868) LR 3 QB 584 . . . 57

Bairstow v Queens Moat Houses plc [2001] 2 BCLC 531 . . . 83, 176

Balkis Consolidated Co v Tomkinson [1893] AC 396 . . . 57

Balston Ltd v Headline Filters Ltd [1990] FSR 385 . . . 91

Bamford v Bamford [1970] Ch 212 . . . 58, 78

Bamford v Harvey [2012] EWHC 2858 (Ch) . . . 124, 128

Bank of India [2005] EWCA Civ 693 . . . 159

Barclays Bank v Quistclose Investments Ltd [1970] AC 567 . . . 216

Barings plc (No 5), Re [2000] 1 BCLC 523 . . . 82, 86, 222

Barrett v Duckett [1995] 1 BCLC 243 . . . 125

Barron v Potter [1914] 1 Ch 895 . . . 103

Barton Manufacturing Ltd, Re [1999] 1 BCLC 740 . . . 217

Bayoil SA, Re [1999] 1 WLR 147 . . . 208, 209

Beattie v E & F Beattie Ltd [1938] Ch 708 . . . 36, 40

Beckett Investment Management Group Ltd v Hall [2007] ICR 1539 . . . 20

Bell v Lever Bros [1932] AC 161 . . . 82

Bell Houses Ltd v City Wall Properties Ltd [1966] 1 QB 207 . . . 153

Belmont Finance Corpn Ltd v Williams Furniture Ltd [1979] Ch 250 . . . 179, 182

Belmont Finance Corpn Ltd v Williams Furniture Ltd (No 2) [1980] 1 All ER 393 . . . 181

Ben Hashem v Ali Shayif [2009] 1 FLR 115 . . . 20, 24, 25

Bentinck v Fenn (1887) 12 App Cas 652 . . . 244

Bhullar v Bhullar [2003] 2 BCLC 241 . . . 90

Birch v Cropper (1889) 14 App Cas 25 . . . 61

Bird Precision Bellows Ltd, Re [1984] Ch 419 . . . 138

Bishopsgate Investment Management Ltd v Maxwell (No 2) [1994] 1 All ER 261 . . . 87

BNY Corporate Trustee Services Ltd v Eurosail-UK plc [2013] UKSC 28 . . . 207, 208

Borland's Trustee v Steel Brothers & Co Ltd [1901] 1 Ch 279 . . . 51, 53

Boulting v Association of Cinematograph, Television and Allied Technicians [1963] 2 QB 606 . . . 81

Bradford Investments plc (No 2), Re [1991] BCLC 688 . . . 166, 170

Brady v Brady [1989] AC 755 . . . 177, 180, 181, 182

Bratton Seymour Service Co Ltd v Oxborough [1992] BCLC 693 . . . 34, 35, 37, 44, 53, 233

Bray v Ford [1896] AC 44 . . . 89

Braymist Ltd v Wise Finance Co Ltd [2002] Ch 273 . . . 144

Brazilian Rubber Plantations and Estates Ltd, Re [1911] 1 Ch 425 . . . 86

Brian D Pierson Ltd, Re [1999] BCC 26 . . . 221

Brightlife Ltd, Re [1987] Ch 200 . . . 187

British America Nickel Corpn Ltd v O'Brien Ltd [1927] AC 369 . . . 67

British and Commonwealth Holdings plc v Barclays Bank plc [1996] 1 WLR 1 . . . 179

Brooks v Armstrong [2015] EWHC 2289 (Ch) . . . 221

Brumark Investments Ltd, Re see Agnew v IRC

Bugle Press Ltd, Re [1961] Ch 270 . . . 20

Bushell v Faith [1970] AC 1099 . . . 31, 42, 46, 66, 104, 111

Campbell v Paddington Corporation [1911] 1 KB 869 . . . 157

Canadian Aero Service Ltd v O'Malley (1973) 40 DLR (3d) 371 . . . 90, 239

Cane v Jones [1980] 1 WLR 1451 . . . 31, 44

Capitol Films Ltd, Re [2010] EWHC 2240 (Ch) . . . 154

Cardiff Savings Bank, Re; Marquis of Bute's Case [1892] 2 Ch 100 . . . 86

Carlen v Drury (1812) 35 ER 63 . . . 232

Carney v Herbert [1985] 1 All ER 438 . . . 181

CAS (Nominees) Ltd v Nottingham Forest FC plc [2002] 1 BCLC 613 . . . 77

Chandler v Cape Industries plc [2012] 1 WLR 3111 . . . 21

Charnley Davies Ltd (No 2), Re [1990] BCLC 760 . . . 130

Charterbridge Corporation v Lloyds Bank Ltd [1970] Ch 62 . . . 81–2

Charterhouse Investment Trust Ltd v Tempest Diesels Ltd [1986] BCLC 1 . . . 180

Chatterley-Whitfield Colliers Ltd, Re [1948] 2 All ER 593, CA; aff'd sub nom Prudential Assurance Co Ltd v Chatterley-Whitfield Collieries Ltd [1949] AC 512, HL . . . 62

Cheyne Finance Ltd, Re [2008] 1 BCLC 741 . . . 207

Chez Nico (Restaurants) Ltd, Re [1992] BCLC 192 . . . 72

Citco Banking Corporation NV v Pusser's Ltd [2007] BCC 205 . . . 33

City Equitable Fire Insurance Co Ltd, Re [1925] Ch 407 . . . 82, 85, 86, 87

CL Nye Ltd, Re [1971] Ch 442 . . . 193

Clayton's Case (1816) 1 Mer 572 . . . 218

Clough Mill v Martin [1985] BCLC 64 . . . 216

Cohen v Selby [2001] 1 BCLC 176 . . . 87, 244

Coleman v Myers [1977] 2 NZLR 225 . . . 72

Colin Gwyer and Associates Ltd v London Wharf (Limehouse) Ltd [2003] 2 BCLC 153 . . . 74

Coloursource Ltd, Re [2005] BCC 627 . . . 59

Commonwealth Oil & Gas Co Ltd v Baxter [2009] CSIH 75 . . . 82

Continental Assurance Co of London plc, Re [1997] 1 BCLC 48 . . . 182

Cornhill Insurance v Improvement Services [1986] BCLC 26 . . . 207

Coroin Ltd, Re; McKillen v Misland (Cyprus) Investments Ltd [2013] EWCA Civ 781 . . . 134, 135, 137

Cosslett (Contractors) Ltd, Re [2002] 1 BCLC 77 . . . 188, 192

Cotman v Brougham [1918] AC 514 . . . 153

Cotronic (UK) Ltd v Dezonie [1991] BCLC 721 . . . 146

Cream Holdings Ltd v Davenport [2010] EWHC 3096 (Ch) . . . 37

Creasey v Beachwood Motors Ltd [1993] BCLC 480 . . . 20

Cumbrian Newspapers Group Ltd v Cumberland & Westmorland Herald Newspaper & Printing Co Ltd [1987] Ch 1; [1986] BCLC 286 . . . 32, 42, 52, 66, 233

Dafen Tinplate Co Ltd v Llanelly Steel Co (1907) Ltd [1920] 2 Ch 124 . . . 32

Daimler Co Ltd v Continental Tyre and Rubber Co (Great Britain) Ltd [1916] 2 AC 307 . . . 19

Daniels v Daniels [1978] Ch 406 . . . 124

Denney v John Hudson [1992] BCLC 901 . . . 214

DHN Food Distributors Ltd v Tower Hamlets London Borough Council [1976] 1 WLR 852 . . . 19, 20

Dimbleby v National Union of Journalists [1984] 1 WLR 427 . . . 19

D'Jan of London Ltd, Re [1994] 1 BCLC 561 . . . 86, 87

DKG Contractors Ltd, Re [1990] BCC 903 . . . 12, 221, 244

DKLL Solicitors v HMRC [2008] 1 BCLC 112 . . . 205

Dorchester Finance Co Ltd v Stebbing [1989] BCLC 498 . . . 82, 86

DPP v Kent and Sussex Contractors Ltd [1944] KB 146 . . . 157

Duckwari plc, Re [1999] Ch 253 . . . 92

Duomatic Ltd, Re [1969] 2 Ch 365 . . . 44

Ebrahimi v Westbourne Galleries Ltd [1973] AC 360 . . . 130, 132, 137, 138, 235

Eclairs Group Ltd v JKX Oil plc [2015] UKSC 71 . . . 76, 77, 78, 238

Eddystone Marine Insurance Co, Re [1893] 3 Ch 9 . . . 165, 237

Edwards v Halliwell [1950] 2 All ER 1064 . . . 123

EIC Services Ltd v Phipps [2004] 2 BCLC 589 . . . 155

Eley v Positive Government Security Life Assurance Co Ltd (1876) 1 Ex D 88 . . . 36, 40, 41

Elgindata Ltd, Re [1991] BCLC 959 . . . 132

Equitable Life Assurance Society v Hyman [2002] 1 AC 408 . . . 37

Erlanger v New Sombrero Phosphate Co (1878) 3 App Cas 1218 . . . 17

Exchange Banking Co, Re, Flitcroft's Case (1882) 21 Ch D 519 . . . 174

Extrasure Travel Insurances Ltd v Scattergood [2003] 1 BCLC 598 . . . 76, 77, 243

F & E Stanton Ltd, Re [1929] 1 Ch 180 . . . 196

Fairline Shipping Co v Adamson [1974] 2 All ER 967 . . . 12

Fairway Magazines Ltd, Re [1992] BCC 924 . . . 197

First Energy (UK) Ltd v Hungarian International Bank Ltd [1993] BCLC 1409 . . . 154

Folkes Group plc v Alexander [2002] 2 BCLC 254 . . . 37

Foss v Harbottle (1843) 2 Hare 461 . . . 47, 83, 121, 123, 126, 127, 128, 129, 233, 234, 237, 239

Foster Bryant Surveying Ltd v Bryant [2007] BCC 804 . . . 91

Franbar Holdings Ltd v Patel [2008] EWHC 1534 (Ch) . . . 125

Freeman & Lockyer v Buckhurst Park Properties (Mangal) Ltd [1964] 2 QB 480 . . . 151, 154

Fulham Football Club (1987) Ltd v Richards [2011] EWCA Civ 855 . . . 46

Fulham Football Club Ltd v Cabra Estates plc [1994] 1 BCLC 363 . . . 81

Gaiman v National Association for Mental Health [1971] Ch 317 . . . 72

Gamlestaden Fastigheter AB v Baltic Partners Ltd [2007] 4 All ER 164 . . . 134, 235

GBI Investments, Re [2010] 2 BCLC 624 . . . 208

Ghyll Beck Driving Range Ltd, Re [1993] BCLC 1126 . . . 137

Giles v Rhind [2003] 1 BCLC 1 . . . 128

Gilford Motor Co Ltd v Horne [1933] Ch 935 . . . 20, 25

Governments Stock and Other Securities Investment Co Ltd v Manila Railway Co Ltd [1897] AC 81 . . . 186

Grace v Biagioli [2006] 2 BCLC 70 . . . 130, 138

Graham v Every [2014] EWCA Civ 191; [2015] 1 BCLC 41 . . . 59, 135

Gray's Inn Construction Ltd, Re [1980] 1 WLR 711 . . . 213, 217

Greenhalgh v Arderne Cinemas Ltd [1946] 1 All ER 512 . . . 62, 66

Greenhalgh v Arderne Cinemas Ltd [1951] Ch 286 . . . 33

Greenhalgh v Mallard [1943] 2 All ER 234 . . . 45

Greenwell v Porter [1902] 1 Ch 530 . . . 46

Gross v Rackind [2004] 4 All ER 735 . . . 134

Guidezone Ltd, Re [2000] 2 BCLC 321 . . . 133, 137, 138

Guinness plc v Saunders [1990] 2 AC 663 . . . 115

Halliwells LLP, Re [2011] 1 BCLC 345 . . . 205

Halt Garage (1964) Ltd, Re [1982] 3 All ER 1016 . . . 116, 177

Harborne Road Nominees Ltd v Karvaski [2011] EWHC 2214 . . . 134, 139

Hawkes v Cuddy [2009] 2 BCLC 427 . . . 72, 133, 138

Hawkes Hill Publishing Ltd, Re [2007] BCC 937 . . . 221

Heald v O'Connor [1971] 1 WLR 497 . . . 181

Hellas Telecommunications, Re [2010] BCC 295 . . . 205

Hely-Hutchinson v Brayhead Ltd [1967] 3 All ER 98 . . . 149

Hendy Lennox v Grahame Puttick [1984] 1 WLR 485 . . . 216

Hickman v Kent or Romney Marsh Sheep-Breeders'
  Association [1915] 1 Ch 881 . . . 35, 40, 41, 45, 47,
  53, 233
HL Bolton (Engineering) Ltd v TJ Graham & Sons Ltd
  [1957] 1 QB 159 . . . 158
HMRC v Portsmouth FC [2010] EWHC 2013
  (Ch) . . . 203
Hogg v Cramphorn Ltd [1967] Ch 254; [1966] 3 All ER
  420 . . . 58, 78
Holders Investment Trust Ltd, Re [1971] 1 WLR 583 . . . 67
Holland v Commissioners for Revenue & Customs; Re
  Paycheck Services 3 Ltd [2010] UKSC 51; [2010] 1
  WLR 2793 . . . 94, 95, 238
Hong Kong and China Gas Co Ltd v Glen [1914] 1 Ch
  527 . . . 172, 237
House of Fraser plc v ACGE Investments Ltd [1987] AC
  387 . . . 62–3
Howard Smith Ltd v Ampol Petroleum Ltd [1974] AC
  821 . . . 58, 77, 78, 238
Hutton v West Cork Railway (1883) 23 Ch D 654 . . . 115
Hydrodam (Corby) Ltd, Re [1994] 2 BCLC 180; [1994]
  BCC 161 . . . 94, 95, 242

Iesini v Westrip Holdings Ltd [2009] EWHC 2526
  (Ch) . . . 124, 128, 129
Illingworth v Houldsworth see Yorkshire Woolcombers
  Association Ltd, Re
In a Flap Envelope Co Ltd, Re [2004] 1 BCLC
  64 . . . 181
Industrial Development Consultants Ltd v Cooley
  [1972] 1 WLR 443 . . . 90, 239
Introductions Ltd, Re [1970] Ch 199 . . . 153
Irvine v Irvine [2007] 1 BCLC 349 . . . 138
Irvine v Union Bank of Australia (1877) 2 App Cas
  366 . . . 234
Island Export Finance Ltd v Umunna [1986] BCLC
  460 . . . 90, 239
Item Software (UK) Ltd v Fassihi [2004] EWCA Civ
  1244; [2005] 2 BCLC 91 . . . 72, 81, 127

J. Leslie Engineering, Re [1976] 1 WLR 292 . . . 213
Jetivia SA v Bilta (UK) Ltd [2015] UKSC 23 . . . 160
John Smith's Tadcaster Brewery, Re [1953] Ch
  308 . . . 66
Johnson v Gore Wood & Co [2002] 2 AC 1 . . . 128, 234
Jones v Lipman [1962] 1 WLR 832 . . . 20
JSF Finance v Akma Solutions [2001] 2 BCLC
  307 . . . 207

Kayford Ltd, Re [1975] 1 All ER 604 . . . 216
Kayley Vending, Re [2011] 1 BCLC 114 . . . 205
Kaytech International plc, Re [1999] 2 BCLC 351;
  [1999] BCC 390 . . . 94, 95, 238, 242
Kelner v Baxter (1866) LR 2 CP 174 . . . 144, 145, 228
Kiani v Cooper [2010] EWHC 577 (Ch) . . . 125
Kinsela v Russell Kinsela Pty Ltd [1986] 4 NSWR
  722 . . . 73, 74, 243
Kleanthous v Paphitis [2011] EWHC 2287 . . . 125
Kuwait Asia Bank EC v National Mutual Life Nominees
  Ltd [1991] 1 AC 187 . . . 73

Landhurst Leasing plc, Re [1999] 1 BCLC 286 . . . 87
Lee Panavision Ltd v Lee Lighting Ltd [1992] BCLC
  22 . . . 76, 78, 238
Leeds United Holdings plc, Re [1996] 2 BCLC
  545 . . . 136, 235
Leigh Estates Ltd, Re [1994] BCC 292 . . . 209
Lennard's Carrying Co Ltd v Asiatic Petroleum Co Ltd
  [1915] AC 705 . . . 158, 159
Lewis's Will Trusts, Re [1985] 1 WLR 102 . . . 12
Lexi Holdings (In Administration) v Luqman and Ors
  [2009] EWCA Civ 117 . . . 86
Leyland Daf Ltd, Re [2004] UKHL 9 . . . 212
Littlewoods Mail Order Stores Ltd v Inland Revenue
  Commissioners [1969] 1 WLR 1241 . . . 20
Living Images Ltd, Re [1996] 1 BCLC 348 . . . 222
Lo-Line Electric Motors Ltd, Re [1988] Ch 477 . . . 95, 244
London and Cheshire Insurance Co Ltd v Laplagrene
  Property Co Ltd [1971] Ch 499 . . . 191
London and Mashonaland Exploration Co Ltd v
  New Mashonaland Exploration Co Ltd [1891] WN
  165 . . . 82, 83
London School of Electronics Ltd, Re [1986]
  Ch 211 . . . 138
Lovett v Carson Country Homes [2009]
  2 BCLC 196 . . . 57

Macaura v Northern Assurance Co Ltd [1925]
  AC 619 . . . 11, 52
Macdougall v Gardiner (1875) 1 Ch D 13 . . . 47, 234
Madoff Securities International Ltd v Raven [2013]
  EWHC 3147 . . . 243
Mann v Goldstein [1968] 1 WLR 1091 . . . 208, 209
Marquis of Bute's Case see Cardiff Savings Bank, Re
MC Bacon Ltd, Re [1990] BCLC 324 . . . 197, 198, 217
Mechanisations (Eaglescliffe) Ltd, Re [1966]
  Ch 20 . . . 193

Meridian Global Funds Management Asia Ltd v Securities Commission [1995] 2 AC 500 . . . 142, 157, 158, 159, 160

Mission Capital plc v Sinclair [2008] EWHC 1339 (Ch) . . . 125

Monolithic Building Co, Re [1915] 1 Ch 643 . . . 192

Montgomery v Wanda Modes Ltd [2002] 1 BCLC 289 . . . 209

Morris v Bank of India [2005] EWCA Civ 693 . . . 159

Mourant Trustees v Sixty UK Ltd [2011] BCLC 383 . . . 203

Multinational Gas and Petrochemical Co v Multinational Gas and Petrochemical Services Ltd [1983] Ch 258 . . . 73

Natal Land Co & Colonization Ltd v Pauline Colliery and Development Syndicate Ltd [1904] AC 120 . . . 144, 229

National Telephone Co, Re [1914] 1 Ch 755 . . . 61

New British Iron Co, ex p Beckwith, Re [1898] 1 Ch 324 . . . 36, 41, 233

New Bullas Trading Ltd, Re [1993] BCC 251 . . . 188

Newborne v Sensolid (Great Britain) Ltd [1954] 1 QB 45 . . . 144, 145, 228

Nicholas v Nicholas [1984] FLR 285 . . . 25

Norman v Theodore Goddard (A Firm) [1991] BCLC 1028 . . . 86

North Holdings Ltd v Southern Tropics Ltd [1999] 2 BCLC 625 . . . 134, 139

North-West Transportation Co Ltd v Beatty (1887) 12 App Cas 589 . . . 102

Northern Engineering Industries plc, Re [1994] 2 BCLC 704 . . . 63

Northumberland Avenue Hotel Co, Re (1886) 33 Ch D 16 . . . 145, 229

Novatrust Ltd v Kea Investments Ltd [2014] EWHC 4061 . . . 123

Oak Investment Partners XII Ltd Partnership v Boughtwood [2010] 2 BCLC 459 . . . 133, 135

Oasis Merchandising, Re [1995] 2 BCLC 493 . . . 219

O'Donnell v Shanahan [2009] 2 BCLC 666 . . . 90, 239

O'Neill v Phillips [1999] 1 WLR 1092 . . . 47, 122, 129, 131, 132, 133, 134, 135, 137, 138, 139, 235, 240

Ooregum Gold Mining Co of India v Roper [1892] AC 125 . . . 165, 171

Ord v Belhaven Pubs Ltd [1998] 2 BCLC 447 . . . 20

Oshkosh B'Gosh Inc v Dan Marbel Inc & Craze [1989] BCLC 507 . . . 16, 146

Ossory Estates plc, Re [1988] BCLC 213 . . . 167, 171

P & J MacRae Ltd, Re [1961] 1 WLR 229 . . . 209

Panama, New Zealand and Australian Royal Mail Co (1870) 5 Ch App 318 . . . 186

Panorama Developments (Guildford) Ltd v Fidelis Furnishing Fabrics Ltd [1971] 2 QB 711 . . . 57, 150

Patrick and Lyon Ltd, Re [1933] Ch 786 . . . 244

Pavlides v Jensen [1956] 2 All ER 518 . . . 124, 128

Paycheck Services 3 Ltd, Re see Holland v Commissioners for Revenue & Customs

Pender v Lushington (1877) 6 Ch D 70 . . . 35, 40, 234

Pennell Securities Ltd v Venida Investments Ltd (1974), 25 July, unreported . . . 46, 47

Percival v Wright [1902] 2 Ch 421 . . . 72

Peskin v Anderson [2001] 1 BCLC 372 . . . 72

Peso Silver Mines Ltd v Cropper [1966] SCR 673 . . . 90, 239

Petrodel Resources Ltd v Prest [2012] EWCA Civ 1395 . . . 24

Phillips v Brewin Dolphin [2001] 1 WLR 143 . . . 217

Phillips v Fryer [2012] EWHC 1611 (Ch) . . . 125

Phoenix Office Supplies Ltd, Re [2003] 1 BCLC 76 . . . 133

Phonogram Ltd v Lane [1982] QB 938 . . . 17, 144, 145, 146, 229

Plus Group v Pyke [2002] EWCA Civ 370; [2002] 2 BCLC 201 . . . 82

Prest v Petrodel Resources Ltd [2013] UKSC 34 . . . 5, 12, 19, 20, 21, 22, 23, 25, 26, 229

Produce Marketing Consortium Ltd (No 2), Re [1989] BCLC 520 . . . 221, 222, 230, 244

Progress Property Co Ltd v Moorgarth Group Ltd [2010] UKSC 55 . . . 177

Prudential Assurance Co Ltd v Newman Industries Ltd (No 2) [1982] Ch 204 . . . 124, 128

Punt v Symons & Co Ltd [1903] 2 Ch 506 . . . 31, 78

Purpoint Ltd, Re [1991] BCC 121 . . . 12

Queensland Mines v Hudson (1978) 52 ALJR 379 . . . 90

Quin & Axtens Ltd v Salmon [1909] AC 442 . . . 36, 40, 41, 42, 233, 234

R v Andrews-Weatherfall Ltd [1972] 1 WLR 118 . . . 158

R v Cotswold Geotechnical Holdings Ltd [2011] EWCA Crim 1337 . . . 160

R v HM Coroners for East Kent, ex p Spooner (1987) 3 BCC 636 . . . 159

R v ICR Haulage Ltd [1944] KB 551 . . . 157, 158

R v Kite and OLL Ltd (1994) *The Independent*, 9 Dec . . . 159

R v P&O Ferries (Dover) Ltd (1991) 93 Cr App Rep 72 . . . 159

R v Registrar of Companies, *ex p* Attorney-General [1991] BCLC 476 . . . 16

R v St Regis Paper Company Ltd [2012] 1 Cr App R 14 . . . 159–60

R v Sale [2014] 1 WLR 663 . . . 25

RA Noble & Sons (Clothing) Ltd, Re [1983] BCLC 273 . . . 138

Ratiu v Conway [2005] EWCA Civ 1302 . . . 22

Rayfield v Hands [1960] Ch 1 . . . 35, 45

Regal (Hastings) Ltd v Gulliver [1942] 1 All ER 378 . . . 90, 91, 239

Richborough Furniture Ltd, Re [1996] 1 BCLC 507 . . . 94

Roberts v Frohlich [2011] 2 BCLC 625 . . . 244

Roberts and Cooper Ltd, Re [1929] 2 Ch 383 . . . 61

Rod Gunner Organisation Ltd, Re [2004] 2 BCLC 110 . . . 221

Rolled Steel Products (Holdings) Ltd v British Steel Corpn [1986] Ch 246 . . . 153

Rover International Ltd v Cannon Films Ltd [1989] 1 WLR 912 . . . 146

Royal Bank of Scotland plc v Sandstone Properties Ltd [1998] 2 BCLC 429 . . . 57

Royal British Bank v Turquand (1856) 6 El & Bl 327 . . . 142, 148, 149, 151, 152, 155, 156

Royal Brunei Airlines Sdn Bhd v Tan Kok Ming [1995] 2 AC 378 . . . 181

Ruben v Great Fingall Consolidated [1906] AC 439 . . . 57

Russell v Northern Bank Development Corpn Ltd [1992] 1 WLR 588 . . . 30, 31, 45, 48

Salomon v A Salomon & Co Ltd [1897] AC 22 . . . 4, 5, 10, 12, 14, 19, 20, 21, 22, 23, 53, 72, 165, 228, 229, 230

Sam Weller & Sons Ltd, Re [1990] Ch 682 . . . 138

Saul D Harrison & Sons plc, Re [1995] 1 BCLC 14 . . . 129, 130, 133, 137, 240

Scandinavian Bank Group plc, Re [1988] Ch 87 . . . 52

Scott v Frank F Scott (London) Ltd [1940] Ch 794 . . . 37

Scottish Insurance Corp v Wilsons & Clyde Coal Co Ltd [1949] AC 462; [1949] 1 All ER 1068 . . . 54, 62, 172, 176

Secretary of State for Business, Innovation and Skills v Chohan [2013] EWHC 680 (Ch) . . . 95

Secretary of State for Trade and Industry v Deverell [2001] Ch 340; [2000] 2 WLR 907 . . . 94, 95, 238

Secretary of State for Trade and Industry v Hollier [2007] BCC 11 . . . 242

Secretary of State for Trade and Industry v Taylor [1997] 1 WLR 407 . . . 245

Secretary of State for Trade and Industry v Tjolle [1998] BCC 282 . . . 94, 242

Secretary of State for Trade and Industry v Van Hengel [1995] 1 BCLC 545 . . . 116, 222

Selectmove Ltd, Re [1995] 1 WLR 474 . . . 208

Sevenoaks Stationers (Retail) Ltd, Re [1991] Ch 164 . . . 222, 223, 245

Sharma v Sharma [2013] EWCA Civ 1287 . . . 83

Shaw & Sons (Salford) Ltd v Shaw [1935] 2 KB 113 . . . 101, 102

Sheffield Corporation v Barclay [1905] AC 392 . . . 56–7

Shoe Lace Ltd, Re; Power v Sharp Investments Ltd [1994] 1 BCLC 111 . . . 196, 213, 218

Short v Treasury Commissioners [1948] AC 534 . . . 52

Shuttleworth v Cox Brothers & Co (Maidenhead) Ltd [1927] 2 KB 9 . . . 33, 66

Sidebottom v Kershaw, Leese & Co Ltd [1920] 1 Ch 154 . . . 33

Siebe Gorman & Co Ltd v Barclays Bank Ltd [1979] 2 Lloyd's Rep 142 . . . 188

Sikorski v Sikorski [2012] EWHC 1613 . . . 47

Simpson v Westminster Palace Hotel Co (1860) 8 HL Cas 712 . . . 234

Smith v Croft (No 2) [1987] 3 All ER 909 . . . 125

Smith and Fawcett Ltd, Re [1942] Ch 304 . . . 72, 76

Smith, Stone & Knight v Birmingham Corporation [1939] 4 All ER 116 . . . 21, 230

Smithton Ltd v Naggar [2014] BCC 482 . . . 94

South London Greyhound Racecourses Ltd v Wake [1931] 1 Ch 496 . . . 57

Southard Ltd, Re [1979] 1 WLR 1198 . . . 20

Spectrum Plus Ltd, Re [2005] 2 AC 680 . . . 184, 188

Stainer v Lee [2010] EWHC 1539 (Ch) . . . 125

Standard Chartered Bank v Pakistan National Shipping Corpn (Nos 2 and 4) [2002] 3 WLR 1547 . . . 13

Staples v Eastman Photographic Materials Co [1896] 2 Ch 303 . . . 61

Stimpson v Southern Landlords Association [2009] EWHC 2072 (Ch) . . . 125

Stone & Rolls Ltd v Moore Stephens [2009] 1 AC 1391 . . . 113

Sugarman v CJS Investments LLP [2015] 1 BCLC 1 . . . 37

Sukhoruchkin v Van Bekestein [2014] EWCA Civ 399 . . . 96

Supply of Ready Mixed Concrete, Re (No 2) [1995] 1 BCLC 613 . . . 158

Swabey v Port Darwin Gold Mining Co (1889) 1 Meg 385 . . . 36, 41

Tallington Lakes Ltd v Ancasta International Boat Sales Ltd [2012] EWCA Civ 1712 . . . 208

Taylor's Industrial Flooring Ltd v M & H Plant Hire (Manchester) Ltd [1990] BCLC 216 . . . 207

Teleomatic, Re [1994] 1 BCLC 90 . . . 192

Tesco Supermarkets Ltd v Nattrass [1971] 2 All ER 127 . . . 158

Thompson v Renwick Group plc [2014] EWCA Civ 635 . . . 21

Thundercrest Ltd, Re [1995] 1 BCLC 117 . . . 58

Tobian Properties Ltd, Re [2012] EWCA Civ 998 . . . 133, 134, 235

Transbus International, Re [2004] 1 WLR 2654 . . . 205

Trevor v Whitworth (1887) 12 App Cas 409 . . . 165, 169–70, 171, 173, 174, 175, 176, 177

Trustor AB v Smallbone (No 2) [2001] 1 WLR 1177 . . . 20

Tunstall v Steigman [1962] 1 QB 593 . . . 11

Turquand's Case see Royal British Bank v Turquand

Tweeds Garages Ltd, Re [1962] 1 Ch 406 . . . 208

Twycross v Grant (1877) 2 CPD 469 . . . 17

Ultraframe (UK) Ltd v Fielding [2005] EWHC 1638 . . . 94, 96

Uniq plc, Re [2011] EWHC 749 . . . 180

Unisoft Group Ltd (No 3), Re [1994] 1 BCLC 609 . . . 95, 132

Universal Project Management Ltd v Fort Gilkicker Ltd [2013] EWHC 348 . . . 123

Vivendi SA v Richards [2013] EWHC 3006 (Ch) . . . 96, 103, 238

VTB Capital plc v Nutritek International Corp [2013] UKSC 5 . . . 19, 20, 21, 23, 25

Wallersteiner v Moir (No 2) [1975] 1 QB 373; [1976] 1 All ER 849 . . . 125, 129, 240

Weavering Capital (UK) Ltd v Dabhia and Platt [2013] EWCA Civ 71 . . . 85

Webb v Earle [1875] LR 20 Eq 556 . . . 52, 61

Welsh Irish Ferries Ltd, Re [1985] BCLC 327 . . . 190

West Mercia Safetywear Ltd v Dodd [1988] BCLC 250 . . . 73, 243

Westcoast (Holdings) Ltd v Wharf Land Subsidiary (No 1) Ltd [2012] EWCA Civ 1003 . . . 47

Westmid Packing Services Ltd, Re; Secretary of State for Trade and Industry v Griffiths [1998] 2 All ER 124 . . . 86, 222

White v Bristol Aeroplane Co [1953] Ch 65 . . . 32, 62, 65, 233

Will v United Lankat Plantations Ltd [1914] AC 11 . . . 61

William C Leitch Bros, Re [1932] 2 Ch 71 . . . 244

Williams v Natural Life Health Foods Ltd [1998] 1 WLR 830; [1998] 1 BCLC 689 . . . 12, 21

Wood v Baker [2015] EWHC 2536 (Ch) . . . 26

Woodroffes (Musical Instruments) Ltd, Re [1985] 3 WLR 543 . . . 187

Woolfson v Strathclyde DC 1978 SC (HL) 90 . . . 19, 20, 23

Wragg Ltd, Re [1897] 1 Ch 796 . . . 165, 172, 237

Yagerphone Ltd, Re [1935] 1 Ch 392 . . . 218

Yenidje Tobacco Ltd, Re [1916] 2 Ch 426 . . . 138–9

Yeovil Glove Co Ltd, Re [1965] Ch 148 . . . 218

Yeung Kei Yung v Hong Kong & Shanghai Banking Corpn [1981] AC 787 . . . 57

Yorkshire Woolcombers Association Ltd, Re; Houldsworth v Yorkshire Woolcombers Association Ltd [1903] 2 Ch 284, CA; aff'd sub nom Illingworth v Houldsworth [1904] AC 355, HL . . . 185, 186, 188

YP v MP and Petrodel Resources Ltd [2011] EWHC 2956 . . . 23

Yukong Line Ltd of Korea v Rendsburg Investments Corpn of Liberia (No 2) [1998] 1 WLR 294 . . . 21, 96, 230, 243

Table of legislation

UK statutes

Bribery Act 2010 . . . 160

Companies Act 1948
  s 20 . . . 35
  s 210 . . . 132
Companies Act 1980 . . . 165
Companies Act 1985 . . . 144, 153, 190
  s 3A . . . 153
  s 14 . . . 34, 35
  s 35A . . . 155
  s 309 . . . 73
  s 459 . . . 132
Companies Act 1989 . . . 153
Companies Act 2006 . . . 9, 31, 52, 53, 71, 72, 76, 79,
  84, 85, 86, 89, 96, 112, 117, 122, 123, 124, 125,
  146, 152, 153, 154, 155, 156, 164, 170, 174, 177,
  178, 179, 189, 234
  s 3(2) . . . 7, 10
  s 7 . . . 15
  s 8 . . . 15, 31
  s 9 . . . 15
  s 9(2) . . . 15
  s 9(4)(a) . . . 15
  s 9(4)(c) . . . 15
  s 9(5)(b) . . . 15
  s 10 . . . 15
  s 12 . . . 15
  s 13 . . . 15
  s 14 . . . 15
  s 15 . . . 15
  s 16 . . . 16, 144, 228
  s 17 . . . 44
  s 18(2) . . . 45
  s 18(3) . . . 45
  s 20 . . . 15, 45, 102
  s 21 . . . 30, 33, 37, 42, 44, 46, 62, 66, 67, 102, 103,
    104, 111, 233
  s 21(1) . . . 30, 32
  s 22 . . . 30, 37, 42, 46, 233
  s 22(1) . . . 31

  s 22(3) . . . 31
  s 23 . . . 31
  s 25 . . . 32
  s 26 . . . 46
  s 31 . . . 142, 148, 150, 152, 154
  s 33 . . . 30, 34, 35, 38, 40, 44, 53, 232
  s 33(1) . . . 35
  s 35 . . . 154
  s 35A . . . 155
  s 39 . . . 142, 148, 150, 152, 154, 155
  s 40 . . . 142, 148, 149, 150, 151, 152, 154, 155, 156
  s 40(1) . . . 149
  s 40(2)(a) . . . 149, 155
  s 40(2)(b) . . . 149, 155
  s 40(4) . . . 149, 155
  s 40(5) . . . 149, 155
  s 41 . . . 142, 148, 151, 155
  s 41(2) . . . 150, 155
  s 41(3) . . . 150
  s 41(4) . . . 155
  s 42 . . . 155
  s 51 . . . 16, 17, 144, 145, 146, 227, 228, 229, 231
  s 51(1) . . . 144
  Pt 5 (ss 53–85) . . . 16
  s 53 . . . 16
  s 54 . . . 16
  s 55 . . . 17
  s 59 . . . 16
  s 66 . . . 17
  s 67 . . . 17
  ss 69–74 . . . 17
  s 77(1) . . . 16
  s 82 . . . 17
  ss 90–96 . . . 7
  s 112 . . . 56
  s 157 . . . 107
  s 168 . . . 83, 103, 104, 111, 115, 118, 130, 137, 150
  s 168(2) . . . 104
  s 169 . . . 111
  s 170 . . . 71, 80
  s 170(1) . . . 72, 238, 239, 242

s 170(2)(a) . . . 90
s 170(3) . . . 77, 84, 89
s 170(4) . . . 77, 84, 89, 238
s 170(5) . . . 96, 103, 238
s 171 . . . 77
ss 171–177 . . . 72, 76, 80, 84, 104
s 171(a) . . . 76, 148, 149, 150, 151, 154, 155
s 171(b) . . . 58, 75, 76, 77, 78, 79, 130, 181, 238,
    239, 240
s 172 . . . 58, 70, 71, 72, 73, 74, 75, 76, 77, 78, 79,
    81, 82, 83, 84, 87, 124, 125, 127, 128, 130, 181,
    239, 240, 241, 242, 243, 245
ss 172–175 . . . 83
s 172(1) . . . 72, 73, 243
s 172(1)(a) . . . 81
s 172(1)(a)–(f) . . . 73, 242, 243
s 172(1)(d) . . . 81
s 172(1)(f) . . . 50
s 172(3) . . . 74, 243
s 173 . . . 80, 81
s 174 . . . 82, 83, 84, 85, 86, 87, 127, 230, 243
s 175 . . . 71, 76, 82, 83, 88, 89, 90, 91, 92, 238,
    240
ss 175–177 . . . 89
s 175(1) . . . 89
s 175(2) . . . 89, 90, 238
s 175(3) . . . 91
s 175(4) . . . 83, 239
s 175(4)(a) . . . 90
s 175(7) . . . 83
s 177 . . . 88, 91, 92, 150
s 177(2) . . . 91
s 177(6)(b) . . . 91
s 178 . . . 81, 82, 84
s 179 . . . 76, 80, 240
s 182 . . . 91, 92
ss 188–189 . . . 108, 115
s 190 . . . 88, 89, 91, 92, 150
ss 190–196 . . . 150, 151
s 191 . . . 92
s 195 . . . 92
s 195(2) . . . 150
s 195(3)–(4) . . . 92
ss 215–222 . . . 115
ss 227–230 . . . 108, 115
s 238(1) . . . 66
s 238(6) . . . 66
s 239 . . . 76

s 250 . . . 95
s 251 . . . 94, 103, 238
ss 252–254 . . . 91
ss 252–256 . . . 155
s 252(2)(a) . . . 150
s 253(2)(e) . . . 150
s 260 . . . 123, 240
ss 260–264 . . . 74, 128, 234, 239
s 260(1) . . . 123, 128
s 260(1)(a) . . . 239
s 260(1)(b) . . . 239
s 260(3) . . . 123, 128, 234, 239
s 260(4) . . . 124, 128
s 260(5) . . . 128
s 261 . . . 123, 239
s 261(1) . . . 124
s 261(2) . . . 124, 128, 239
s 261(3) . . . 126
s 262 . . . 123
s 263 . . . 123, 128, 234
s 263(2) . . . 124, 239
s 263(2)(a) . . . 124, 128
s 263(2)(b)–(c) . . . 124, 128
s 263(3) . . . 124, 125, 129, 239
s 263(3)(b) . . . 124
s 263(4) . . . 125, 129, 239
s 264 . . . 123
s 270(1) . . . 15
ss 281–283 . . . 102
s 281(4) . . . 44
s 283 . . . 31
s 288 . . . 31
s 288(2) . . . 104
s 321 . . . 42
ss 382–383 . . . 8
s 412 . . . 115
s 417 . . . 74
s 420 . . . 115
s 439A . . . 115
s 441 . . . 17
s 475 . . . 113
s 477 . . . 8
s 495 . . . 113
s 540(1) . . . 52
s 541 . . . 53, 54
s 542(1) . . . 52
s 544(1) . . . 53
s 550 . . . 58

s 551 . . . 58, 59
s 560 . . . 58, 63
ss 560–577 . . . 58
s 561 . . . 58, 59, 63
s 562 . . . 58
s 563(2) . . . 58
s 564 . . . 59
s 565 . . . 59
s 566 . . . 59
s 567 . . . 59
s 568 . . . 59
s 569(1) . . . 59
ss 570–571 . . . 59
s 580 . . . 169
ss 580–609 . . . 165
s 580(1) . . . 165, 171
s 580(2) . . . 171
s 582 . . . 165, 166, 170
s 582(1) . . . 237
s 584 . . . 165, 170
s 585(1) . . . 167
s 585(2) . . . 167
s 587(1) . . . 167
s 587(2) . . . 167
s 588 . . . 167, 169, 171
s 588(2) . . . 167
s 589 . . . 167
s 590 . . . 167, 169, 171
s 593 . . . 166, 167, 170, 237
ss 593–597 . . . 170
ss 593–609 . . . 169
s 593(1) . . . 170
s 593(3) . . . 166, 170
s 594 . . . 166
s 595 . . . 166
s 596 . . . 166
s 596(1) . . . 170
s 596(2) . . . 170
s 597 . . . 166, 170
s 598 . . . 166
ss 599–600 . . . 166
s 601 . . . 166
s 605 . . . 166
s 606 . . . 170
s 606(1) . . . 166
s 606(2) . . . 166
s 606(4) . . . 166, 170
s 607 . . . 166, 170

s 609 . . . 167
s 618 . . . 42, 65
s 630 . . . 32, 42, 46, 66, 233
ss 630–635 . . . 52
ss 630–640 . . . 62, 65, 67
s 630(4) . . . 67
s 630(6) . . . 42, 66
s 633 . . . 67
s 633(3) . . . 67
s 633(4) . . . 67
s 638 . . . 171
s 641(1)(a) . . . 172, 175
s 641(1)(b) . . . 171, 176
ss 641–649 . . . 175
ss 641–653 . . . 169
s 641(3) . . . 175
s 641(4) . . . 175
s 641(4)(b)(i) . . . 172
s 642 . . . 172
ss 642–644 . . . 175
s 643 . . . 172
ss 645–647 . . . 172
ss 645–651 . . . 176
s 651 . . . 172
s 653 . . . 59
s 656 . . . 175
s 658 . . . 171, 172, 176, 238
ss 658–669 . . . 169
s 658(2) . . . 171
s 658(2)(b) . . . 171
s 658(3) . . . 171
s 659(1) . . . 171
s 659(2)(c) . . . 238
s 677 . . . 179
ss 677–683 . . . 179
s 677(1)(b)(i) . . . 179
s 677(1)(d)(i) . . . 179
s 678 . . . 177, 179
s 678(1) . . . 180
s 678(2) . . . 180
s 678(2)(a) . . . 180
s 678(2)(b) . . . 180
s 678(4) . . . 180
s 678(4)(a) . . . 180
s 678(4)(b) . . . 180
s 680(1) . . . 181
s 680(2) . . . 181
s 681 . . . 181

s 682 . . . 181
s 684 . . . 176
s 687 . . . 176
ss 690–708 . . . 171, 176
s 690(1) . . . 171
s 692 . . . 176
s 692(1ZA) . . . 172, 176
s 692(2) . . . 171
s 693 . . . 171
ss 709–723 . . . 176
s 761 . . . 7, 166
s 762 . . . 7
s 763 . . . 7, 11, 172
s 768(1) . . . 56
s 770 . . . 56
s 775(3) . . . 57
s 779 . . . 52
s 830 . . . 60, 176
s 831(1) . . . 176
s 859(4) . . . 192
Pt 25 (ss 859A–894) . . . 190
Pt 25, Chpt A1 (ss 859A–859Q) . . . 191
s 859A . . . 191, 193
s 859A(6) . . . 191
s 859D . . . 191
s 859E . . . 192
s 859F(3) . . . 192
s 859H . . . 192, 195
s 859H(4) . . . 192
s 859I(7) . . . 193
s 859O . . . 193
s 859P . . . 193
s 859Q . . . 193
Pt 25, Chpt 1 (ss 860–877) . . . 190
s 860 . . . 191, 192
s 873 . . . 192
s 874 . . . 192
s 874(3) . . . 192
s 876 . . . 193
Pt 25, Chpt 2 (ss 878–892) . . . 190
s 894 . . . 190
ss 895–901 . . . 202
s 994 . . . 33, 47, 59, 63, 67, 68, 125, 129, 131, 132,
    133, 134, 135, 136, 137, 138, 234, 235, 240
s 996 . . . 68, 125, 130, 138, 240
s 996(1) . . . 33
s 996(2)(d) . . . 33

s 1127 . . . 221
ss 1150–1153 . . . 166, 170
s 1157 . . . 78, 83, 87, 91, 97, 244
s 1163 . . . 91
Pt 41 (ss 1192–1208) . . . 16
Company Directors Disqualification Act 1986 . . . 8,
    86, 87, 220, 222
s 1A . . . 223
s 6 . . . 86, 103, 116, 182, 220, 222, 223, 230, 241,
    244, 245
s 7(2A) . . . 223
s 7A . . . 222
s 8 . . . 86, 116
s 10 . . . 220, 222, 223, 244
s 12C . . . 222
s 15 . . . 223
s 15A . . . 223, 231
s 15A(2) . . . 223
s 15B . . . 223
s 22(5) . . . 94
Sch 1 . . . 86, 222
Contracts (Rights of Third Parties) Act 1999 . . . 145
s 1(3) . . . 145
Corporate Manslaughter and Corporate Homicide Act
    2007 . . . 143, 157, 160
s 1(1) . . . 160
s 1(3) . . . 160

Employment Rights Act 1996
s 205A . . . 52
Enterprise Act 2002 . . . 202, 203, 204, 212, 213
Enterprise and Regulatory Reform Act 2013 . . . 109,
    115, 116, 118
European Communities Act 1972
s 9(2) . . . 144

Growth and Infrastructure Act 2013 . . . 52

Insolvency Act 1986 . . . 182, 195, 203
Pt 1 (ss 1–7B) . . . 203
s 4 . . . 203
s 6 . . . 203
s 86 . . . 216
s 122(1)(f) . . . 202, 206, 230
s 122(1)(g) . . . 47, 129, 135, 136, 138, 139, 234
s 123 . . . 195, 197, 206, 213, 217
s 123(1)(a) . . . 206, 207
s 123(1)(b) . . . 206, 207

s 123(1)(e) . . . 206, 207, 208
s 123(2) . . . 206, 207
s 125(2) . . . 138
s 127 . . . 211, 213, 217
s 129 . . . 213
s 129(1) . . . 216
s 129(2) . . . 216
s 143(1) . . . 211, 215
s 175 . . . 212
s 175(2) . . . 187, 212
s 176A . . . 187, 213, 216
s 176ZA . . . 187, 212
s 178 . . . 216
s 189 . . . 214
s 205 . . . 214
s 212 . . . 12, 97, 218, 220, 230, 241, 244
s 213 . . . 12, 218, 220, 230, 244
s 214 . . . 8, 12, 19, 74, 95, 103, 211, 218, 220, 222, 230, 241, 243, 244, 245
s 214(1) . . . 222, 244
s 214(2) . . . 220
s 214(3) . . . 220, 221, 244
s 214(4) . . . 85, 86, 221, 244
s 214(5) . . . 221
s 217 . . . 12
s 238 . . . 182, 217, 230
s 238(4) . . . 217
s 238(5) . . . 217
s 239 . . . 186, 194, 195, 197, 211, 213, 216, 217
ss 239–245 . . . 217
s 239(5) . . . 197, 198, 217
s 239(6) . . . 197, 217
s 240(1)(a)–(b) . . . 197, 217
s 240(2) . . . 217
s 241 . . . 197, 217, 218
s 241(2) . . . 218
s 241(2A) . . . 218
s 244 . . . 218
s 245 . . . 186, 187, 194, 195, 196, 197, 198, 211, 213, 216, 218
s 245(2) . . . 196
s 245(3) . . . 213
s 245(3)(a) . . . 196
s 245(3)(b) . . . 195
s 245(4) . . . 196, 218
s 245(5) . . . 196
s 246ZD . . . 218
s 249 . . . 196, 213

s 251 . . . 94, 187
s 423(3) . . . 218
s 425 . . . 218
s 435 . . . 196, 213
s 435(6) . . . 196
Sch A1 . . . 203
Sch B1 . . . 187, 203
  para 3 . . . 204
  para 14 . . . 204
  para 84 . . . 205
Sch 6 . . . 212

Landlord and Tenant Act
  s 30(1)(g) . . . 11
Limited Liability Partnership Act 2000 . . . 7
Limited Partnerships Act 1907 . . . 7

Matrimonial Causes Act 1973 . . . 24
  s 24 . . . 23

Partnership Act 1890 . . . 6
  s 1(1) . . . 6, 14

Small Business, Enterprise and Employment Act 2015 . . . 8, 52, 103, 218, 219, 222, 223, 238
  s 89 . . . 96

UK statutory instruments

Companies Act 2006 (Amendment of Part 25) Regulations 2013 (SI 2013/600) . . . 189, 190, 191, 193
Companies (Model Articles) Regulations 2008 (SI 2008/3229) . . . 15, 45
  Sch 1 Private Companies . . . 39–40, 76, 238
    Art 3 . . . 102, 111, 154
    Art 4 . . . 103, 149
Companies (Trading Disclosures) Regulations 2008 (SI 2008/495) . . . 17
Company, Limited Liability Partnerships and Business Names (Sensitive Words and Expressions) Regulations 2014 (SI 2014/3140) . . . 17

Insolvency Rules 1986 (SI 1986/1925)
  r 4.19 . . . 209
  r 4.90 . . . 209, 216
  r 4.218 . . . 212

Codes of Practice

Cadbury Code (Code of Best Practice) . . . 106, 107

Combined Code . . . 100, 106

Greenbury Code (Code of Best Practice for Directors' Remuneration) . . . 106

Stewardship Code . . . 100, 107, 108, 110, 112

UK Corporate Governance Code . . . 104, 105, 106, 107, 108, 109, 110, 112, 113, 114, 115, 116, 117

EU legislation

Directives

Directive 68/151/EEC (First Company Law Directive) (OJ L65/8, 14 March 1968) . . . 156
Art 7 . . . 144
Directive 77/91/EEC (Second Company Law Directive) (OJ L26/1, 31 January 1977) . . . 165

Exam Skills for Success in Company Law

1

This chapter provides some general advice on approaching exams and exam questions in company law. To get the most benefit from the advice both here and in the following chapters, you should first consider your own position. In particular:

- **Know your course:** check your syllabus and focus your time and efforts on those topics. By all means explore more widely, but only after you feel confident about all the topics your exam could include.

- **Know your assessment:** company law exams come in a variety of forms—number/type of questions, time available, permitted material (if any), and so on. Check the format of your own exam so you are not surprised on exam day. Past exam papers can help to familiarise you with the format and the question-setter's approach, but check there have been no significant changes in course delivery.

- **Reflect on prior experience:** consider any feedback you've had from other law exams (whether implicit or explicit) and work on the skills you need to improve. An exam seeks to test your knowledge and understanding of topics and your ability to apply and analyse the law with unseen problems and issues, all within a highly pressured environment—where do your strengths and weaknesses lie?

Dealing with Questions: Essays

Essay questions appear in various forms: the most common are statements followed by an instruction such as 'discuss', or a query (eg 'to what extent is it true that …'), but they also include tasks such as writing a case note or legislative comment, or considering where law reform is needed. To do well in an essay question, remember to pull apart the question to identify the relevant issues, and focus your discussion accordingly. Don't be tempted to provide a general discussion of the topic.

PEA is a common acronym for an approach to essay writing: Point, Explain (or Evidence), Analysis (or Assess). Using PEA is a good way to ensure you cover all the points, explain and provide evidence for them, and assess and analyse each point. All this is essential to doing well. But there is no need for it to become too formulaic: PEA should be your slave and not your master. Don't lose sight of the essence of PEA—you need to cover all these elements—but you can add interest by raising an argument from the start, bringing in wider and deeper critical thought, and sometimes merging the P, the

E, and the A to be more concise and show your mastery of the law (while still ensuring each element is present).

Dealing with Questions: Problems

Problem questions give a series of facts and ask you to advise one or more of the parties. You need to identify the legal issues arising, keeping an eye on all the facts. Don't just ignore facts that seem inconvenient–even if you conclude a particular point is not legally relevant, you need to indicate why (otherwise the examiner may think you simply missed the point). Focus on who you are advising and direct your response accordingly; this shows the examiner you are really thinking about the problem and not the topic generally.

IRAC is a well-known approach to problem questions. It stands for Issue, Rule (or Relevant Law), Apply, Conclude. (It also appears as ILAC or IPAC—Issue, Law (or Point), Apply, Conclude.) Just as with PEA, IRAC is a tool and not an end in itself. IRAC ensures you have covered the things you need to cover and particularly if you lack confidence, is a good way of keeping calm and working steadily through the issues. The slight danger with IRAC is that if applied to the essay as a whole (setting out all the issues, followed by all the law, then the application, and then a conclusion), the discussion of the law can be quite descriptive without a focus on the facts, and the application and analysis may be limited if you are running out of time. In many ways IRAC is more effectively used within sections, rather than the essay as a whole—use it to check that for each of the points you identified, you have clearly identified the issue, set out the law, applied the law to the facts, and concluded on that point.

Tips for Exam Success

Prepare actively: Revision needs to establish solid foundations—knowledge and understanding of the syllabus topics—but should also ensure you can analyse, criticise, and apply the law convincingly. A good student moves beyond describing the relevant law, and is able to apply it, recognise problems, inconsistencies, and 'grey areas', consider its significance and effect, critique the approach of statute or the courts, consider how it could (or should) be applied in new situations, etc. Conventional revision such as reading, thinking, note-making, and mind-mapping is important, but you should also develop your skills through practice—test your knowledge and understanding against questions and other challenges and critically evaluate your own efforts. Practice can also help you cope better with time pressures and stress come the exam itself.

Answer the question: Too often students don't get the marks they expect because they discuss a topic too generally, rather than answering the question set. It is answering the question that shows the examiner you have really understood the subject, and can use (and not simply reproduce) your knowledge. Focus on the question, and explicitly identify the issues. Concentrate on these, even if this means you have to jettison some knowledge that you'd really hoped to share with the examiner. Never seek to reproduce a prepared answer.

Be time-aware: Split your time in the exam sensibly, allocating enough time to each question. If you spend too long on the first question(s) it is highly unlikely that any extra marks you might gain will compensate for an incomplete or missed answer at the end. Similarly don't spend too long in any answer on an introduction or setting out the basics—get on to the main issues as quickly as you can. Taking a few minutes to plan your answer before starting to write will help enormously with this.

Make connections: The interlinking nature of topics in company law means it is very important in the exam to concentrate on the question and not jump to conclusions about what topic(s) it covers. When studying and revising, you will naturally focus on individual topics, but you should also aim to understand the subject as a whole and the connections between topics, rather than viewing each topic as entirely self-contained. Your own course of study (as well as your reading) will help you both grasp the principles and see the connections—mind-mapping helps here too.

Be structured: A clear structure allows you to work steadily and logically through the issues that arise, so taking a few minutes to plan your answer is invaluable. There is no single 'right' way to structure a company law answer (subject to anything your lecturer says to the contrary) but remember that every answer needs a start, a middle, and an end. The start is the introduction. For an essay, this could identify the context and issues, explain your approach and/or argument, and ideally link explicitly to the question. In a problem question, keep it brief, just identifying the area of law and/or issues, so you don't get distracted by general discussion. The middle contains the main sections of your essay. Separate issues into paragraphs (and don't be afraid to use sub-headings); explain and analyse each issue, linking to the question and/or applying the law to the problem, reaching interim conclusions on each point. Splitting the issues in this way helps to encourage analysis and comment as you go along, rather than waiting until the final paragraph. The end of your essay is the conclusion. This should wrap up your discussion, pulling together any threads of argument, and linking back to the question (ensuring the essay is addressed, or advice provided).

Stand out from the crowd: Examiners love to see a student really focusing on the question, critiquing (as well as confidently explaining) the law, and engaging with (not just reciting) the material, including further reading. You could also show off your wider appreciation of (relevant) developments in the legal and commercial worlds and topical issues. Don't overplay this—your first priority must be to deal with the law—but deeper awareness and interest in the subject is valuable. You can also bring in relevant elements of legal theory and/or commercial practice, using your own course (both the syllabus and the teaching) as a guide to what your examiners might expect.

Keep calm: Easier said than done, but thinking (and writing) clearly requires a calm head. Initial panic can make questions seem incomprehensible, but take a deep breath and read them again. Remember that if you've attended classes, prepared the work, undertaken the revision, and practised your skills, there is nothing you can't tackle. Ultimately an exam is there to test you, but not to trick you—enjoy the ride.

2

Companies and Corporate Personality

ARE YOU READY?

- Forms of business enterprise and distinguishing features
- Forms of company and distinguishing features
- Consequences of incorporation
- Company formation requirements and procedure
- Company name restrictions and considerations
- Issues arising in the pre-formation period—promoters and pre-incorporation contracts
- Corporate personality and the *Salomon* case
- Lifting/piercing the veil of incorporation
- Connections (in particular) with: directors, constitution, management and governance, corporate liability, insolvency
- Note: The coverage of many of these issues—particularly forms of business enterprise, the nature of the corporate form, and the registration process—can vary widely between courses, so please check your own course syllabus

KEY DEBATES

Debate: Availability/appropriateness of business vehicles and limited liability

There has long been discussion about whether the available business vehicles adequately meet the needs of modern businesses. One particular issue surrounds the requirements of small businesses, and whether it is appropriate or necessary to offer limited liability with the additional formalities and restrictions that brings, and various papers by Judith Freedman and Andrew Hicks address this point. A relatively new addition to the range of business vehicles, the LLP in 2001, also gave rise to much discussion, and some criticism.

Debate: The nature of the company and the role of company law

What is the status of the company—a purely private contractual arrangement, or a 'concession' or privilege granted by the State? What should be the proper role of company law in supporting, enabling, and regulating companies? Although these issues can seem largely theoretical, these notions underpin much thinking on corporate regulation and topical issues such as corporate social responsibility. There can be very different perspectives on companies and company law, for example contrast Cheffins, B., *Company Law: Theory, Structure and Operation* (Oxford, 1997) and Parkinson, J., *Corporate Power and Responsibility: Issues in the Theory of Company Law* (Cambridge, 1993). The Company Law Review (see in particular *The Strategic Framework*, 1999) touched on these issues when considering company law reforms.

Debate: How far should the courts be willing to lift/pierce the veil of incorporation?

Whether and to what extent the veil of incorporation should be pierced has been a very long-running debate, and, although not in those terms, underpins *Salomon v A. Salomon & Co Ltd* itself. While some (including the courts in this jurisdiction, see *Prest v Petrodel Resources Ltd*) favour commercial certainty and a strict approach, others would prefer a more interventionist and proactive approach, particularly in relation to involuntary creditors. This debate of course links to the wider debate about the availability and risks of limited liability.

 QUESTION | 1

While studying Art at University, Mo has been designing and making his own greetings cards to send to friends and family. Following positive feedback he has now decided to develop this into a business and his friend Gok (a business studies graduate) is going to join him to provide business and marketing expertise. The business will need some initial capital to obtain appropriate premises and stock. Mo and Gok seek your advice on the most appropriate business form for their new enterprise and the benefits and drawbacks of that choice. They are anxious to protect their personal assets from business risk.

Advise Mo and Gok.

 CAUTION!

- Don't just describe the different types of business enterprise—the examiner wants to see that you really appreciate what the key features are and how they relate to the problem facts
- Avoid a simple list of advantages and disadvantages of incorporation

DIAGRAM ANSWER PLAN

Identify the issues	■ Identify Mo and Gok's key concerns and requirements ■ Identify the different options available
Relevant law	■ Different business vehicles: particularly partnerships, LLPs, and companies ■ Definitions, benefits, and drawbacks for each
Apply the law	■ Apply to the facts ■ Consider which benefits and drawbacks will be most significant and why
Conclude	■ Advise on most appropriate form

SUGGESTED ANSWER

This essay will consider which of several possible business forms would be most appropriate for Mo and Gok, taking particular account of their wish to protect their personal assets and the need to raise capital for the business. As there is no indication that Mo and Gok want to run the business as a social enterprise, specialist vehicles such as the Community Interest Company (CIC) will not be considered.[1]

[1] Rather than waste time going through every possible business form, explain why you are narrowing down your choices

The simplest form of business vehicle is the sole trader, but as it appears that Mo and Gok will be running the business jointly, this is not an option. Unless they take steps to create a specific legal form for the business, by working together Mo and Gok would create a partnership—defined in the **Partnership Act 1890 (PA 1890), s. 1(1)** as 'the relation which subsists between persons carrying on a business in common with a view of profit'.[2] It is sometimes called a 'general partnership' to distinguish it from other types of partnership.

[2] Use statutory material sparingly; you don't need more than this here

A (general) partnership comes into existence as soon as the definition is fulfilled; there is no need for registration or any formal written agreement. This means there is no cost for Mo and Gok, although they might choose to create a formal written partnership agreement anyway (particularly if they wanted to avoid the default provisions of **PA 1890** on matters such as the division of profits). There is no need to disclose information, meaning no loss of business confidentiality, a further advantage. Capital could be brought in through investment by the partners, whether jointly or in different shares, or by a loan from a bank or other source. However a partnership does not exist as a separate legal entity in England and Wales (the position is different in Scotland), and the partners remain personally liable for the business debts to the full extent of their personal wealth. This would obviously concern Mo and Gok.[3] They could be advised that the risks inherent in their proposed business would be low, and they might be able to achieve a high level of protection through adequate insurance (admittedly with cost implications) so there may be little need to protect their personal assets further,[4] but if they want the benefit of 'limited liability' then they will need to choose a different business form.

This would require the friends to take formal steps to create a business structure through registration, most sensibly either a Limited Liability Partnership (LLP), or a private limited company. The other form of partnership giving limited liability, the Limited Partnership, under the **Limited Partnerships Act 1907**, would not be suitable here[5] as all the partners will be active in the business. The friends will need to pay a registration fee, but this is not a large amount (£40 for paper filing, less online).

An LLP is a relatively new creation, formed under the **Limited Liability Partnerships Act 2000**, that combines elements of the partnership (particularly internally) and the limited company. An LLP is a separate legal entity (distinct from its members, as partners in an LLP are called) and members are not liable for the LLP's debts. However it has the same drawbacks as a company—it has to be registered (involving formality, disclosure of information, and cost), and the benefits of limited liability may be more apparent than real in practice. From the information we are given an LLP would not seem to offer Mo and Gok any advantages over a company, while not offering quite the flexibility or familiarity of the company form. Mo and Gok might wish to obtain specialist advice on the differing tax treatments[6] of LLPs and companies, but subject to that advice, a company would probably be better suited to their requirements.

There are several types of company: unlimited, limited by guarantee, and limited by shares. As this will be a normal trading business, the company limited by shares (members' liability is limited to the amount (if any) unpaid on their shares, **Companies Act 2006 (CA 2006), s. 3(2)**) is the most appropriate form for Mo and Gok. They can take either equal or different proportional shareholdings to reflect their individual stakes in the company, and will both be directors.

Companies limited by shares can be private or public. Here a private limited company is most appropriate,[7] as a public company cannot trade without a minimum issued share capital of £50,000 (**CA 2006, s. 761–3**) and is subject to more onerous regulation. The company could be re-registered as a public company (**CA 2006, ss. 90–6**) in the future should this become desirable.

[3] This shows that you have understood the relevance of the point you make to the information given in the question

[4] This sentence as a whole shows you have thought about the practical position as well as the more obviously 'company law' points

[5] This gives you credit for recognising the LP, while ensuring that you do not waste time describing it when it is not a good option

[6] You won't be expected to know what the tax position is, but you can raise the point to show you understand its significance when choosing a business form

[7] This links your explanation to the question itself

A private company is cheap and simple to form and offers the advantage to Mo and Gok that their liability would be limited to their capital contribution as opposed to their being exposed to unlimited personal liability. It also provides a bit more flexibility in respect of the provision of capital.[8] Mo and Gok could provide the capital themselves, either by way of shareholder investment (in return for their shares) or by way of a loan, but would then be at risk of losing the money in the event of the business failing. They could issue shares to friends and family in return for investment, but should bear in mind that the increased numbers of shareholders could lead to later disputes and disagreements. More likely, the capital investment would come from a loan, probably from a bank, and the business may benefit from slightly better rates because it could offer a floating charge (as well as a fixed charge) over business assets as security for the loan, whereas sole traders and (general) partnerships are not able to grant a floating charge. In reality, as well as taking security for the loan, the bank will probably require Mo and/or Gok to act as guarantor/surety for the debts of the company meaning that they would effectively lose the benefit of limited liability in respect of these debts. Research by Freedman indicates that over half of small business proprietors have given personal guarantees ('Small businesses and the corporate form: burden or privilege?' (1994) 57 MLR 55).[9] This insistence on personal guarantees from banks (and other providers of credit) means that the benefit of limited liability is not as extensive as might be supposed.

Mo and Gok should also be aware that using a limited company does not protect their personal assets in all circumstances, particularly if they do not act responsibly if the company gets into financial difficulty. As directors, they could be made personally liable in the event of the company's insolvency, for example for wrongful trading, under **Insolvency Act 1986 s. 214**, or could be disqualified from acting as directors under the **Company Directors Disqualification Act 1986**, which can now (following reforms in the **Small Business, Enterprise and Employment Act 2015**) also lead to a Compensation Order being granted against them.

Another possible drawback of using the corporate form is that some company information will be available for public inspection—known as 'the price of incorporation'. However, as long as the company qualifies as a 'small' company under **CA 2006, ss. 382–3**, as seems likely here, the extent of the disclosure of its affairs would be greatly reduced, and it will be exempt from the audit requirement of **CA 2006, s. 477**. The criteria are: two out of three (tested every other year) of: turnover—not more than £10.2m; balance sheet total—not more than £5.1m; number of employees—not more than 50 (**CA 2006, ss. 382–3**). To this extent, the threat of disclosure is greatly diminished and the company can enjoy almost the same degree of

[8] Deal expressly with capital as it is raised in the question

[9] This shows both that you appreciate the reality of business life, and that you have engaged with academic work

privacy as a partnership. Companies are subject to more regulation, and thus a higher administrative burden than partnerships, but some of this administrative burden has been reduced for small companies by the **CA 2006** (the reform agenda explicitly followed a 'Think Small First' approach to reduce the legislative burden on small companies[10]) so for example Mo and Gok will not need to appoint a company secretary and will not need to hold Annual General Meetings.

[10]This indicates that you have read more widely about the reform of company law and understand some of the policy thinking behind the legislation

For Mo and Gok a private limited company is a sensible option (and one chosen by many small businesses: there are over 3 million companies on the register, the majority of them small private companies). It is not without its drawbacks and some of the apparent benefits may prove to be limited but as their prime concern appears to be to minimise their risk, a company is the easiest way of achieving this aim, in part at least. To reduce the scope for later disagreements they should consider making specific provision in the company's articles of association (the main constitutional document of the company) and/or enter into a separate shareholder agreement to deal with the resolution of disputes between them.

LOOKING FOR EXTRA MARKS?

■ Engage with some of the relevant research in the area to support your points and show your deeper understanding of the issues

■ Evaluate the benefits of limited liability; don't just assume that it is invariably a 'good thing' for all businesses

QUESTION | 2

'Despite being viewed as the key advantage of incorporation, the benefit of limited liability may prove to be illusory and so be outweighed by the disadvantages of incorporation.'

Discuss.

CAUTION!

■ Avoid a simple list of advantages and disadvantages of incorporation, this would not give you any scope for analysis and would not adequately address the question

■ Don't provide a general account of 'lifting the veil'—this question is focused on limited liability in the wider context rather than veil-lifting

DIAGRAM ANSWER PLAN

> Potential advantages of incorporation—is limited liability the 'key' advantage?

> Lack of benefit of limited liability in practice for many companies

> Drawbacks to incorporation—weighing up benefits and disadvantages

> Continuing potential for personal liability

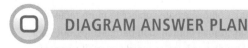 **SUGGESTED ANSWER**

On registration, members of a limited company gain the advantage of limited liability—their liability is limited (for a company limited by shares) to the amount unpaid on their shares (**Companies Act 2006 (CA 2006), s. 3(2)**). Accordingly, while a member would lose their investment in the event of the company becoming insolvent, the rest of their personal wealth is safe, protected by the 'veil of incorporation' that separates the company from its members. As a member in a small company will commonly invest only a small amount (often as little as £1), there may be little financial risk. This contrasts with the position of a sole trader or partnership where the trader/partners are personally liable for the business debts. Understandably this benefit of limited liability is often seen as the key advantage of incorporation.[1]

The case of *Salomon v A. Salomon & Co Ltd* **[1897] AC 22** established that the veil of incorporation applies just as much to 'one-man companies' as it does to the multi-member large corporations initially envisaged by Parliament, so members even of very small companies can benefit from limited liability. Although the decision has been criticised (eg Kahn-Freund described the decision as 'calamitous' and tempting traders to incorporate when there was no business need to do so: 'Some reflections on company law reform'(1944) 7 MLR 54),[2] the availability of limited liability to practically all traders who seek it is now firmly established.

It is generally assumed most traders choosing to use a limited company do so largely to benefit from this protection. However, research by both Freedman and Hicks indicates[3] this protection is only one of many factors influencing a trader—other factors as diverse as tax and prestige/credibility can also be highly influential (Freedman, 'Small businesses and the corporate form: burden or privilege?' (1994) 57

[1] This shows that your initial explanation of the essential points—limited liability, the veil, risk, etc is all directed to answering the question

[2] Judicious citation of academic work can show you have read more widely and understand different points of view

[3] Engage with the academic articles—here you can use them to bring together the law, practice, and respected research

MLR 555; Hicks, 'Corporate form: questioning the unsung hero' [1997] JBL 306). Incorporation also brings other benefits, such as flexibility of organisational structure and increased financing options including the ability to bring in outside investors. Accordingly while limited liability may be the 'key' benefit of incorporation, it is not the only benefit.[4] Furthermore, as the question indicates, the benefit of limited liability may prove to be illusory, particularly for small businesses, while the potentially negative consequences of incorporation may be unforeseen.

The inadequate capital of many small companies may mean the company cannot borrow money or buy in goods and services against the security of its own assets. Private companies have no minimum capital requirement and often have only a nominal capital (a public company by way of contrast must have a minimum capital of £50,000 (**CA 2006, s. 763**)). This makes it difficult for the company to obtain credit from banks and suppliers without external support. Banks commonly require some form of security for any loans (Freedman's research revealed over 50 per cent of respondents had personal guarantees to the bank), and suppliers may also seek protection through a third party guarantee. This means those seeking protection in the form of limited liability are likely to be liable as guarantors for any corporate loans or lines of credit, and so face personal losses (even bankruptcy) in the event of the company's failure. If the loan is secured over personal assets such as the family home, as is often the case, then there is the risk that these assets may be sold to recover the loans. The benefit of limited liability is indeed illusory in such situations[5] and as Freedman has observed, some traders may be incorporating to 'obtain the unattainable'.[6]

Companies are often formed without the benefit of legal advice and entrepreneurs may fail to appreciate fully the consequences of forming a company. The research of Freedman and Hicks shows the majority of entrepreneurs are not particularly aware of, or interested in, the precise legal form their business will take. That is regrettable as the veil of incorporation may have negative as well as positive effects. For example, in[7] ***Macaura v Northern Assurance Company*** **[1925] AC 619,** Macaura was unaware that his transfer of property to a company in which he was virtually the sole shareholder, meant he no longer owned the property. As a result, a policy taken out in his name, but covering property that now belonged to the company, was not covered by the insurance since he no longer had an insurable interest in the property.

A further example is ***Tunstall v Steigman* [1962] 1 QB 593** where Steigman, the landlord of a pair of shops, gave notice to the lessee of one on the ground (**Landlord and Tenant Act 1954, s. 30(1)(g)**) that she intended to occupy the premises for the purpose of her business.

[4] This shows you are keeping an eye on the question but also challenging the statement

[5] Use terms from the question itself to show you are answering it

[6] Don't spend much time trying to memorise long passages, but if you can remember a few pithy comments from your reading, whether cases or articles, it can add interest and depth to your work.

[7] The following paragraph and a half look at relevant cases and show how important it is to be able to summarise the relevant facts and points of law very succinctly

However, the court held that she had not met the requirements of the Act as the business was not to be carried on by her but by her company—which was a separate legal entity. A similar lack of awareness of the separation of the company and its proprietor meant that in *Re Lewis's Will Trusts* **[1985] 1 WLR 102** Lewis' bequest of 'my freehold farm and premises' to his son failed because the farm had been transferred to a company. Although Lewis owned three-quarters of the shares in the company (his son owned the other shares) the bequest failed as the farm was owned by the company, not Lewis. Other cases concern shareholder/directors who fail to recognise that the company is a separate legal person and who treat their company's assets and bank accounts as mere extensions of their private assets: *Attorney-General's Reference (No. 2 of 1982)* **[1984] QB 624** established that a sole shareholder of a company could nevertheless be guilty of stealing from 'his' company.

Generally company proprietors are safe from the courts piercing the veil of incorporation to impose liability on them for company debts. The reluctance of the higher courts to pierce the veil as seen in *Salomon v A. Salomon & Co Ltd* has been confirmed recently in *Prest v Petrodel Resources Ltd* **[2013] UKSC 34**.[8] However statute may remove the protection of the veil of incorporation. Directors may find themselves liable to contribute to the assets of a company in insolvent liquidation where they have engaged in fraudulent or wrongful trading (**Insolvency Act 1986 (IA 1986), ss. 213–4**), or to meet the claims of creditors where they have misused the name of a company that had previously gone into insolvent liquidation (**IA 1986, s. 217**). This liability may be extensive; for example in *Re DKG Contractors Ltd* **[1990] BCC 903** directors were ordered to contribute £400,000 for wrongful trading. Liquidators may also use the misfeasance procedure (**IA 1986, s. 212**) to recover assets wrongly used or transferred out of the company by company proprietors, as in *Re Purpoint Ltd* **[1991] BCC 121** where the proprietor of a company was ordered to reimburse the company where company money had been used for the proprietor's new business venture. In these cases the benefits of limited liability were significantly reduced.

Directors may also be found personally liable for torts committed within the company environment, depending on the circumstances. It is not common for directors to be found personally liable for negligent misstatements in the context of company activity as the courts require evidence that the director assumed personal responsibility (see *Williams v Natural Life Health Food Ltd* **[1998] 1 WLR 830**) but where a director does assume personal responsibility, liability can follow. This can be demonstrated by *Fairline Shipping Co v Adamson* **[1974] 2 All ER 967** where the court was influenced by the fact that the director communicated in the first person and

[8]Make reference to important recent decisions to show you are up to date with the law

on personal notepaper. Directors have also been held personally liable for other torts, eg in *Standard Chartered Bank v Pakistan National Shipping Corpn (Nos. 2 and 4)* [2002] 3 WLR 1547 the court held the managing director liable in deceit. The veil of incorporation will not protect all those behind it in respect of all their actions.

In conclusion,[9] it has been seen that while limited liability is an attractive proposition for many entrepreneurs, it is not the only reason for incorporation in practice. Furthermore its benefits are often illusory and it does not guarantee total protection from personal liability. Incorporation may result in unplanned and undesired outcomes, particularly when an entrepreneur does not fully appreciate the consequences of separate legal personality. In addition, the 'privilege' of limited liability is balanced by the need to comply with formalities and disclose information at Companies House. This increases the administrative burden through the need to file documents such as annual returns (due to be replaced by confirmation statements from June 2016), as well as reducing privacy. Disclosure obligations are reduced for small companies but even small additional burdens with the attendant cost of compliance and potential loss of privacy may be too much if the benefits of limited liability are not fully available. For some traders the disadvantages of incorporation could indeed outweigh the apparent benefit of limited liability.[10]

[9] Let the examiner know where you are in your structure—it shows you are still in control

[10] It can be helpful to make a clear link back to the question at the end

LOOKING FOR EXTRA MARKS?

- Engage with relevant research to support points and show your deeper understanding of the issues
- Consider how the merits and drawbacks of incorporation might differ for businesses of different sizes and types
- Recognise how some statutory provisions (or other legal mechanisms) may impose personal liability on individuals despite otherwise limited liability

QUESTION | 3

Gerhard and Angeline are friends who recently graduated from the University of Exford and decided to set up a fashion design business. Having considered their options, they have decided to set up a company to conduct the business. They are considering calling their business either 'F U Fashion' or 'Great University Trends'.

Advise Gerhard and Angeline on the steps they will need to take, and any issues or restrictions they should bear in mind, in creating and naming their company.

CAUTION!

- Avoid just describing the registration process or the name restrictions—assess the different elements and provide advice based on the facts of the question

- Don't just copy out statutory material: make sure you link relevant material to the facts

- Don't go into detail on the merits of the corporate form as the question tells us that the decision about the business form has already been made

DIAGRAM ANSWER PLAN

Identify the issues	■ Identify the issues: creating and naming a company
Relevant law	■ Registration process including documents and fees ■ Buying 'off-the-shelf': benefits and problems ■ Company name requirements and restrictions ■ Promotion and pre-incorporation contracts ■ Ongoing obligations including filing requirements
Apply the law	■ Apply to the facts
Conclude	■ Conclude

SUGGESTED ANSWER

Gerhard and Angeline should be aware that the company will (unlike a partnership) have its own separate legal personality and so they would not normally be liable for the company's debts or other liabilities (*Salomon v A. Salomon & Co Ltd* [1897] AC 22). From the facts of the question it appears that they intend to be the only directors and shareholders of the company, but the flexibility of the company form means they could easily involve others if they wanted—whether by appointing someone as director to share management of the business, or by providing shares to people, eg family members who wish to invest without running the business. However, unlike a partnership (which can arise under the **Partnership Act 1890, s. 1(1)** without any need for formality),[1] Gerhard and Angeline will need to observe various formalities in order to create a company.

[1] Shows, in passing, that you appreciate the difference between a company and a partnership

Creating the Company

Gerhard and Angeline can choose between creating the company by registering it themselves, or purchasing a company 'off the shelf'.[2] A shelf company is one that has already been created by a company formation agent and is available for immediate purchase.

[2]Very many companies are 'purchased' rather than created from scratch by their eventual users

If Gerhard and Angeline choose to register their own company (**Companies Act 2006 (CA 2006), ss. 7–13**) they will need to complete various documents and send these to the registrar of companies at Companies House (based in Cardiff for companies registered in England and Wales) either in paper form or electronically:

[3]In this and other 'bullet points' that follow, the basic information is combined with references to the facts of the problem to show the question is being addressed

- Memorandum of association[3] (**s. 8**)
  - Gerhard and Angeline must subscribe their names to the memorandum—the document that forms the company. It is no longer part of the company's constitution.
- Application for registration (**s. 9(2)**)
  - This states the company's basic details including its proposed name, the address of its registered office, and that it is (in this case) a private company.
- Articles of association (**s. 9(5)(b)**)
  - Articles (the company's constitution) need not be filed if Gerhard and Angeline wish to use model (standard form) articles. The current model articles are found in the **Companies (Model Articles) Regulations 2008**. If Gerhard and Angeline want to have some bespoke articles, they could register these and the model articles would then fill any gaps by virtue of **s. 20**.
- Statement of capital and initial shareholdings (**ss. 9(4)(a) and 10**)
  - This states the company's share capital and shareholdings. Most small private companies (as this will be) have minimal share capital, eg Gerhard and Angeline could have a share capital of £2 with each taking a single £1 share.
- Statement of proposed officers (**ss. 9(4)(c) and 12**)
  - It is assumed that Gerhard and Angeline will be the company's first directors so their names, addresses, and consent to act should go in here. As it will be a private company they do not need a company secretary[4] (**s. 270(1)**).

[4]Recognises the change to the law in the CA 2006

- Statement of compliance (**s. 13**)
  - Gerhard and Angeline must state that all the registration requirements have been complied with and the registrar can take this statement as evidence of compliance.

Gerhard and Angeline must also pay a registration fee, which is currently £40 for paper registration (less for electronic registration).[5] Same-day registration can be obtained for a higher fee. If all documents are in order the registrar registers them under **CA 2006, s. 14** and issues a Certificate of Incorporation (**CA 2006, s. 15**) which

[5]Impress the examiner by showing that you are aware of wider practical points as well as the legal points

is conclusive evidence that the registration requirements have been complied with. The company comes into existence at the point of registration (**CA 2006, s. 16**).

If Gerhard and Angeline did not want to prepare and send the incorporation documentation they could buy a shelf company, which is ready to use straight away. It costs more to buy a shelf company than register a company yourself, but it is not expensive (£50 is fairly standard, but cheaper options are available). There are potential disadvantages to buying a company off the shelf as it will not be in exactly the form Gerhard and Angeline might have chosen, so they should make changes to the articles to avoid problems later on. A shelf company will not have the desired name but the name can be changed by means of a special resolution (or other procedure specified in the articles) under **CA 2006, s. 77(1)**, or they could leave the company's name unchanged and trade under a different business name. As a company comes into existence on registration (not on purchase from the company formation agent or change of name) they should bear in mind that their company exists prior to their purchase. This is not normally a problem but can lead to complications, eg the

⁶Use your knowledge of other, connected, topics to add weight to your consideration of shelf companies

pre-incorporation contract provisions (**CA 2006, s. 51**)[6] do not apply where a company is already in existence at the time of the contract but under a different name (*Oshkosh B'Gosh Inc v Dan Marbel Inc Ltd* **[1989] BCLC 507**).

Naming the Company

There are some important requirements and restrictions in the choice of name for the company (see **CA 2006, Part 5**), and the restrictions also apply to business (or trading) names under **CA 2006, Part 41**. First, as a private company the company's name must end with 'limited' or 'Ltd' (or the Welsh equivalent if the company were to be registered in Wales, rather than England and Wales) (**CA 2006, s. 59**). Further, a company must not be registered if, in the opinion of the Secretary of State, use of its name would constitute an offence or be offensive (**CA 2006, s. 53**). It is possible that 'F U Fashions'[7]

⁷Try to relate your knowledge of the naming restrictions to the specific names suggested

would be perceived as offensive, *R v Registrar of Companies, ex parte Attorney-General* **[1991] BCLC 476** revealed that the registrar had rejected 'Prostitutes Ltd' and 'Hookers Ltd' as possible names for a new company (although he accepted 'Lindi St Claire (Personal Services) Ltd').

Approval of the Secretary of State is required if a company's proposed name would be likely to give the impression that the company is associated with the government, local authority, or specified public authorities (**CA 2006, s. 54**). This does not seem to be a problem in this case. The Secretary of State's approval must also be obtained if the name contains any word or expression specified in regulations under CA 2006, s. 55—currently the **Company, Limited Liability Partnerships and Business Names (Sensitive Words and Expressions) Regulations 2014.** This list has been reduced under the government's 'Red Tape Challenge' (designed to reduce the legislative burden on business)[8] since the previous regulations in 2009, but does include 'University'[9] so Gerhard and Angeline would have to go through the process of obtaining approval of the Secretary of State if they wanted to use this name.

The company name must not be the same as, or too similar to, any other company name on the register (**CA 2006, s. 66**). To avoid this problem Gerhard and Angeline can check the register of company names via the Companies House website. If the company was registered with a name that is the same as, or too similar to, another company's name then it could be directed to change it under **CA 2006, s. 67.** Furthermore, if someone were to complain that the company name is sufficiently similar to a name associated with them so as to be likely to mislead by suggesting a connection between them, there is an adjudication process under **CA 2006, ss. 69–74** which could also lead to a direction to change the company's name.

The company's name (whether or not a business name is used) must be disclosed at the registered office, any business premises, on all business communications, and on websites (**CA 2006, s. 82** and the **Companies (Trading Disclosures) Regulations 2008**).

Other Issues

Gerhard and Angeline should keep in mind that during the pre-formation process they can be regarded as company promoters[10] as they are taking the necessary steps to form a company with reference to a particular project (**Twycross v Grant (1877) 2 CPD 469**). As promoters they owe fiduciary duties to the company (see, eg ***Erlanger v New Sombrero Phosphate Co (1878) 3 App Cas 1218***) and they must ensure that all material facts are disclosed and any profits they make personally must be accounted for to the company. They should also be aware that any contracts entered into prior to incorporation will operate as contracts with them personally under **CA 2006, s. 51** (***Phonogram Ltd v Lane* [1982] QB 938**). Once the company is incorporated, it will only be bound by such contracts if the parties novate the contract and so Gerhard and Angeline should ensure this is done following incorporation to avoid any potential personal liability.

Once the company is registered, there are ongoing responsibilities. Annual accounts and annual reports must be filed at Companies House (**CA 2006, s. 441**) unless the company is exempt and any changes to the company's constitution, directorships, membership, etc must also be notified to Companies House. Filing fees are due each time so there are ongoing financial consequences attached to the 'privilege' of forming a company.

LOOKING FOR EXTRA MARKS?

- Show your practical knowledge—consider the possibility of buying a company 'off the shelf' as well as forming the company from scratch

- Bring in some awareness of other connected issues, such as promoters and pre-incorporation contracts, while taking care not to go off point

- Recognise recent developments in the law, such as the updating of the name regulations in 2014/15

QUESTION | 4

Which of the following statements more accurately reflects the current law on lifting (or piercing) the veil of incorporation and why?

'Salomon is in the shadow. It is still alive but no longer occupies the centre of the corporate stage.'

(Schmitthoff, C.M., 'Salomon in the shadow' [1976] JBL 305)

'The veil of incorporation is as opaque and impassable as an iron curtain.'

(Samuels, A., 'Lifting the veil' [1964] JBL 218)

CAUTION!

- The quotes are being used here as a trigger for a wider discussion, so don't be tempted simply to recite the arguments from the articles (and don't be put off the question just because you haven't read those particular articles)

- Analyse the current law, don't just describe the cases chronologically

- Remember to assess the impact of recent decisions—particularly those from higher courts

DIAGRAM ANSWER PLAN

Lifting/piercing the veil: concept, terminology, and current trend

Single economic unit: explain and explore

'Mere facade' or 'evasion': explain and explore

Agency, tort and other legal principles: explain and explore

Conclude: reconsider trend, and relate discussion to quotes

The quotes reflect the changing approaches of the law to lifting the veil of incorporation over the years. This essay will show that, despite the attempts of some judges (notably Lord Denning) to move the principle of separate corporate personality into the shadow, the current law is much more in line with Samuels' quote than Schmittoff's,[1] particularly with recent restrictive Supreme Court decisions in **VTB Capital plc v Nutritek International Corp [2013] UKSC 5 (VTB)** and **Prest v Petrodel Resources Ltd [2013] UKSC 34 (Prest)**.[2]

The veil of incorporation is a metaphor for the separation of a company and its members. Ever since the House of Lords in **Salomon v A. Salomon & Co Ltd [1897] AC 22 (Salomon)** recognised the validity of Salomon's 'one-man company',[3] attempts have been made to lift this veil, whether to impose liability on those behind the veil or for some other purpose (eg attributing 'enemy alien' status: **Daimler Co Ltd v Continental Tyre and Rubber Co Ltd [1916] 2 AC 307**). The veil can be lifted by statute (**Dimbleby v National Union of Journalists [1984] 1 WLR 427**), but such provisions are uncommon and usually impose additional liability on individuals rather than ignoring separate personality (eg **Insolvency Act 1986, s. 214**). Accordingly this essay will focus on the approach of the courts.

Over the years different phrases have been used, sometimes indicating different categories of veil-lifting (eg Ottolenghi, 'From peeping behind the corporate veil, to ignoring it completely' (1990) 53 MLR 338). Following **Prest**, this essay will restrict 'piercing' the veil to occasions when the court rejects the consequences of **Salomon** and imposes liability on members behind the veil.[4] 'Lifting' the veil may encompass a wider range of circumstances where liability is imposed on members or directors or the veil is looked through, including occasions where the **Salomon** principle remains intact.

In general terms the trend of the courts is very much towards the Samuels statement. Suggestions that courts could lift the veil whenever justice required (eg **Re a Company [1985] BCLC 333**) were rejected in **Adams v Cape Industries plc [1990] Ch 433 (Adams)** as was the argument that the veil could be lifted where a company and its members form a 'single economic unit' (**DHN Food Distributors v Tower Hamlets LBC [1976] 1 WLR 852 (DHN)**). **Woolfson v Strathclyde Regional Council, 1978 SC (HL) 90 (Woolfson)** stated the 'only' ground for lifting (or rather, 'piercing') the veil is where the involvement of a company is a 'mere facade concealing the true facts' and this has been generally accepted (**Adams** and **Prest**). This essay will first assess the 'single economic unit' and 'mere facade' grounds, and then consider the use of agency, tort, or other means to avoid (rather than pierce) the veil.[5]

---

[1] Using your introduction to set out your argument is an effective technique to encourage a critical and analytical approach

[2] Reassure the examiner that you know about recent cases

[3] This shows the examiner that you know your stuff, without wasting time setting out the detailed facts and judgment of *Salomon*

[4] At first sight this is just about terminology, but it also reveals a good awareness of *Prest*

[5] This tells the examiner where you are going. Often this would come in the first paragraph, but this essay has used an extended introduction to establish the main argument, cover the basic principles succinctly, and try to grab the examiner's attention.

Single Economic Unit

The principle of separate corporate personality applies to corporate groups as it does to companies with human members (*The Albazero* [1977] AC 774; *Re Southard* [1979] 1 WLR 1198). However, in *Littlewoods Mail Order Stores Ltd v Inland Revenue Commissioners* [1969] 1 WLR 1241 and *DHN* Lord Denning considered the economic reality—if a group was a 'single economic unit' in fact then it should be treated as such in law. Schmittoff's quote dates from this period where courts were more willing to lift the veil, pushing *Salomon* into the shadow.[6] But in *Woolfson* the House of Lords doubted this approach. This was accepted in *Adams*, holding the veil could be lifted on the basis of 'single economic unit' only where this was the true construction of a statute or contract. This allows veil-lifting on occasion (eg *Beckett Investment Management Group Ltd v Hall* [2007] ICR 1539) but is very limited in scope. Under this ground, the veil is indeed largely 'opaque and impassable'.[7]

Mere Facade Concealing the True Facts

The courts stated the veil can only be lifted/pierced if the company is a 'mere facade concealing the true facts', but *Adams* recognised there was sparse guidance on what that means. It seems there must be some impropriety on the part of those using the company (although not necessarily when forming the company: *Ben Hashem v Ali Shayif* [2009] 1 FLR 115) and this impropriety must be relevant—there must be a connection between the impropriety and the use of the corporate form: *Trustor AB v Smallbone (No. 2)* [2001] 1 WLR 1177. This was emphasised in *Prest* which located veil-piercing within the wider policy that 'statute must not be used as an engine of fraud', and focused on the concept of 'evasion'.[8]

The motivation of the individual is important. Where the corporate form was used deliberately to evade an existing liability the veil has been lifted (eg *Jones v Lipman* [1962] 1 WLR 832; *Gilford v Horne* [1933] Ch 935), as did the use of a company to hide misappropriated money (*Trustor AB v Smallbone (No. 2)* [2001] 1 WLR 1177) or abuse legislation (*Re Bugle Press* [1961] Ch 270), although *VTB* and *Prest* raise doubts as to whether all these are true examples of veil-piercing. Merely using separate personality to push liability onto another member of a group is not impropriety ('the right to use a corporate structure in this manner is inherent in our corporate law': *Adams v Cape Industries plc*).[9] *Ord v Belhaven Pubs Ltd* [1998] 2 BCLC 447, rejecting *Creasey v Breachwood Motors Ltd* [1993] BCLC 480, showed even transferring assets from a company after a potential liability had arisen would not justify piercing the veil where this was not done with the purpose of evading that liability (the transfer was part of a group reorganisation of assets). Similarly

---

[6] Link back to the quotes to show you are not producing a generic response to a veil-lifting question

[7] Interim conclusions (as you deal with each point) can be very helpful to keep your eye on the question and convince the examiner that you understand the relevance of the points you make.

[8] This shows an awareness of how the *Prest* analysis fits within the previously accepted categories

[9] Using a short quote can help to support the point being made

restrictively, **VTB** denied the veil could be lifted to impose liability on a person behind a 'dishonorable' transaction, and in **Prest** an individual's impropriety in matrimonial proceedings was not considered relevant in lifting the veil.

Accordingly, while the courts remain willing to lift the veil on this ground, the principle is applied restrictively, leaving the current law closer to the statement of Samuels than Schmittoff.

Agency, Tort, and Other Legal Principles

If a company is agent of its shareholder, liability for the company's debts will fall on the shareholder, by-passing the corporate veil (although not disturbing separate personality). The House of Lords in **Salomon** rejected the idea the company was Salomon's agent; the fact a company has a single member or is a wholly-owned subsidiary is not enough to make it the agent of its member or parent company. In the past, courts have found an agency relationship between subsidiary and parent (eg **Smith, Stone & Knight v Birmingham Corpn [1939] 4 All ER 116**) but **Adams** made clear agency cannot be presumed from the closeness of operations between parent company and subsidiary (see also **Yukong Line Ltd of Korea v Rendsburg Investments Corpn of Liberia (No. 2) [1998] 1 WLR 294**). The current law shows it is very unlikely that an agency relationship will be found on the facts, leaving the veil intact.

Where a member (or director) has personally committed a tort then personal or joint liability could follow. However, courts are generally reluctant to impose tortious liability on those behind the veil, recognising the potential for damage to the principle of separate personality (**Williams v Natural Life Health Foods Ltd [1998] 1 BCLC 689**). One area of topical interest is tortious liability of parent companies relating to their subsidiaries' activities. **Chandler v Cape Industries plc [2012] 1 WLR 3111** held that while responsibility does not arise by mere fact of the corporate relationship, on the facts the parent company had assumed a direct duty of care to the subsidiary's employees. This provides some scope for imposing liability notwithstanding the veil, but **Thompson v Renwick Group plc [2014] EWCA Civ 635** shows the courts will not often find a duty of care on parent companies.

In **Prest**, despite declining to pierce the veil, the Supreme Court obtained the same result by applying trusts principles. This case was not about imposing liability on a member for debts of the company, but nonetheless indicates courts may be willing to 'lift' the veil in the wide sense by exploring the facts (described as the 'concealment principle' in **Prest**), and this may lead to the application of other legal principles through which the veil could be by-passed.

Conclusion

The high-point of veil-lifting recognised in Schmittoff's quote is long gone. Despite occasional indications of Denning-esque views (eg *Ratiu v Conway* [2005] EWCA Civ 1302) recent decisions show a clear reluctance to depart from the principle of separate corporate personality and lift/pierce the veil except where there is abuse of the corporate form. This is so regardless of the seriousness or moral force of the claimant's position, although the courts are willing to explore the use of other legal principles to achieve the same end. Largely in line with Samuels' quote, the current law starts from the assumption that the veil is indeed an 'iron curtain'; contrary to Schmittoff's statement *Salomon* is very much 'centre stage'.[10]

[10] After summarising the position to show that the writer's initial view has been supported, the conclusion uses the quotes themselves to link back to the question

LOOKING FOR EXTRA MARKS?

■ Clearly relate the question quotes to attitudes to lifting/piercing the veil, eg a generally permissive approach (as suggested by the Schmittoff quote) or a more strict approach (Samuels)

■ Refer back to the particular stances reflected in the question quotes from time to time to show that you are really engaging with the question

■ Having identified what the approach of the law is; think about whether this is how it should be, or not, and why.

QUESTION | 5

Write a case note on *Prest v Petrodel Resources Ltd* [2013] UKSC 34 focusing on the company law issues raised in the case.

CAUTION!

■ Be careful not to spend too much time simply reciting the case facts; you need to leave enough time to analyse the judgments and issues

■ Don't examine the case in isolation—explore how it fits within the broader legal context and alongside other cases

■ Practise preparing case notes (or case comments) as well as more conventional essays to develop your writing skills and deepen your knowledge and understanding

DIAGRAM ANSWER PLAN

Introduction: why the case is significant; brief case facts

Judgments: approach of lower courts; approach of Supreme Court

Identify and assess important elements of the judgments

Conclusion: summarise key points and evaluate significance of the case

SUGGESTED ANSWER

Prest v Petrodel Resources Ltd **[2013] UKSC 34 (*Prest*)** gave the Supreme Court a second chance in only a few months (the first being *VTB Capital plc v Nutritek International Corp* **[2013] UKSC 5 (*VTB*)**) to consider the law on lifting the veil of incorporation. Prior to these cases the most recent authoritative guidance was that of *Adams v Cape Industries plc* **[1990] Ch 433 (*Adams*)** and *Woolfson v Strathclyde Regional Council* **1978 SC (HL) 90**. Since lifting (or, as the Supreme Court prefers, 'piercing') the veil means ignoring the separate personality of a company and its members (as established in *Salomon v A. Salomon & Co Ltd* **[1897] AC 22**)[1] and thus potentially undermining the 'unyielding rock' of company law (Templeman, Lord, 'Forty years on' (1990) 11 Co Law 10), this issue is of great importance.

The case concerned proceedings for ancillary relief following the divorce of Yasmin Prest from her oil-tycoon husband, Michael, who was found to be the effective sole owner and controller of several companies holding UK properties. Mr Prest had not been co-operative—his conduct of the proceedings was 'characterised by persistent obstruction, obfuscation and deceit'[2] and refusal to comply with court orders (Lord Sumption).

At first instance[3] (*YP v MP and Petrodel Resources Ltd* **[2011] EWHC 2956**) Moylan J ordered the transfer of properties held by Mr Prest's companies. Although the judge concluded he could not pierce the veil under general principles (as Mr Prest's impropriety did not relate to the use of the companies), Moylan J interpreted the **Matrimonial Causes Act 1973 (MCA 1973), s. 24** widely by construing 'property' to include property over which an individual exercises control.

[1] Shows you understand and can explain the concept, but deals with the basics very concisely

[2] In a 'closed book' exam you probably wouldn't remember the exact words, but you could still give a flavour of the court's view of Mr Prest's behaviour

[3] Deal with the lower courts' decisions concisely as the bulk of the essay needs to be devoted to the Supreme Court's approach and evaluation of this

In the Court of Appeal (*Petrodel Resources Ltd v Prest* [2012] **EWCA Civ 1395**) the majority (Rimer and Patten LJJ) found in favour of the companies, rejecting both the piercing of the veil and Moylan J's interpretation of **MCA 1973**. The majority criticised the generous approach of the family courts to piercing the veil and decreed this 'must now cease' (Patten LJ). However Thorpe LJ favoured the looser approach to lifting the veil in family cases, memorably describing the alternative as offering 'an open road and a fast car to the money maker'.

The Supreme Court Judgment

The Supreme Court reversed the Court of Appeal decision, with the seven Justices unanimously finding in favour of Mrs Prest, but not by piercing the veil of incorporation, nor by restoring Moylan J's interpretation of **MCA 1973**. Instead the court re-assessed the facts, concluding Mr Prest had provided the purchase money for the properties, giving rise to a presumption (that was not rebutted) that the properties were held by the companies on resulting trust for him. Nonetheless the Supreme Court offered extensive (albeit obiter) discussion of veil-piercing.

The main judgment was given by Lord Sumption (whose reasons were expressly accepted, in the main, by Lords Neuberger, Mance, Clarke, and Walker). Lord Sumption recognised the principle of separate corporate personality is in some sense a fiction, but is one that amounts to 'the whole foundation of English company and insolvency law'. Although a foundational principle should presumably not be easily disturbed, the Supreme Court accepted a limited jurisdiction to pierce the veil, allied to the broader principle that absolute legal principles can be overturned in the event of fraud. Lord Sumption indicated 'piercing the veil' happens only where separate personality is disregarded. He separated authorities into 'evasion' cases—where the corporate form was being used improperly—and 'concealment' cases—where regard was simply had to facts behind the veil;[4] only the first category were properly examples of veil-piercing.

The veil should, therefore, be pierced only where necessary to prevent the abuse of corporate legal personality, such abuse being using the company to evade the law or to frustrate its enforcement, and 'only for the purpose of depriving the company or its controller of the advantage they would otherwise have obtained' (Lord Sumption). This should be a remedy of 'last resort',[5] following the approach of Munby J in *Ben Hashem v Al Shayif* [2009] 1 FLR 115, to be used only 'when all other more conventional remedies have proved to be of no assistance' (Lord Clarke).

[4] A key part of *Prest* was this distinction between 'concealment' and 'evasion' so make sure you deal with it

[5] Another important point. You could develop this with reference to some of the academic writing about *Prest* and whether veil-piercing should be a last resort

Comment

The Supreme Court's judgment provides some clarity. The explicit acknowledgement that a veil-piercing jurisdiction exists is helpful after doubts were sown by Lord Neuberger in **VTB**. It is also clear that family law cannot take an independent approach to this issue, contrary to dicta in cases such as **Nicholas v Nicholas [1984] FLR 285**.

Lord Sumption's distinction between 'concealment' and 'evasion' may help in assessing the different ways in which a court approaches the veil of incorporation and in reducing occasions where it is thought necessary to pierce it. Nonetheless, as Lord Sumption recognised, many cases combine both elements, while Lady Hale doubted whether all cases could be classified in this way.[6] There is scope for confusion as Lords Sumption and Neuberger disagreed on whether to class some cases (eg **Gilford Motor Co Ltd v Horne [1933] Ch 935**) as evasion or concealment. Whether these concepts can be applied clearly and distinctly in future cases remains unclear, but post-**Prest**, in **R v Sale [2014] 1 WLR 663** the Court of Appeal explicitly distinguished the evasion principle (which did not apply) from the concealment principle (which did, the court holding the company and the individual were interlinked, allowing liability to be quantified on the basis of the company's profits).

It should be noted that not all Justices fully accepted a strict limitation on the principle to 'evasion' cases, eg Lord Mance felt it would be 'dangerous' to foreclose all possible future situations in which the principle might arise. Be that as it may, the Court of Appeal has subsequently indicated that any development of the law will be difficult: **Antonio Gramsci Shipping Corporation v Lembergs [2013] EWCA Civ 730**,[7] per Beatson LJ.

The connecting of veil-piercing with the principle that statute should not be used as an engine of fraud shows clearly that veil-piercing relies on the corporate form being used for some deliberately dishonest purpose. This is in line with the approach of the Court of Appeal in **Adams**. The impropriety must thus be relevant impropriety—bad behaviour in itself does not justify piercing the veil. What matters is an improper purpose in the use of the company, although there need not have been an improper purpose in creating the company (**Ben Hashem v Al Shayif**).

Furthermore, although it was acknowledged that Mr Prest had himself ignored the corporate veil and misapplied corporate assets (the group was described as his 'money box which he uses at will' (Moylan J)), such behaviour does not allow a court to disregard the corporate veil in the same way. This focus on the 'relevance' of the impropriety, limits and justifies the engagement of the veil-piercing jurisdiction and thus promotes commercial certainty. Yet the consequence is that

[6] Recognise that the Justices took different approaches at times, even while coming to the same result

[7] Bring in later cases to show the impact of *Prest* on the law

[8] Don't be afraid to comment on the merits of an approach. You could develop this into a deeper discussion of approaches to veil-lifting (perhaps comparing this jurisdiction to others) and potentially conflicting concerns

the law offers continued protection and advantage to individuals who many might feel should have forfeited those rights.[8] Interestingly, *Prest* has not stifled all enthusiasm for veil-piercing in the lower courts: in *Wood v Baker* **[2015] EWHC 2536 (Ch)** the High Court (albeit without the benefit of legal argument from both sides) explicitly pierced the veil to freeze assets of companies used by a bankrupt to hide assets from his trustee-in-bankruptcy.

Conclusion

Arguably *Prest* made few changes to company law: it confirms the existence of a principle that was not in serious doubt and, to a significant extent, confirms earlier case law on when it should apply. However, the case emphasises the principle's status as a 'last resort'—where no other legal principle can aid the claimant. It also provides further guidance on the limited circumstances in which veil-piercing

[9] Show you have thought about the consequences of the case for future legal actions

may be permitted. It might be expected that the number of cases seeking to pierce the veil will reduce and claims evoking the principle will be more carefully formulated.[9] Any future attempt to expand veil-piercing beyond 'evasion' cases will have little support; even Lord Mance (who, along with Lady Hale, declined to limit the principle) discouraged the thought that any further exception would be easy to establish (further supported by *Antonio Gramsci Shipping Corporation v Lembergs*).

[10] Reflect also on the particular situation at the heart of the case

Despite Mrs Prest's success, *Prest* does not give someone in her position much comfort from company law.[10] Only if the company is being used in order to evade liability or frustrate enforcement will the veil be pierced, and only impropriety in that sense is relevant to the court's determination. This conclusion is undoubtedly positive from the sense of legal and commercial clarity but may be unappealing to a layperson who would, like Mr Prest himself, view the company and controller as one and the same. The use of trusts gives hope to the non-controlling spouse in these cases, but arguably re-opens uncertainty as to the ownership of 'corporate' assets that the case had otherwise sought to close, potentially creating the commercial uncertainty that the restrictive approach to veil-piercing had sought to prevent.

 LOOKING FOR EXTRA MARKS?

- Deal with the different approaches taken by the individual Justices and consider the impact this might have on the development of the law
- Explore later cases where the case has been considered to evaluate its impact
- Consider how the approach compares to that taken in other jurisdictions

TAKING THINGS FURTHER

▪ Cheng-Han, T., 'Veil-piercing—a fresh start' [2015] JBL 20

Argues that veil-piercing is based on the privilege of incorporation having been abused and welcomes Prest *as a 'significant attempt to formulate a principled approach'.*

▪ Day, W., 'Skirting around the issue: the corporate veil after *Prest v Petrodel*' [2014] LMCLQ 269

*Recognises the importance, particularly post-*Prest, *of the use of conventional legal principles to by-pass the corporate veil.*

▪ Freedman, J., 'Small businesses and the corporate form: burden or privilege?' (1994) 57 MLR 555

Explores the motivations behind the choice of particular business forms.

▪ Freedman, J. and Finch, V., 'The limited liability partnership: pick and mix or mix-up?' [2002] JBL 475

Questions the value of the LLP—'this strange hybrid entity'—to both large and small businesses and raises areas of legal and practical uncertainty.

▪ Hannigan, B., 'Wedded to *Salomon*: evasion, concealment and confusion on piercing the veil of the one-man company' (2013) 50 Irish Jurist 11

A typically well-written, comprehensive, and critical consideration of Prest.

▪ Hicks, A., 'Corporate form: questioning the unsung hero' [1997] JBL 306

Considers and challenges the relevance and availability of limited liability to small businesses. See also Griffin, S., 'Limited liability: a necessary revolution?' (2004) 24 Co Law 99.

▪ Kahn-Freund, O., 'Some reflections on company law reform' (1944) 7 MLR 54

Includes an evaluation of the Salomon *decision and considers the wider merits of providing limited liability to small businesses.*

▪ Lower, M., 'What's on offer? A consideration of the legal forms available for use by small- and medium-sized enterprises in the United Kingdom' (2003) 24 Co Law 166

A quick review of the main business forms, focusing on the elements important to SMEs and considering policy issues.

▪ Moore, M., 'A temple built on faulty foundations' [2006] JBL 180

*A pre-*Prest *plea for 'reconceptualization' of the test for piercing the veil, arguing for a move away from the notion of 'sham' or 'façade' to the company's 'genuine ultimate purpose'.*

▪ Muchlinski, P., 'Limited liability and multinational enterprises: a case for reform?' (2010) 34 Camb J Econs 915

Considers the basis and justification of limited liability generally, and particularly in relation to corporate groups and large tort claims. See also, eg Leebron, D. W., 'Limited liability, tort victims and creditors' (1991) 91 Columbia L R 1565; Hansmann, H. & Kraakman, R., 'Toward unlimited shareholder liability for corporate torts' (1991) 100 Yale LJ 1879.

▪ Ottolenghi, S., 'From peeping behind the corporate veil, to ignoring it completely' (1990) 53 MLR 338

Categorises veil-lifting cases using distinctive terminology: consider whether you agree with the categories, and whether they remain valid in light of subsequent legal developments.

■ Tjio, H., 'Lifting the veil or piercing the veil?' [2014] LMCLQ 19

A generally thoughtful explanation of Prest *and consideration of its potential impact.*

 Online Resource Centre   www.oxfordtextbooks.co.uk/orc/qanda/

Go online for extra essay and problem questions, a glossary of key terms, online versions of all the answer plans and audio commentary on how selected ones were put together, and a range of podcasts which include advice on exam and coursework technique and advice for other assessment methods.

The Corporate Constitution

3

ARE YOU READY?

- Articles of association
- The model articles
- Alteration of the articles
- Entrenchment
- Legal effect of the articles of association—the statutory contract
- Shareholder agreements
- Connections (in particular) with: management and governance, shareholder rights and remedies

KEY DEBATES

Debate: to what extent do the articles of association bind the parties to it?

There was some lively academic discussion, particularly during the 1970s and 80s, about the enforceability of the 'statutory contract' but without any clear resolution of the matter. The most helpful articles are probably Wedderburn (1957) and Drury (1986), but see also Goldberg (1972), Gregory (1981) and Prentice (1980), all cited in this chapter's 'Taking Things Further' section. The debate was touched upon by the Company Law Review Steering Group but the resulting legislation left the area unchanged.

QUESTION | 1

'**Section 21(1) of the Companies Act 2006** provides only one part of a much bigger picture relating to the alteration of a company's articles of association.'

Discuss.

CAUTION!

- Don't forget to move beyond the statutory provisions on alteration of the articles; you must include consideration of the 'bona fide for the benefit of the company' test

- Avoid just describing the law on alteration of the articles; think about how all the elements work together to create the 'bigger picture'

DIAGRAM ANSWER PLAN

Indroduction: CA 2006, s. 21

Contracting out: *Russell v Northern Bank*

Entrenchment: s. 22 and alternative methods

Statutory restrictions on alteration: additional contributions and class rights

The 'bona fide for the benefit of the company' test: meaning and complexities

Conclusion: summarise main points

SUGGESTED ANSWER

The company's articles of association are the key constitutional document of the company, containing its internal regulations, and bind the company and the members: **Companies Act 2006 (CA 2006), s. 33.** Under **CA 2006, s. 21**, companies can alter their articles at any time by special resolution. This requires a 75 per cent majority of those voting (**CA 2006, s. 283**) and the written resolution procedure (**CA 2006, s. 288**) can be used. Articles can also be altered by unanimous agreement of the members, without a formal meeting or resolution (***Cane v Jones* [1980] 1 WLR 1451**). This essay will show[1] that although the statutory right of alteration is very important, the true picture of alteration of the articles is indeed much bigger, with many statutory and common law restrictions on this right.

[1] Using the introduction to indicate the argument helps you to focus on the key issues from the start

Contracting out of the Right to Alter[2]

[2] Subheadings can be useful to keep to a clear structure and deal with all the points

Companies cannot contractually restrict themselves from exercising their statutory right of alteration. For example, in ***Punt v Symons & Co Ltd* [1903] 2 Ch 506** it was held that the company's agreement not to alter its articles to remove a restriction on the appointment of directors was unlawful. However, in ***Russell v Northern Bank Development Corpn Ltd* [1992] 1 WLR 588** the House of Lords accepted that while any such agreement was not binding on the company itself, an agreement between all the shareholders agreeing not to vote in favour of an alteration was effective and enforceable.

Entrenchment

Although a special resolution is normally sufficient to alter the company's articles, it is possible to 'entrench' an article, making it harder to alter that article. Prior to **CA 2006,**[3] it was possible to 'embed' a constitutional provision by inserting it, with protection from alteration, within the company's memorandum of association. Post-2006 a company's memorandum is no longer part of the company's constitution (it is the document that forms the company: **CA 2006, s. 8**) and so this is not an option. Provision for entrenchment within the articles of association is now possible. Under **CA 2006, s. 22(1)** a company's articles may provide that specified clauses of the articles may be amended or repealed only if conditions are met, or procedures are complied with, that are more restrictive than a special resolution. Entrenched articles therefore cannot be altered by special resolution alone, but only by following the provisions by entrenchment (or by unanimous agreement of the members or order of the court: **CA 2006, s. 22(3)**).[4] The registrar of companies must be notified of provisions for entrenchment and also of their removal: CA 2006, s. 23.

[3] This shows your awareness of how the position has changed and so the need for the new 'entrenchment' provisions

[4] Follow through your discussion to demonstrate the effect of the provision and make explicitly clear the relevance of the point to your argument

Companies can also effectively entrench articles by making use of weighted voting.[5] If some shares are weighted to carry more than 25 per cent of the votes on a resolution to alter a particular article, then it becomes impossible for a special resolution to be passed against the wishes of that shareholder, effectively entrenching the article. The validity of this was confirmed in ***Bushell v Faith* [1970] AC 1099**—although a company could not validly create an article depriving it

[5] Making the connection between statutory entrenchment and other devices for achieving similar effects

of the right to alter its articles by special resolution, it could give weighted voting rights that could have the same effect.

Statutory Restrictions on the Right to Alter

[6] This provides your link between sections of your essay

Even articles that are not entrenched or subject to weighted voting[6] may be subject to restrictions on alteration, or alteration may be ineffective to some extent. Alterations made after the date a person becomes a member, will not bind that member so far as it requires them to take or subscribe for shares other than those held at the date of the alteration, or increases their liability to contribute to the company's share capital or otherwise pay money to the company: **CA 2006, s. 25**.

Where the alteration of the articles constitutes a variation of class rights, the alteration cannot be made under **CA 2006, s. 21(1)**, but only in accordance with **CA 2006, s. 630**. This requires alteration to be in accordance with any provision in the company's articles for the variation of those rights, or, if there is no such provision, with the agreement of a three-quarter majority of that class of shareholders (whether in writing or resolution at a separate class meeting):

[7] As this essay is not really about class rights you cannot risk spending too much time on this point, but you can still show your good understanding of it by making a few key points very succinctly

Cumbrian Newspapers Group Ltd v Cumberland & Westmorland Herald Newspaper & Printing Co Ltd **[1986] BCLC 286**. Although 'variation' has been construed narrowly and so not every alteration of articles concerning class rights will trigger **CA 2006, s. 630** (see *White v Bristol Aeroplane Co Ltd* **[1953] Ch 65**),[7] this is nonetheless a significant restriction on the company's right to alter its articles by special resolution.

Further Restrictions: the Bona Fide Test

Arguably the most important restriction on companies' freedom to alter their articles is where the court decides the alteration is not bona fide for the benefit of the company as a whole but is an abuse of majority power. The power of the courts to police proposed alterations of the articles was established in *Allen v Gold Reefs of West Africa Ltd*

[8] This is an important case so it is worth including a few salient case facts

[1900] 1 Ch 656. In this case the company altered its articles to give a lien on shares of any member in respect of any debts or liabilities of the member to the company. At the time, the alteration only affected one member, who owed arrears of calls on his shares.[8] The court held the power of the company to alter its articles under what is now **CA 2006, s. 21(1)** had to be exercised, not only in the manner required by the law, but also bona fide for the benefit of the company as a whole. However the fact the alteration only applied to a single member at the time of alteration did not mean that it was an abuse of majority power and that it was not for the benefit of the company as a whole.

How should the court decide whether the alteration is bona fide in the interests of the company as a whole? There was initially some disagreement as to whether the test should be objective (*Dafen Tinplate Co Ltd v Llanelly Steel Co* **[1920] 2 Ch 124**) or subjective

(*Sidebottom v Kershaw, Leese & Co Ltd* [1920] **1** Ch **154**), but in *Shuttleworth v Cox Brothers & Co Ltd* [1927] **2 KB 9** the court opted for the subjective test. Accordingly the court is merely concerned to establish whether the shareholders, in voting for the alteration, believed that they were acting in the best interests of the company as a whole; it is not for the court itself to determine whether or not the proposed alteration was in the interests of the company.[9] It is hard to challenge an alteration where the test is subjective, but not impossible. As held in *Shuttleworth v Cox Brothers & Co Ltd*, even with a subjective test, if an alteration is so oppressive as to cast doubt on the shareholders' honesty, or so extravagant that no reasonable man could consider it for the company's benefit, the alteration will not be allowed.

[9] Think PEA: the point that the test is 'subjective' has been identified (and supported with case authority), now this part explains what that means in this context, and from here the paragraph goes on to assess how this still allows the courts to challenge the alteration

A particular problem is how to determine what is in the interests of the company as a whole when the proposed alteration only concerns membership matters (as here the company has no separate interest). In *Greenhalgh v Arderne Cinemas Ltd* [1951] **Ch 286** the court stated that in these circumstances the court should ask whether the alteration was for the benefit of 'an individual hypothetical member', and whether the effect of the alteration was to discriminate between majority and minority shareholders. This test has met with criticism, but the court in *Citco Banking Corporation NV v Pusser's Ltd* [2007] **BCC 205** declined to disturb it despite recognising it has not been found 'entirely illuminating'.

[10] Recognise the increasing importance of statutory shareholder remedies in this area

Although this area is complex and difficult to apply, its significance is now much reduced.[10] Now where a minority shareholder alleges that there has been an alteration of the articles which constitutes an abuse by the majority of their power, the claim would normally be brought as a claim of unfair prejudice under **CA 2006, s. 994**. If a claim is brought under this section and the court decides in favour of the claimant, the court has unlimited power to make orders under **CA 2006, s. 996(1)** which include an order requiring the company not to make any, or any specified, alterations in its articles without the leave of the court: **s. 996(2)(d)**.

Conclusion

It can be seen that **CA 2006, s. 21** only provides a starting point for considering the alteration of the articles by a company. Not only can the articles be altered otherwise than by way of a special resolution; in many circumstances the company's right to alter the articles is restricted in some way, whether by statute or by the courts. Furthermore the importance of the company's right to alter its articles contained in **CA 2006, s. 21** is reduced through court decisions allowing the use of weighted voting and shareholder agreements that effectively prevent alteration while not technically disturbing the principle of an unfettered statutory right of alteration.

LOOKING FOR EXTRA MARKS?

- Show that you recognise the links between this topic and other areas such as shareholder relations and remedies
- Explore the relevant cases in some detail, particularly in relation to the 'bona fide' test
- Consider more recent developments such as entrenchment, comparing it to the pre-2006 position and making sure you relate your discussion to the question

QUESTION | 2

'By virtue of **s. 14** [now **CA 2006, s. 33**] the articles of association become, upon registration, a contract between a company and members. It is, however, a statutory contract of a special nature with its own distinctive features' (per Steyn LJ, ***Bratton Seymour Service Co Ltd v Oxborough*** **[1992] BCLC 693**).

Discuss.

CAUTION!

- Before attempting this question you need really sound understanding of the topic—you need to be able to provide both breadth and depth of content
- Don't be tempted to write about the articles of association generally; focus on the nature of the articles, the 'statutory contract'
- Concentrate on the main points of interest (enforcement and alteration), but don't forget to mention other, more minor, points of similarity or difference as well

DIAGRAM ANSWER PLAN

> Introduction: identify key points for discussion

> The articles as a binding contact: CA 2006, s. 33

> Enforceability of the statutory contract: insider and outsider rights

> Alteration of the articles compared with alteration of contracts

Inapplicability of usual contractual rules

Conclusion: assess statement overall

SUGGESTED ANSWER

Companies Act 2006 (CA 2006), s. 33 establishes the contractual nature of the articles of association: the provisions of the 'company's constitution' (the articles) bind the company and its members as if there were covenants on both sides to observe the provisions. The articles are termed a 'statutory contract'[1] as their contractual nature derives from statute rather than the operation of conventional contract law requiring offer, acceptance, and consideration. In many ways the contract contained in the articles is of a special nature, many are highlighted in *Bratton Seymour Service Co Ltd v Oxborough* **[1992] BCLC 693** itself. The most significant are[2] the limits on the ability of members to enforce their contractual rights, and the ability to vary the terms of the statutory contract by majority vote, but other distinctive features such as the implication of terms and the availability of contractual remedies will also be considered.

CA 2006, s. 33(1) is in equivalent terms to its predecessor, **CA 1985, s. 14** (and before that **CA 1948, s. 20**), with slight modifications, including recognising that post-2006 the memorandum of association is no longer part of the company's constitution. It has long been established that the articles, in accordance with their contractual nature, can be enforced by the company against the members of the company; by a member against a member; and by a member against the company. So, it has been held[3] that the company can enforce compliance with an obligation to refer disputes between the company and a member to arbitration if the articles contain a valid reference to an arbitration clause (see *Hickman v Kent or Romney Marsh Sheep-Breeders' Association* **[1915] 1 Ch 881**), while in *Pender v Lushington* **(1877) 6 Ch D 70** the plaintiff sued to enforce his right as a member to have his vote recorded. In *Rayfield v Hands* **[1960] Ch 1** the court established a member could enforce against another member the obligation to acquire shares which that member wished to sell where such an obligation was contained in the articles.

But complications arise in respect of quite which provisions of the articles are enforceable under the statutory contract, and in this regard the articles do appear special in nature compared with a traditional contract.[4] In *Hickman v Kent or Romney Marsh Sheep-Breeders' Association*, Astbury J expressed the view that an 'outsider' given

[1] It is a good idea to clearly but concisely explain the key concept at the start of the essay

[2] Even if you don't set out your full argument, your introduction can give an indication of the direction of your work

[3] The rest of this paragraph deals with important cases with just enough of the facts to show the examiner that you know the cases, without wasting time

[4] Show that you are thinking about the question itself and not just producing a standard answer by using the same words as appear in the question quote

rights in his capacity as an outsider could not enforce those rights under the articles, whether or not he was or became a member (ie an 'insider'). Normal principles of contract law generally prevent an outsider from suing on a contract to which he is not party, but the statutory contract takes this a step further in denying that right even to an 'insider' if he is seeking to enforce rights in his capacity as an 'outsider'. This was applied in *Beattie v E & F Beattie Ltd* [1938] **Ch 708** to a claim brought by a director/shareholder since the claim related to his capacity as a director not as a member, while in *Eley v Positive Government Security Life Assurance Co Ltd* (1876) **1 Ex D 88** Eley was not permitted to enforce a right contained in the company's articles that he should remain the company's solicitor. The definition of outsider rights is broad and includes remuneration rights of directors contained in the articles. In *Re New British Iron Co, ex p Beckwith* [1898] **1 Ch 324** the court held the articles did not constitute a contract between the company and the directors (although, since the directors had accepted office on the basis of the article, the terms were incorporated as an implied term in their service contract). Similarly, *Swabey v Port Darwin Gold Mining Co* (1889) **1 Meg 385** held the implied term was subject to prospective alteration in the normal way of any article. These latter cases show 'outsider' rights may be enforceable under contracts extrinsic to the articles, even though they are apparently not enforceable under the statutory contract itself.

[5] Make sure that you recognise the complexities of the legal position by looking at potentially contradictory cases

The position on enforceability of the terms of the articles is complicated further by other cases, particularly *Quin & Axtens Ltd v Salmon* [1909] AC 442.[5] In that case, the company's two managing directors, Salmon and Axtens, were also shareholders. The company's articles gave each a veto on director resolutions relating to the acquisition of certain properties. A meeting of the directors resolved to acquire properties despite Salmon's dissent, and at a subsequent general meeting the shareholders passed similar resolutions. The House of Lords held that the shareholders' resolutions were inconsistent with the articles and restrained the company from acting on them. Was this enforcing 'outsider' rights (ie the director's veto) under the articles?

[6] Make good use of your wider reading by introducing academic discussion and showing you understand the key arguments

Lord Wedderburn has explained the case as showing that members have an enforceable right for the company to be managed in accordance with its constitution (see Wedderburn, 'Shareholder rights and the rule in *Foss v Harbottle*' [1957] CLJ 194) and, provided that[6] they sue in their 'member' capacity, can thus indirectly enforce outsider rights by enforcing their right to have all the provisions of the constitution observed. This analysis has been subjected to further refinements by Goldberg, Prentice, and Gregory[7]

[7] If you have time you can draw out these refinements and provide a more critical assessment of the debate; where time is short you will need to indicate your understanding of the ideas but focus on particular points—in this essay the focus has been placed on Wedderburn and Drury as they take different approaches.

(see Goldberg, 'The enforcement of outsider-rights under section 20(1) of the Companies Act 1948' (1972) 35 MLR 362, Prentice, 'The enforcement of "outsider" rights' (1980) 1 Co Law 179, and Gregory, 'The section 20 contract' (1981) 44 MLR 526), although none of the arguments

THE CORPORATE CONSTITUTION

seem fully to reconcile the cases. Taking a slightly different perspective, Drury argued that the statutory contract should be viewed as a dynamic 'relational contract' characterised by longevity and incompleteness (see 'The relative nature of the shareholder's right to enforce the company contract' [1986] CLJ 219) which provides a basis for understanding why rights in the articles should not be absolutely and uniformly enforceable. It also shows an appreciation of the limits of contractual analysis in relation to the articles, further confirming the 'special' nature of the statutory contract.

Another way in which the statutory contract is of a special nature, distinct from a traditional contract, relates to amendment of the contract. Unlike a standard contract,[8] the articles can be altered by means of a special resolution under **CA 2006, s. 21**, that is by majority vote rather than agreement of all the parties. Although articles can now be entrenched (**CA 2006, s. 22**), and this entrenchment can provide for unanimity, this would be the exception rather than the rule. The court imposes restrictions on the alteration of the articles, such that they can only be altered 'bona fide in the interests of the company as a whole' (**Allen v Gold Reefs of West Africa Ltd [1900] 1 Ch 656**), but this is not equivalent to requiring the consent of all parties to the contract. Indeed if anything it highlights the special nature of the statutory contract as it shows the parties must have the company's, and not just their own, interest in mind, unlike in a traditional contract.

There are other ways in which the statutory contract has its own special nature and distinctive features. First, not all contractual remedies apply to the statutory contract: misrepresentation, mistake, undue influence, and duress are not applicable (**Bratton Seymour Service Co Ltd v Oxborough**). In **Scott v Frank F Scott (London) Ltd [1940] Ch 794**, the court refused to rectify the articles to make them accord with the intention of the members at the time of the company's registration. Similarly the court will not imply a term to change the articles by implication from extrinsic circumstances (**Bratton Seymour Service Co Ltd v Oxborough**). A term can be implied where necessary to give business efficacy to the language of the articles in their commercial setting (**Equitable Life Assurance Society v Hyman [2002] 1 AC 408**) and this has sometimes been approached quite generously (**Folkes Group plc v Alexander [2002] 2 BCLC 254, Cream Holdings Ltd v Davenport [2010] EWHC 3096 (Ch)**), but implication of terms by the court should not improve upon the document: **Attorney General of Belize v Belize Telecom Ltd [2009] UKPC 10**. In **Sugarman v CJS Investments LLP [2015] 1 BCLC 1**, the Court of Appeal refused to imply a term where the article was clear and unambiguous, and even if unusual and not within the court's view of 'business common sense', was not absurd.

[8] Draw the contrast explicitly to show you have understood the significance of your discussion

In conclusion it can be seen that while **CA 2006, s. 33** gives contractual force to the articles of association, the contract is indeed of a special nature with some distinctive features.[9] The contractual nature can be justified because the hallmark of a company is that of a voluntary relationship, like a contract (see Drury, 'The relative nature of the shareholder's right to enforce the company contract'), but the contractual analysis cannot be pushed too far. Given the very significant differences it is understandable that some have criticised the 'contractual straitjacket' (Sealy, L. and Worthington, S., *Cases and Materials on Company Law* (10th edn, 2013)) of **CA 2006, s. 33**.

[9] Use your conclusion to link back to the question. You should also show you have engaged with the fundamental notion of a contractual relationship—so the conclusion goes on to question whether the contractual concept is justified or not

 LOOKING FOR EXTRA MARKS?

■ Recognise the many ways in which the statutory contract differs from a 'normal' contract, but focus your energies on the key elements of alteration and enforcement

■ Engage with the academic work in this area: try to convince the examiner that you have really thought about the arguments and are not just repeating textbook summaries

■ Explore whether a contractual analysis is justified, considering whether there are any other alternative analyses

 QUESTION | **3**

Grimaldi Ltd was incorporated in 2010 and its directors are Coco, Joey, and Krusty. Coco also holds the title of 'Executive Advisor'. The company's 100 shares are held equally by Coco, Joey, Krusty, Bozo, and Tumble. Grimaldi Ltd relies on the model articles, with the following additional clauses:

1.1 Any resolution of the directors relating to the purchase of new premises shall be valid only with the agreement of any director holding the title of 'Executive Advisor'

1.2 The company's sales manager shall receive an annual bonus equal to 5 per cent of the company's profits

1.3 On any resolution to alter the company's share capital, any shares voted by Bozo shall be allocated five votes per share on a poll.

At the last board meeting, Joey and Krusty voted in favour of Grimaldi Ltd purchasing new premises for the business. Coco disagreed and sought to exercise his veto over such decisions but Joey and Krusty have ignored this. The other shareholders support Joey and Krusty's decision.

All five of the shareholders believe that the company's sales manager's bonus is too high and propose altering the articles to pay him a bonus of only 2 per cent (the sales manager's contract makes no separate provision for a bonus).

Coco, Joey, and Krusty have proposed a resolution to consolidate the company's share capital into five shares, with each shareholder holding one share. Tumble is happy to support this resolution but they are concerned that Bozo is likely to demand five votes per share in accordance with the articles, which would prevent the resolution being passed.

Advise the parties.

CAUTION!

- Don't just discuss the articles of association generally—focus on the issues raised by the facts of the problem and relate your discussion to the problem

- To avoid getting confused, don't start writing until you are clear about the positions and concerns of all the parties

DIAGRAM ANSWER PLAN

| Identify the issues | ■ Identify the main issues: board veto; manager's bonus; capital alteration |

| Relevant law | ■ Enforceability of articles of association
■ Insider and outsider rights
■ Interplay of articles of association and extrinsic contract
■ Weighted voting
■ Class rights |

| Apply the law | ■ Apply the law to the facts |

| Conclude | ■ Conclude and advise on each point |

SUGGESTED ANSWER

The model articles relevant to Grimaldi Ltd, as a private company incorporated in 2010, will be **Companies (Model Articles) Regulations**

2008, Sch 1. The issues that arise in the question largely concern the operation, alteration, and enforceability of the articles of Grimaldi Ltd, in particular the additional clauses outlined in the question.[1]

Coco's Veto

Coco's right of veto is within the articles of association, which raises questions about its enforceability. The articles are a 'statutory contract' by virtue of **CA 2006, s.33** and its provisions bind the company and the members. This means the articles can be enforced by the members against the company, the company against the members, and the members *inter se*. For example in *Hickman v Kent or Romney Marsh Sheep-Breeders' Association* [1915] 1 Ch 881[2] a member was bound by an article that required disputes to be submitted to arbitration.

[2] You could provide more examples to support your point, but be careful not to use up too much time

This might suggest Coco can simply enforce his veto as a matter of contract through the articles. However in *Hickman v Kent or Romney Marsh Sheep-Breeders' Association* Astbury J stated that the articles are enforceable only so far as they relate to a member's interests in his capacity as a member ie 'insider' rights. 'Outsider' rights, ie those that relate to an interest in some other capacity, could not be enforced under the statutory contract. This principle can be seen in operation in *Beattie v E & F Beattie Ltd* [1938] **Ch 708** (rights given qua director) and *Eley and Positive Government Security Life Assurance Co Ltd* (1876) **1 Ex D 88** (*Eley*) (rights given qua solicitor). These cases indicate that outsider rights cannot be enforced even if the individual seeking to rely on them is also a member, and only true 'membership' rights (such as the right to vote at general meeting: *Pender v Lushington* (1877) **6 Ch D 70**) are enforceable. It is arguable that this interpretation is not justified by **CA 2006, s. 33** itself (or its predecessors) which places no limit on which terms should be regarded as binding,[3] but the principle is probably too well established now to challenge other than in the highest court. This would indicate that Coco cannot enforce his right of veto, as the right is given to him in his capacity as director and is not a 'membership right'.

[3] This shows that you have understood some of the criticisms of Astbury J's approach

However, in *Quin & Axtens Ltd v Salmon* [1909] AC 442 (*Quin*), where similarly to the facts of this problem a director/shareholder had a veto over board decisions, his right was enforced, albeit indirectly. In that case the director/shareholder was granted an injunction restraining the company from acting contrary to its articles. Following the analysis of Lord Wedderburn (Wedderburn, 'Shareholder rights and the rule in *Foss v Harbottle*' [1957] CLJ 194), this indicates Coco can enforce his right, provided he sues in his capacity as member, enforcing his right to ensure the company is run in accordance with the constitution, rather than in his capacity as director seeking to enforce

[4]If you have time you can develop the other academic arguments and consider whether the different approaches would make any difference to the present case

a right of veto. Wedderburn's thesis has been variously modified and explained further by other academics,[4] and it remains difficult to predict when the courts will enforce particular provisions in the articles. As Drury has pointed out in 'The relative nature of the shareholder's right to enforce the company contract' [1986] CLJ 219, it is not possible to say that any provision of the articles is enforceable in an absolute sense as the contract is a relational one. The Company Law Review did consider reform, including a suggestion that all obligations in the articles should be enforceable unless otherwise provided, but the resulting legislation has left this issue unresolved. As this case

[5]Even where the law is not entirely clear you should make an effort to reach a conclusion

is very close to *Quin* on the facts, Coco can be advised[5] he has a good chance of enforcing the veto, provided he acts qua member rather than qua director.

Sales Manager's Bonus

The sales manager is not a member and so is not a party to the statutory contract. He thus cannot enforce the articles directly, and even if he was a member, the right is an 'outsider' right and so enforcement would be barred (***Hickman v Kent or Romney Marsh Sheep-Breeders' Association***). Furthermore, a member (even if inclined to help the manager) is unlikely to be able to enforce the right indirectly under *Quin* as the right to a bonus does not relate to the proper functioning of the company—the case is much more like *Eley* where the 'outsider' right was not enforceable, even by a member. However, the sales manager may still be able to enforce his right to be paid a 5 per cent bonus for time already completed under *Re New British Iron Co, ex p Beckwith* **[1898] 1 Ch 324**. There the claimants had served the company as directors without express agreement for remuneration, but the articles provided for board remuneration (£1,000 per annum) to be divided between them as they thought fit. On the company's liquidation, they claimed arrears of directors' fees. The court held that this provision did not constitute a contract between the company and the directors for the payment of fees to the directors but held that, by accepting office on the understanding that the terms of the article applied, the article provision was impliedly incorporated in the contract of service between the company and the directors and they were entitled to payment. In *Swabey v Port Darwin Gold Mining Co* **(1889) 1 Meg 385**, the company's articles provided that for directors to be remunerated at £200 per annum but subsequently, the company altered the articles to set remuneration at £5 per month. One director resigned and claimed for unpaid remuneration at the old rate. The Court of Appeal held in his favour on the grounds that, even though article provisions incorporated into a contract of service must be on the understanding that the articles are alterable, the alteration can only be prospective and not retrospective.

Applying these decisions to the sales manager,[6] it appears that, although the members can alter the articles to reduce the bonus to be awarded, the alteration will only have prospective effect. If the sales manager has completed a period of service prior to the alteration on the basis of the incorporation of the article provision prior to its alteration, he can sue for the bonus for that period to be calculated at the old rate.

Bozo's Voting Rights

Companies can consolidate (or subdivide) their share capital by ordinary resolution: **CA 2006, s. 618**. On the facts this resolution can only be passed if Bozo's shares are not given the additional weighting provided for in the articles. The case of **Bushell v Faith [1970] AC 1099** shows that such a provision is valid, even where it effectively restricts the use of a statutory power (in that case the power to remove a director). Accordingly, on any poll (Bozo would be able to demand a poll: **CA 2006, s. 321**)[7] Bozo is entitled to have his votes counted in full and can defeat the resolution.

[7]This shows you have an understanding of other areas of company law

The other shareholders might seek therefore to alter the articles to remove this clause. The clause is not entrenched (**CA 2006, s. 22**) so alteration would prima facie only require a special resolution to amend or remove it (**CA 2006, s. 21**). Although alteration must be made 'bona fide for the benefit of the company as a whole', the mere fact that an alteration affects only one shareholder does not of itself breach that requirement (**Allen v Gold Reefs of West Africa Ltd [1900] 1 Ch 656**). The problem for the other members is that this provision creates a class right:[8] in **Cumbrian Newspapers Group Ltd v Cumberland & Westmorland Herald Newspaper & Printing Co Ltd [1986] BCLC 286**, the weighted voting rights in **Bushell v Faith** were identified as a class right, even though not explicitly attached to a separate class of shares. This means that the clause cannot be varied (removal of the right would be a variation: **CA 2006, s. 630(6)**) unless the consent of a three-quarter majority of the class affected is obtained: **CA 2006, s. 630**.[9] As the class is made up of Bozo alone, he is unlikely to consent and so his weighted voting rights cannot be altered.

[8]When looking at alteration of the articles, always keep an eye out for class rights

[9]The model articles do not contain any provisions for the variation of class rights, so the variation must be in accordance with the three-quarter majority requirement

Conclusion[10]

[10]A conclusion is less important in a question like this as you can conclude on each point as you go along but it is still helpful—it is a check that you have covered all the issues and a final chance to raise any points (possibly practical rather than legal) relevant to the problem as a whole

Coco's right of veto over the board decision is probably enforceable following **Quin**, although the enforceability of such 'outsider' rights is a complex area where it is difficult to predict the court's approach. The sales manager cannot prevent the members from altering the articles to change the bonus for the future, but he can claim the bonus at the higher rate for years completed, provided the court is satisfied that the term was incorporated into an extrinsic contract with the company. As for the proposed consolidation of share capital, Bozo's vote should be weighted in accordance with the articles which will prevent the resolution being passed, and his right to weighted votes on this matter cannot be altered without his consent.

LOOKING FOR EXTRA MARKS?

- Concentrate on the particular issues raised but support this with strong knowledge and understanding of the fundamental principles
- In a problem question you can use academic work to show you have read more widely and understand there are debates and disagreements on points of law, but you might want to avoid detailed discussion of more theoretical points

Q QUESTION | 4

Critically evaluate the use of shareholder agreements as a supplement to a company's constitution.

CAUTION!

- You could structure this answer in terms of advantages and disadvantages of shareholder agreements, but it would be tempting to be very descriptive. By examining different issues instead, it is easier to be more analytical
- Remember that you'll need a good understanding of the articles of association as well as shareholder agreements to do well in this question

DIAGRAM ANSWER PLAN

> Introduction: key areas for discussion

▼

> Shareholder agreements and the constitution

▼

> Parties: who is bound?

▼

> Formalities, registration, privacy

▼

Enforcement of terms

▼

Alteration of terms

▼

Conclusion: evaluate benefits in different circumstances

SUGGESTED ANSWER

Shareholder agreements may be entered into when the company is formed or subsequently. They are usually formal contracts and are often used, particularly in small private companies, to modify or supplement the company's constitution (contained in the articles of association) to provide additional rights or protections for shareholders. **By considering their nature, enforcement, and alteration, this essay will show shareholder agreements offer a useful tool for supplementation of the constitution but are not universally advantageous.** [1]

[1] It can be effective to indicate both the areas you are going to cover and the thrust of your argument

Contract and Constitution

Shareholder agreements are governed by contract law, providing some certainty regarding the applicable legal rules. This is advantageous compared with the articles where, although a 'statutory contract' by virtue of **Companies Act 2006 (CA 2006), s. 33**, contract law does not fully apply. For example mistake, misrepresentation, duress, undue influence, rectification, and implication of terms do not normally apply to the articles (***Bratton Seymour Service Co Ltd v Oxborough*** **[1992] BCLC 693**). In contrast, [2] in ***Antonio v Antonio*** **[2010] EWHC 1199** the court accepted a shareholder agreement could be set aside for duress.

[2] To make your points about shareholder agreements clearly, it can be helpful to distinguish them from the articles of association explicitly

Although normally seen as just a supplement to the constitution, shareholder agreements can become part of the constitution. [3] Under the unanimous consent rule [4] (or ***Duomatic*** principle': ***Re Duomatic Ltd*** **[1969] 2 Ch 365**) unanimous agreement/consent of the shareholders is equivalent to a resolution of the company. ***Cane v Jones*** **[1980] 1 WLR 1451** established this can alter the articles, even though statute requires a special resolution (**CA 2006, s. 21**). The unanimous consent rule has been criticised (Grantham argues it wrongly conflates the company and the members: 'The unanimous consent rule in company law' [1993] CLJ 245) but is recognised in **CA 2006, s. 281(4)**, and **CA 2006, s. 17** extends the constitution to include such agreements.

[3] The separation of contract and constitution is not complete so show you understand how one can lead into the other

[4] By bringing in connected areas such as the unanimous consent rule (where relevant to the point you are making) you can show that you have got a broad understanding of the course as a whole

Parties: Who is Bound?

Shareholder agreements can be between all or only some share-holders. To be fully effective it should include all shareholders, making shareholder agreements of most use to small companies.[5]

Shareholder agreements bind the parties to them, which will normally be the members only. The articles bind the members and the company, and the members *inter se* (**Hickman v Kent or Romney Marsh Sheep-Breeders' Association** [1915] 1 Ch 881; **Rayfield v Hands** [1960] Ch 1). Shareholder agreements could include the company as a party, but this risks the company wrongfully restricting its statutory powers, as in **Russell v Northern Bank Development Corpn Ltd** [1992] 1 WLR 588. Here the shareholders and company agreed not to increase share capital without the consent of all parties, and a shareholder objected when the board subsequently proposed an increase. The House of Lords accepted the agreement was binding but on the shareholders only, not the company as this would restrict the company's statutory right to increase capital. Although the company was not bound, the effect was the same while the original sharehold-ers remained in place, leading to some criticism (Ferran, 'The decision of the House of Lords in *Russell v Northern Bank Development Corporation Limited*' [1994] CLJ 343).[6]

A disadvantage of shareholder agreements compared with the articles is that shareholder agreements will not bind new members to whom shares have been allotted, nor will obligations run with the shares to bind someone acquiring shares from existing shareholders (**Greenhalgh v Mallard** [1943] 2 All ER 234). If new members are to be bound by shareholder agreements, they must agree to be bound.

Formalities, Registration, and Privacy

The articles must follow statutory requirements: contained in a single document, divided into paragraphs numbered consecutively (**CA 2006, s. 18(3)**), and must be registered on formation unless the company uses model articles (**CA 2006, s. 18(2)**, **Companies (Model Articles) Regulations 2008 (SI 2008/3229)**). If a company does not register its own articles, or to the extent its articles do not exclude or modify the model articles, then model articles take effect (**CA 2006, s. 20**). This facilitates the efficient creation of companies by ensuring those wishing to form a company do not need to start from scratch in creating a constitution.[7] It is not a service offered in relation to shareholder agreements—the legislature does not offer 'standard form' shareholder agreements.

Unlike the articles, for shareholder agreements there are no prescribed requirements and they need not be in writing. The court has been prepared to find an oral shareholder agreement, and even imply additional terms into that agreement: in **Pennell Securities Ltd v Venida Investments Ltd (25 July 1974)** (**Pennell Securities**) (unreported but discussed in Burridge, S., 'Wrongful Rights Issues' (1981) 44 MLR 40) the court found the parties had impliedly agreed to maintain a particular share split and not increase share capital without consent.

Registration of the articles means they (and any alterations, which must be notified to the registrar: **CA 2006, s. 26**) are available for public inspection at Companies House. As shareholder agreements do not need to be registered they offer greater privacy than terms in the articles, making them useful for matters the parties prefer to keep confidential. [8]

Alteration

Unlike the articles, the terms of a shareholder agreement cannot be altered by majority vote (special resolution: **CA 2006, s. 21**). This offers greater protection to minority shareholders who are party to the agreement than a clause in the articles.

However this difference may not be as significant as first appears. [9] If a term of the articles creates a class right then any variation needs the consent of a three-quarter majority of the class (or compliance with any provisions of the articles for variation of class rights): **CA 2006, s. 630**, offering some protection against alteration. Or an article could be entrenched under **CA 2006, s. 22**, providing protection against alteration by the majority without need for a shareholder agreement. Alternatively rights could be entrenched by the use of weighted voting as in **Bushell v Faith [1970] AC 1099**. Entrenchment means protection is available to new members as well, as protection is not limited to those who are party to the shareholder agreement.

Enforcement

As a contract, shareholder agreements are, in principle, enforceable as of right. The court may even restrict a shareholder's vote: in **Greenwell v Porter [1902] 1 Ch 530** an injunction was granted restraining shareholders from opposing re-election of a director they had agreed to vote for. Even where an agreement purports to oust legal rules, **Fulham Football Club (1987) Ltd v Richards [2011] EWCA Civ 855** indicates it will normally be enforced, provided it does not interfere with third-party rights or is contrary to public policy, an approach welcomed by Cheung ('Shareholders' Agreements—shareholders' contractual freedom in company law' [2012] JBL 504).

By way of contrast, company law remedies are usually discretionary. Even a clear breach of articles may not be directly enforceable by a shareholder. Under the rule in *Foss v Harbottle* (1843) **2 Hare 461** 'mere irregularities' cannot be litigated by a shareholder (*Macdougall v Gardiner* (1875) **1 Ch D 13**). Further, in *Hickman v Kent or Romney Marsh Sheep-Breeders' Association* **[1915] 1 Ch 881** Astbury J indicated only 'insider' rights can be enforced by members; rights given in an 'outsider' capacity cannot be enforced, even by a member, a distinction that would not apply to terms of a shareholder agreement. [10]

[10] If you have more time you could expand this to show that the position on 'outsider rights' is more complex than this, but make sure you don't lose sight of the focus which is shareholder agreements rather than the articles generally

Agreements and Shareholder Remedies

Shareholder agreements can be important in resolving shareholder disputes, particularly where articles do not provide for dispute resolution or an exit route. Shareholder agreements may offer some protection to a minority shareholder, whether through enforcing the agreement directly, or in support of a claim under statutory shareholder remedies.

The existence of a shareholder agreement may be relevant to a claim of unfair prejudice (**CA 2006, s. 994**) or just and equitable winding up (**Insolvency Act 1986, s. 122(1)(g)**). Although the first strand of 'unfairness' identified by Lord Hoffmann in *O'Neill v Phillips* **[1999] 1 WLR 1092** was through breach of a binding agreement, breach of a shareholder agreement will not necessarily amount to unfair prejudice: *Sikorski v Sikorski* **[2012] EWHC 1613**. The interplay of shareholder agreements and shareholder remedies (both under just and equitable winding up and unfair prejudice) can be seen in cases such as *Re A & B C Chewing Gum Ltd* **[1975] 1 All ER 1017** and *Pennell Securities*. *Westcoast (Holdings) Ltd v Wharf Land Subsidiary (No. 1) Ltd* **[2012] EWCA Civ 1003** shows the importance of clear drafting if an agreement is to be relied upon in a dispute.

Conclusion

Shareholder agreements, particularly those encompassing all shareholders, provide a useful tool to supplement the constitution. Their importance is recognised in some jurisdictions (eg Canada) by giving them statutory force, but while not the case here, they remain significant in regulating shareholder relations, protecting minorities, and restricting directorial action, particularly in smaller companies and in areas such as joint ventures and management buy-outs. They have advantages over the articles in offering additional certainty and privacy, but will only cover shareholders for the time being and provisions need to be drafted carefully to be effective.

LOOKING FOR EXTRA MARKS?

- Contrast shareholder agreements with the articles of association to show you understand the differences

- Provide detailed analysis of important decisions such as *Russell v Northern Bank* and an awareness of criticism of key cases

- Draw links with topics such as shareholder remedies and the unanimous consent rule to show your deeper understanding of the issues

TAKING THINGS FURTHER

- Cheung, R., 'The use of statutory shareholder agreements and entrenched articles in reserving minority shareholders' rights: a comparative analysis' (2008) 29 Co Law 234

  Considers whether entrenched articles can offer similar protection to shareholders to that offered by the North American statutory unanimous shareholder agreement.

- Cheung, R., 'Shareholders' Agreements—shareholders' contractual freedom in company law' [2012] JBL 504

  Explores the approach of the courts to enforcing shareholder agreements—how far should private shareholder agreements be permitted to trump legal rules? Identifies an increasing trend in respecting freedom in private contracting.

- Drury, R. R., 'The relative nature of the shareholder's right to enforce the company contract' [1986] CLJ 219

  Compares the statutory contract with commercial 'relational contracts' to explore the relative enforceability of its provisions. Also contains a useful summary of the other main academic arguments on the nature of the statutory contract.

- Ferran, E., 'The decision of the House of Lords in *Russell v Northern Bank Development Corporation Limited*' [1994] CLJ 343

  Critically examines whether companies should be prevented from fettering their statutory powers through contract, and the distinction (with 'little to commend it') drawn in Russell *between that and effective fettering of a company's powers through shareholder agreements.*

- Grantham, R., 'The unanimous consent rule in company law' [1993] CLJ 245

  A critical evaluation of the unanimous consent rule, examining and challenging the rule from different perspectives.

- Griffin, S., 'Companies Act 2006 s. 33: altering the contractual effect of the articles of association?' (2010) Co LN 1

  Provides a summary of the statutory contract and with a controversial interpretation of s. 33 and s. 168 (removal of a director) argues that it might be possible to restrict the operation of s. 168.

- Rixon, F. G., 'Competing interests and conflicting principles: An examination of the power of alteration of articles of association' (1986) 49 MLR 446

  Assesses the ability of a shareholder to challenge an alteration of the articles, both directly (providing a detailed examination of the Allen v Gold Reefs *test) and through the unfair prejudice remedy.*

- Savirimuthu, J., 'Thoughts on *Russell*—killing private companies with kindness' (1993) 14 Co Law 137

   A case note on Russell v Northern Bank Development Corp Ltd, *criticising the House of Lords' reasoning. Contrast Savirimuthu's view of whether the company and the members should be viewed as separate entities, with that of Grantham (1993), and see also Ferran (1994). A more positive view on the case can be seen in Sealy, L. S., 'Shareholders' agreements—an endorsement and a warning from the House of Lords' [1992] CLJ 437.*

- Wedderburn, K. W., 'Shareholder rights and the rule in *Foss v Harbottle*' [1957] CLJ 194

   Considers the enforceability of the articles of association: seeks to reconcile important cases in the area, and draws the connection with shareholder remedies. See further Goldberg, G. D., 'The enforcement of outsider rights under s. 20(1) Companies Act 1948' (1972) 35 MLR 362 and (1985) 48 MLR 158; Gregory, R., 'The section 20 contract' (1981) 44 MLR 526; Prentice, G. N., 'The enforcement of outsider rights' (1980) 1 Co Law 179.

Online Resource Centre   www.oxfordtextbooks.co.uk/orc/qanda/

Go online for extra essay and problem questions, a glossary of key terms, online versions of all the answer plans and audio commentary on how selected ones were put together, and a range of podcasts which include advice on exam and coursework technique and advice for other assessment methods.

4 Shares and Shareholders

ARE YOU READY?

- Definitions and characteristics of a share
- Different types of share, particularly ordinary and preference shares
- Transfer of shares and rights of pre-emption
- Shareholders and members
- Share certificates
- Variation of class rights
- Connections with (in particular): the constitution, capital, directors' duties, shareholder remedies

 KEY DEBATES

Debate: the nature and characteristics of a share

The complexity of the share allows writers to focus on different elements to raise different issues or support particular approaches. It links into other areas of company law such as the nature of the company's constitution, shareholder primacy and stakeholding, shareholder remedies, and issues of corporate management and governance.

Debate: respective rights of shareholders of different classes and variation of those rights

In exercising the duty to promote the success of the company directors must have regard to the need to act fairly between shareholders (CA 2006, s. 172(1)(f)) but with different classes of share, shareholders will have different rights, and these rights will need to be balanced in the company's interest. The courts have consistently limited the statutory protection given to shareholders in respect of variation of their class rights, leading to some criticism.

QUESTION | 1

'The complex nature of a share makes it difficult to define concisely and comprehensively.'

Discuss.

CAUTION!

- Different classes of share will have different features, but don't just describe them, use the features as a way of illustrating the complexity of a share

- Although the question is potentially quite broad, don't drift too much into peripheral issues such as share allotment or transfer as this will tempt you away from deeper discussion about the nature of a share

DIAGRAM ANSWER PLAN

> Introduction: recognising the problem

▼

> Types of share and shareholder

▼

> Characteristics of a share: the *Borland's Trustee* description

▼

> Characteristics of a share: Sealy & Worthington's three factors

▼

> Conclusion: reflect on problem of definition

SUGGESTED ANSWER

Shares are fundamental to company law (the vast majority of companies are limited by shares) but are difficult to define comprehensively and concisely. That is because, not only are there different types of share, shares' features differ in importance depending on the interests of the shareholder.[1] Shareholders may be as diverse as an owner-manager in a one-person company, or an investor holding shares in multiple companies, and the nature of a share looks very different

[1] This identifies the main theme of the discussion from the start

from those different perspectives. Accordingly, while the general notion of a share is tolerably clear, finding a workable and meaningful definition is difficult. This essay will examine definitions and features of shares to address why it is difficult to define.

A share measures a shareholder's interest in the company—the shareholder's proportional share in a company's share capital and (assuming the articles of association provide for one vote per share) proportional voting power. Shares must have a nominal value under **Companies Act 2006 (CA 2006), s. 542(1)** (usually a small amount, eg £1). But this is not the 'value' of the share, which is worth what someone is willing to pay for it, or, in the event of winding up, the proportional share of the company's assets less its liabilities.

Most shares are ordinary shares, the residual category of shares. If a company has only one class of shares, these are ordinary shares, and every company must have at least one ordinary share. These usually carry a right to a variable dividend (declared lawfully in accordance with **CA 2006** and the articles) and a right to share in the company's net assets on winding up. The other main type of share is preference shares. These typically carry rights to a fixed (and usually cumulative: ***Webb v Earle* [1875] LR 20 Eq 556)**[2] dividend and a preferential right to return on capital on winding up. These rights are described as 'preferential' as they have priority over the rights of ordinary shareholders; they are not 'better' than ordinary shares (as 'preferential' might suggest), simply different.[3]

Companies may issue any number of different classes of share provided the articles allow, potentially carrying different nominal values (even in different currencies: ***Re Scandinavian Bank Group plc* [1988] Ch 87**) and different rights (including redeemable shares: **s. 684**). Any rights that attach to a particular class of shares, but not generally, are regarded as 'class rights' (see ***Cumbrian Newspapers Group Ltd v Cumberland & Westmoreland Herald Newspapers and Printing Co Ltd* [1987] Ch 1**) and provisions exist to protect shareholders in respect of variations to these rights (**ss. 630–5**). Shares can also be used to promote social aims,[4] eg allowing employees to exchange certain employment rights for shares with tax benefits to encourage 'employee-ownership' (**Employment Rights Act 1996, s. 205A**, inserted by **Growth and Infrastructure Act 2013**), and the abolition of 'bearer shares', where the holder is not registered, to enhance transparency (**CA 2006, s. 779**, amended by **Small Business, Enterprise and Employment Act 2015**).

A share does not give its holder any share in the company's property (***Short v Treasury Commissioners* [1948] AC 534**); the company as a separate entity owns its assets (***Macaura v Northern Assurance Co* [1925] AC 619**[5]). The member's share is in the company's share capital (**s. 540(1)**). **CA 2006** also provides that shares are personal

[2] By adding in a few points in passing you can demonstrate the depth of your knowledge to the examiner without wasting time

[3] It is important to show you understand that 'preferential' doesn't necessarily mean 'better'

[4] This recognises that shares have wider significance than just their importance to the individual or company; it also gives you the opportunity to show you have kept up to date with recent developments in the area

[5] An important link between the topic of corporate personality and this topic, but it doesn't need much elaboration here

property (**s. 541**) and transferable in accordance with the articles (**s. 544(1)**). These statutory provisions indicate some features of a share but do not explain what a share is.

The classic analysis of a share comes from **Borland's Trustee v Steel Brothers & Co Ltd** [1901] 1 Ch 279: '... the interest of a shareholder in the company measured by a sum of money, for the purpose of liability in the first place, and of interest in the second, but also consisting of a series of mutual covenants entered into by all the shareholders *inter se* in accordance with [**CA 2006 s. 33**]'[6] (Farwell J). This is a partial description rather than a complete definition (see Pennington, 'Can shares in companies be defined?' (1989) 10 Comp Law 140), but the features identified by Farwell J should be further explored.

First, Farwell J recognises that the interest of a shareholder is 'in' the company. This indicates how the shareholders are very much part of the company—unlike a creditor, whose interests are 'against' the company. A share thus creates a different type of interest from that of a purely contractual interest.

Secondly, a share is an interest measured by a sum of money, but is not itself a sum of money. As discussed earlier, the nominal value is measured in monetary terms, but this provides a proportional measurement rather than a statement of monetary value. Farwell J mentions the share having elements of both liability and interest. Liability arises from the taking up of the shares—a shareholder is liable to pay for the shares, either on issue or on later call, but beyond that a shareholder has no further financial liability (shareholders are not liable for the company's debts: **Salomon v A. Salomon & Co Ltd** [1897] AC 22). In terms of interest, the shareholder's financial interest or return on his investment (whether by distribution of dividends or return of capital) is measured by reference to his proportional share.

The reference to 'mutual covenants' relates to the rights of shareholders under the articles—commonly known as the 'statutory contract' under what is now **CA 2006, s. 33**.[7] This deeming provision creates a contract between the company and the shareholders (and the shareholders *inter se*). This relationship is not identical to a traditional contract (**Bratton Seymour Service Co Ltd v Oxborough** [1992] BCLC 693); for example contractual remedies of rescission and mistake are not available, and not all provisions of the articles are directly enforceable by members (see, eg **Hickman v Kent or Romney Marsh Sheepbreeders' Association** [1915] 1 Ch 881: only membership rights can be enforced). Nonetheless this statutory contract indicates the voluntary and binding nature of the relationship and the importance of the provisions of the articles. A shareholder will have further rights and obligations arising from the provisions of the **CA 2006**.

A share is essentially a bundle of different rights and obligations. This is supported by Sealy and Worthington, *Cases and Materials on Company Law* (10th edn, Oxford, 2013)[8] who identify three key features. The first is a reflection of the shareholder's financial stake in the company; it indicates the member's level of financial interest and liability—the share measures the amount a shareholder might have to contribute to a company's capital, and provides the proportional measurement for financial returns. Secondly, a share is a measure of the shareholder's interest in the company as an association of members—a share gives its holder rights as a member of an association, including voting rights, as set out by the articles. Thirdly, a share is a species of property in its own right. This aspect is not included in Farwell J's analysis (but is reflected in **CA 2006, s. 541**)—a share is an item of property and thus capable of being bought, sold, charged, and split into legal and beneficial interests. The three elements are memorably described by Worthington as 'property, power and entitlement' ('Shares and shareholders: property, power and entitlement—Part I' (2001) 22 Co Law 258).

Clearly the importance of these features will differ according to the type of share and reasons for holding it.[9] As a shareholder in a small private company, the second element—rights in the association—is likely to be most important. For a holder of preference shares the first element—the financial return by way of a fixed dividend payment—is likely to be most important. For investors in a listed public company, the third element is more important as financial gains are often made through purchase and sale of shares rather than dividend payments, and voting rights are largely irrelevant (as each shareholding is a tiny proportion of the company's shares).

It is similarly difficult to define shares by way of contrast with other investments in companies such as debentures (loans, usually secured on a company's assets). While in essence the concepts are very different, in practice, they can become blurred. For example, preference shares providing for a fixed return and no voting rights in many ways look more like a loan than a share (and have been so regarded by the courts, eg *Scottish Insurance Corporation Ltd v Wilsons & Clyde Coal Co Ltd* [1949] 1 All ER 1068) and are often termed 'hybrid securities'.

Pennington concludes that shares are 'a species of intangible movable property which comprise a collection of rights and obligations relating to an interest in a company of an economic and proprietary character, but not constituting a debt'. This definition is not one many shareholders would find illuminating, but may be the closest we can come to being both 'concise and comprehensive',[10] recognising that a more meaningful definition depends on who is the shareholder.

LOOKING FOR EXTRA MARKS?

- Show how the important elements of a share differ according to the position of the shareholder

- Balance legal knowledge, practical understanding, and awareness of the academic discussion

- Engage with the cases and key academic work in this area

- Link to other topics such as the statutory contract created by the articles of association, or the rights of shareholders more generally

QUESTION | 2

Nick is the holder of registered shares in both Diabolo Ltd and Lucifero Ltd.

Michelle stole the share certificate relating to Nick's Diabolo shares from Nick's study and, pretending to be Nick, deposited the certificate and a signed blank transfer form with Southern Bank plc as security for a loan. When Michelle defaulted on the loan, Southern Bank plc transferred the shares to Paolo, sending the certificate and transfer form to Diabolo Ltd. On receipt of the share certificate and the transfer form, Diabolo Ltd replaced Nick with Paolo on the register of members and issued a share certificate to Paolo. Paolo later transferred the shares to Quentin. When Nick queried the fact he had not received any dividends from Diabolo Ltd, he was informed that he was no longer a shareholder.

Nick has learned that the directors of Lucifero Ltd have decided to allot a significant number of shares to Rafael. Nick is unhappy as this allotment will dilute his shareholding and he has not been offered the opportunity to buy any further shares. Lucifero Ltd has only one class of shares and Nick is a minority shareholder.

Advise the parties.

CAUTION!

- Consider the two different shareholdings separately as distinct issues arise

- Work through the issues step by step to avoid getting muddled

- This question covers estoppel by share certificate, forged transfers, and statutory pre-emption rights—check your course outline as not all courses cover these issues in depth

DIAGRAM ANSWER PLAN

| Identify the issues | ■ Identify the main problems in the two scenarios |

| Relevant law | ■ Shareholders and the register
■ Share certificates and estoppel
■ Forged transfers
■ Power to allot shares
■ Pre-emption rights and disapplication |

| Apply the law | ■ Apply the relevant law to the different scenarios |

| Conclude | ■ Conclude separately for each scenario |

SUGGESTED ANSWER

[1] Introductions for problem questions can be short, but do identify the main problems or points of law to show you are heading in the right direction

[2] If you separate the problem into two parts it is fine to conclude on each separately, rather than repeating yourself in a further overall conclusion. But it is worth checking back at the end to make sure that you have concluded properly in relation to each part of the question

[3] This makes the important point that a share certificate is not the share itself, but only evidence of title

This question concerns two particular problems relating to share ownership, transfer, and rights—estoppel by share certificate and rights of pre-emption.[1] The two companies will be considered separately to advise the parties[2] on their legal position.

Diabolo

Diabolo Ltd has certificated shares: title is evidenced by a share certificate, and transfer of legal title must be through a proper instrument of transfer (**Companies Act 2006 (CA 2006), s. 770**). Membership of a company requires entry on the company's register of members (**CA 2006, s. 112**) but although the company entered Paolo on the register as a member, the original transfer form was a forgery and the share certificate issued to Paolo incorrect.

A share certificate is only prima facie evidence of title[3] (**CA 2006, s. 768(1)**). As the transfer was a forgery, and the share certificate issued in error, the transfer is void and Nick is still the true shareholder. Diabolo Ltd must pay damages to Nick (including dividend payments not received) and retransfer to his name the shares currently registered to Quentin. Diabolo Ltd can claim indemnity from Southern Bank in respect of losses arising from the sending in of the forged transfer, even if Southern Bank is entirely innocent, as by presenting the transfer, the presenter impliedly warrants that the transfer is genuine (**Sheffield Corporation v Barclay [1905] AC**

392 and *Yeung Kei Yung v Hong Kong & Shanghai Banking Corpn* **[1981] AC 787**). Southern Bank could claim against Michelle if she can be found.

As far as Quentin is concerned,[4] he relied on the share certificate issued to Paolo by Diabolo Ltd. A company may be estopped from denying the truth of an incorrect certificate it has issued, where the certificate has been relied upon by a bona fide purchaser of the shares. In *Re Bahia and San Francisco Rly Co* **(1868) LR 3 QB 584**

[5] It is worth making reference to case facts where you recognise that they are similar to those in the problem before you—it supports your argument and shows the examiner that you are really thinking about the problem

(which is similar to the present facts[5]) the company was estopped from denying the title of the individual in whose name it had wrongly issued the share certificate (based on a forged transfer and stolen share certificate) and the innocent purchasers from that individual were entitled to damages from the company. In *Balkis Consolidated Co v Tomkinson* **[1893] AC 396** the vendor of the shares (in whose name the certificate had been issued, but who had not been party to any fraud or error) was also able to rely on the estoppel.

[6] Deal with potentially unhelpful authorities as well as those that support your case

The availability of an estoppel in cases of forgery was called into question by *Ruben v Great Fingall Consolidated* **[1906] AC 439**.[6] Here the company secretary forged a share certificate, providing it to stockbrokers as security for a loan. The company refused to register the brokers as holders and they sued for damages. The House of Lords held that the company was not estopped and was not liable as the forged certificate was a pure nullity (see also *South London Greyhound Racecourses Ltd v Wake* **[1931] 1 Ch 496**). However, these cases have since been distinguished and can be restricted to the point that an estoppel arises only where the statement is made with authority (and at the time a company secretary's ostensible authority to bind the company was thought much less extensive than is now accepted: *Panorama Developments (Guildford) Ltd v Fidelis Furnishing Fabrics Ltd* **[1971] 2 QB 711**). Accordingly a forgery is not necessarily a nullity, and a party may be estopped from denying its validity (eg *Lovett v Carson Country Homes* **[2009] 2 BCLC**

[7] Apply the law to the facts explicitly

196). We can thus be confident that an estoppel would arise against Diabolo Ltd to protect Quentin.[7]

Accordingly, as Diabolo Ltd has issued a share certificate in Paolo's name, the company is estopped from denying that Paolo was the registered holder of the shares. Quentin can therefore claim damages from Diabolo Ltd for the loss of the shares. He could alternatively claim damages against Diabolo Ltd for negligent certification (**CA 2006, s. 775(3)**). As before, Diabolo Ltd will be entitled to claim damages from Southern Bank as the presenter of the initial forged transfer even if Southern Bank was unaware of the forgery (see also *Royal Bank of Scotland plc v Sandstone Properties Ltd* **[1998] 2 BCLC 429**), and Michelle would also be liable, if she can be found.

Lucifero

Directors can generally only allot shares if authorised to do so by a resolution or the articles (**CA 2006, s. 551**). However, **CA 2006, s. 550** gives directors of a private company with one class of shares the power to allot shares without express authorisation unless prohibited from so doing by the articles. The question does not suggest any prohibition so the **s. 550** power can be exercised. It must be noted though that directors must 'only exercise powers for the purposes for which they are conferred': **CA 2006, s. 171(b)**[8] and this duty (the 'proper purposes' rule) has often been invoked in relation to the allotment of shares (eg *Hogg v Cramphorn Ltd* **[1967] Ch 254**; *Bamford v Bamford* **[1970] Ch 212**). The reasons for the allotment would have to be examined, but provided the 'substantial purpose' (*Howard Smith Ltd v Ampol Petroleum Ltd* **[1974] AC 821**) is within the proper scope of the power (usually the raising of capital) the directors will not be in breach of their duty to the company. If the directors were acting outside the scope of their powers then the allotment would be invalid. Directors must also be aware of their overriding duty to act in good faith to promote the success of the company (**CA 2006, s. 172**). The question does not suggest the directors are acting otherwise than for a proper purpose and in a manner they believe will promote the success of the company and so in the absence of further information this does not offer a route for Nick.

Nick is concerned that he has not been offered the chance to purchase more shares to maintain his proportional shareholding. Existing shareholders are given statutory pre-emption rights (**CA 2006, ss. 560–77**)[9] in respect of an allotment of 'equity securities', which includes ordinary shares (**s. 560**). Before an allotment, **s. 561** requires a company to make an offer to each person holding ordinary shares (communicated in accordance with **s. 562**) to allot to him 'on the same or more favourable terms' a proportion of those securities matching his existing proportional shareholding. An allotment cannot be made until the period for acceptance of such an offer (at least 21 days) has expired or the company has received notice of acceptance or refusal of the offer.

If an allotment is made in contravention of **CA 2006, ss. 561–2**, the company and every officer who knowingly authorised or permitted the contravention are jointly and severally liable to compensate the person to whom an offer should have been made for any loss, damage, costs, and expenses incurred as a result: **s. 563(2)**. An allotment in contravention of **ss. 561–2** is not invalid, although an allotment made in favour of the directors themselves was set aside in *Re Thundercrest Ltd* **[1995] 1 BCLC 117**.

The important thing for Nick to be aware of is that **CA 2006, s. 561** is subject to several exceptions. Those relating to the issue of bonus

---

[8] Directors' duties may be relevant in almost any company law question

[9] You'll need to be familiar with the statutory provisions, and ideally have the statute in front of you (if this is permitted), before dealing with pre-emption rights

shares (**s. 564**) and securities held under employee share schemes (**s. 566**) do not seem to apply here. However allotments for non-cash consideration are also excluded (**s. 565**) and this would be an easy way for the directors to avoid Nick's pre-emption rights. Furthermore, the articles of a private company can exclude all or any of the statutory pre-emption requirements whether generally or in relation to allotments of a particular description: **s. 567**.

There are also ways in which pre-emption rights can be disapplied. Particularly relevant here is the ability of private companies with only one class of shares to disapply the rights, giving the directors power by the articles, or by special resolution, to allot equity securities as if **s. 561** did not apply to the allotment, or applied as modified by the directors: **s. 569(1)**. (Rights can also be disapplied where a company has a provision in its articles to that effect (**s. 567**) or where the company's articles make separate provision for pre-emption rights in relation to a class (**s. 568**), while **ss. 570–1** provide for disapplication generally or for a specific allotment where the authority to allot arises under **s. 551**.)

Accordingly, while the directors' proposed allotment to Rafael would seem to be in breach of Nick's rights of pre-emption, there are many routes by which these rights could be avoided or disapplied. If the rights have not been excluded or disapplied then Lucifero Ltd and its directors will be liable to compensate Nick, although the new issue is not invalidated (**CA 2006, s. 653**). Nick might also petition under **CA 2006, s. 994**[10] arguing the allotment is unfairly prejudicial to his interests as a member: eg *Re Coloursource Ltd* [2005] **BCC 627** and *Graham v Every* [2014] **EWCA Civ 191**.

[10] Show your wider understanding by indicating other avenues that a claimant might be able to pursue

LOOKING FOR EXTRA MARKS?

- Keep linking your discussion of the law to the facts of the problem; doing this moves your answer from being just a relevant description of the law, to a clear application showing understanding as well as knowledge

- Spread your time sensibly across both parts of the question

- Show excellent awareness of the statutory provisions, how they link together, and how they apply to the facts, without just copying out chunks of statutory material

QUESTION | 3

'Suspended midway between true creditors and true members ... [preference shareholders] may get the worst of both worlds, unless the instrument creating the preference shares is carefully drafted.' (Davies, P. and Worthington, S., *Gower's Principles of Modern Company Law* (9th edn, London, 2012))

Discuss.

CAUTION!

- You need to reflect on the similarities and differences between preference shareholders and both ordinary shareholders and creditors
- Avoid just listing the differences between ordinary and preference shares; contrast and comment upon their features to assess the position of preference shareholders

DIAGRAM ANSWER PLAN

> Introduction: classes of share

> Characteristics/rights of preference shares: dividends, capital, and voting

> Protection of class rights

> Use of preference shares instead of ordinary shares or debt

> Conclusion: review position overall

SUGGESTED ANSWER

Share capital can be issued in different classes of share provided the articles of association give power to do so (***Andrews v Gas Meter Co* [1897] 1 Ch 361**). The rights of each class will depend on the articles and terms of issue. 'Preference' shares give priority to the holder[1] over ordinary shareholders in one or more areas, usually ranking ahead of ordinary shares as to payment of dividend or return of capital (or both), and often with different voting rights.

In order to evaluate the statement this essay will examine the rights attached to preference shares (and how they are protected) and consider why preference shares are used, contrasting preference shareholders' position with that of both ordinary shareholders and creditors.[2]

Dividend

The right to a dividend arises where the company makes a distributable profit ('accumulated, realised profits ... less ... accumulated, realised losses ...' (**CA 2006, s. 830**)) and declares a dividend. For

[1] A very brief 'definition' in the introduction means you can get straight into deeper discussion in the main parts of your essay

[2] Setting out your approach in the introduction gives the examiner confidence that you have thought about the question

ordinary shareholders the dividend varies from year to year according to profit. In contrast, a preference dividend is generally a fixed percentage of the share's nominal value, eg '3 per cent preference shares', giving the advantage of certainty of income over ordinary shareholders. In this regard preference shareholders appear more like creditors,[3] but with weaker rights as, in the case of creditors, interest is payable pursuant to the loan terms, and is not reliant on the company making a distributable profit.

[3] As you deal with each point, link it explicitly to the question by indicating the similarity or contrast with ordinary shareholders or creditors as appropriate

Preference dividends (unlike ordinary dividends) are cumulative unless otherwise stated, so failure to pay a dividend in a financial year means the right will be carried forward until paid: *Webb v Earle* **[1875] LR 20 Eq 556**. So although, unlike creditors,[4] preference shareholders do have to wait for a dividend to be declared; overall they should not be financially disadvantaged (provided the presumption of accumulation is not rebutted by the issue terms: *Staples v Eastman Photographic Materials Co* **[1896] 2 Ch 303**). There is a risk that preference shareholders will lose any accrued right to unpaid dividend on winding up (*Re Roberts and Cooper Ltd* **[1929] 2 Ch 383**) but this can be avoided by careful drafting[5] providing for payment on liquidation whether declared or not.

[4] Another example of how, very briefly, you can keep linking to the question

[5] The question statement mentions the need for careful drafting so impress the examiner by picking up on this point as well as the 'compare and contrast' element of the question

Compared with ordinary shareholders, preference shareholders benefit from a more certain income return but suffer because a preferential right will be treated as an exhaustive statement of the shareholder's right in that respect (*Re National Telephone Co* **[1914] 1 Ch 755**). Accordingly preference shareholders with a preferential dividend have no right to share in additional profits after payment of the fixed dividend: *Will v United Lankat Plantations Ltd* **[1914] AC 11**. This puts preference shareholders in a less favourable financial position than ordinary shareholders and more akin to a creditor in this regard.

Return of Capital

Shares are presumed to have equal rights to return of capital unless specifically provided (*Birch v Cropper* **(1889) 14 App Cas 25**), but it is common for preference shares to carry priority over return of capital so that on a winding up, preference shareholders will be paid before ordinary shareholders. The preference normally relates to the nominal value and not any premium paid, but careful drafting can give priority for the full amount and so improve preference shareholders' position. Preference shareholders really benefit from their priority when the company has insufficient assets on winding up to pay all claimants—their priority means they are more likely to be paid in full than ordinary shareholders. However, creditors (particularly secured creditors) are in a stronger position, as creditors rank ahead of shareholders on winding up.

Another problem for preference shareholders is that, as a statement of right is deemed to be exhaustive, if there is a preferential return of capital, there is no right to share in any surplus assets. Accordingly, in *Scottish Insurance Corporation Ltd v Wilsons & Clyde Coal Co Ltd* [1949] AC 462, the court allowed the company to pay off preference shareholders (so removing them from the company) as only ordinary shareholders had a right to share in the company's surplus assets. Interestingly, the court expressly likened the preference shareholders' position to that of creditors. See also *Re Chatterley-Whitfield Collieries Ltd* [1948] 2 All ER 593, confirmed *Prudential Assurance Co Ltd v Chatterley-Whitfield Collieries Ltd* [1949] AC 512.

Voting

A preference shareholder has the right to exercise any votes attached to his shares. Preference shareholders' voting rights are often restricted by the terms of issue, putting them in a weaker position than ordinary shareholders and making their position closer to that of creditors. Even if a preference shareholder has voting rights, these may have little impact where the shares constitute only a small proportion of the total issued shares. Preference shareholders may actually have less power than creditors, as in practice major creditors can wield significant influence over decision-making, even without specific provisions in the loan contract, because of the importance of their continued financial support.[6]

[6] This paragraph shows the importance of recognising 'practical' as well as strictly 'legal' points

Protection of Class Rights

Preference shareholders' rights would be further weakened if alterable by special resolution as for the articles generally: **CA 2006, s. 21**. Accordingly, statute offers additional protection against 'variation of class rights',[7] requiring the consent of a three-quarter majority of the affected class, or compliance with the company's own provisions as to variation, with additional rights for an aggrieved minority to apply for cancellation (**CA 2006, ss. 630–40**).

[7] Although the question doesn't directly mention variation of class rights, it is relevant as it relates to the strength (or weakness) of the preference shareholder's position

This protection is much reduced by the courts' restrictive interpretation of what constitutes a variation of class rights. In *White v Bristol Aeroplane Co* [1953] Ch 65 the court distinguished between a change in the right (a variation) and a change in the enjoyment of that right (not a variation and so not within the statutory scheme). Accordingly diluting a preference shareholder's voting power by increasing the class of ordinary shares is not a variation of his rights: *Greenhalgh v Arderne Cinemas Ltd* [1946] 1 All ER 512. Furthermore early repayment of preference shareholders and cancellation of their shares on a reduction of capital was not a variation of their rights but a 'fulfilment or satisfaction of [their] contractual rights': *House of Fraser plc v ACGE Investment Ltd* [1987]

AC 387. Careful drafting can offer some protection by providing that such a reduction is deemed to be a variation, as in *Re Northern Engineering Industries plc* [1994] 2 BCLC 704, but a preference shareholder may not be sufficiently well-informed to demand that protection. Changes not amounting to a variation may give rise to a claim of unfair prejudice under **CA 2006, s. 994**, but this falls short of specific protection for preference shareholders.

Use of Preference Shares[8]

Preference shares have been described as 'a somewhat unique anomaly' that reflect no credit on the law (Pickering, 'The problem of the preference share' (1963) 26 MLR 499),[9] but they remain part of corporate funding. This suggests they can offer benefits to the company, the holder, or both.

Preference shares may be used by venture capital firms investing in companies. Bankers and creditors may find preference shares more acceptable than a large loan with preference shareholders ranking behind creditors on winding up, while the company's balance sheet will be less highly geared and look more solid to potential suppliers and customers. It can offer the venture capitalist a dividend stream and, with careful drafting, the possibility of weighted voting rights to give power over decisions such as voluntary winding up or appointing or removing directors.

Preference shares may also be used to raise capital more cheaply than through a loan (depending on prevailing rates), and on refinancing by converting debt into preference shares. By using preference shares with restricted voting rights, this can be done without disturbing the control of existing members. They may also be used to raise further capital without triggering pre-emption rights, provided the shares are not convertible into ordinary shares: **CA 2006, ss. 560–1**. In addition, the value of preference shares can be less volatile than that of ordinary shares, as the price fluctuates in relation to the level of fixed dividend as against interest rates, and may be less affected by general company and market activity.

Conclusion

Preference shareholders typically benefit from greater certainty of income and capital return compared with ordinary shareholders, but sacrifice any share in further profits or capital. Voting rights may also be restricted compared with ordinary shareholders. Compared with creditors, preference shareholders are disadvantaged both in relation to certainty of income, and on return of capital. While preference shareholders have some protection against variation of their rights, the courts' restrictive interpretation limits the value of this, further weakening their position.

[8] Having identified many problems of preference shares, it is important to consider why they are ever used

[9] Use your additional reading to add depth and show you have engaged fully with the topic

[10]It is good practice to link back to the question in the conclusion

There is thus every prospect that preference shareholders will get the 'worst of both worlds'.[10] There can be good reasons to use preference shares, but it is essential that the terms of issue are carefully drafted to protect the preference shareholder as far as possible. Otherwise, as Pickering observes, preference shares offer 'largely illusory' membership benefits and weaker rights than creditors, and so constitute 'a potential trap for the less informed'.

LOOKING FOR EXTRA MARKS?

- Explore the practical benefits and drawbacks of preference shares compared with ordinary shares and debt, as well as strictly legal differences
- Think about how preference shareholders' rights are protected by the law and evaluate the strengths and weaknesses of the current provisions on the variation of class rights
- Make use of your further reading to support or challenge the view expressed in the question

QUESTION | 4

Moby Ltd has 200 issued shares, each of £1 nominal value: 100 ordinary shares and 100 5 per cent preference shares. All shares carry full voting rights. Ahab is the holder of 20 of the 100 issued preference shares. All other preference shareholders apart from Ahab also hold ordinary shares. The articles of association state that Ahab has the right to veto any director's appointment while he retains a shareholding in the company.

At a recent general meeting at which all shareholders were present and voted, Moby Ltd passed two resolutions: (i) under authority given in its articles, to subdivide the ordinary shares, each into 10 shares of 10 pence nominal value, and (ii) altering the articles to remove Ahab's right to appoint a director. Furthermore, at a separate class meeting, a resolution has been passed removing the right of preference shareholders to receive their dividends cumulatively. Ahab voted against all resolutions (the only shareholder voting against).

Advise Ahab.

CAUTION!

- Identify the complaints at the start so that you focus on the problem facts and reduce the temptation to provide a general discussion on the topic
- Deal with each complaint separately to ensure you identify all the issues and reach a conclusion; if the same point arises in more than one complaint you can refer back to your earlier discussion rather than repeat yourself

DIAGRAM ANSWER PLAN

Identify the issues	■ Identify the complaints
Relevant law	■ Alteration of articles ■ Class rights ■ Variation of class rights ■ Statutory protection against variation of class rights
Apply the law	■ Apply to the facts
Conclude	■ Conclude

SUGGESTED ANSWER

Various rights connected with Ahab's shares have been disturbed. The subdivision of shares has diluted the overall voting power of his shares (from 10 per cent to 2 per cent) while his veto over director appointments and his right to receive preference dividends cumulatively have been removed.[1] Ahab's legal position will differ according to whether these changes constitute 'variations of class rights' or not, as if they are, protection is offered under **Companies Act 2006 (CA 2006), ss. 630–40**. Ahab's three complaints will be considered in turn.

Subdivision

Companies can subdivide shares provided there is authority in the articles under **CA 2006, s. 618**, which Moby Ltd has. But if the subdivision is a variation of Ahab's class rights, the resolution would be invalid as not satisfying **CA 2006, ss. 630–40** (in essence requiring separate agreement of the class affected).

The right to vote is a valuable feature of a share and the subdivision of ordinary shares has significantly reduced the relative voting power of Ahab's shares. But this would not trigger **ss. 630–40**, as the courts have interpreted 'variation' very narrowly, effectively distinguishing between direct and indirect variation of shareholders' rights.

The classic authority is ***White v Bristol Aeroplane Co* [1953] Ch 65** which held that issuing additional preference and ordinary shares to the ordinary shareholders did not 'vary' the rights of existing preference shareholders, drawing a distinction between a change in the right, and in the 'enjoyment' of that right (see also *Re John Smith's Tadcaster Brewery* [1953] Ch 308). Particularly pertinent to Ahab's case is *Greenhalgh v Arderne Cinemas Ltd* [1946] 1 All ER 512[2] where the company subdivided one class of shares, giving much greater proportional voting power to members of that class. This was held not to vary the rights of the other class of shareholders (as each shareholder still had the same right, namely one vote per share), it merely affected the enjoyment of that right.

[2] Shows you have recognised which case is most relevant

While this approach has received justifiable criticism (eg Reynolds, 'Shareholders' class rights: a new approach [1996] JBL 554), the case law is well established.[3] It therefore has to be concluded that Ahab cannot challenge the resolution as a variation of class rights. Other routes for redress will be considered at the end of the answer.

[3] There is less scope in problem questions for engaging with academic work; but you can still make some use of your further reading

Right of Veto

The company has sought to remove Ahab's right of veto through a resolution in general meeting; provided proper notice was given (**CA 2006, s. 238(6)**) this will be a special resolution (not less than 75 per cent: **s. 238(1)**) as we are told that all members were present and voting and only Ahab voted against. Accordingly, the requirements of **CA 2006, s. 21** for alteration of the articles were met.[4] Alteration of the articles must also be 'bona fide for the benefit of the company' (***Allen v Gold Reefs of West Africa Ltd* [1900] 1 Ch 656**), but this is a subjective test and a challenge is unlikely to succeed, unless the change was so 'oppressive' that it casts doubt on the majority's good faith (***Shuttleworth v Cox Brothers & Co Ltd* [1927] 2 KB 9**).

[4] See how this passage combines the problem facts and points of law—establishing and applying the law as you go can be much more concise and effective than setting out all the law and then applying it, but you do need confidence

However, a special resolution will be insufficient if Ahab's right of veto is a 'class right', as removing the right would be a 'variation' and not simply an interference with its enjoyment (variation includes 'abrogation': **CA 2006, s. 630(6)**). Class rights are conventionally those rights that explicitly attach to a class of shares, such as the right to a stated dividend. This would not obviously include the right of veto given to an individual shareholder but not attached to a class of shares. However, in ***Cumbrian Newspapers Group Ltd v Cumberland & Westmoreland Herald Newspapers and Printing Co Ltd* [1987] Ch 1** 'class right' was extended to include rights given to an individual in their capacity as shareholder. The court held that the right to appoint a director while the shareholder held a certain proportion of shares was a class right, and gave as a further example the weighted voting right in ***Bushell v Faith* [1970] AC 1099**.

[5] Make clear where you are applying the law

Following this authority,[5] the right to veto would be a class right, with Ahab the only member of that class. Under **CA 2006, s. 630** variation must be in accordance with any procedure in the company's constitution (we will assume Moby Ltd has no specific provision as there is none in the model articles), or follow the statutory require-ments. That requires consent in writing from the holders of at least three-quarters in nominal value of the issued shares of that class, or a special resolution passed at a separate class meeting: **s. 630(4)**. Ahab has not consented to the change and so the resolution is invalid.

Cumulative Dividends

The right to receive preference dividends cumulatively will be a class right, as it attaches to the class of shares. It is valuable as it means that once a dividend is declared, the company has also to make up unpaid dividends to preference shareholders from earlier years, prior to paying a dividend to ordinary shareholders.

As a class right it cannot be varied through the normal statutory provisions for altering the articles (special resolution under **CA 2006, s. 21**), but, as explained in relation to the veto point, only by following any variation procedure in the company's constitution or following **CA 2006, ss. 630–40**, which requires agreement of at least three-quarters of the class. In relation to this particular right, it appears that the company has already complied with the correct procedure. Ahab is the only member voting against, indicating that 80 per cent of the preference shareholders voted in favour, meeting the requirement.

The vote could be challenged[6] as members of a class must vote with regard to the interests of the class as a whole. In **British America Nickel Corpn Ltd v O'Brien [1927] AC 369**, the vote was invalidated because a shareholder was induced to support the resolution by the promise of additional shares, but there is no evidence of anything like that here. **Re Holders Investment Trust Ltd [1971] 1 WLR 583** is closer to Ahab's position. There the majority preference shareholders were also ordinary shareholders and so gained from the variation— they were found to have voted in their own interests without regard to what was best for the class. Ahab may be able to challenge the vote on this basis: the other preference shareholders will benefit from the variation as the removal of the cumulative right potentially increases profits available for distribution to ordinary shareholders.[7]

There is also a final layer of protection for Ahab. Under **CA 2006, s. 633** a shareholder with no less than 15 per cent of the issued shares in the class in question who did not vote in favour of the variation can apply to the court to have the variation cancelled on the ground that his rights as a member of the class have been unfairly prejudiced. Ahab holds 20 per cent of the class and voted against the variation, so can make an application[8] (this must be within 21 days of the variation (**s. 633(4)**)), and the variation will then have no effect unless and until it is confirmed by the court (**s. 633(3)**)). There is a dearth of authority on the interpretation of 'unfair prejudice' in relation to this provision, but it can be argued that it should follow the jurisprudence on **CA 2006, s. 994**. In such cases much often depends on the circumstances

[6] Don't assume that just because the basic procedure has been followed, that is an end to the issues

[7] Demonstrate you are really thinking about the problem: having identified a line of attack, think now about how you can argue it on the basis of the facts and your wider knowledge of the topic

[8] Think IRAC: having identified the issue and the rule that applies, now apply it expressly and conclude appropriately

in which the member joined the company which is information we do not have, but Ahab's case for 'unfairness' is clearly supported by his being the only shareholder who would suffer only detriment and no benefit from the variation.

[9] A final conclusion wraps up the individual points, and also here allows you to raise other options, such as s. 994, that could easily have taken over the question if dealt with in the body of the essay

Conclusion[9]

It would be difficult to challenge the subdivision resolution as a variation of class rights, as the case law is strongly against Ahab. However, he could consider a claim under **CA 2006, s. 994** on the basis that it is unfairly prejudicial to his interests as a member. This offers a wide range of remedies under **s. 996**, the most common of which is a share purchase order.

Ahab's position on the removal of his veto is much stronger: the resolution appears invalid, as it is strongly arguable that it is a class right and so consent of the class was needed. Even if it were valid, the alteration of the article could amount to unfair prejudice under **s. 994**, depending on the circumstances of the case.

Moby Ltd has followed the correct procedure for variation of the cumulative dividend right, but Ahab can still challenge it, either claiming the vote was invalid because the majority were not acting for the benefit of the class, or applying for cancellation as unfairly prejudicing his interests as a member of the class. While Ahab's chances of success seem quite high, if he is considering bringing a claim under **s. 994** in respect of his other complaints it might be advisable instead to add this complaint to that claim, opening up a wider range of remedies.

LOOKING FOR EXTRA MARKS

- Don't look at a topic in isolation; here you need to make the connections with alteration of the articles and shareholder remedies
- Add some concise details of relevant cases to add depth to your discussion; explicitly identify which cases are most pertinent to the facts of the question and show how you are applying them
- Don't assume that in a problem question there is no scope for deeper comment and criticism of the law; bring in your further reading and analysis where you can

TAKING THINGS FURTHER

- Pennington, R., 'Can shares in companies be defined?' (1989) 10 Co Law 140
  A helpful exploration of the nature of shares, particularly in the context of the historical development of companies and shareholding.

- Pickering, M. A., 'The problem of the preference share' (1963) 26 MLR 499

  Examines class rights and the 'somewhat unsatisfactory' features of preference shares. Challenges the preference share for failing to provide shareholders with certainty and protection while meeting business needs.

- Reynolds, B., 'Shareholders' class rights: a new approach' [1996] JBL 554

  Criticises the prevailing approach to interpreting variation of class rights, arguing that class rights should be interpreted widely and indirect alteration does amount to a variation.

- Worthington, S., 'Shares and shareholders: property, power and entitlement—Parts I and II' (2001) 22 Co Law 258, 307

  Considers the nature of shares ('property, power and entitlement'), and links shareholding to wider corporate governance questions. Argues shareholders' entitlements should be limited to the right to have the company's business conducted in accordance with the law and constitution, and not extend to the enhancement of 'shareholder value', reducing the primacy of shareholders within the class of stakeholders.

Online Resource Centre

www.oxfordtextbooks.co.uk/orc/qanda/

Go online for extra essay and problem questions, a glossary of key terms, online versions of all the answer plans and audio commentary on how selected ones were put together, and a range of podcasts which include advice on exam and coursework technique and advice for other assessment methods.

5 Directors' Duties

ARE YOU READY?

- Directors' duties: purpose, origins, and codification
- De facto and shadow directors; application of duties beyond de jure directors
- Duty to act within constitution and powers
- Duty to promote the success of the company; shareholder primacy and stakeholding
- Duty to exercise independent judgment
- Duty to exercise reasonable care, skill, and diligence
- Duty to avoid conflicts of interest
- Duty not to accept benefits from third parties
- Duty to declare interest in proposed transaction or arrangement; substantial property transactions, loans and quasi-loans
- Consequences of breach of duty
- Ratification and relief from liability
- Connections (in particular) with: management and governance, company contracts, shareholder remedies, capital, corporate insolvency

KEY DEBATES

Debate: to whom should directors owe their duties?

This debate is particularly expansive, stretching from interesting but fairly limited questions of whether individual shareholders should be owed duties by directors, to creditor interests and directors' obligations on insolvency, to fundamental notions of stakeholding and shareholder primacy. The proposals of the Company Law Review and the introduction of CA 2006, s. 172, were catalysts for a great deal of discussion on these points. The literature is extensive, with much of interest, but

⊙

the work of Andrew Keay, both on creditor interests, and his extensive writing on the corporate objective, is both readable and stimulating.

Debate: how strict should the law be in regulating conflicts of interest?

Differing attitudes to liability for conflict of interest can be seen both in the cases and in academic commentary. While some argue that a strict prophylactic rule (as exemplified by older authorities) is appropriate, others argue strongly for a more nuanced and flexible approach. There is still discussion as to what level of flexibility CA 2006, s. 175 incorporates, as well as fears from some that the ability to authorise breaches creates too wide a hole in the duty.

QUESTION | 1

Taking into account **Companies Act 2006, s. 172**, is it true to say that a director owes his duties to the company alone?

CAUTION!

- For this question you will need to have an appreciation of the difference between shareholder primacy and stakeholding approaches, and the concept of 'enlightened shareholder value' from CA 2006
- The focus of this question is to whom duties are owed rather than CA 2006, s. 172 itself, so don't provide a lengthy discussion of all aspects of the section (such as the 'good faith' point) that would be relevant in a more general analysis of s. 172

◻ DIAGRAM ANSWER PLAN

> Duties owed to the company: s. 170 and common law

▼

> The position of shareholders

▼

> 'Having regard to' interests of other constituents

▼

> The position of creditors

▼

> Enforcement of s. 172 and stakeholding considerations

▼

> Conclusion: limitations and impact of s. 172

[1] Nominee directors are an interesting group when it comes to directors' duties, but there is too much else to fit into this particular essay to explore this further

Companies Act 2006 (CA 2006), s. 170(1) states that a director owes his general duties (**ss. 171–7**) to the company. Even nominee directors owe their duties to the company[1] rather than the person appointing them (*Hawkes v Cuddy* **[2009] 2 BCLC 427**).

CA 2006, s. 170(1) confirms the approach taken at common law prior to codification of directors' duties in the **CA 2006** (following the Company Law Review) but does not elaborate on the meaning of 'the company' in this context. The company is both a separate entity (*Salomon v A. Salomon & Co Ltd* **[1897] AC 22**) and an association of its members, while relying and impacting on myriad other stake-holders, from employees to the environment. This essay will explore whether a director owes duties only to the company and what this means, considering the impact of **CA 2006, s. 172** in this area.[2]

[2] Having established the very basic points of law that underpin the issues, it is sensible to link explicitly to the question

At common law directors had to act bona fide in what they considered to be the interests of the company (*Re Smith & Fawcett Ltd* **[1942] Ch 304**); the interests of the company were the interests of the shareholders as a general body (*Gaiman v National Association for Mental Health* **[1971] Ch 317**). Slightly differently,[3] **s. 172** requires a director to 'act in the way he considers, in good faith, would be most likely to promote the success of the company for the benefit of its members as a whole …'. This is the fundamental duty to which a director is subject: *Item Software (UK) Ltd v Fassihi* **[2004] EWCA Civ 1244**. **CA 2006, s. 172(1)** thus recognises the dual nature of the company—first as a separate entity that can succeed or fail, and secondly as an association of members who will benefit from the company's success. In so far as duties are owed to shareholders though, this is through the medium of the company, and not in their individual capacity.

[3] Show that you are contrasting the pre- and post-2006 law

Percival v Wright **[1902] 2 Ch 421** made clear that directors do not owe duties to shareholders directly, whether individually or collectively. In rare cases directors may owe duties directly to shareholders: where they act as the shareholder's agent (*Allen v Hyatt* **(1914) 30 TLR 444**) or where the nature of the company and director–shareholder relationship is such that directors have taken on direct responsibilities to shareholders (*Coleman v Myers* **[1977] 2 NZLR 225**; *Re Chez Nico (Restaurants) Ltd* **[1992] BCLC 192**). This was confirmed in *Peskin v Anderson* **[2001] 1 BCLC 372** where former members of the Royal Automobile Club claimed directors owed them a duty to disclose the details of a pending sale. The court confirmed that a director's duty is to the company alone, other than in special relationships where directors are in 'direct and close contact' with shareholders. This position is not changed by **CA 2006, s. 172**.[4]

[4] This final sentence shows that you not only understand the case law but you've thought about whether the position remains the same and are therefore reflecting on the question

Duties are thus owed to the company alone save in the rare cases above. But this does not mean the interests of others are irrelevant. **Section 172(1)** requires directors, in fulfilling the duty to promote the success for the benefit of its members, to have regard ('amongst other matters') to a list of factors (paragraphs (a)–(f)) which includes the interests of the company's employees; the need to foster business relationships with suppliers, customers, and others; and the impact on the community and the environment.[5] However this is a long way from directors owing a duty to any stakeholder or other interest listed; the duty is still to the company alone. It is akin to the former **Companies Act 1985, s. 309**[6] which required directors to have regard to employees' interests, while leaving the duty owed to the company itself.

The approach of **s. 172** was labelled 'enlightened shareholder value' (ESV) by the Company Law Review. It is fundamentally a 'shareholder primacy' approach in that companies should be run for the benefit of their members, rather than a 'stakeholder' or 'pluralist' approach (whereby companies should be run to benefit all those with a stake in the business). ESV recognises taking other interests into account can enhance the success of the company which will benefit shareholders, but under ESV these factors are relevant only so far as they achieve that aim; they are not pursued for their own merits. It is a matter for the directors' business judgment how far those factors are relevant, if at all, in promoting the company's success for the members' benefit. The extent to which **s. 172** marks a change in the law is thus a matter of debate, with some (eg Lynch, 'Section 172: a groundbreaking reform of directors' duties, or the Emperor's New Clothes?' (2012) 33 Co Law 196) arguing it makes no meaningful difference.[7]

Because the duty is owed to the company, breach of **s. 172** is enforceable only through the company; groups within the **s. 172(1)** list have no right of action. Even if an action was brought in respect of a failure to take account of a **s. 172(1)** factor, it might be hard to establish any resultant loss to the company. Breach of **s. 172** is in any case difficult to establish because of its subjective nature, requiring only that directors act in the way they believe is appropriate. It is hardly surprising that the major impact of **s. 172** is thought to be educative only.

While directors' duties are owed to the company, the position becomes more complex with regard to creditors. Normally directors do not owe duties to creditors, whether individually or collectively (*Multinational Gas and Petrochemical Co v Multinational Gas and Petrochemical Services Ltd* **[1983] Ch 258**; *Kuwait Asia Bank EC v National Mutual Life Nominees Ltd* **[1991] 1 AC 187**). However, in *West Mercia Safetywear v Dodd* **[1988] BCLC 250** the court adopted the statement in *Kinsela v Russell Kinsela Pty Ltd* **[1986] 4 NSWR 722** that where a company is insolvent directors must have regard to creditors' interests. But this does not mean that a duty is owed to creditors directly; instead creditors' interests displace

[5] It can be difficult to know how far you should set out statutory material in an answer. Here you do need to establish the law, but it is much better to summarise the key elements than simply copy out from a statute book

[6] Not an essential point but it indicates some awareness of the pre-2006 position

[7] If you had time this would be a good place to explore the academic discussion in more depth

those of the members: 'It is in a practical sense their assets and not the shareholders' assets that, through the medium of the company, are under the management of the directors' (Street CJ in *Kinsela v Russell Kinsela Pty Ltd*). This applies on insolvency or where the company is 'of doubtful solvency or on the verge of insolvency' (*Colin Gwyer and Associates Ltd v London Wharf (Limehouse) Ltd* [2003] 2 BCLC 153). Further, **Insolvency Act 1986, s. 214** imposes liability on a director[8] if he permits the company to continue to trade beyond the point when he knew or ought to have known there was no reasonable prospect of avoiding insolvent liquidation. Again this does not impose a duty owed to creditors individually; enforcement is through the liquidator and benefits unsecured creditors as a body, rather than those specific creditors who have suffered loss as a result of breach of **s. 214**.

The developing state of the law relating to creditors is reflected in **s. 172(3)**. This provides that the **s. 172** duty has effect subject to 'any enactment or rule of law requiring directors, in certain circumstances, to consider or act in the interests of creditors of the company', allowing further development of these principles in the future.

To conclude, it remains the case that a director owes his duties to the company alone, other than in very limited circumstances where a direct duty to an individual shareholder arises. However, in exercising his overriding duty to act in good faith to promote the success of the company for the benefit of the members, the director must take into account all relevant matters which will include the interests of a range of stakeholders and other considerations. **Section 172** thus provides important guidance to directors, but does not give rise to a duty owed to anyone other than the company. Furthermore, since duties are enforceable by the company, any action taken in respect of any breach must be through the company, either through the directors or, more likely, the members in a derivative action under **CA 2006, ss. 260–4**. This means that even if **s. 172** is breached, action is unlikely, and even if a claim were brought successfully, any remedy would benefit the company rather than the aggrieved stakeholder.

The changes wrought by **s. 172** thus do not change the law in terms of to whom the duties are owed but reflect a more general cultural change in recognising wider interests and responsibilities.[9] This can also be seen in the business review required under **CA 2006, s. 417** (other than for small companies) which requires analysis of the company's business and the principal risks and uncertainties facing the company and, for quoted companies, information on matters such as employees, community, and the environment. These developments reflect a growing awareness of the importance of corporate responsibility for both social and economic gain, but do not alter the legal position that duties are owed to the company alone.[10]

[8] Be careful not to spend time going into IA 1986, s. 214 in depth—its relevance here is in its overlap with duties to creditors

[9] Quite how far s. 172 does this is a matter for debate that you could look at in more depth

[10] This finishes off the essay by tying the conclusion back to the question itself

LOOKING FOR EXTRA MARKS?

- Develop the discussion on stakeholding, engaging with the academic debates, but remember to link this back into s. 172 as the question demands. Consideration of other approaches such as Keay's 'entity maximisation and sustainability model' could also provide scope for critiquing the current legal approach.

- Show an awareness of the reform process (the Company Law Review) that resulted in s. 172 arguably being more than a straightforward 'codification' of existing law

| | QUESTION | 2 |

'A director must use his powers only for proper purposes.'

Discuss.

CAUTION!

- Make sure you are familiar with both the new and old terminology with respect to directors' duties—here the reference to 'proper purposes' relates to what is now CA 2006, s. 171(b)

- Don't just describe the current law or its origins; you need to provide some explanation but more importantly you need to assess how the law operates and any problems/benefits

DIAGRAM ANSWER PLAN

Introduction: s. 171(b) and its origins in the 'proper purposes' rule

⬇

Relationship with other duties

⬇

The purpose for which a power is conferred

⬇

The purpose for which a power is exercised

⬇

Relevance of good faith

⬇

Conclusion: balance criticisms against merits

The 'proper purposes' doctrine is an important part of the duties imposed by law on directors. The articles of association invariably give directors power to manage the company (eg Article 3 of the Model Articles for Private Companies (**Companies (Model Articles) Regulations 2008, Sch 1**) and leave little power in shareholders' hands.[1] To balance directors' extensive power, the law imposes duties on directors—now codified as the 'general duties of directors' in **Companies Act 2006 (CA 2006), ss. 171–7**.

[1] This briefly recognises the link between duties, governance, and division of powers

CA 2006, s. 171(b) requires a director to 'only exercise powers for the purposes for which they are conferred'. This is based on the long-established fiduciary duty to act only for 'proper purposes'[2] or not for any ulterior purpose (eg to benefit themselves). Accordingly, when exercising a power, a director must exercise it only for its proper purpose. If he fails to do so he will be in breach of duty and the exercise of the power will be invalid, although the company in general meeting can choose to affirm the exercise of power and/or ratify the director's breach (**CA 2006, s. 239**). The duty has been applied in areas as diverse as entering into agreements (***Lee Panavision Ltd v Lee Lighting Ltd*** [1992] BCLC 22) and dealing with company assets (***Extrasure Travel Insurances Ltd v Scattergood*** [2003] 1 BCLC 598), and the recent Supreme Court decision in ***Eclairs Group Ltd v JKX Oil plc*** [2015] UKSC 71 (***Eclairs Group***) indicates it continues to apply over the full range of directors' powers.[3]

[2] Show early on that you understand where the current law deals with the 'proper purposes' doctrine

[3] This was important as the majority of the Court of Appeal in this case had indicated the duty did not apply to the exercise of all powers in all circumstances

At common law the proper purpose duty was combined with the duty to act bona fide in the interests of the company.[4] For example, in ***Re Smith and Fawcett Ltd*** [1942] Ch 304 it was said directors must act: 'bona fide in what they consider—not what a court may consider—is in the interests of the company, and not for any collateral purpose' (Lord Greene MR). However, codification in the **CA 2006** has split them with the 'bona fide' duty, reformulated as the duty to promote the success of the company for the benefit of its members, found in **s. 172**. It is clear that a director cannot escape liability by saying that only one of the duties has been breached but despite splitting the duties, there are still clear links between the two as will be discussed later in this answer. The duty in **s. 171(b)** also overlaps with **s. 171(a)** as a director who fails to 'act in accordance with the company's constitution' may also, depending on the purpose for which he was exceeding his authority, be in breach of **s. 171(b)**. A director may also be at risk of breaching **s. 171(b)** when considering other directors' duties, such as **s. 175** (conflict of interest) as 'more than one of the general duties may apply in any given case' (**s. 179**).

[4] This paragraph takes the opportunity offered by needing to explain how s. 171(b) differs from the previous law to consider the extent to which s. 171(b) relates to or overlaps with other duties

Howard Smith Ltd v Ampol Petroleum Ltd [1974] AC 821*(Howard Smith)* established that in assessing the proper purposes duty the first stage is to ascertain the nature of the power and, 'in the light of modern conditions' the limits within which it may be exercised. In *Eclairs Group*, Lord Sumption indicated that ascertaining the purpose of the power depends on an inference from the mischief of the provision, including the court's understanding of the business context.[5] The power may be specific (as in *Howard Smith*) or general (the general power of management: *CAS (Nominees) Ltd v Nottingham Forest FC plc* [2002] 1 BCLC 613) and the limits of the power will depend upon the breadth of the power itself. On this point the interrelation of **s. 171** and **s. 172** may be relevant as if a director is to avoid breaching **s. 172** (the duty to promote the success of the company for the benefit of the members as a whole) then he must exercise his powers for the ultimate purpose of promoting the success of the company as well as any more specific, narrower purpose.

The limits to the exercise of a power are not necessarily narrow. In *Howard Smith*, it was held that the power to allot shares could properly be exercised not just to raise capital for the company but also to foster business connections, ensure the requisite number of shareholders, and to reach the best commercial agreement for the company. However, it could not be exercised in order to alter the majority shareholding, even though done without any intention of personal gain on the part of the directors. In *Extrasure Travel Insurances Ltd v Scattergood*[6] the court considered that in transferring company assets to another company within the group, the directors were exercising their power to deal with the assets of the company in the course of trading. The purpose for which such a power was conferred was the broad notion of promoting the company's commercial interests, but this meant exercising the power to enable the other company to meet its liabilities was not a proper exercise of that power.

A problem arises where a power is exercised for more than one purpose, one of which is 'proper' and one of which is not—when should this be regarded as exercising the power for the purpose for which it was conferred? In *Howard Smith*, the House of Lords determined that once the power had been identified and its limits ascertained, it was necessary to establish the 'substantial purpose' for which it was exercised, and then address whether that substantial purpose was within the previously identified limits of the power. If so, then the power was exercised properly (even if there were other 'improper' purposes), if not the directors were in breach of duty (even if they had acted in good faith, and even if there was a proper subordinate purpose). In *Eclairs Group*, the Supreme Court confirmed that the 'substantial purpose' test continues to apply under **s. 171(b)**: the statutory codification reflects the previous law (**ss. 170(3)–(4)**).[7]

[5] You could consider whether the most recent formulation is identical to, or subtly different from the earlier test

[6] In an exam you need to be sparing with case facts to leave enough time to discuss the law and address the question, but this paragraph shows sometimes case facts are essential to support the point being made

[7] This sentence fulfils two purposes—it shows both an awareness of an important recent case, and explicitly compares the old and new law

In assessing the 'substantial purpose', *Howard Smith* requires the court to engage in an objective assessment of the situation, considering the directors' subjective motives. By assessing objectively how 'critical or pressing' a particular issue might have been, the court can evaluate the assertions of directors as to the importance of this factor in their minds when exercising the power, although the directors' judgment on matters of management should be respected. Where directors are primarily motivated by aims other than the purpose for which the power was conferred, they will be in breach of duty and the exercise of power will be invalid. This can be seen in several cases, eg *Hogg v Cramphorn Ltd* **[1966] 3 All ER 420** where the directors' allotment of shares was invalidated when made primarily to retain control of the company for the directors and their supporters (and see also *Punt v Symons & Co Ltd* **[1903] 2 Ch 506** and *Bamford v Bamford* **[1970] Ch 212**). In *Eclairs Group*, Lord Sumption indicated that the critical point in determining whether the purpose is 'substantial' is whether it was causative of the power being exercised, but this point was not adopted by all the Justices.

[8] An important point that should be made expressly

The fact that directors have acted in good faith and in what they honestly believed to be the best interests of the company will not prevent a breach of **CA 2006, s. 171(b)**.[8] This can be seen in *Lee Panavision Ltd v Lee Lighting Ltd* where directors were in breach of duty for committing the company to a management agreement, even though they thought it in the company's interests to do so, and similarly in *Eclairs Group*, where the bona fides of the directors was not in doubt. While good faith does not prevent a breach of duty, it may still be relevant to a director in seeking relief from liability as if a director acted 'honestly, reasonably and ought fairly to be excused' then he may seek relief from the court under **CA 2006, s. 1157**.

In conclusion, a director must indeed exercise his powers only for the purpose for which they have been conferred, even if otherwise complying with his duties. The duty has received some criticism, notably that it allows courts to replace directors' business judgment with their own judgment (eg Sealy, 'Directors' duties revisited' (2001) 22 Co Law 79). Furthermore, directors do not have clear boundaries as it

[9] It is fine to make the point in your own words if you can't remember a quote in an exam

has been declared 'impossible' to 'define in advance exact limits beyond which directors must not pass' (*Howard Smith*).[9] Nonetheless, **s. 171(b)** provides an important objective protection, contrasting with the largely subjective nature of **s. 172** under which a director only needs to act in the way he considers in good faith will promote the success of the company. *Eclairs Group* shows the importance of

[10] The final sentence both links back to the question and reminds the examiner that you've done your best to evaluate and not simply describe the law

the duty in protecting the balance of power between directors and shareholders. Accordingly, following codification of the law on directors' duties, directors must still exercise their powers only for 'proper purposes' and this is as it should be.[10]

LOOKING FOR EXTRA MARKS?

- Although your focus must be on s. 171(b), don't look at it entirely in isolation—show that you recognise links between s. 171(b) and other aspects of directors' duties, and use this to explore the significance of the proper purpose doctrine

- Recognise how CA 2006 separated the previously 'composite' duty into two duties—s. 171(b) and s. 172. You could consider the Company Law Review approach to this if you wanted to explore this further

- Explore the cases and academic commentary to add depth to your discussion, in particular taking note of recent Supreme Court authority

QUESTION | 3

Gatto Ltd, a property development company, has four directors: Honey, Cherry, Florentine, and Victoria. Honey and Cherry are the children of the original founder of the business, Madeleine, who is now retired. Honey and Cherry promised Madeleine, who has a passion for local environmental issues, that they would never take any action that affects the wildlife reserve based on nearby Maryland Meadow.

In 2015, the board decided that the company should pursue new developments in the local area and asked Victoria to investigate possible new development sites. She identified two possible options: (i) Holly Wood, a brownfield site (previously developed land), and (ii) Berry Park, a greenfield site (undeveloped land) situated on the edge of Maryland Meadow. Holly Wood required decontamination prior to development and so offered lower profits than development at Berry Park, but development at Berry Park would inevitably have a negative impact on the wildlife reserve. At board discussions, Honey and Cherry refused to consider Berry Park because of their promise to Madeleine, and Victoria went along with their preference. Florentine was not present at the discussions: since last year when she became director of another company (Torta Ltd), also in the construction industry, she has rarely attended Gatto Ltd's board meetings. Decontamination of the Holly Wood site has proved very expensive and Gatto Ltd is set to lose money on the development.

Advise Gatto Ltd.

CAUTION!

- Don't work through each duty in order—this wastes time and indicates to the examiner that you are struggling to identify the relevant law. Although more than one duty can (and often does) apply, you should work out the most relevant duties and start with those

- Try to balance explanation of the law with applying the law to the facts

- Read the question carefully—as you are told to advise the company, you don't need to worry about shareholder remedies

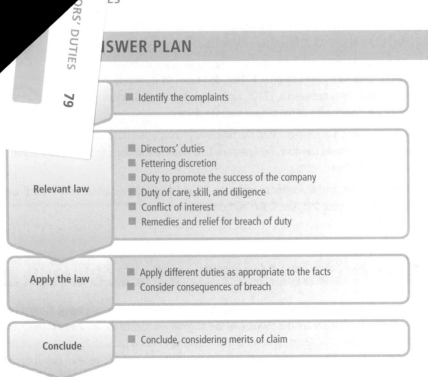

SWER PLAN

Identify the complaints

Relevant law
- Directors' duties
- Fettering discretion
- Duty to promote the success of the company
- Duty of care, skill, and diligence
- Conflict of interest
- Remedies and relief for breach of duty

Apply the law
- Apply different duties as appropriate to the facts
- Consider consequences of breach

Conclude
- Conclude, considering merits of claim

SUGGESTED ANSWER

The general duties the directors owe to Gatto Ltd (**Companies Act 2006 (CA 2006), s. 170**) are set out in **CA 2006, ss. 171–7** and are of both fiduciary and common law origin. There have been several possible breaches of duty[1] relating to the purchase of Holly Wood and involvement with Torta Ltd. These, and the consequences of breach, will be considered, bearing in mind that more than one duty may apply at any time (**CA 2006, s. 179**).

Holly Wood

The first issue to consider in relation to the Holly Wood purchase is Honey and Cherry's promise to Madeleine, which led to their refusal to consider the other (more profitable) alternative, Berry Park. Under **CA 2006, s. 173** a director 'must exercise independent judgment',[2] which originates in the fiduciary duty on a director not to fetter his judgment. This prevents a director entering into an agreement

[1] You could set out in the introduction which particular duties will be most relevant, but don't go into too much detail in the introduction as you risk repeating yourself later

[2] This duty doesn't come up often in problem questions, but do keep all the duties in mind when assessing the facts to make sure you don't miss relevant duties

preventing later consideration of his duties (***Boulting v Association of Cinematograph, Television and Allied Technicians* [1963] 2 QB 606**), although it does not prevent a director, in the proper exercise of his powers, making a decision to bind the company to a future course of action even though this restricts future decisions (***Fulham Football Club Ltd v Cabra Estates plc* [1994] 1 BCLC 363**). While Honey and Cherry have not contractually committed themselves to acting in accordance with Madeleine's wishes, by following a pre-agreed policy rather than considering the issue on its merits, they are clearly not exercising independent judgment. As this appears not to be a decision made at the time for the benefit of the company, but for family reasons, it is probable that **s. 173** has been breached. The consequences of breach[3] are the same as if the corresponding equitable principle applied (**CA 2006, s. 178**) which would include rescission of a contract made in breach of duty or equitable compensation for loss.

[3] Use your own course as a guide to how much depth you will be expected to go into on remedies

The directors may also have breached **CA 2006, s. 172** which is the 'fundamental' duty of directors (***Item Software (UK) Ltd v Fassihi* [2005] 2 BCLC 91**). It requires directors to act in the way they consider, in good faith, to be most likely to promote the success of the company for the benefit of the members as a whole. In most cases this will mean the most profitable course of action, but the potential for damage to a company's reputation will be relevant as it could harm the longer-term interests of the members.

Under **s. 172** directors are required to have regard, 'amongst other things', to a list of factors, which includes the long-term consequences of any decision (**s. 172(1)(a)**) and the 'impact of the company's operations on the community and the environment' (**s. 172(1)(d)**). This 'enlightened shareholder value' approach maintains shareholder primacy, whereby companies are run in the interests of shareholders, not other stakeholders. Accordingly directors must have regard to environmental issues only in order to promote the success of the company.[4] It appears that Cherry and Honey have breached **s. 172** if they are taking this factor into account only because of the promise to Madeleine, and not because they honestly believe this to be in the best interests of the company. Victoria will also be in breach if she has failed to consider the question for herself.

[4] Don't just explain the ESV approach—apply it to the facts

Nonetheless Gatto Ltd might have difficulty in proving breach, as the duty is subjective (what the director thinks is best, not what is, objectively, best)[5] and the directors might convince the court they genuinely believed Holly Wood was best for the company. It can also be difficult to establish loss if a director properly fulfilling the duty could reasonably have reached the same decision (as could be the case if Berry Park would cause damage to the company's reputation). This effectively brings in an objective element to **s. 172**, allowing the court to judge the director's own decision against that of an 'intelligent and honest man' (***Charterbridge Corporation Ltd v Lloyds***

[5] Remember the duty only requires a director to act in good faith in what he considers to be the best interests of the company

Bank Ltd [1970] **Ch 62**). It would therefore be difficult to establish breach of **s. 172**.

Florentine's Position

It seems that Florentine has not met the standard of care, skill, and diligence expected of a director. This requires a director to act with 'reasonable care, skill and diligence' as measured by a dual objective/ subjective test—an objective minimum of the standard reasonably expected of someone in that position in that company, increased by any general knowledge, skill, or experience of the particular individual (**CA 2006, s. 174**). Although early cases indicated a director's duties were only of an 'intermittent nature' (*Re City Equitable Fire Assurance Co Ltd* [1925] **Ch 407**),[6] later cases show a director must pay adequate attention to the company's affairs (eg *Dorchester Finance Co Ltd v Stebbing* [1989] **BCLC 498**). Ongoing failures to attend meetings and take any interest in the company, as here,[7] would be a breach of duty. The other directors could also be in breach of this duty by allowing Florentine to pay no attention to the company, as all directors have ongoing monitoring and supervisory obligations (*Re Barings plc (No. 5)* [2000] **1 BCLC 523**).

The origins of the duty of care, skill, and diligence in **s. 174** lie in the common law duty of care, and the consequences of breach are the same as if the corresponding common law rule applied (**CA 2006, s. 178**). This would be common law damages as compensation for loss. However it might be difficult for Gatto Ltd to establish causation and loss as it is hard to say that Berry Park would necessarily have been favoured even if Florentine had been present at the meeting. Even if the matter had been discussed properly between all four directors, Honey and Cherry's view might still have prevailed, or they might have all concluded that Holly Wood was the right option.

There is a further possibility that Florentine has breached her duty to avoid a conflict of interest (**CA 2006, s. 175**) by joining the board of Torta Ltd.[8] In *London and Mashonaland Exploration Company Ltd v New Mashonaland Exploration Co Ltd* [1891] **WN 165 (Mashonaland)**, Chitty J held there was no prohibition on a director acting as a director of a rival company, but he approached this on the basis of contractual restraints and confidentiality, rather than fiduciary duties. This decision was cited with approval in *Bell v Lever Bros* [1932] **AC 161**, but questioned in later cases. In *Plus Group Ltd v Pyke* [2002] **EWCA Civ 370**, [2002] **2 BCLC 201** the Court of Appeal indicated that, in general, the holding of competing directorships would require the approval of the companies in question, but stressed the situation was 'fact specific'. More recently, the Scottish courts in *Commonwealth Oil & Gas Co Ltd v Baxter* [2009] **CSIH 75** cast doubt on the judgment in *Mashonaland* and limited the case to its own facts.

[6] Don't be tempted to give too much description of the earlier cases and the development of the duty, there simply isn't time and it is more important to apply the law to the facts

[7] Make the link to the facts explicitly

[8] The law on breach of duty through the holding of more than one directorship is still not entirely clear so requires a reasonable amount of consideration

The codification of the conflict duty in **CA 2006, s. 175** makes explicit that the duty applies equally to a conflict of duty and duty as to a conflict of interests (or interest and duty) (**s. 175(7)**). A breach of **s. 175** can thus arise if Florentine is acting for two companies, because the duties owed to two different companies will in all likelihood pull in two different directions. Accordingly, while *Mashonaland* suggests there would not appear to be a breach by merely joining the board of a rival company, by acting in that position Florentine is highly likely to be in breach of **s. 175**. She could avoid this by ensuring that both companies are fully aware of the position and agree to it but in this case there seems to have been neither formal authorisation of the board (**s. 175(4)**), nor prior approval of the shareholders (*Sharma v Sharma* **[2013] EWCA Civ 1287**). On balance it seems likely that Florentine is in breach of duty in acting as director of Torta Ltd, and would accordingly be liable to account for any profits made from this position.

Conclusion

[9] As conclusions have been made on each point as they appeared, this final conclusion can be short and the opportunity can be taken to provide more general and pragmatic advice

To conclude,[9] there are potential breaches of **ss. 172–5** by the directors, although there could be some problems in proving breach, causation, and loss, particularly in relation to **s. 172** and **s. 174**. The directors might also seek relief under **CA 2006, s. 1157**, claiming they acted honestly and reasonably and ought fairly to be excused, although it must be doubted whether they acted reasonably on the facts, particularly as reasonableness is measured objectively: *Bairstow v Queens Moat Houses plc* **[2001] 2 BCLC 531**. Accordingly, Gatto Ltd might be better advised not to throw good money after bad in pursuing its directors, and instead should consider refreshing its management team by removing some or all of its directors by ordinary resolution under **CA 2006, s. 168**. In any event, action against the directors will be very difficult while they remain in power because of the rule in *Foss v Harbottle* **(1843) 2 Ha 461** and the difficulties for shareholders in bringing a derivative claim.

LOOKING FOR EXTRA MARKS?

■ Clearly relate the discussion on duties to particular complaints and particular facts to show you are applying the law and not just discussing duties generally

■ Remember to consider the consequences of breach (and, if relevant, avoidance of or relief from liability), using your own course as a guide to how much time to allocate to these elements of the question

■ A recognition of wider debates, even in a problem question, will impress the examiner, but don't go too far off point

'The formulation of the duty of skill and care in the **Companies Act 2006** shows an important sea-change in the law's expectations on directors.'

Discuss.

CAUTION!

- It is tempting to approach the law chronologically as the simplest way of explaining the position, but this may well encourage a descriptive approach. Instead try starting with the current law, and consider the extent to which it reflects the pre-existing common law

- Remember that there had already been important developments in the common law prior to the 2006 Act

DIAGRAM ANSWER PLAN

Introduction: context and approach

⬇

Relevant law: the dual objective/subjective test

⬇

Contrast earlier law with current law; explore reasons for development

⬇

Assessment and conclusion: 'sea-change' or not?

SUGGESTED ANSWER

The 'duty of skill and care' is now found within the general duties of directors in **Companies Act 2006 (CA 2006), ss. 171–7**, as the 'duty of care, skill and diligence': **s. 174**. As the general duties are based on the common law rules and equitable principles and have effect in their place (**s. 170(3)**), this would indicate no change in the law in this area, let alone a 'sea-change'.[1] However **CA 2006** is not a true 'codification' of the law, as some duties have been developed (eg **s. 172**), some aspects have not been codified (eg remedies, **s. 178**), and the common law is explicitly retained as a guide to interpreting and applying the duties (**s. 170(4)**).

[1] Indicate a focus on the question right from the start

[2] If you have planned your essay sufficiently to know where you are going, it can be very effective to indicate your argument within your introduction

This essay will argue that **s. 174** is not a 'sea-change' in the law, but merely reflects pre-2006 common law development.[2] However, its approach is based on a more modern view of the role of a director and is stricter than at least early judicial formulations of the duty. The essay will assess the current statutory duty, and compare this with the pre-existing common law, to evaluate the significance of the statutory formulation and its merits.

Section 174

Under **CA 2006, s. 174** a director must exercise 'reasonable care, skill and diligence': that exercised by a 'reasonably diligent person' with both (a) the general knowledge, skill, and experience reasonably expected of someone carrying out the functions of that individual in that company, and (b) the general knowledge, skill, and experience that the individual has. The formulation is modelled on **Insolvency Act**

[3] Show you understand what IA 1986, s. 214(4) relates to, but don't be sidetracked into discussion of wrongful trading more generally

1986 (IA 1986), s. 214(4) which relates to the knowledge required for liability for wrongful trading,[3] and, as will be seen, had already been adopted in some common law cases before **CA 2006**.

[4] This is a limited but very concise way of indicating some personal evaluation of the law

The minimum objective standard provided in paragraph (a) cleverly[4] varies according to the nature of the company and the position of the director, ensuring the law imposes higher standards on directors with greatest responsibility, thus reflecting modern expectations on directorial behaviour, particularly in larger companies. Paragraph (b) adds a further subjective layer where a director has skills or experience beyond that expected in his position. This operates only to increase the expectations on directors in relevant cases, it does not take the standard below the objective minimum. Although the level of skill, care, and diligence thus differs according to the director and the company, judges need not set out the precise knowledge, skills, and experience expected in a particular case: *Weavering Capital (UK) Ltd v Dabhia and Platt* [2013] EWCA Civ 71, reducing the scope for appeals.

The Common Law Standard

[5] By starting with the modern law, the discussion of the previous law now appears to be much more thoughtful and directed, as it is no longer a simple chronological account of legal development

By way of contrast[5] with the fundamentally objective nature of **s. 174**, the common law as established by Romer J in *Re City Equitable Fire Assurance Co Ltd* [1925] Ch 407 (*City Equitable*) appears to be much more subjective and imposed fairly lax expectations on directors. *City Equitable* established three principles. The first required a director only to show that degree of skill that 'may reasonably be expected from a person of his knowledge and experience'. The second held that a director was 'not bound to give continuous attention to the affairs of his company' with duties only of 'an intermittent nature'. Thirdly, directors were entitled to trust in officials to whom duties had been (justifiably) entrusted.

These propositions reflected the generous attitude of the time towards 'gentlemen-directors'. For example, in *Re Cardiff Savings Bank, Marquis of Bute's Case* [1892] 2 Ch 100 the Marquis became chairman at the age of six months and attended only one board meeting in 38 years but was not in breach of duty. *Re Brazilian Rubber Plantations and Estates Ltd* [1911] 1 Ch 425 held that directors need not 'bring any special qualifications to their business'; and need have no awareness of the nature of the company's business.

Comparing the Standards

On that basis it is tempting to regard **s. 174** as a sea-change in the law—from a lax subjective approach, to a strict objective one. However the common view of the *City Equitable* standard has been challenged, as it does arguably incorporate an objective element based on the reasonable director.[6] More importantly, even if one accepted that the *City Equitable* standards were lax and entirely subjective, in fact the law had evolved from this position even before **CA 2006** and so the new law does not mark a 'sea-change'.[7]

In *Norman v Theodore Goddard (A Firm)* [1991] BCLC 1028, Hoffmann J was willing to assume that the test of the director's duty of care should be based on the dual objective/subjective test imposed in respect of wrongful trading under the **Insolvency Act 1986 (IA 1986), s. 214(4)**. He restated this as the law in *Re D'Jan of London Ltd* [1994] 1 BCLC 561 *(Re D'Jan)*.

The second and third propositions of *City Equitable* had also been qualified prior to **CA 2006**. In *Re Barings plc (No 5)* [2000] 1 BCLC 523, Jonathan Parker J highlighted the 'inescapable, personal duties' of a director, holding that directors must acquire and maintain a sufficient knowledge and understanding of the company's business to enable them properly to discharge their duties as directors, and that while functions can be delegated, there is an ongoing obligation to supervise delegated functions (see also *Re Westmid Packing Services Ltd, Secretary of State for Trade and Industry v Griffiths* [1998] 2 All ER 124 (*Westmid*)). Cases such as *Dorchester Finance Co Ltd v Stebbing* [1989] BCLC 498 and *Lexi Holdings (In Administration) v Luqman and Ors* [2009] EWCA Civ 117 show that directors cannot escape liability for the consequences of another director's fraud, where their own inactivity has enabled that fraud to take place.

A major influence in the development of the duty of skill and care at common law was disqualification of directors for unfitness[8] under **Company Directors Disqualification Act 1986 (CDDA 1986), ss. 6 and 8**, where any breach of duty by the director is relevant in determining unfitness (**CDDA 1986, Sch 1**). The courts have explicitly acknowledged that the main purpose of disqualification under the **CDDA 1986** is to protect the public, and part of this protection is by raising standards of conduct among directors generally: *Westmid*.

[6] You could engage with the academic discussion on this point if you had time to do so

[7] Explicitly using the language of the question (and making interim conclusions) throughout the essay can be an effective technique to reassure the examiner that you are continuing to focus on the question

[8] This is an interesting area where directors' duties and liability on insolvency interlink—it could be relevant both in questions on directors' duties and in questions on corporate insolvency

In *Bishopsgate Investment Management Ltd v Maxwell (No. 2)* **[1994] 1 All ER 261** Hoffmann LJ linked the evolution of directors' duties with changing public attitudes as reflected in **CDDA 1986**. In *Re Landhurst Leasing plc* **[1999] 1 BCLC 286**, Hart J appeared to align the standard of the duty at common law and the standard for unfitness under the **CDDA 1986** with the *Re D'Jan* test (as now accepted in **s. 174**), although it should be remembered that a breach of the duty of care and skill is not a prerequisite for a finding of unfitness (eg *Cohen v Selby* **[2001] 1 BCLC 176**).

Conclusion: Development or Sea-change?[9]

[9] The conclusion here also contains a fair amount of evaluation of the question, so this has been made clear in the sub-heading

Section 174 thus reflects a developing jurisprudence, rather than a sea-change. The choice was made to resolve any conflict between *City Equitable* and *Re D'Jan* in favour of the latter, increasing the expectations on directors in line with modern views on director responsibility and making it easier to establish liability. But it is highly probable that the courts would have favoured the later authorities in any event and continued to develop the law in this direction, even without statutory involvement. This trend had been seen in relation to all three of the basic propositions regarding a director's duty of care, skill, and diligence. The formulation in **s. 174** makes clear that incompetence, inactivity, or abrogation of responsibility (however honest, and however limited the director's own ability) are no longer acceptable, if they ever were. It brings the old common law into line with more modern concepts such as wrongful trading and disqualification, ensuring consistency of approach.

[10] This paragraph raises some points that challenge the approach of the law, providing some additional analysis to strengthen the overall response to the question

It could be argued[10] that an objective approach is potentially unfair when no qualification is expected of directors—the law permits individuals to become directors however ill-suited they might be, and even though potentially incapable of meeting the objective standards set for them. This contrasts with other professions where qualifications are required, ensuring a level of competence. However the modern approach reflects public expectations and growing awareness of the power of directors, whose decisions and competence can impact on whole communities and economies, not just shareholders. Similar attitudes can be seen in other areas of directors' duties, particularly **s. 172**, where the opportunity was taken to develop and not simply codify the law. The potential for unfairness is reduced through **s. 174**'s variable objective standard, which allows the court to set expectations at appropriate levels for different companies, and through **s. 1157** which offers the possibility of relief where a director has acted 'honestly and reasonably' even when in breach of the duty of care and skill (*Re D'Jan*). The importance of **s. 174** thus lies not in any sea-change in the law but in ensuring modern values and practice are properly reflected and balanced in the law.

LOOKING FOR EXTRA MARKS?

- Show that you understand how the duty of care, skill, and diligence is linked with wrongful trading and disqualification

- Consider the reasons for the change in approach, and also whether the modern approach has any downsides

- Consideration of the Company Law Review deliberations can add value to discussion of directors' duties, particularly where the law has developed during the codification process

QUESTION | 5

Brianna, Alvin, Dilip, and Clara are the directors of Tweedy Ltd, manufacturers of traditional cloth. A fifth director, Joella, left the company in August, having been released from her post following a period of ill health.

In October, the directors discovered that Joella is now working with one of their former customers, Megacrush plc, developing an innovative new fabric from recycled plastics. Megacrush plc had discussed this project with Tweedy Ltd in March (all the directors being present at the meetings) but the directors had concluded this would be a distraction from Tweedy Ltd's core business and so decided not the pursue the project further. It now appears that Joella commenced work on the project with Megacrush plc very soon after her departure from Tweedy Ltd in August. Industry rumours suggest the project is likely to be very profitable.

In November, the directors agreed to place a large order for computer supplies (worth £50,000) with Futurco Ltd, and this contract has now been completed. All the directors have been aware throughout that Clara and her husband are the only shareholders of Futurco Ltd.

Advise Tweedy Ltd.

CAUTION!

- It is very easy in the panic of an exam to muddle CA 2006, ss. 175 and 177 or forget about one of them. They both deal with conflicts of interest but deal with different factual matrices, and approach the issue in a different way, so keep a clear head. Remember that s. 177 concerns transactions with the company itself, and if s. 177 applies, s. 175 doesn't.

- Where you have a transaction with the company, remember to consider the possibility that it is a substantial property transaction under CA 2006, s. 190.

DIAGRAM ANSWER PLAN

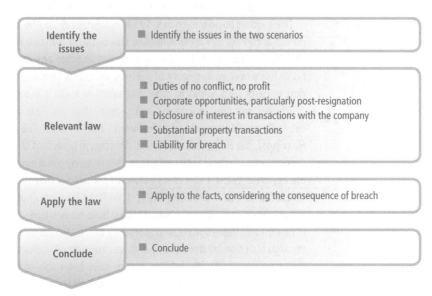

Identify the issues	▪ Identify the issues in the two scenarios
Relevant law	▪ Duties of no conflict, no profit ▪ Corporate opportunities, particularly post-resignation ▪ Disclosure of interest in transactions with the company ▪ Substantial property transactions ▪ Liability for breach
Apply the law	▪ Apply to the facts, considering the consequence of breach
Conclude	▪ Conclude

SUGGESTED ANSWER

[1] A very brief summary of the key duties is all that is required in the introduction

To advise Tweedy Ltd, the fiduciary duties of 'no conflict' and 'no profit' should be considered—a director cannot (without the company's agreement) have an interest that conflicts (or may conflict) with the interests of the company, nor profit from his position.[1] These duties have traditionally been strictly applied to ensure a director is not tempted to further his own interests at the expense of the company (*Bray v Ford* [1896] AC 44). The duties are now codified in **Companies Act 2006 (CA 2006), ss. 175–7** but the case law remains relevant in interpreting and applying them (**CA 2006, s. 170(3)–(4)**). Additional specific duties also need to be considered, particularly that relating to substantial property transactions (**CA 2006, s. 190**).

Joella

[2] Focus immediately on the current law, ie the codified duty, and bring the case law into this, rather than establishing the pre-2006 law and only then moving on to CA 2006

By working with Megacrush plc on the project discussed with Tweedy Ltd, Joella may be in breach of **CA 2006, s. 175**.[2] This section requires a director to avoid a situation in which s/he has a conflict of interest between his own interest and that of the company (**s. 175(1)**) and applies in particular to the exploitation of 'any property, information or opportunity' (**s. 175(2)**). Joella may be exploiting information or an opportunity of Tweedy Ltd in moving on to work with Megacrush plc. Although Joella has left the company, the duty continues to apply even after her departure in relation to information or opportunities of which she became aware when she was a director (**s. 170(2)(a)**).

[3] This is a way of getting in knowledge that you want to show off, but isn't actually relevant to the question. However you must be careful in doing this as it is very easy to spend too much time establishing law that isn't pertinent to the problem

There would be no breach of **s. 175** had the directors authorised the potential conflict (s. 175(4), reflecting **Queensland Mines v Hudson (1978) 52 ALJR 379**), but the facts do not indicate any authorisation.[3] It is therefore necessary to see how the courts have applied the duty to cases such as this to determine whether Joella is in breach.

The key authority indicates a strict approach to conflicts of interest. In **Regal (Hastings) Ltd v Gulliver [1942] 1 All ER 378 (Regal Hastings)**, the House of Lords found directors in breach of duty even though acting in good faith and where the company could not take up the opportunity itself. This is supported by **Industrial Development Consultants Ltd v Cooley [1972] 1 WLR 443**, where (not unlike

[4] This is a simple and very quick way of linking your discussion of the law to the facts of the problem, without having to follow a strict IRAC process

the present case)[4] a director was released from his position (claiming ill health) and then took up an opportunity that he was aware of only through his previous directorship—it was considered irrelevant that the company was highly unlikely ever to have been able to take up the opportunity itself. **Section 175(2)** now expressly states that it is immaterial whether the company could take advantage of the information or opportunity. On this basis Joella would be liable as she was only aware of the opportunity through Tweedy Ltd. Nonetheless, a softer line is present in other cases—making use of information or an opportunity post-resignation is not invariably a breach—and s. 175(4)(a) recognises there is no breach if the situation cannot reasonably be regarded as likely to give rise to a conflict of interest.

Commonwealth courts in particular have taken a more flexible line, for example **Canadian Aero Service Ltd v O'Malley (1973) 40 DLR (3d) 371** indicated liability depends on whether all the facts reveal adoption of a 'maturing business opportunity'. A similar approach was taken in the UK in **Island Export Finance Ltd v**

[5] Recognising academic discussion can add interest to a problem question, although there is usually not much scope for exploring the arguments in depth

Umunna [1986] BCLC 460. The flexible approach has been welcomed by many academics (eg Lowry and Edmunds 'The corporate opportunity doctrine: the shifting boundaries (1998) 61 MLR 515).[5] In relation to Joella, a potentially important point is that the opportunity was apparently rejected in good faith by the company's board. In **Peso Silver Mines Ltd v Cropper [1966] SCR 673**, a director was not liable when he took up a mining opportunity that had been rejected bona fide by the company. On this basis, Joella would not be in breach.

Although the courts of England and Wales have tended to take a stricter approach, exemplified by **Regal Hastings** and more recent cases such as **Bhullar v Bhullar [2003] 2 BCLC 241** and **O'Donnell v Shanahan [2009] 2 BCLC 666**, there seems a greater willingness to engage in a balancing exercise in cases of post-resignation conflict (as is the case here).[6] In *Balston Ltd v Headline Filters Ltd* [1990] **FSR 385**, there was no breach in setting up a business post-resignation to supply a former customer of the director's previous company, as no competitive activity had taken place prior to departure. This more nuanced approach with greater flexibility has been welcomed by writers such as Lowry and Sloszar ('Judicial pragmatism: directors' duties and post-resignation conflicts of duty' [2008] JBL 83). As recognised explicitly in *Foster Bryant Surveying Ltd v Bryant* [2007] **BCC 804**, the area is 'highly fact sensitive' and based on common sense. Much may therefore depend on quite what steps, if any, Joella took towards working with Megacrush plc prior to her departure.[7]

If Joella were liable under **s. 175** (and was not relieved under **CA 2006, s. 1157** on the ground she acted honestly and reasonably and ought fairly to be excused), she would be liable for an account of profits. This shows the duty can operate somewhat unfairly and provide a windfall (as in *Regal Hastings*): it would effectively give Tweedy Ltd the benefit of an opportunity it would not have secured. On balance though, at least on the limited facts provided, Joella is unlikely to be liable for breach of duty, because the company rejected the opportunity in good faith before she took it up, and she appears to have left the company on genuine rather than manufactured grounds without (as far as we can tell) taking active steps to take up the opportunity prior to her departure.

Clara

The contract with Futurco Ltd reveals a conflict of interest for Clara. However, in this case **s. 175** does not apply as the conflict arises in relation to a transaction with the company (**s. 175(3)**).[8] Other duties should be considered.

Under **s. 177** a director with an interest (direct or indirect) in a proposed transaction with the company must disclose that interest to the other directors, normally at a meeting or by notice (**s. 177(2)**). However, there is no obligation to declare an interest where the other directors are already aware of it (**s. 177(6)(b)**), and this is the case here. Accordingly there was no breach of **s. 177** in failing to make a declaration prior to the transaction, neither is there any breach of **CA 2006, s. 182** in not making a declaration after the transaction has been entered into.

However, in this particular case there may still be a breach of duty. Under **CA 2006, s. 190** a company may not acquire a 'substantial non-cash asset' from a director or a person connected with a director unless this is approved by a resolution of the company's members. Futurco Ltd is connected with Clara, as she and her husband own all the shares in the company (**CA 2006, ss. 252–4**). The asset is clearly 'non-cash' (defined **s. 1163**) and will be 'substantial' if its value exceeds £100,000 (which is not the case here), or if it exceeds both £5,000 and 10 per cent of the company's asset value (**s. 191**). Accordingly whether or not Tweedy Ltd should have obtained members' approval depends on whether its asset value (by reference to its most recent statutory accounts) is above or below £500,000.

[9] As you are not given the necessary financial information you have no choice but to give both alternatives

If above there is no breach of **s. 190**, but if below then the failure to obtain members' approval means that the transaction is voidable at the instance of the company and the directors (and Futurco Ltd) are liable to account for any gains made and indemnify the company for any losses resulting (**s. 195**).[9] This can have major consequences, for example in *Re Duckwari plc* **[1999] Ch 253**, losses included those caused by a market fall in the value of the asset.

[10] The conclusion can be brief as the points are concluded within the main text, but it is still worthwhile to draw everything together

Conclusion[10]

If the traditional strict approach to conflicts of interest is followed, Joella appears to be in breach of **s. 175**. If so Tweedy Ltd could claim an account of profits from her. However, the more balanced approach in the post-resignation cases indicates Joella would escape liability. That conclusion would change if more damning evidence about her plans and activities prior to departure came to light.

Although Clara has an interest in the transaction between Futurco Ltd and Tweedy Ltd, there has been no breach of **s. 177** or **s. 182**. However, there may have been a breach of **s. 190** in failing to get the approval of Tweedy Ltd's members. This depends on Tweedy Ltd's asset value, as this will determine whether the acquisition was of a substantial non-cash asset. If there has been a breach of **s. 190**, then the contract is voidable (unless one of the exceptions in **s. 195** applies). In addition, Clara, the other directors, and Futurco Ltd will be liable for any gains they have made or losses the company suffers under **s. 195(3)–(4)**.

 LOOKING FOR EXTRA MARKS?

- Demonstrate you are confident with both the statutory provisions and the case law, and combine them effectively
- Show an awareness of academic discussion about the duty to avoid conflicts of interest and the requirement to declare interests in transactions with the company
- Be very clear in applying the law to the facts of the problem

 QUESTION | **6**

Critically assess the extent to which directors' duties apply to those who are not formally appointed as directors.

CAUTION!

- You need to be able to examine and critique the concepts of de facto and shadow director and the relationship between them

- It is essential that you also consider the extent to which duties apply to such individuals—this is a topical issue that has been considered in recent cases and in statutory reform

- In order to 'critically assess' you should consider not just what the legal position is but also evaluate that position—is the law right? Even without a direct steer from the question, you should always try to enhance your analysis by questioning the aim, effect, and value of the law

DIAGRAM ANSWER PLAN

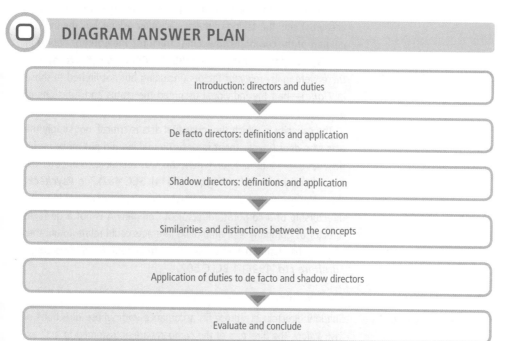

Introduction: directors and duties

↓

De facto directors: definitions and application

↓

Shadow directors: definitions and application

↓

Similarities and distinctions between the concepts

↓

Application of duties to de facto and shadow directors

↓

Evaluate and conclude

SUGGESTED ANSWER

Directors' duties seek to prevent abuse of the extensive powers given to directors; they require that directors act competently and in the interests of the company and apply to all those duly appointed, ie 'de jure directors'. But if duties applied only to those formally appointed to the role of director, the protection duties offer could be easily subverted. Duties may therefore extend to those not formally appointed—to de facto and shadow directors. This essay will examine those concepts and assess the extent to which duties apply to such individuals.[1]

[1] Reassure the examiner that you know you've got to discuss both what de facto and shadow directors are, and how far directors' duties apply to them

De facto directors

[2] Be brave and jump straight in with recent authority, rather than always starting from the beginning; it tends to encourage a more thoughtful approach

There is no single test for a de facto director, and the test may differ according to context: *Holland v Commissioners for Revenue & Customs; Re Paycheck Services 3 Ltd* [2010] UKSC 51 (*Paycheck*).[2] In *Re Hydrodam (Corby) Ltd* [1994] 2 BCLC 180 (*Hydrodam*), Millett J focused on whether an individual was held out and claimed to be a director, and undertook functions only a director could properly discharge. Subsequent cases have shown these are factors to be taken into account, rather than determinative. In *Secretary of State for Trade and Industry v Tjolle* [1998] BCC 282 (*Tjolle*), Jacob J identified various relevant factors, including holding out, the use of the title 'director', access to proper information (eg management accounts), and the taking of major decisions, asking was the individual part of the corporate governing structure? The Court of Appeal in *Re Kaytech International plc* [1999] 2 BCLC 351 (*Kaytech*) held there were many relevant factors (including but not limited to those in *Tjolle*)—had the individual assumed the status and functions of a director?

[3] Ideally slightly more detail would be provided to illustrate the point, but when time is short, a statement of the principle is adequate

The capacity in which the individual acts is critical, not simply the acts s/he does: involvement in decision-making did not make an individual a de facto director, where this was referable to another capacity (*Smithton Ltd v Naggar* [2014] BCC 482).[3] In *Paycheck*, the majority concluded an individual whose acts are referable to his directorship of a corporate director of Company A is not a de facto director of Company A. If an individual's acts could relate to another capacity, he should have the benefit of the doubt: *Re Richborough Furniture Ltd* [1996] 1 BCLC 507.

Shadow Directors

[4] It is impossible to avoid setting out the statutory provision to some extent, but summarising it at least in part indicates more personal thought than simply copying it out

Shadow directors are those 'in accordance with whose directions or instructions the directors of the company are accustomed to act', excluding those giving advice in a professional capacity[4] (**Companies Act 2006 (CA 2006), s. 251**; see also **Company Directors Disqualification Act 1986, s. 22(5), Insolvency Act 1986 (IA 1986), s. 251**).

Hydrodam held it was necessary to identify who are the directors of the company (de facto or de jure) and show: the alleged shadow director directed them how to act, they acted in accordance with such directions, and that they were accustomed to do so. Later cases emphasise there is no need to add to the requirements of the statute, so *Secretary of State for Trade and Industry v Deverell* [2000] 2 WLR 907 (*Deverell*) held the instructions or directions did not need to extend over all or most corporate activities, and could include advice. *Ultraframe (UK) Ltd v Fielding* [2005] EWHC 1638 (*Ultraframe*) held it was sufficient if a consistent majority of the directors (not necessarily the whole board) was accustomed to act in accordance with directions/instructions.

The courts have held that an initial focus on control and secrecy was somewhat misplaced. *Re Unisoft Group Ltd* [1994] **1 BCLC 609** referred to 'the puppet master' with the board as his 'cat's paw', while *Hydrodam* said a shadow director 'lurks in the shadows'. However in *Deverell* the Court of Appeal said this was unnecessary and more than the statute required.

Overlapping Concepts

A particular issue has been whether the concepts are distinct or overlap. In *Hydrodam*, Millett J saw them as essentially different; they were alternatives and usually mutually exclusive. The Court of Appeal in *Kaytech* agreed the concepts were, in most cases, mutually exclusive but said they had in common the exercise of real influence in the corporate governance of the company, whether concealed or open or a mixture.

The line between them has become increasingly blurred. In *Paycheck* the Supreme Court recognised the distinction between the concepts of de facto and shadow directors was eroded, and an individual could fulfil both roles, consecutively or simultaneously. Someone exercising power sometimes directly and sometimes indirectly, could be both a de facto and shadow director: *Secretary of State v Chohan* [2013] EWHC 680.

[5] This is an interesting article, and if you had time, further engagement with the arguments would add depth to the essay

The blurring of the concepts has received some criticism (Noonan and Watson 'The nature of shadow directorship: ad hoc statutory intervention or core company principle?' [2006] JBL 763).[5] However by accepting an overlap, the courts ensure that individuals exercising power in a company cannot escape responsibility simply because they exercise their power in a variety of ways.

Application of Duties

[6] 'Director' includes 'any person occupying the position of a director, by whatever name called'. This obviously includes those properly appointed but using a different title, but also arguably includes those not appointed but nonetheless fulfilling a director's role

Whether duties apply to de facto directors will depend on a construction of the provision (*Re Lo-Line Electric Motors Ltd* [1988] **Ch 477**) but generally all duties applying to de jure directors will apply to de facto directors, including the general duties. A de facto director arguably comes within the definition of 'director' in **CA 2006, s. 250**[6] but even if this were not the case it seems obvious that someone acting as a director (and often held out as such) should be subject to all the duties attaching to that position, even if not properly appointed.

[7] This is a question that has arisen in recent cases and law reform so you need to be aware of the issue and able to address it

More problematic is whether directors' duties apply to shadow directors.[7] Where statute expressly imposes liability on shadow directors, such as for wrongful trading (**IA 1986, s. 214**) and disqualification, the matter is clear, but what if statute is silent? Shadow directors do not fall within the **CA 2006, s. 250** definition of directors and the Supreme Court indicated (obiter) in *Paycheck* that they are subject only to obligations explicitly extended to them. This can be justified through statutory construction, and because shadow directors are not in the same position (in direct control of the company) as de jure and de facto directors. Against this, it is hard to justify treating shadow directors more favourably than the directors they are directing. Furthermore, the blurring of the distinction between de facto and shadow directorship makes it important that the same obligations should attach to both, to avoid nice distinctions depending on how an individual exercised power at any particular time.[8]

[8] This provides a good link back to the discussion on whether the concepts overlap and shows its importance in the context of what duties apply

The courts have not been consistent. While *Yukong Line of Korea Ltd v Rendsburg Corp Investments of Liberia Inc* **[1998] 1 WLR 294** assumed shadow directors owed fiduciary duties to the company, in *Ultraframe* Lewison J held they did not. In *Vivendi SA v Richards* **[2013] EWHC 3006** (*Vivendi*) Newey J disagreed with *Ultraframe* and held a shadow director does owe fiduciary duties, at least in relation to the directions given by him. Although this development was widely welcomed, in *Sukhoruchkin v Van Bekestein* **[2014] EWCA Civ 399** the Court of Appeal indicated the law remains unsettled.

CA 2006 initially left the matter open, providing that the general duties applied to shadow directors 'where and to the extent' the 'corresponding common law rules or equitable principles apply' (**s. 170(5)**). However, following *Vivendi*, **s. 170(5)** was amended to indicate more strongly that shadow directors should be subject to the duties—the general duties now apply to shadow directors 'where and to the extent that they are capable of so applying'.[9] The Secretary of State is authorised to make regulations relating to the application or adaptation of the general duties to shadow directors (**Small Business, Enterprise and Employment Act 2015, s. 89**). It seems likely that the courts will now, where appropriate, find shadow directors liable for breach of general duties, as well as specific provisions such as wrongful trading.

[9] If you have a new statute book, the amended formulation of s. 170(5) will be in there, so you need to remember at least the gist of the original formulation in order to appreciate the reform

Conclusion

Individuals without formal appointment can be subject to duties of directors if found to be a de facto or shadow director. The courts have provided guidance on these concepts, while retaining flexibility, and the distinction between them has become blurred as the courts seek to ensure individuals cannot escape liability solely because they do not fit neatly within one category. It is clear though that liability falls only on those able to exercise power and control (whether direct or indirect, open or secret). This must be right: responsibilities of a director should fall on those genuinely part of the corporate governance structure, but not on someone outside.[10] Anything else would either allow someone in a position of influence and control to avoid responsibility, or attach responsibility to someone in fact unable to effect change.

[10] This shows a willingness to engage in personal reflection on the legal position and is something that examiners are very keen to see, particularly when backed up with reasons

The courts have rightly subjected de facto directors to the full responsibilities of a de jure director. Liability of shadow directors has
been less clear but there is increasing acceptance that shadow directors are indeed subject to all a director's duties, albeit with adaptation
if necessary. Again, this must be right: shadow directors should not
be held to a lower standard of conduct than the directors whom they
direct and instruct.

LOOKING FOR EXTRA MARKS?

- Explore whether and why it matters if the concepts of de facto director and shadow director overlap

- Consider what the position is and should be in relation to a shadow director's liability for misfeasance (IA 1986, s. 212) and their ability to seek relief from liability (CA 2006, s. 1157)

- Identify, explain, and comment upon recent law reform in the area

TAKING THINGS FURTHER

- Aherne, D., 'Directors' duties, dry ink and the accessibility agenda' (2012) 128 LQR 114
  An interesting article on the approach to (and limitations of) the CA 2006 codification of directors' duties, described here as 'a sui generis codification' which attempts 'to have the best of both worlds' and engenders 'both confusion and opposition'.

- Arden, M., 'Regulating the conduct of directors' (2010) 10 JCLS 1
  Considers the origins of CA 2006, and in particular the decision to codify directors' duties. Explores the choice of an 'enlightened shareholder value' approach in s. 172, expressing the view that s. 172 creates a new balance between companies and society and instils 'a measure of corporate social responsibility'.

- Ho, J. K. S., 'Is s. 172 of the Companies Act 2006 the guidance for CSR?' (2010) 31 Co Law 207
  Considers the background to and scope of CA 2006, s. 172's 'enlightened shareholder value' approach and its value in providing guidance to companies on corporate social responsibility (CSR).

- Keay, A., 'Directors taking into account creditors' interests' (2003) 24 Co Law 300
  Considers whether a duty on directors to take creditors' interests into account exists, and if so when this duty arises and its scope. Includes consideration of UK and Commonwealth authorities and the Company Law Review proposals.

- Keay, A., 'The duty of directors to exercise independent judgement' (2008) 29 Co Law 290
  Examines the origins of CA 2006, s. 173 (the duty to exercise independent judgment), concluding that s. 173 is not identical in its ambit to the pre-2006 common law.

- Keay, A. 'Ascertaining the corporate objective: an entity maximisation and sustainability model' (2008) 71 MLR 663

Formulates an alternative approach to stakeholding or shareholder primacy that focuses on the company as an entity in its own right with a need both for wealth maximisation and survival. See also other publications including, 'The ultimate objective of the company and the enforcement of the entity maximisation and sustainability model' (2010) 10 JCLS 35.

- Keay, A., 'Good faith and directors' duty to promote the success of their company' (2011) 32 Co Law 138

    An exploration of the 'most interesting and controversial' of the duties, s. 172, but, unlike most articles, focusing on the 'good faith' element of the duty rather than enlightened shareholder value.

- Lim, E., 'Directors' fiduciary duties: a new analytical framework?' (2013) 129 LQR 242

    Examines conflicts of interest, in particular exploring when a situation 'cannot reasonably be regarded as likely to give rise to a conflict of interest' under s. 175(4)(a), linking this to 'scope of business' and 'maturing business opportunity' questions.

- Lowry, J. and Sloszar, L. 'Judicial pragmatism: directors' duties and post-resignation conflicts of duty' [2008] JBL 83

    Welcomes the more nuanced approach of cases such as Foster Bryant *to considering conflict of interest where a director has resigned, allowing the courts to view all the facts of the case.*

- Lynch, E., 'Section 172: a ground-breaking reform of directors' duties, or the emperor's new clothes?' (2012) 33 Co Law 196

    A critical evaluation of s. 172, viewing it as little more than a restatement of the previous legal position. Concludes it is 'all bark and no bite', but that the 'bark' may have some value in educating directors about good corporate management and social responsibility.

- Moore, I., 'Duties of a shadow director: recent developments considered' (2013) 345 Co LN 1

    Welcomes Vivendi *as an appropriate development in applying duties to shadow directors and argues for the definition of director to be expanded to include shadow directors to improve clarity and consistency.*

- Noonan, C. and Watson, S., 'The nature of shadow directorship: ad hoc statutory intervention or core company principle?' [2006] JBL 763

    Argues that shadow and de factor directorship should be conceptually and factually distinct, and a clear concept of shadow directorship is necessary to maintain a proper distinction between a director and a member.

- Sealy, L., 'Directors' duties revisited' (2001) 22 Co Law 79

    An entertaining (and relatively short) view of trends in directors' duties, including challenging the widespread use of the term 'duty'.

- Worthington, S., 'Reforming directors' duties' (2001) 64 MLR 439

    A critical review of directors' duties reform, pre-dating the Company Law Review's final report. Interesting to read these thoughtful criticisms of both general approach and specific suggestions in light of the eventual reform that appeared in CA 2006.

- Yap, J. L., 'De facto directorships and corporate directorships' [2012] JBL 579

    Examines the Supreme Court decision in Paycheck, *in particular critiquing the law relating to de facto directors and more generally the existence of corporate directorships.*

Online Resource Centre   www.oxfordtextbooks.co.uk/orc/qanda/

Go online for extra essay and problem questions, a glossary of key terms, online versions of all the answer plans and audio commentary on how selected ones were put together, and a range of podcasts which include advice on exam and coursework technique and advice for other assessment methods.

6 Company Management and Governance

ARE YOU READY?

- Role of directors in management and governance; executive and non-executive directors
- Relationship between directors and shareholders; the separation of ownership and control
- Accountability and disclosure of information
- Governance reports and codes and the principle of self-regulation
- The UK Combined Code on Corporate Governance; the 'comply or explain' principle
- The role of auditors in corporate governance
- Shareholder engagement
- The role of institutional investors and the Stewardship Code
- Executive remuneration
- Connections (in particular) with: incorporation, directors' duties, corporate social responsibility, the constitution, shareholder rights and remedies

KEY DEBATES

Debate: the balance of power between directors and shareholders

The separation of directors (the 'managers') from shareholders (often, but controversially, called the 'owners'), encourages efficient use of resources, but also creates tensions, not least through potential misalignment between the interests of directors and shareholders. Evaluating these tensions and considering how best to manage them has been a hot topic ever since the early days of corporate law theorising.

Debate: the effectiveness of self-regulation in corporate governance

The role of the State in corporate management and governance (as in other areas of corporate life) is an important question, and the balance to be held between legal regulation, self-regulation, and full deregulation is a difficult one. The current approach of using 'soft law' through non-legally-binding codes on a 'comply or explain' basis has been widely accepted, but is not without its limitations and critics.

Debate: balance on the board of directors

The right balance on the board of directors remains a topical subject, and ranges from older (but still relevant) debates surrounding the role of non-executive directors and the chairman, through issues such as employee representation on the board, to more recent debates such as gender and ethnic minority balance.

QUESTION | 1

'If powers of management are vested in the directors, they and they alone can exercise these powers.' (Greer LJ, *Shaw & Sons (Salford) Ltd v Shaw* [1935] **2 KB 113**)

Discuss.

CAUTION!

- There are a lot of different but connected issues within this apparently simple question, so think carefully about how to organise your discussion
- Avoid simply setting out directors' and shareholders' powers and contrasting them—you also need to explore the wider director-shareholder relationship

DIAGRAM ANSWER PLAN

Introduction: the split of powers between directors and shareholders

▼

Shareholders' powers: decision making; power to direct; default power; removal of directors

▼

Balancing the power of directors and shareholders: further thoughts

▼

Conclusion: review quote in light of discussion

The company's powers of management are habitually vested in directors (as indicated in the quote) by virtue of the company's articles of association.[1] This can be seen in the standard form articles (taking effect unless excluded: **Companies Act 2006 (CA 2006), s. 20**), for example Article 3, Model Articles for Private Companies: **Companies (Model Articles) Regulations 2008, Schedule 1**. Accordingly the courts have held that shareholders cannot act for the company, nor instruct the directors what to do. This can be seen in cases such as ***Automatic Self-Cleansing Filter Syndicate Co v Cuninghame* [1906] 2 Ch 34** where directors were not obliged to comply with a resolution of the shareholders directing a sale of the business,[2] as well as ***Shaw & Sons (Salford) Ltd v Shaw* [1935] 2 KB 113** itself.

So the management powers of the company are indeed in the hands of the directors alone. This reflects one of the key benefits of incorporation, the ability to bring together investors (shareholders) and expert managers (directors), while allowing the directors to operate the business largely without interference to maximise economic efficiency. But the quote does not tell the full story:[3] shareholders are not entirely without power, nor are directors' powers entirely unconstrained. There is and needs to be a balance of power between the directors and the shareholders, and so this essay will firstly consider what powers shareholders do have and then reflect further on the relationship between shareholders and directors.

Shareholders and Decision-making

Greer LJ's statement does not mean that shareholders are excluded entirely from decision-making. Many important decisions are reserved to the company's shareholders (such as alteration of the articles (**CA 2006, s. 21**)), whether through ordinary or special resolution (**CA 2006, ss. 281–3**). Shareholders are generally free to vote in their own interests (***North-West Transportation Co Ltd v Beatty* (1887) 12 App Cas 589,** subject to some constraints to prevent oppression of the minority[4] such as ***Allen v Gold Reefs of West Africa Ltd* [1900] 1 Ch 656**), but a resolution in general meeting is treated as a decision of the company itself, the general meeting being an organ of the company, rather than simply representing the shareholders. Valid decisions can also be made without a resolution, if made with unanimous consent of the shareholders. This pragmatic rule recognises the power of shareholders acting unanimously, but only operates to give an alternative way of reaching valid decisions; it does not vest management powers in shareholders.[5]

[1] This shows immediately that you know the status of the powers being discussed

[2] Very brief case facts show you know about the case and the context in which the point of law has been developed, without taking up too much time

[3] This links explicitly to the quote, showing you are addressing the question, and also indicates a critical approach by indicating that you don't agree fully with the quote

[4] It might be tempting to discuss this point further if you've revised it fully, but be careful to stick to the main issues raised by the question

[5] This links the point about the unanimous consent rule to the issue in the question, otherwise it risks appearing to be just general discussion about decision-making in companies

Power to Direct

Shareholders commonly retain a right to restrain or direct the directors by special resolution, as in the standard form articles (eg Article 4, Model Articles for Private Companies: **Companies (Model Articles) Regulations 2008, Sch 1**). This is because shareholders could change the articles by special resolution under **CA 2006, s. 21** and thereby re-vest powers in the general meeting in any event. But in practice shareholders do not choose to restrain or direct the directors as a matter of course. Most shareholders are happy to leave management decisions to the directors, and it would normally be difficult to secure a three-quarter majority to take such a step. Furthermore, a majority shareholder who habitually directed the directors would risk being found to be a shadow director[6] (**CA 2006, s. 251**) and thus potentially liable for breaches of duty (*Vivendi SA v Richards* [2013] EWHC 3006 (Ch)** and **CA 2006, s. 170(5)** (as amended by the **Small Business, Enterprise and Employment Act 2015**)[7]), wrongful trading (**Insolvency Act 1986, s. 214**), and disqualification (**Company Directors Disqualification Act 1986, s. 6**).

[6] Connect different topics to show your understanding

[7] Bring in recent developments so the examiner knows your knowledge is up to date

Default Powers

In unusual circumstances powers otherwise vested in directors will revert to the shareholders (the company in general meeting). This 'default' power of shareholders arises only where the board is incapable or unwilling to exercise its powers. The classic example is *Barron v Potter* [1914] 1 Ch 895 where a deadlock between the two directors meant that their powers could not be exercised. The court held that the power to appoint additional directors (conferred on the directors by the articles) reverted to the company in general meeting. Another example where the court accepted the general meeting had 'residual authority' to use the company's powers is *Alexander Ward and Co Ltd v Samyang Navigation Co Ltd* [1975] 1 WLR 673.

This default or residual power of the general meeting clearly recognises the power of shareholders to act 'as' the company where necessary, even where this means taking over powers vested in directors. However its very limited scope means that it has no real impact on the essence of Greer LJ's statement.[8]

[8] Think PEA: the point about default powers has been made, explained, and evidenced; it is then important to assess it by considering its significance in relation to the question

Removal of Directors

The most significant power of shareholders is arguably the ability to remove a director before the expiration of any term of office by ordinary resolution, notwithstanding any agreement between the director and the company: **CA 2006, s. 168**. This ensures that even though, as recognised in the title quote, management powers are vested in directors, and shareholders cannot exercise them, if a majority of shareholders are unhappy with the exercise of those powers they could choose to remove the directors responsible. Not only does this power keep shareholders in ultimate control as they choose who they want to manage the company, it also provides further incentive for directors to act in shareholders' interests to keep their own position secure.

Despite the importance of this power, in practice its use is limited. Although the articles cannot override **s. 168** to require more than an ordinary resolution, it is still possible for directors to entrench their positions using devices such as weighted voting (**Bushell v Faith [1970] AC 1099**). Even without such restrictions, shareholders may lack sufficient information to allow them to question management behaviour and in many companies, particularly larger ones, it can be difficult to engage sufficient numbers of shareholders to secure the necessary 50 per cent majority of those voting to remove a director. In addition, special notice must be given (**CA 2006, s. 168(2)**) and a written resolution cannot be used (**CA 2006, s. 288(2)**). Accordingly, while shareholders do technically retain ultimate power over the management of a company (albeit not over day-to-day decisions) which might call Greer LJ's statement into question, in practice a company's management is usually free to act without much fear of challenge.

The Balance of Power

It has been seen that shareholders' powers are limited and do not normally encompass management powers.[9] As this position comes from the articles, the shareholders could choose to change this balance of power (by altering the articles by special resolution, **CA 2006, s. 21**) if the majority saw fit. However, the standard form article remains because this split between shareholders and directors is viewed as the most efficient and effective way of running a company and excessive shareholder interference could be a recipe for economic disaster.

But there are disadvantages in placing powers disproportionately in the hands of directors. This goes to the heart of the separation of ownership and control within the corporate structure, most notably recognised by Berle & Means in 'The Modern Corporation and Private Property' (1932) but much discussed ever since. This separation can give rise to problems of corporate governance as human self-interest means that directors may use their powers for their own benefit.[10] Although directors are constrained by legal principles such as directors' duties (**CA 2006, ss. 171–7**), these are difficult to enforce, particularly without effective shareholder oversight. This is often lacking, particularly in larger companies with dispersed shareholdings. Similarly corporate governance principles in the UK Corporate Governance Code (which applies to listed public companies) are of limited effectiveness without an engaged shareholder body to challenge the board over instances of non-compliance. Even if shareholders do become dissatisfied with directors' management decisions, the temptation at least in public companies is for shareholders simply to exit by selling their shareholding rather than stay and exercise

[9] This sentence looks back to the preceding discussion to show the examiner how the answer fits together

[10] In this part of the essay you can show how issues of 'company management' overlap significantly with the wider notion of 'corporate governance'

the powers they do have, reducing further any constraint on director power.

Conclusion

While the quote is right that powers of management are in the hands of directors, and shareholders do not normally have the right to exercise them, this does not mean shareholders are without power. However, the powers of shareholders are limited, and even more importantly, shareholders are often inhibited in exercising them. In most cases the separation of powers accords with the wishes of all those in the company but can potentially lead to the interests of the shareholders (and other stakeholders) being neglected in favour of the interests of the directors themselves. It is therefore important, if a company is to be run effectively in the interests of its primary (and arguably other) stakeholders, for shareholders to use the powers they have. The key is thus maintaining the delicate balance of power within the company, while recognising that day-to-day management powers are indeed rightly vested in the directors.

LOOKING FOR EXTRA MARKS?

- Make the connection between principles of company management and wider notions of corporate governance
- Explore the problem of shareholder engagement and the notion of the separation of ownership and control; this could develop further into some appreciation of basic stakeholder arguments
- Demonstrate strong underlying understanding of company management and decision-making without just describing the law

QUESTION | 2

Critically assess the role of the UK Corporate Governance Code in encouraging and enforcing good corporate governance in the UK.

CAUTION!

- Explore how the self-regulatory Code works ('comply and explain') as well as what it requires
- You will need to explain some of the origins and purpose of the Code to provide context, but avoid giving a purely historical account of the corporate governance regime
- Make sure you evaluate the effectiveness of the Code in ensuring good corporate governance and don't just explain what it does

DIAGRAM ANSWER PLAN

Introduction: context and approach

The UK Corporate Governance Code: origins and 'soft law'

Governance themes (the board): constitution of board; qualifications; NEDs; chairman/chief executive

Governance themes (other points): remuneration; appointrnent; use of committees

The effectiveness of self-regulation: 'comply or explain'; benefits and problems

Conclusion: final evaluation

SUGGESTED ANSWER

The UK Corporate Governance Code (the Code), published by the Financial Reporting Council (FRC) (the independent regulator for corporate reporting and governance), is a code of best practice applying to public companies listed on the Stock Exchange. This essay will consider the Code's origins, principles, and self-regulation to assess how far it encourages and enforces good corporate governance.[1]

The Code originated as the Code of Best Practice (or 'Cadbury Code') following the Cadbury Report (Report of the Cadbury Committee on the Financial Aspects of Corporate Governance, 1992). Cadbury focused on encouraging a strong and balanced board, to ensure that chief executives were not without challenge. This was to be achieved in particular through using independent non-executive directors, separating the roles of chairman and chief executive and using sub-committees on appointment, remuneration, and audit—all still very important today.[2]

In 1995 the Cadbury Code was supplemented by the Greenbury Code (Code of Best Practice for Directors' Remuneration) and in 1998 the Hampel Committee consolidated the two codes, with some further recommendations, into the 'Combined Code'. Further reports, including that of Higgs on non-executive directors (2003), led to several revisions. In 2010, following review by the FRC, the Combined Code was updated (taking account of the Walker Report on corporate

[1] Use your introduction to tell the examiner what you are going to do, and show that you are thinking about the question itself

[2] There is a risk that discussion on the origins of the Code becomes too descriptive; by making even brief pertinent comments you can show you are not just reciting knowledge governance in UK banks in 2009) and renamed the UK Corporate Governance Code. There have been further refinements since, with notable reports by Davies (2011) on women on boards and Kay (2012) on markets and long-term decision-making. The FRC has also initiated The Stewardship Code to encourage more active engagement by institutional investors.

The Code is an example of 'soft law'.[3] It does not have the force of statute, but works on a 'comply or explain' basis: listed companies are obliged (under Stock Exchange Listing Rules) to make a compliance statement and explain to shareholders (in the annual report) if they are not compliant and why. However, as statute provides little on governance (other than on meetings, resolutions, and service contracts), the Code is very important in the corporate governance of listed companies.

The Code indicates best practice on corporate governance in a number of areas, many of which first appeared in essence in the Cadbury Code. The Code is split into five sections—Leadership, Effectiveness, Accountability, Remuneration, and Relations with Shareholders—each consisting of main and supporting principles. Some significant aspects of the Code will be explored to demonstrate how it encourages good corporate governance.[4]

In terms of board constitution, the Code does not specify any particular size but warns it should not be too small or too large to operate effectively. The Code does not specify particular qualifications required of directors. This is consistent with the underlying law: statute only imposes a minimum age qualification of 16 (**Companies Act 2006 (CA 2006), s. 157**) and while the Institute of Directors offers a 'Chartered Director' qualification, this is entirely optional.[5] The board should have a balance of skills, experience, independence, and knowledge of the company. Diversity on boards, and particularly gender balance, is very topical,[6] with an eye to taming excessive risk-taking such as contributed to the banking crisis. There has been significant improvement in this area following the Davies Report (2011), hitting the target of 25 per cent representation of women on FTSE100 boards in 2015. Although the Code does not set any definite requirements, specific reference is now made to the need to consider 'diversity, including gender' on the board.

Independent non-executive directors (NEDs) are seen as key to good corporate governance, by providing an important check on the activities of executive directors. The Code expects half the board (or at least two directors in smaller companies) to consist of independent NEDs, with NEDs being dominant on committees (and making up all the members of the remuneration committee). Independence (considering, eg family and current and former business relationships and also length of time on the board) is essential, although independence is to be determined by the board itself which provides some scope for manoeuvre. A senior independent director should be appointed so NEDs

[3] Think PEA: this paragraph makes the point about soft law, explains what this means, and then assesses the importance of the Code despite its non-legally binding status—further assessment of the merits of the 'soft law' point comes later on in the essay

[4] This shows the examiner that you are still thinking about the question and not just working through the provisions of the Code

[5] There isn't always much scope for conventional legal authority in essays on corporate governance, but by bringing in a bit of your legal and practical knowledge where appropriate, you can provide support and contrast for the points you make

[6] Show your awareness of topical issues in corporate governance

and shareholders can express any concerns through him/her. The Code emphasises that the roles of chairman and managing director should be held by different people to provide balance, with no individual having 'unfettered powers of decision' and executive directors should not be appointed chairman on their retirement from executive office. The Code also requires companies to enter into dialogue with shareholders. In order to encourage greater shareholder engagement with corporate governance, institutional investors are expected to comply with the FRC's Stewardship Code,[7] also on a 'comply or explain' basis.

[7] Link the Code with other developments such as the Stewardship Code

Director remuneration has been a concern of corporate governance for many decades. The Code expects remuneration to be designed to promote 'long-term success of the company'. Remuneration policy and pay levels should be set (following a 'formal and transparent procedure') by a remuneration committee made up entirely of NEDs; remuneration of NEDs is set by the board. Remuneration of each director must be stated in the company's annual report to ensure transparency. Similarly, appointments to the board must be under a 'formal, rigorous and transparent procedure'. A nomination committee should make recommendations to the board and every director should be up for re-election annually (for FTSE 350 companies). Service contracts must be open to inspection by members (**CA 2006, ss. 227–30**) and are limited to two years' duration without members' prior authorisation (**CA 2006, ss. 188–9**).

[8] It is not enough just to consider the main principles of the Code, it is necessary to assess potential barriers to the achievement of the Code's aims in order to address the question

However admirable its principles, the Code is valuable only if it actually encourages and enforces good corporate governance.[8] As there are no penalties for failure to comply with its provisions, the Code's ability to encourage and enforce good corporate governance could be doubted. Companies have indeed sometimes ignored key principles, for example[9] Marks & Spencer plc has previously allowed the same person to hold both chairman and chief executive roles (most recently Stuart Rose). However, in practice the Code is largely followed. It seems the 'comply or explain' requirements of the Listing Rules impose just enough pressure, and directors are aware that if the Code were seen to be failing more rigid regulation might well take its place. Although the self-regulatory system cannot ensure full compliance with best practice, successive governments have chosen to leave governance as primarily self-regulatory in nature.

[9] Support the points you make with examples if you can—in corporate governance essays this is more likely to be business examples rather than legal cases

The self-regulatory system has the benefit of flexibility, both by allowing alterations to the Code to reflect changes in practice and by allowing businesses freedom to operate within guidelines rather than rigid limits. By focusing on principles rather than strict rules the Code encourages compliance with the spirit of the rules rather than just a box-ticking exercise. Further, involving experts in drawing up the Code ensures provisions better reflect real practices so that self-regulation is generally accepted by those it regulates in a way that statutory regulation could never expect. However, there are obvious concerns where those making the rules are the people who will benefit most from a relaxed system.

The current system of self-regulation is not without its critics. It has not prevented a series of corporate failures and significant public disquiet with corporate activities, although it is not clear these would have been avoided even if the Code were legally binding. Despite the limits of the Code in preventing corporate failure and promoting public confidence (particularly in relation to excessive pay), the government has not seen fit to legislate wholesale on corporate governance (and the 'comply and explain' system has been adopted in very many other jurisdictions), although there has been some statutory 'interference' for example in **Enterprise and Regulatory Reform Act 2013 (ERRA 2013)**. This suggests that while the Code might need tightening, it is not without merit, or possibly that governments are not up for the fight with the City that such a change would entail (tellingly the provisions of **ERRA 2013** are significantly weaker than initially proposed).

[10] Use your conclusion to pull together the main strands of your argument and balance some of the positive and negative points that can be made

To conclude,[10] good corporate governance is essential if investors are to have confidence in UK companies and so needs to be encouraged and enforced. The Code is obviously an important part of this and provides an important guide to good practice. The Code and its predecessors can take much credit for improvements in corporate governance since 1992. However, the Code has its failings, as corporate failures and continuing debates over excessive remuneration have shown and it remains a matter of debate whether the Code simply needs strengthening, or the system itself is inadequate.

An obvious weakness of the Code in promoting good corporate governance is its application only to listed companies—the vast majority of companies are not listed. For unlisted companies, there is little encouragement to apply good corporate governance practice proactively (as the Code does for listed companies) although failures of governance can be used as a post-failure stick against directors (eg as factors in director disqualification). If the Code is to encourage good corporate governance, then its principles should be applied more widely, and its enforcement mechanisms strengthened to further encourage observance.

LOOKING FOR EXTRA MARKS?

- Balance your arguments—for example don't just explain what self-regulation is; think about its benefits and problems

- Show you understand the context of the Code—where it comes from, to whom it applies, how it is enforced, etc

- Link your discussion to your wider awareness of corporate governance matters—this could be by making reference to events in the corporate sphere or to recent reforms or proposed reforms

QUESTION | **3**

Evaluate the roles of shareholders and auditors in achieving good corporate governance in listed companies.

CAUTION!

- Split your time carefully to ensure you cover both shareholders and auditors in sufficient depth
- As well as explaining the role that shareholders and auditors should play in corporate governance, think about the factors that might inhibit the proper fulfilment of those roles.
- Remember to consider the particular role of institutional investors when considering the role of shareholders

DIAGRAM ANSWER PLAN

> Introduction: corporate governance and different roles

⬇

> Shareholders (general): removal of directors; proxy votes and apathy; availability of information

⬇

> Institutional investors: active engagement, the Stewardship Code

⬇

> Auditor: audit requirement; audit committee; independence

⬇

> Conclusion: final evaluation

SUGGESTED ANSWER

[1] Take a critical approach to the question from the start by assessing what 'good' corporate governance means

Corporate governance is 'the system by which companies are directed and controlled' (Cadbury Report, 1992). Good corporate governance[1] should ensure directors do not operate the company for their own benefit rather than the company's members. This potential problem arises from the long-recognised (Berle and Means, 'The Modern Corporation and Private Property', 1932) separation of ownership (the members) and control (the directors) in large companies. For listed companies, the UK Corporate Governance Code (the Code) provides principles of best practice for corporate governance with the Listing Rules requiring companies to 'comply or explain' as a condition of listing. This essay will examine the roles of shareholder and auditor to evaluate how and whether they can encourage good corporate governance.[2]

[2] As well as setting the scene, use your introduction to explain what you are going to do and link explicitly to the question—this reassures the examiner

Shareholders

The company's constitution invariably gives the board of directors the power to manage the company on a day-to-day basis (Article 3, Model Articles for Private Companies: **Companies (Model Articles) Regulations 2008, Sch 1**) and members have no power to instruct the directors how to act or overrule their decisions (*Automatic Self-Cleansing Filter Syndicate Co Ltd v Cuninghame* **[1906] 2 Ch 34**). Statute reserves some limited matters to shareholders, including changes to the company's constitution (**Companies Act 2006 (CA 2006), s. 21**), but shareholders have a very minor role in the running of the company. However, shareholders still have an important role to play in corporate governance. While shareholders' powers are limited, and there are significant barriers to using what powers they have, shareholders are the ultimate beneficiaries of good corporate governance and accordingly need to accept responsibility in enforcing it.

[3] This paragraph identifies the power of shareholders, but also identifies barriers to its use—both legal and practical.

Some of shareholders' power lies in their ability to dismiss directors[3] by ordinary resolution before expiry of a term of office (**CA 2006, s. 168**), which can be exercised notwithstanding any provisions in a director's service contract. It is highly unlikely that entrenching mechanisms such as that used in *Bushell v Faith* **[1970] AC 1099** (weighted votes) would be permitted by the Stock Exchange, so directors in listed companies are always at risk of dismissal without need to show cause. However, in practice shareholders would have to be very determined to go through the special notice process of **ss. 168–9**. Furthermore, if a director is removed before the expiration of his term of office, there is likely to be generous compensation payable under his service contract (or damages for breach of contract), and this may be a substantial disincentive for shareholders wishing to remove a director (as well as removing any real incentive for a director to keep the shareholders happy, as the pain of any removal is heavily cushioned). Furthermore, even a sizeable portion of unhappy shareholders will struggle to get sufficient votes to pass even an ordinary resolution—particularly when faced with the problem of disengaged shareholders and the use of proxy votes.[4]

[4] This part of the sentence is important structurally, to link the preceding discussion (barriers to exercising shareholder powers) with the discussion that follows (looking more explicitly at engaging shareholders)

The role of shareholders in good corporate governance is limited through lack of engagement. Most shareholders in listed companies hold their shares as an investment, whether for capital gain or dividend income, and often have little interest in the company itself or its governance, provided returns keep coming. If individual shareholders choose to vote at all, they often give proxy votes to the chairman of the meeting—something that further entrenches the power of the board. It is highly unlikely that individual shareholders (other than activists who have taken shares for this purpose and will be a tiny minority) will take the trouble (and expense) to attend meetings and question the board. While the introduction of additional provisions for electronic voting in **CA 2006**[5] is a step in the right direction in encouraging individual shareholder votes, it is unlikely to make a significant difference.

The general lack of engagement of individual shareholders is unsurprising as such a shareholder will typically hold only a tiny proportion of the shares. Since a shareholder's vote would be unlikely to make a difference, shareholders are disinclined to participate in governance, trusting to other shareholders to resolve any issues (the 'free rider' problem[6]), or simply trusting to the executive to keep making profits. Even if a shareholder is inclined to take an active role he faces the problem of asymmetric provision of information—directors have all the information about the company while shareholders have very little. While disclosure and transparency are important elements of statute and the Code, its use to a non-expert individual shareholder is often limited. The problems faced by individual shareholders mean that if shareholder engagement is to be effective, much then rests on those shareholders with more expertise and proportionately larger stakes in the company—institutional investors[7] such as pension funds and unit trusts.

[6] This shows an awareness of wider economic theories and could be explained and developed a bit further, depending on time available and the emphasis put on such matters in your own course

[7] Explains why institutional investors are particularly important in corporate governance and so justifies their inclusion as a distinct issue in the essay

Institutional investors have traditionally been seen as taking too passive a role, rarely challenging the actions of the board and with a tendency to 'rubber stamp' the board's resolutions. The Myners Report of 2001 recommended more active and constructive involvement in corporate governance. Similarly, the Walker Report of 2009 sought greater engagement on the part of institutional shareholders and fund managers, and the Code encourages dialogue between companies and investors, viewing the chairman as a conduit between shareholders and the board. In addition the UK Stewardship Code 'aims to enhance the quality of engagement between institutional investors and companies'. The Stewardship Code was produced by the FRC in 2010 following recommendations in the Walker Report and operates on a 'comply or explain' basis. It requires institutional investors to disclose their policy on stewardship and monitor companies in which they have investments. Investors are reminded that they should not automatically support the board. The Stewardship Code shows that the importance of institutional shareholder engagement is recognised but its impact in practice has been questioned, for example by Roach ('The UK Stewardship Code' (2011) 11 JCLS 463)[8] who argues its scope is too limited and its principles insufficiently high-quality and forward-looking.

[8] Bring in your further reading to support the point you make, providing a bit of information about the arguments in the article to show that you have engaged with the piece

There has been some evidence of shareholders being a little more willing to challenge board decisions, as in the 'Shareholder Spring' of

2012. However, the role of institutional investors is more often 'behind the scenes' than open, preferring to exercise their influence in direct communication with the board rather than in public debate. This, while potentially more effective, does not provide the visible lead that might encourage other small investors to engage.

Auditor

Company accounts must be audited unless the company is exempt by virtue of being a small private company or a dormant company: **CA 2006, s. 475**. This audit is effectively a certification of the validity of the accounts—an independent check on the company finances. Accordingly the role of the auditor is crucial for the financial accountability of the board and for corporate governance more generally.[9]

[9] Remember to link your discussion about the auditor with the issue of good corporate governance, rather than just describing his/her role

Auditors must report on the annual accounts to the members under **CA 2006, s. 495** stating whether the annual accounts have been properly prepared and give a 'true and fair view'. They also state whether the directors' report is consistent with the accounts. Although this is an important protection for shareholders, it must be emphasised that auditors cannot provide a guarantee of accuracy. Furthermore, auditors' duties are owed only to the company and the shareholders, not to creditors (*Stone & Rolls Ltd v Moore Stephens* **[2009] 1 AC 1391**).

Overseeing the audit process is the audit committee, which should have a majority of independent non-executive directors. The audit committee reduces the amount of influence that the management might otherwise have over the audit process, and minimises the risk of auditors being pressured to present information in a favourable light. The audit committee monitors both the company's internal audit function and the external audit process, and makes recommendations on the appointment of external auditors. In FTSE 350 companies, the auditor position must be put up for tender every 10 years.

Concerns about the auditor's role largely relate to independence and the stranglehold that the large accountancy firms have over accountancy and audit work in listed companies. It is rare for companies to change their audit firm, and very few use firms outside the 'Big Four'. There are fears that a 'cosy' relationship can exist between audit firms and directors, with audit firms being so reliant on work from large companies that they could be tempted not to highlight unfavourable information, or might be overly willing to accept an executive's explanation. To counter this (in part), where the auditor also provides non-audit services, the Code requires the annual report to explain how auditor 'objectivity and independence' is assured.

Conclusion

In conclusion, it can be seen that the roles of both shareholders (particularly institutional investors) and auditors are critical to the proper

[10] This allows you to show that you know about other key corporate governance points but that you recognise that this essay is not the place for discussing them

functioning of corporate governance, but that there are very real limits on the extent to which those governance functions are actually fulfilled. This inevitably means that the checks and balances on the activities of directors are not as effective as they could be, and further emphasises the importance of other governance requirements such as independent non-executive directors.[10]

LOOKING FOR EXTRA MARKS?

- Link your discussion to key underlying themes such as the shareholder primacy approach
- Consider how the roles of shareholders and auditors work together to achieve good corporate governance (as well as being significant in their own right)
- Reflect on whether there are other equally (or more) important factors in achieving good corporate governance

QUESTION | 4

Consider the effectiveness of controls on executive remuneration in the UK, considering in particular the role of the non-executive director in this area.

CAUTION!

- Don't just describe the legal (and other) controls; you need to evaluate their effectiveness
- Make sure you examine the role of the non-executive director specifically in the context of executive remuneration as well as more generally

DIAGRAM ANSWER PLAN

Introduction: director remuneration as a topical issue

▼

Legal position: no entitlement to remuneration; statutory restrictions

▼

UK Corporate Governance Code: relevant principles; role of non-executive director

▼

Conclusion: limits and transparency

Director remuneration is a frequent topic of debate. The high, indeed sometimes lavish, pay of some directors has created public disquiet, particularly in the case of former publicly-owned utilities (such as British Gas/Centrica) and companies needing substantial taxpayer assistance (such as Royal Bank of Scotland).[1] This essay will consider the effectiveness of the existing controls on director remuneration and the part non-executive directors play in this area of corporate governance.

[1] Bring in some examples to support the points you make and show the examiner you have taken an interest in the topic more widely

Directors have no outright entitlement to remuneration (***Hutton v West Cork Railway Co* (1883) 23 Ch D 654**), and are accordingly reliant on the articles making provision for payment of directors. This became very clear in ***Guinness plc v Saunders* [1990] 2 AC 663** where the House of Lords held that payment to a director was void when agreed to by a committee of the board rather than the full board as required by the articles. Usually, however, companies comply with the provisions of their articles in paying remuneration (articles almost invariably giving the power to the board) and so this will not be an issue. Statute could impose restrictions on director pay but governments are understandably reluctant to interfere too much in internal corporate matters and so there are few legal restraints. For listed companies additional regulation of remuneration is provided through the UK Corporate Governance Code (the Code) which puts non-executive directors (NEDs) at the heart of this control.[2]

[2] Make the connection between remuneration and NEDs to encourage you to discuss the topics more critically

There are few statutory restrictions on executive remuneration. One important exception is **Companies Act 2006 (CA 2006), ss. 188–9** which limits contracts to two years unless approved by the members. It is designed to stop companies granting long contracts which effectively entrench directors' positions by making it prohibitively expensive to dismiss them. Payments on loss of office other than pursuant to a contractual obligation must also be approved by members (**CA 2006, ss. 215–22**). Furthermore, **Enterprise and Regulatory Reform Act 2013 (ERRA 2013)** amended **CA 2006, s. 439A**[3] to require shareholder approval by ordinary resolution (in quoted companies) of director remuneration policy, although voting on how it has been implemented is advisory only. There is also provision for disclosure of remuneration information: under **s. 412** companies must disclose in the annual accounts aggregate directors' remuneration, while quoted companies must produce a remuneration report (**s. 420**), including individual details of directors' pay; **ss. 227–30** require directors' service contracts to be available for inspection by members.

[3] Recognise recent developments to show your knowledge is up to date

Even where shareholders do have corporate governance powers (eg the ability to dismiss a director under **CA 2006, s. 168**), a lack of engagement by shareholders in larger companies means that these powers are little used. If shareholders do not vote, or always vote in line with the board's wishes, there is little to be gained by giving more power to the general meeting. Even if shareholders were given binding votes on the implementation of remuneration policies or individual pay packages, the reality of the general meeting is that decisions of the board are often 'rubber stamped'. Accordingly, the new binding vote on remuneration policy introduced by **ERRA 2013** may have limited impact.[4]

[4]Use your knowledge and understanding to evaluate the likely impact of developments

The courts have made occasional forays into director remuneration. In *Re Halt Garage (1964) Ltd* [1982] 3 All ER 1016, the court rejected payments made to a director after she had ceased working for the company (although still registered as a director) labelling them a gratuitous distribution out of capital rather than genuine remuneration. Director disqualification may also operate as a restriction on director remuneration, at least for companies in financial difficulty. While it is not in itself 'unfit' (**Company Directors Disqualification Act 1986, ss. 6 and 8**) to pay directors even while the company is insolvent, payment of generous remuneration to directors while creditors are going unpaid is evidence of unfitness, and in setting director pay directors must consider what the company can afford and not just the 'going rate' (*Secretary of State for Trade and Industry v Van Hengel* [1995] 1 BCLC 545). While this will not make much impact in setting director remuneration, it could, provided directors are aware of the risk, operate to reduce remuneration when a company is struggling.

[5]Briefly explain the function and operation of the Code, but don't spend too much time on this as the question isn't about the Code as such

For listed companies the Code sets out best practice for corporate governance including provisions relating to remuneration of directors (Section D). The Code does not have the force of law, taking effect through the Listing Rules which require companies to 'comply or explain'.[5] The Code requires that remuneration levels should be designed 'to promote the long-term success of the company', and while pay should be compared with other companies this should be done with caution and the company should avoid 'paying more than is necessary'. In ensuring good governance of director remuneration, the role of NEDs is very important.

[6]This shows you understand that NEDs have been a critical part of corporate governance from the early days of the Code

The importance of NEDs generally was recognised in the Cadbury Report of 1992,[6] and the role has increased since. Independent NEDs provide a company with complementary expertise and experience that should inform corporate decision-making and improve strategy and profitability. As they are not involved full-time in running the company they are able to provide independent judgment and a check on the executive directors. The Code expects listed companies to have a remuneration committee to set remuneration policy and pay, filled entirely by independent NEDs (as a whole the board of larger companies should consist of at least half independent NEDs). The remuneration committee offers a more transparent and less obviously conflicted process than the former situation where executives decided each other's pay (with an obvious incentive to ensure that pay scales were high).

The question remains whether NEDs are sufficiently independent[7] to exercise real control over remuneration. The Code sets out requirements for 'independence'—including an absence of family and business links and a limit on the time a NED can stay with a company and still be viewed as independent (currently nine years). While independence in this sense is obviously important, it should be remembered that NEDs are often drawn from the same talent pool as executive directors and often sit as executive directors in other companies (or are retired executive directors). There can thus be a commonality of interest and outlook that may limit the extent to which decisions of the managing director might be challenged and this can be exacerbated by gender imbalance on corporate boards (efforts are being made to address gender imbalance following the Davies Report, 2011). While independent NEDs may avoid direct conflicts of interest, there remain indirect conflicts—is a NED truly independent in setting remuneration at Company A, knowing that this will impact on pay awards generally, including at Company B where he is an executive director? Similarly NEDs may overvalue business skills and experience, since it is human nature to put a high price on one's own skills and experience. Since it is the NED's experience that makes him/her of value to a company, it is difficult to formulate a solution to this particular problem, although there are moves to encourage candidates from other walks of life including charities and the public sector.

Another issue is the time a NED has to spend in his/her role in any individual company. These positions are part-time and it is thus not possible for a NED to be fully attuned to the business and operation of a company. In some ways this ensures independence, but it undoubtedly also reduces the ability to question and challenge decisions of the executive. The time spent by NEDs was a concern of the Walker Report (2009)[8] which recommended a significant increase in time NEDs should devote to their role; the Code requires NEDS to undertake that they have 'sufficient time' to meet expectations.

The Code, like **CA 2006**, seeks to control director remuneration through transparency. Unfortunately increased transparency (introduced initially by Cadbury) was not wholly positive—as well as informing shareholders, it meant that directors were able to compare their own pay with that of other directors, with the effect of increasing pay awards. In addition, although transparency is a worthwhile aim, disclosure has little impact if shareholders are unable or unwilling to take action when pay is seen to be excessive. Since members have no power to reject pay packages they would be left with the ultimate sanctions of selling shares or triggering a vote for director removal

[7] This paragraph questions the independence of NEDs by looking not just at the obvious concept of 'independence' as defined by the Code but also other more subtle problems of independence

[8] Link particular points to the relevant Report to show an appreciation of the development of principles

(**CA 2006, s. 168**), which are only effective if sufficient shareholders act. There are rare cases where directors have retreated from generous remuneration awards or payoffs, but this has largely come about through political or media pressure, rather than shareholder action. In light of general shareholder disengagement it is perhaps unsurprising that the new binding vote on remuneration policy in quoted companies (introduced **ERRA 2013**) has done little to encourage shareholders to take a more active role (this was perhaps predictable, see Cheffins and Thomas, 'Should shareholders have a greater say over executive pay? Learning from the US experience' (2001) 1 JCLS 277).[9] As has been seen, there are real difficulties in creating effective controls on executive remuneration in the UK.

[9]Bring in your wider reading to add interest—this point could be explained further if you had the time

LOOKING FOR EXTRA MARKS?

- Show a good understanding of how law, self-regulation, and other factors work together in this area
- Cover recent developments such as Enterprise and Regulatory Reform Act 2013 and evaluate their impact
- Show an awareness of topical issues (bringing in real-life examples) in order to demonstrate your wider engagement with the subject

TAKING THINGS FURTHER

- Adeyeye, A., 'The limitations of corporate governance in the CSR agenda' (2010) 31 Co Law 172

  A short article that links issues of management, governance, and corporate social responsibility (CSR) and discusses problems in bringing CSR more fully into corporate governance.

- Bartlett, S. and Chandler, R., 'The private shareholder, corporate governance, and the role of the annual report' [1999] JBL 415

  Examines the limitations of provision of information to shareholders as a tool of corporate governance, recognising the existence of information asymmetry between private and institutional investors (as well as between directors and shareholders).

- Cheffins, B. R. and Thomas, R. S., 'Should shareholders have a greater say over executive pay? Learning from the US experience' (2001) 1 JCLS 277

  Explores whether shareholders would be likely to exercise additional powers over executive pay, and expresses doubt that this would make a significant impact. Particularly interesting to reflect upon in light of recent changes brought about by the ERRA; 2013, but note that the references to the legal position pre-date the CA 2006.

Gutierrez, M. and Saez, M., 'Deconstructing independent directors' (2013) 13 JCLS 63

Casts doubt on the effectiveness of independent directors, particularly in relation to companies with concentrated (rather than dispersed) ownership structures. Also considers problems in identifying and selecting an effective independent director.

Keay, A., 'Company directors behaving poorly: disciplinary options for shareholders' [2007] JBL 204

Explores the options (legal and practical) shareholders may have against directors, and particularly helpful in identifying some of the practical constraints faced by shareholders.

Moore, M. T., 'The end of "comply or explain" in UK corporate governance?' (2009) 60 NILQ 85

An interesting explanation and analysis of the history and practice of the principle of 'comply or explain'. Addresses the argument that the Code had become too rigid and prescriptive.

Pedamon, C., 'Corporate social responsibility: a new approach to promoting integrity and responsibility' (2010) 31 Co Law 172

Links the recent financial crisis to issues of business ethics and integrity, thus providing fuel for thought on connections between corporate governance and CSR more generally.

Petrin, M., 'Executive compensation in the UK: past, present and future' (2015) Co Law 196

An easy-to-read review of the regulation of executive remuneration. Includes an explanation and evaluation of recent reforms in ERRA 2013, concluding reforms are 'weak at best'.

Roach, L., 'The UK Stewardship Code' (2011) 11 JCLS 463

A helpful account of the Stewardship Code: its origins, aims, application, and principles. Argues that while it represents a step for corporate governance, its impact is not likely to be significant.

Sweeney-Baird, M., 'The role of the non-executive director in modern corporate governance' (2006) 27 Co Law 67

Examines the historical development and modern role of the NED in corporate governance and considers whether greater regulation of NEDs is desirable. (Note: some discussion relates to the pre-CA 2006 law and draft Companies Bill.)

Villiers, C., 'Executive pay: beyond control?' (1995) 14 LS 260

A thoughtful consideration of remuneration issues (including the gap between pay and performance and the problems of disclosure and monitoring) that remains very relevant today. Assesses the case for 'fair pay' based on wider notions of justice.

Villiers, C., 'Controlling executive pay: institutional investors or distributive justice?' (2010) 10 JCLS 309

Explores the role of institutional investors in controlling executive remuneration levels, through the prism of increasing dissatisfaction with wide pay gaps and 'corporate greed' in a time of austerity. Argues for alternative methods of setting/monitoring pay.

Wheeler, S., 'Non-executive directors and corporate governance' (2009) 60 NILQ 51

Considers the role of NEDs in corporate governance and their effectiveness, touching on issues such as the finite pool of potential NEDs and the 'circularity' of accountability.

Online Resource Centre   **www.oxfordtextbooks.co.uk/orc/qanda/**

Go online for extra essay and problem questions, a glossary of key terms, online versions of all the answer plans and audio commentary on how selected ones were put together, and a range of podcasts which include advice on exam and coursework technique and advice for other assessment methods.

Minority Shareholder Remedies

7

ARE YOU READY?

- The rule in *Foss v Harbottle*: proper claimant and majority rule principles
- Exceptions to the rule in *Foss v Harbottle*
- Derivative claims
- Personal claims, including reflective loss
- Just and equitable winding up
- Unfairly prejudicial conduct
- Legal and practical position of a minority shareholder within a company
- Connections (in particular) with: directors' duties, company management, corporate governance, shares, the constitution, shareholder agreements

KEY DEBATES

Debate: the nature of shareholders' rights and remedies

The ability of a minority shareholder to bring proceedings notwithstanding the rule in *Foss v Harbottle* has been the topic of a number of classic articles, sometimes linking to the statutory contract. Further connected debates have considered the difference between corporate and personal wrongs, and whether a shareholder can ever claim personally for 'reflective' loss.

Debate: derivative claims and the 2006 statutory changes

The complexity of derivative claims has long resulted in plenty of academic comment, often highly critical of the courts' approach. Proposals for a statutory derivative claim triggered further debates over the value and scope of such claims, with particular concerns that it would increase shareholder activism to undesirable levels when combined with a statutory statement of directors' duties.

⊙

Debate: the meaning and scope of 'unfairness' and 'just and equitable'

Quite what 'unfairness' should encompass within the 'unfair prejudice' remedy, and how flexible or bounded it should be, has been an ongoing question, only partially resolved by *O'Neill v Phillips*. A related issue is what impact this has on the just and equitable winding up jurisdiction, and how far these remedies overlap or remain distinct.

QUESTION | 1

'Although an improvement on the preceding law, the statutory derivative claim introduced in the **Companies Act 2006** still offers only very limited value to a minority shareholder unhappy with the management of the company.'

Discuss.

CAUTION!

- You need to be aware of the differences between the statutory derivative claim and the former common law derivative claim

- Don't spend too much time setting the scene generally on shareholder remedies as this will be too descriptive; you need to focus on derivative claims

- In order to assess its 'value', think about various elements of the remedy, including the requirements of the claims, the problems a minority shareholder may face in bringing a claim, and the remedy a successful claim would attract

DIAGRAM ANSWER PLAN

Introduction: derivative claims

▼

Requirements of claim; contrast with common law

▼

Procedural requirements; contrast with common law

▼

Other considerations: remedies and costs

▼

Conclusion: assessing the value of the statutory derivative claim

The statutory derivative claim (**Companies Act 2006 (CA 2006), ss. 260–4**) is indeed an improvement on the preceding law. However the improvement is not hugely significant[1] and such claims remain unattractive for shareholders wanting to remedy problems with the company's management. In order to assess the improvements and value of the statutory derivative claim, this essay will explain its origins, and compare the pre- and post-2006 law,[2] looking in particular at the requirements (substantive and procedural), remedy, and costs.

[1] Immediately indicating the line of argument can be effective to grab the examiner's attention

[2] Comparison is essential, but structure this within themes, rather than setting out the pre-2006 law followed by the post-2006 law, otherwise the essay will be very descriptive

Derivative Claims—Statute and Common Law

The derivative claim is a true exception to the rule in ***Foss v Harbottle*** **(1843) 2 Hare 461** that the proper claimant in an action in respect of a wrong to a company is the company (the rule also encompasses the majority rule principle: where a wrong may be made binding by a simple majority, no individual member can maintain an action in respect of it, ***Edwards v Halliwell*** **[1950] 2 All ER 1064**). The rule reflects the separate personality of the company, and prevents multiplicity of claims, futile claims, and harassment of management by minority shareholders, but may lead to injustice where the wrongdoers are in control of the company.[3] Because of this last point, shareholders may bring derivative claims on behalf of the company in limited circumstances.

[3] This brings in background understanding (the justifications for the rule in *Foss v Harbottle*) but still keeps the focus on derivative claims

Derivative claims were a common law creation (requiring 'fraud on the minority') but were placed on a statutory footing in **CA 2006** following proposals by the Law Commission, ('Shareholder Remedies', Law Com No. 246, 1997) who sought to simplify and modernise the law and improve its accessibility. The proposals were supported by the Company Law Review Steering Group ('Developing the Framework', 2000). The statutory claim supersedes the common law, other than for multiple derivative claims (where the claimant is not a shareholder in the company to which the complaint relates, but is a shareholder in the company's parent company under the same 'wrongdoer control') (***Universal Project Management Ltd v Fort Gilkicker Ltd*** **[2013] EWHC 348**) and claims against foreign companies (***Novatrust Ltd v Kea Investments Ltd*** **[2014] EWHC 4061**). In these (unusual) situations the statute offers shareholders no improvement at all.[4]

[4] Multiple derivative claims aren't directly relevant to the question but it would be misleading to state that the statutory claim entirely supersedes the common law

Basis of Claim

Under **CA 2006, s. 260(1)** a derivative claim is brought by a member in respect of a cause of action vested in the company, seeking relief on behalf of the company. The cause of action must arise from an actual or proposed act or omission involving negligence, default, breach of duty, or breach of trust by a director (**s. 260(3)**) whether the cause of action arose before or after the claimant became a member of the company (**s. 260(4)**). (This latter point emphasises that this is a corporate, not a personal remedy.) This is slightly wider than before,[5] as at common law 'fraud' covered most breaches of duty but did not cover negligence (***Pavlides v Jensen* [1956] 2 All ER 518**) unless resulting in profit to a director (***Daniels v Daniels* [1978] Ch 406**).

The common law also required 'wrongdoer control'—actual voting control, not mere de facto control through dominance of shareholding and management position: ***Prudential Assurance Co Ltd v Newman Industries Ltd (No. 2)* [1982] Ch 204**. Wrongdoer control is no longer a condition for a statutory derivative claim, but remains relevant as if the company could commence proceedings itself, this is an important element in the court's decision whether to allow the claim to continue (***Bamford v Harvey* [2012] EWHC 2858 (Ch)**). Accordingly a claimant's position is only marginally improved.[6]

Procedural Hurdles

At common law, derivative claims were equitable and discretionary. The procedural hurdles could be off-putting, and claims could be rejected for many reasons. This position has been little altered by **CA 2006**, although the process and grounds on which a claim may be dismissed are clearer.

Members must apply to the court for permission to continue the claim (**s. 261(1)**), which will be refused if the application and evidence filed do not disclose a prima facie case: **s. 261(2)**. *Iesini v Westrip Holdings Ltd* [2009] EWHC 2526 (Ch) held the court should take a provisional view on the strength of the claim, not hold a mini-trial of the action. The court must also refuse permission to continue if satisfied that a person acting in accordance with **CA 2006, s. 172** (duty to promote the company's success) would not seek to continue the claim: **s. 263(2)(a)**. Gibbs argues that the prima facie stage is 'seemingly redundant' as weak cases pass this, but then fall at this stage ('Has the statutory derivative claim fulfilled its objectives?' (2011) Co Law 41).[7] In *Iesini v Westrip Holdings Ltd* the court held **s. 263(2)(a)** required the court to be satisfied that no director acting in accordance with **s. 172** would seek to continue the claim. If some would and others would not then it is simply a factor to be considered in the exercise of discretion under **s. 263(3)(b)**. The court must also refuse permission where the action arises from a prospective act or omission that has been authorised by the company or from an existing act or omission that was previously authorised or subsequently ratified: **s. 263(2)(b)–(c)**.

If the claim is not rejected under **s. 263(2)**, the court considers whether to give permission. **Section 263(3)** gives a (non-exhaustive) list of relevant factors, many of which echo the approach of the courts at common law.[8] For example, the court must consider whether the member is acting in good faith in seeking to continue

[5] Remember to make your comparison

[6] Link your discussion to the focus of the question—improvement and value to shareholders

[7] Bring in some wider reading to show your appreciation of how the procedure works

[8] This demonstrates concisely (when combined with the case examples) an awareness of common law cases as well as the new statutory procedure

the claim—at common law in *Barrett v Duckett* **[1995] 1 BCLC 243** the claimant's ulterior motive led the court to refuse permission to continue. Other factors are whether authorisation or ratification is likely (reflecting the general principle of majority rule); whether the company has decided not to pursue the claim; whether the act or omission gives rise to a personal cause of action for the member, and the importance someone with the duty under **s. 172** would attach to continuing the claim. The court must also have particular regard to the views of any independent members (**s. 263(4)**), echoing the approach taken in *Smith v Croft (No. 2)* **[1987] 3 All ER 909** at common law).

More than one factor can be relevant. In *Mission Capital plc v Sinclair* **[2008] EWHC 1339 (Ch)**, the court refused permission as it felt the notional director would not attach great weight to continuing the claim, and was also influenced by the availability of an unfair prejudice petition (see also *Franbar Holdings Ltd v Patel* **[2008] EWHC 1534 (Ch)** and *Stimpson v Southern Landlords Association* **[2009] EWHC 2072 (Ch)**). Although the existence of an alternative remedy is relevant it is not decisive (*Kiani v Cooper* **[2010] EWHC 577 (Ch)**): a derivative claim was allowed to proceed notwithstanding the existence of a **s. 994** claim in *Phillips v Fryer* **[2012] EWHC 1611 (Ch)**. As well as the **s. 263(3)** factors, the courts will consider any other relevant matters, including in *Kleanthous v Paphitis* **[2011] EWHC 2287**, the fact that any recoveries from directors would largely be returned to them as majority shareholders.

Remedy and Costs

Under **CA 2006**, as under the common law, a successful derivative claim leads to relief for the company. It thus benefits a shareholder claimant only indirectly (as well as benefiting all other shareholders), which may discourage action being taken. Other remedies, particularly **CA 2006, s. 994**, offer greater flexibility,[9] although the tendency to favour buy-out orders under **s. 996** may not suit a shareholder who wants to stay in the company.

A member bringing a derivative claim is potentially liable for costs, though acting on behalf of the company. This could deter claims but the courts have long been willing to order the company to indemnify claimants where it was reasonable to bring an action and it was brought in good faith: *Wallersteiner v Moir* (No. 2) **[1975] 1 QB 373**. If the action is not thought reasonable an indemnity may be rejected: *Smith v Croft*. The power to make costs indemnity orders is unchanged under the statute and when granting permission to continue the courts have granted indemnities for the claimant's reasonable costs subject to limits: *Stainer v Lee* **[2010] EWHC 1539**; *Kiani v Cooper* **[2010] EWHC 577**.

[9] Show an awareness of how derivative claims relate to other shareholder remedies

Conclusion

The statutory derivative claim has improved the law for minority shareholders by widening the cause of action, and clarifying the procedure and grounds for dismissal. Nonetheless, as it deliberately mirrors the common law, it retains many of its problems—even when a shareholder can discover sufficient information to bring a claim (**s. 261(3)** provides for the court to order the production of evidence), the procedural hurdles are significant and the remedy inflexible. The fact that the statutory claim has not resulted in the flood of cases feared by some shows it has retained strict limitations.[10] Accordingly, although derivative claims are an important exception to the rule in *Foss v Harbottle*, in most cases a shareholder unhappy with a company's management will seek an alternative remedy.

[10] This point could be expanded a little, using some academic literature as support, to show the initial concerns and how things have worked in practice

LOOKING FOR EXTRA MARKS?

- Reflect on whether the statutory derivative claim differs significantly from the common law—here you could engage with the academic discussion surrounding the introduction of the statutory remedy

- Show your wider appreciation of the issues by considering whether the derivative claim can better operate as a tool of corporate governance now it is on a statutory footing

- Indicate an awareness of the other options available to a minority shareholder, but don't lose focus on the question itself

- Recognise gaps in the reform, such as the multiple derivative claim

QUESTION | 2

Until recently Ellie was one of the five directors of Drango plc. The shares in Drango Ltd are owned by Lily, Millie, Nelly, Ollie, and Polly. At the end of last year Ellie's negligence caused a loss of £250,000 to Drango plc. Her actions have resulted in a drop in the value of the company's shares.

Ellie has now left the company but the remaining directors have decided that it is not in the company's interest to take any action against her. Polly is not happy with this decision and would like to bring proceedings against Ellie or otherwise recoup her losses.

Advise Polly on the options open to her as a shareholder in this position.

CAUTION!

- Look carefully at the question: the company is a public limited company, so you need to reflect on this in your response

- Make sure that you identify what a shareholder is complaining about so that you can focus your legal discussion and application appropriately

- As the instruction is broad you will need to consider all the potential shareholder remedies, but think through your answer before you start so that you can focus on those that are most relevant

DIAGRAM ANSWER PLAN

Identify the issues	■ Identify the complaints and issues
Relevant law	■ Position of minority shareholders ■ Personal claims and reflective loss ■ Derivative claims ■ Unfairly prejudicial conduct ■ Just and equitable winding up ■ Exit routes
Apply the law	■ Apply to the facts ■ Reflect on what the shareholder wants to achieve
Conclude	■ Conclude, indicating the best route(s)

SUGGESTED ANSWER

Drango plc appears to have a prima facie case against Ellie for breach of the duty of care, skill, and diligence under **Companies Act 2006 (CA 2006), s. 174**, and possibly also for breach of **CA 2006, s. 172** if she failed to declare her wrongdoing to the company (***Item Software (UK) Ltd v Fassihi* [2004] EWCA Civ 1244**). The company is not taking action against Ellie however, and Polly is unhappy about this, particularly as she has suffered financial loss (through the loss in value of her shares) as a consequence of the breach. As the wrong has been done to the company, members are normally prohibited from bringing action under the rule in ***Foss v Harbottle* (1843) 2 Hare 461**, but there are exceptions to this rule[1] which will be considered in order to advise Polly of her options.

[1] There is a lot to cover in this question, so the background has to be dealt with very concisely

Personal Claim

A personal claim would be outside the rule in *Foss v Harbottle*, which relates to wrongs done to the company rather than wrongs done to a shareholder personally.[2] Polly has suffered financial loss through the drop in share value, which might indicate she could bring a personal claim. However, *Prudential Assurance Co Ltd v Newman Industries Ltd (No2)* **[1982] Ch 204**, held that a shareholder could not bring a personal action in respect of a fall in the value of his shares caused by the wrongdoing of the company controllers who had disposed of a corporate asset at an undervalue. This approach was confirmed in *Johnson v Gore Wood and Co* **[2002] 2 AC 1**—a member cannot claim personally for a loss that is merely a reflection of the loss suffered by the company. Although *Giles v Rhind* **[2003] 1 BCLC 1** provides a limited ability to claim for reflective losses where the company's inability to pursue the claim is caused by the wrongdoing itself, this does not assist Polly. Polly will not be able to bring a personal action in respect of the loss in value of her shares.

Derivative Claim

Polly may be able to bring a derivative claim against Ellie under **CA 2006, ss. 260–4**, relating to a cause of action vested in the company. Unlike the common law derivative claim, it is no longer necessary to establish a 'fraud' against the company, 'mere' negligence is now sufficient (contrast this with *Pavlides v Jensen* **[1956] 2 All ER 518** at common law).[3] Any breach of duty by a director (including former directors: **s. 260(5)**) is sufficient cause of action: **s. 260(3)**. Neither is there any longer a need to establish that the wrongdoers are in control of the company (*Bamford v Harvey* **[2012] EWHC 2858 (Ch)**). Polly would thus bring the claim on behalf of Drango plc seeking relief on its behalf (**s. 260(1)**) against Ellie. The company would be joined as a defendant to make it party to the proceedings.

However Polly would face a number of hurdles in bringing a derivative claim. At the first stage she would have to ensure that her application and supporting evidence disclose a prima facie case, if not the court would refuse permission to continue the claim: **s. 261(2)**. The 'prima facie' stage is intended to remove unmeritorious cases at an early stage rather than conduct a 'mini-trial' (*Iesini v Westrip Holdings Ltd* **[2009] EWHC 2526 (Ch)**), and it seems likely that Polly could satisfy this stage. The court would then have to consider whether or not to grant permission to continue, having regard to the provisions of **s. 263**. If the court considers a person acting to promote the interest of the company in accordance with **CA 2006, s. 172** (duty to promote the success of the company), known as 'the hypothetical director', would not seek to continue the claim (**s. 263(2)(a)**), or that the breach was authorised or ratified by the company (**263(2)(b)–(c)**),

[2] You could expand this to explore the nature of corporate and personal wrongs, but do keep your focus on the problem

[3] An essential point to make given the nature of the director's wrongdoing

it must refuse permission. As (a) requires the court to be satisfied that no such hypothetical director would seek to continue the claim, and not just that some would and some wouldn't (*Iesini v Westrip Holdings Ltd*), it seems probable (depending on all the surrounding facts) that the claim would not be dismissed on this ground, neither does it appear that the breach has been authorised or ratified.[4]

But even if Polly does pass this hurdle, the court must then exercise its discretion as to whether or not to give permission, and in so doing must in particular take into consideration the factors in **s. 263(3)**: whether Polly is acting in good faith in bringing the claim, the importance the hypothetical director would attach to continuing the claim; whether authorisation or ratification is likely, whether the company has decided not to pursue the claim, and whether the act gives rise to a cause of action that the member could pursue in his own right. The court must have particular regard to the views of members of the company who have no personal interest in the matter (**s. 263(4)**). Taking the factors into account (particularly the hypothetical director and the company's decision), the court might well refuse permission, although we need more information on the views of the other shareholders, and the reasons why the directors had chosen not to proceed against Ellie.[5]

Even if Polly were to be granted permission to bring a derivative claim, any remedy would go to the company, not to her directly, and so Polly's financial position would only benefit indirectly. Polly would have to weigh this benefit against the difficulties of bringing the claim, the risk of a costs order against her (although the court will commonly order the company to indemnify a claimant acting reasonably for her costs: *Wallersteiner v Moir (No. 2)* [1975] **1 All ER 849**), and the fact that the publicity from any action might impact negatively on the share price (a risk recognised by Arsalidou, 'Litigation culture and the new statutory derivative claim' (2009) Co Law 205).[6]

Unfair Prejudice

Another possible option for Polly would be an unfair prejudice petition under **CA 2006 s. 994**. (As Polly has no apparent wish to 'kill' the company, a petition under **Insolvency Act 1986, s. 122(1)(g)**—winding up on the just and equitable ground—will not be considered.)[7] **Section 994** requires there to have been conduct of the company's affairs that unfairly prejudices the interests of a member. This can include wrongs done to the company—**s. 994** can be used to 'outflank' the rule in *Foss v Harbottle* (*Re Saul D Harrison & Sons plc* [1995] **1 BCLC 14**). There is clearly financial prejudice to her interests, but Polly would also need to show unfairness, which normally requires either a breach of the terms of membership, or the use of legal rules in an inequitable manner (*O'Neill v Phillips* [1999] **1 WLR 1092**).

---

[4] Explicitly consider how the law applies to the facts of the problem

[5] It is fine to take a provisional view and indicate where you would need more facts to advise more confidently

[6] Bringing in a practical point shows you have really thought about the issues; in this particular instance it also allows you to show your wider reading

[7] If you don't think a particular option is relevant, it can be helpful to give a reason for your view—that way the examiner knows you haven't just forgotten it

It is highly unlikely that equitable constraints would be found here as this does not appear to be a quasi-partnership company (***Ebrahimi v Westbourne Galleries Ltd* [1973] AC 360**) and the courts are very reluctant to impose equitable constraints in a public company[8] (***Re Astec (BSR) plc* [1998] 2 BCLC 556**). Is there any breach of the terms of association? Negligent conduct of an individual director may not fall within **s. 994** (***Re Charnley Davies Ltd (No. 2)* [1990] BCLC 760**) but Polly could possibly argue the directors' failure to take action against Ellie is unfair as a breach of their duties (under **s. 171(b)** or **s. 172**), although this will be difficult to establish without clear bad faith, and this is not apparent on the facts. The courts do not commonly find unfair prejudice in public companies, where the commercial nature of the company tends to be foremost (***Re Saul D Harrison & Sons plc***), and the shareholder has alternative options, such as selling their shares.

Even if Polly could establish unfairness, the likely remedy under **s. 996** would be an order for the purchase of her shares (***Grace v Biagioli* [2006] 2 BCLC 70**). This does not appear to be what Polly wants, as although recouping her investment, she will lose the potential for future dividends and capital growth. She would also bear the risk of costs if unsuccessful.[9]

[8]Remember that the company is a public company, so you need to indicate where this is relevant to how the law applies

[9]Consider what the client wants, and think about the drawbacks as well as any benefits

Conclusion

Polly's position shows how limited the rights of a minority shareholder can be. A derivative claim is possible if she is determined to try to remedy the breach and stay in the company, but she will face significant hurdles in bringing the claim. Her other legal options are arguably even less attractive. Pragmatically Polly might be better advised to seek to persuade her fellow shareholders to put pressure on the directors to bring an action, or to seek sufficient support to remove the directors (needing a simple majority under **CA 2006, s. 168**).[10] If Polly has no support and is really unhappy with the way the company is being run, she might be better off selling up and investing elsewhere, as legal proceedings may prove expensive and futile.

[10]This shows you are not just producing a 'standard form' answer but are considering what the particular client could possibly do, as well as demonstrating wider knowledge

 LOOKING FOR EXTRA MARKS?

- Think about what a shareholder wants to achieve and compare this with what different remedies offer, so you can advise more specifically

- Recognise that the position of a minority shareholder in a public company might differ from a shareholder in a private limited company in the availability or application of the remedies available

- Focus on the legal options available, but don't forget also to consider the client's position from a practical perspective

Assess the significance of the House of Lords' decision in *O'Neill v Phillips* [1999] 1 WLR 1092 to the unfair prejudice remedy under **Companies Act 2006, section 994**.

CAUTION!

- You will need a good understanding of the unfair prejudice remedy generally in order to assess the decision in *O'Neill v Phillips* effectively

- The question is about the significance of the case, and not about the case generally, so don't waste time setting out case facts in great detail

- Don't just look at the concept of 'unfairness'; look at other important elements of the case such as the advice given on how to approach an offer to purchase the petitioner's shares

DIAGRAM ANSWER PLAN

> Introduction: issues to be considered

▼

> Context of *O'Neill v Phillips*

▼

> Unfairness: meaning and scope

▼

> Unfairness and 'legitimate expectations'

▼

> Offer to purchase and effect on petition

▼

> Evaluation of broader significance

▼

> Conclusion: summarise points

SUGGESTED ANSWER

This essay will argue that *O'Neill v Phillips* [1999] 1 WLR 1092 (*O'Neill*) has been significant in developing the 'unfair prejudice' remedy (**Companies Act 2006 (CA 2006), s. 994**) but is significant as a strong restatement of principle rather than a fundamental change of approach. After briefly considering the context, two key elements of the case will be analysed—the concept of 'unfairness', and the effect of offers to purchase a petitioner's shares, considering cases and proposed reform before and after *O'Neill*, to evaluate its significance.[1]

[1] It can be effective to both indicate the argument and explain what will be covered in the first paragraph. But if you are not sure how your argument will go before you start writing, you can just explain your approach, linking clearly to the question

Context

CA 2006, s. 994 allows a member to petition for relief when the company's affairs have been conducted in a manner unfairly prejudicial to a member's interests. *O'Neill* was the House of Lords' first opportunity to consider the remedy (then **Companies Act 1985, s. 459**) which had proved very popular in contrast to its predecessor, **Companies Act 1948, s. 210**, which required 'oppression', restrictively interpreted by the courts. But there were concerns about the number, length, and 'appalling' cost of proceedings (*Re Unisoft Group Ltd (No. 3)* **[1994] 1 BCLC 609**), for example, in *Re Elgindata Ltd* **[1991] BCLC 959**, costs of £320,000 were incurred on shares valued at £24,600. These concerns explain the court's generally restrictive approach to the remedy.[2]

[2] This makes the connection between otherwise fairly general points about the remedy and the approach taken in *O'Neill* itself to avoid overly descriptive writing

Unfairness

Lord Hoffmann, giving the only speech in *O'Neill*, identified unfairness as the key element of the remedy. Although this conferred 'a wide power to do what appeared just and equitable',[3] it must be applied judicially and the content based upon rational principles. Lord Hoffmann recognised both that a company has a commercial nature—a legal association for an economic purpose—and that company law developed from the law of partnership, so incorporates equitable concepts of good faith. This, he held, gives two aspects to unfairness. First a member cannot ordinarily complain of unfairness unless there has been some breach of the terms on which he agreed the affairs of the company should be conducted. Secondly, in some cases equitable considerations make it unfair for those conducting the affairs of the company to rely upon strict legal powers. The judge drew a parallel with the approach of *Ebrahimi v Westbourne Galleries Ltd* **[1973] AC 360** (*Ebrahimi*) for just and equitable winding up—legal rights may be subject to equitable considerations in certain circumstances. This is typically justified where the company is a 'quasi-partnership', ie displaying one or more of the characteristics identified in *Ebrahimi*:[4] (i) an association formed or continued on the basis of a personal relationship involving mutual confidence; (ii) an agreement or understanding that the shareholders will participate in the conduct of the business; and (iii) restrictions on the transfer of the shares.

[3] If you can't remember precise phrases when in an exam, don't worry, just give the essence of what was said

[4] You need to be familiar with *Ebrahimi* and be able to set out and apply the quasi-partnership characteristics

In *O'Neill*,[5] O's primary complaint was that P had failed to award him additional shares as expected and discussed. Lord Hoffmann's

[5] This paragraph gives just enough of the facts to show the examiner you know the case well, while using the facts to show a good understanding of how the law (previously explained) is applied

analysis of unfairness led to the conclusion that this was not unfair as the 'promise' to give O more shares was not legally binding. Furthermore, although the company was a quasi-partnership, so excluding O from management would have been unfair, the court found that O had not been forced out; he had chosen to leave.

[6] Pull your discussion back to the question by focusing on 'significance'

This interpretation of unfairness was not particularly significant as it mirrored the analysis (of Hoffmann LJ) in *Re Saul D Harrison & Sons plc* [1995] 1 BCLC 14. More significantly, *O'Neill* explicitly rejected of the concept of 'legitimate expectations',[6] a notion introduced in *Re Saul D Harrison & Sons plc*. In *O'Neill*, Lord Hoffmann held that 'legitimate expectations' was just a label for the equitable restraint and 'should not be allowed to lead a life of its own': a focus on legitimate expectations had led the Court of Appeal to find in favour of O, and (wrongly) loosen the boundaries of unfair prejudice.

Accordingly, while *O'Neill* did not break new ground it made the boundaries clearer. Following the decision, the Law Commission thought the remedy would be less readily available while the Company Law Review Steering Group ('Modern Company Law for a Competitive Economy: Final Report' (2001)) believed it remained substantially unchanged but agreed with the *O'Neill* analysis.[7] There was perceived to be no need for reform, contrary to the views of the Law Commission prior to *O'Neill*, suggesting the judgment was effective in clarifying the boundaries of the remedy.

[7] Awareness of reform proposals is always valuable, but it is particularly helpful to use this knowledge to support your argument, which is what this paragraph goes on to do

Later cases have accepted *O'Neill* as providing the necessary guidance for unfair prejudice: *Oak Investment Partners XII v Boughtwood* [2010] 2 BCLC 459. *Re Tobian Properties Ltd* [2012] EWCA Civ 998 reflects its essence in describing the remedy as 'elastic but not unbounded'. The *O'Neill* analysis means that for the majority of companies, where the relationship is purely commercial, unfairness lies only in a breach of terms of association—such as the articles, company law, or binding agreements. Only where equitable constraints can be justified, as in quasi-partnership companies, can the petitioner rely on a wider notion of 'unfairness'. Even here the petitioner must establish a clear understanding on which the association is based or continued (*Re Guidezone Ltd* [2000] 2 BCLC 321), not just a failure to meet his expectations.

Prior to *O'Neill*, the Law Commission had considered providing a more general exit route for aggrieved shareholders but *O'Neill* made clear the remedy does not provide 'no fault divorce', allowing a petitioner to be bought out wherever trust and confidence has broken down. This was followed in *Re Phoenix Office Supplies Ltd* [2003] 1 BCLC 76. Even deadlock between the shareholders is not enough in itself to trigger s. 994: *Hawkes v Cuddy* [2009] 2 BCLC 427. These limits show how important it is to place dispute resolution mechanisms and exit provisions in the articles or shareholder agreements from the start.[8]

[8] Bring in your wider understanding of a minority shareholder's position

Although *O'Neill* tightened the concept of 'unfairness', in other respects it took a broad approach. For example it held that 'interests of a member' for the purposes of the provision should be interpreted widely and not be 'too narrowly or technically construed'. This has been followed in later cases, eg *Gamlestaden Fastigheter AB v Baltic Partners Ltd* [2007] 4 All ER 164.

Offer to Purchase

Another significant element of *O'Neill* is the guidance given regarding offers to purchase the petitioner's shares—given expressly to encourage parties to avoid litigation. It was already established that an offer could lead to a petition being dismissed—the petitioner having received the full relief that might eventually be awarded (eg *Re A Company (No. 836 of 1995)* [1996] BCLC 192). Lord Hoffmann in *O'Neill* asserted that such an offer prevents conduct from being unfair as the minority is no longer trapped. Providing practical guidance, *O'Neill* set out the principles expected of a 'fair' offer—normally a pro-rata valuation without a minority discount to be determined by a competent expert with both parties having equal access to information and the opportunity to make submissions to the expert. The judge indicated that an offer should usually include legal costs incurred, although a respondent should have 'a reasonable opportunity to make an offer' before any costs obligation arose.

[9] Think PEA: the point about offers to purchase has been made and explained in the previous paragraph, now it is time to analyse its importance (and support this with academic opinion)

Because of its value in bringing petitions to a speedy close, the guidance on offers to purchase is arguably the most significant element of *O'Neill* (see eg Boyle, 'Unfair prejudice in the House of Lords' (2000) 21 Co Law 253)[9] and it has been followed in later cases: *North Holdings Ltd v Southern Tropics Ltd* [1999] 2 BCLC 625. Nonetheless, an offer within the *O'Neill* guidance will not inevitably lead to the striking out of a petition: *Harborne Road Nominees Ltd v Karvaski* [2011] EWHC 2214.

Conclusion

O'Neill is significant because it emphasises the boundaries to **s. 994**, and increases opportunities for resolving disputes out of court. However, it does not change the law materially, nor unduly restrict this important flexible remedy. **Section 994** continues to be praised for its 'adaptability' (Arden LJ in *Re Tobian*, also recognising it as a tool for encouraging good corporate behaviour) and its 'wide and flexible' nature (*Re Coroin Ltd* [2013] EWCA Civ 781). Courts have not been deterred from developing the jurisdiction in appropriate cases, albeit within the constraints of *O'Neill*. For example in *Gross v Rackind* [2004] 4 All ER 735 it was held the conduct of a holding company towards its subsidiary company could be the subject of a complaint by the shareholder of the subsidiary, while in

Oak Investment Partners XII Ltd Partnership v Boughtwood the court accepted that, in principle, the conduct of a senior manager could be relevant.

Unsurprisingly given the restrictions of other shareholder remedies and the limited relief options they offer, **s. 994** continues to be the most favoured option in shareholder disputes. Unfortunately, although helpful in reducing the number and length of proceedings, *O'Neill* has not entirely resolved this problem. In *Re Coroin Ltd*, Arden LJ commented upon 'heavy' and 'resource intensive' **s. 994** cases and the need to reduce hearing times for such cases, making similar observations in *Graham v Every* [2015] 1 BCLC 41,[10] so the significance of *O'Neill* in this regard should not be overstated.

[10] Bringing in more recent cases that can be used to bolster your argument (or, alternatively, provide a slightly different view) can be an effective way of drawing to a close

LOOKING FOR EXTRA MARKS

- Show your wider awareness by reflecting on things such as the reform proposals of the Law Commission and the view of the Company Law Review Steering Group

- Keep your focus on the case itself as the question demands, but bring in both earlier and later cases as ways of assessing the significance of the case

- Link to academic evaluation of the case and its importance to shareholder remedies

- You could also think about whether the case may have impacted on other shareholder remedies (but be careful not to stray too far away from the question itself)

QUESTION | 4

Between 2011 and 2014 Suzie and Tara ran a successful business in partnership. In 2014, they decided to incorporate the business, and to take this opportunity to bring in a mutual friend, Urma, who had previously been working informally with them. Esteyu Ltd was incorporated with an issued share capital of 1000 £1 shares, Suzie and Tara each taking 450 shares, and Urma taking 100 shares. All three became directors of Esteyu Ltd on incorporation.

About a year after incorporation, Suzie and Tara voted to remove Urma from her directorship, and thereafter have not allowed Urma to be involved in management. They claim that she is difficult to get on with and doesn't work as hard as they do. The company has never paid any dividends. Suzie and Tara claim that the company is not profitable enough to pay dividends but Urma says profits are being kept to a minimum because Suzie and Tara are paying themselves substantial remuneration and perks.

Advise Urma, who is very unhappy with the current position, considering both Companies Act 2006, s. 994 and Insolvency Act 1986, s. 122(1)(g). Would your answer differ if Suzie and Tara had recently offered to buy Urma's shares, the value to be determined by the company's auditor?

CAUTION!

- If you are asked to advise in relation to a specific remedy or remedies, keep this focus and don't waste your time discussing shareholder remedies more generally
- Keep linking the law to the facts to avoid being too descriptive
- Don't forget to consider any additional points raised, here the 'offer to purchase' point

DIAGRAM ANSWER PLAN

Identify the issues	■ Identify the shareholder's complaints
Relevant law	■ Quasi-partnership companies ■ Unfair prejudice ■ Just and equitable winding up ■ Relationship between unfair prejudice and just and equitable winding up ■ Effect of offer to purchase shares on shareholder remedies
Apply the law	■ Apply to the facts ■ Consider whether offer to purchase changes the position
Conclude	■ Conclude, evaluating chances of success

SUGGESTED ANSWER

[1] A short introductory paragraph is often all that is necessary in a problem question

Urma is a minority shareholder in Esteyu Ltd. Her complaint relates to her removal as a director and failure to pay dividends. This essay will advise on her chances of success[1] if she were to bring a petition under **Companies Act 2006, s. 994** or **Insolvency Act 1986, s. 122(1)(g)**, also considering the effect of an offer to purchase her shares.

Unfair Prejudice

[2] A neat little device to convince the examiner you are looking at the question—saying 'a member's complaint' would be just as valid, but would give the impression of being less strong on application

Under **CA 2006, s. 994** Urma's complaint[2] must relate to the conduct of the company's affairs. This has been interpreted broadly so provided the complaint does not relate solely to the conduct of an individual's affairs (such as the sale of shares between members: **Re Leeds United Holdings plc [1996] 2 BCLC 545**) this will be satisfied. Suzie and Tara's behaviour would fall within the requirement. Urma must also establish that her interests as a member have been prejudiced. 'Interests as a member' extends beyond pure 'membership rights' and can include participation in management (*O'Neill v Phillips* [1999] 1 WLR 1092 (*O'Neill*)) so is satisfied here. Prejudice is relatively easy to establish, and need not be financial loss (*Re Coroin Ltd* [2013] EWCA Civ 781): here Urma's removal and lack of financial return would amount to prejudice.[3]

[3] Think IRAC: having established the issue, and the rule, remember to apply and conclude on each point. This paragraph uses IRAC concisely to raise and conclude on three minor issues.

The aspect of **s. 994** that is more likely to cause problems for Urma is unfairness. The conduct must not just be prejudicial, but unfairly so: *Re Saul D Harrison & Sons plc* [1995] 1 BCLC 14. 'Unfairness' is a broad concept but must be applied judicially and within established boundaries. The key case is the House of Lords decision in *O'Neill*[4] which held that unfairness will normally (in a standard commercial association) lie only in a (non-trivial) breach of the terms on which it was agreed the company's affairs would be conducted. This would require some breach of the constitution, law, or binding agreement, for example, which does not appear to be the case here, as we will assume Urma's removal was in accordance with **CA 2006, s. 168** (requiring a simple majority and special notice) and there is nothing else prohibiting her removal. Additionally however, unfairness may lie where equitable considerations make it unfair for those conducting the affairs of the company to rely on their strict legal powers. This arises typically only where a company is a 'quasi-partnership company', as identified in *Ebrahimi v Westbourne Galleries Ltd* [1973] AC 360 (*Ebrahimi*): a company formed on the basis of a personal relationship involving mutual confidence with all (or most) members involved in management, and a restriction on the transfer of shares.

[4] You need to be able to set out the *O'Neill* analysis of 'unfairness' confidently (and fairly concisely) in problem questions such as this

Applying the *Ebrahimi* factors to Esteyu Ltd, it appears to be a quasi-partnership. Although Urma was not initially a partner, she had been working with the partners and was brought in as a member and director at incorporation together with Suzie and Tara. Share restrictions are common in private companies (although we are not told expressly) but there will be practical restrictions in any event due to the lack of market for private company shares. Urma seems to have joined the company in reliance on the understanding she would be involved in management (reliance is necessary to give rise to the equitable constraint: *Re Guidezone Ltd* [2000] 2 BCLC 321) and accordingly, it would prima facie be unfair for Suzie and Tara to exclude her. *Re Ghyll Beck Driving Range Ltd* [1993] BCLC 1126 held it was unfair when one of four members in a quasi-partnership was excluded[5] following arguments.

[5] Support your conclusion with reference(s) to a case or cases that are on point

A further factor is the failure to pay dividends, as with Urma no longer a director receiving remuneration, she has no return on her investment. A failure to pay dividends can be unfair, particularly when other members are benefiting from director remuneration (*Re Sam Weller & Sons Ltd* [1990] Ch 682; *Irvine v Irvine* [2007] 1 BCLC 349), as here.

Suzie and Tara might argue the removal was still not unfair,[6] because of Urma's perceived failings. In *Re RA Noble & Sons (Clothing) Ltd* [1983] BCLC 273 exclusion from management was not unfair because the individual had been paying no attention to company affairs, while in *Grace v Biagioli* [2006] 2 BCLC 70 exclusion was not unfair because the individual had been purchasing a competing company. However, unless there is evidence Urma was doing almost no work and/or was deliberately obstructive it seems unlikely that this would be sufficient to render apparently unfair conduct, fair.

On balance Urma seems to have a strong case under **s. 994**. The court has a wide discretion as to the remedy granted (**s. 996**) and Urma must specify the remedy sought (*Hawkes v Cuddy* [2009] BCLC 427). The most common order is a share purchase order buying out the minority shareholder, as it frees the petitioner and removes the possibility of future discord (*Grace v Biagioli*). The valuation date is usually the date of the order (although it can be backdated if losses have been continuing: *Re London School of Electronics Ltd* [1986] Ch 211). In a quasi-partnership company as here, the valuation is usually pro-rata without a minority discount: *Re Bird Precision Bellows Ltd* [1984] Ch 419.

Just and Equitable Winding up

Urma's chances of succeeding on a petition under **Insolvency Act 1986 (IA 1986), s. 122(1)(g)** are much smaller. This is not because she doesn't have a good case per se. Following *Ebrahimi* (see also eg *Re A & BC Chewing Gum Ltd* [1975] 1 WLR 579), in a quasi-partnership company, exclusion from management can make it just and equitable to wind up the company and *O'Neill* drew parallels between the unfair prejudice and 'just and equitable' jurisdictions. *Hawkes v Cuddy* confirmed (rejecting *Re Guidezone Ltd* on this point) that unfair prejudice and just and equitable winding up continue to exist as separate jurisdictions, as well as overlapping to quite some extent.

It is this overlap that means Urma should not pursue a petition

under **s. 122(1)(g)**. Under **IA 1986, s. 125(2)**[7] the court must not wind up a company on the just and equitable ground if it is of the opinion that the petitioner has some other remedy and she is acting unreasonably in seeking winding up instead of pursuing that remedy. As Urma has another remedy (**s. 994**) and it would be unreasonable to wind up a viable company without good reason, her petition under **s. 122(1)(g)** would almost certainly be dismissed. **Section 122(1)(g)** is potentially of most use in a deadlock situation such as *Re Yenidje*

Tobacco Ltd **[1916] 2 Ch 426**—there is no deadlock in this case as Suzie and Tara have a clear majority. Urma should also not be tempted to bring the two petitions in the alternative—this is strongly discouraged because of the serious effect a winding up petition has on a company.

Offer to Purchase

The offer to purchase would potentially change Urma's position. If a reasonable offer to purchase the petitioner's shares is made, an unfair prejudice petition will usually be dismissed. This is because a successful petitioner will most likely obtain a share purchase order—the offer to purchase therefore gives the petitioner all she is likely to achieve (*Re A Company (No. 836 of 1995)* **[1996] BCLC 192**). Lord Hoffmann in *O'Neill* also indicated that an offer means there is no unfairness, as the petitioner is no longer trapped.[8] The same consequence would follow for a petition under **IA 1986, s. 122(1)(g)** as the offer would be an alternative remedy that it would (usually) be unreasonable not to pursue.

The critical factor then is whether the offer is 'reasonable'. In *O'Neill* guidance was given (obiter, but followed in later cases) as to what constitutes a reasonable offer. This will normally be an offer to purchase shares at a 'fair value' on a pro rata basis without minority discount, with the value (if not agreed) to be determined by a competent expert and both parties having access to information to make submissions to the expert. The offer should also normally include payment of the petitioner's costs to date. Here it is not clear that the offer is reasonable as the valuation is by the company's auditor, who will probably not be regarded as sufficiently independent[9] (*North Holdings Ltd v Southern Tropics Ltd* **[1999] 2 BCLC 625**). Furthermore, no allowance is made for costs, although this may not matter if the offer is made promptly: *O'Neill*. A court may still allow a petition to proceed notwithstanding an offer to purchase within the *O'Neill* guidelines, depending on all the facts: *Harborne Road Nominees Ltd v Karvaski* **[2011] EWHC 2214**.

Conclusion[10]

On balance Urma has good prospects of success if she brings an unfair prejudice petition, provided Suzie and Tara have not made (or do not make) a reasonable offer to purchase her shares within the *O'Neill* guidelines. If successful she is likely to be bought out, rather than reinstated as a director, with the valuation not discounted for its minority status. She should not, however, bring a petition for just and equitable winding up, as this is unlikely to succeed.

[8] Although this doesn't make any difference to your conclusion, it is a valuable additional point as it shows you have a deeper appreciation of the issues

[9] Even if unaware of authority on this point, you should think about the significance of the valuation being by the auditor—it must be in the case facts for a reason! The examiner wants to see you've thought about, even if your conclusion differs from theirs

[10] A brief conclusion is fine if you've concluded on points as you've gone along

LOOKING FOR EXTRA MARKS?

- Support your points with authority as much as you can, giving case facts sparingly and only where pertinent to save time for analysis and application

- Structure your work carefully to show you have understood all the relevant points and can work through to a logical conclusion

- Application of the law to the facts and advising the client clearly is critical in a question like this—always try to pull together your discussion and analysis to reach a conclusion for each point

 ## TAKING THINGS FURTHER

- Arsalidou, D., 'Litigation culture and the new statutory derivative claim' (2009) 30 Co Law 205
  Reviews the benefits of the statutory derivative claim generally and in light of cases under the new provisions, reflecting on whether there is a risk of additional litigation against directors.

- Baxter, C., 'The true spirit of *Foss v Harbottle*' (1987) 38 NILQ 6
  An entertaining analysis of the rule in Foss v Harbottle *and its exceptions following the case of* Prudential Assurance v Newman. *There is much of value here as it ranges through a number of 'mind-bending problems', but remember that it pre-dates the introduction of the statutory derivative claim.*

- Boyle, A. J., 'Unfair prejudice in the House of Lords' (2000) 21 Co Law 253
  A brief case note on O'Neill v Phillips, *highlighting the practical importance of the guidance on a 'reasonable' offer to purchase a petitioner's shares.*

- Cheung, R., 'Corporate wrongs litigated in the context of unfair prejudice claims: reforming the unfair prejudice remedy for the redress of corporate wrongs' (2008) 29 Co Law 98
  Examines the basis on which complaints about corporate wrongs (such as breach of directors' duties) can be made and redressed within an unfair prejudice claim.

- Gibbs, D., 'Has the statutory derivative claim fulfilled its objectives? Parts 1 and 2' (2011) 32 Co Law 41 and 76
  Assesses the shortcomings of the statutory derivative claim, examining the mandatory and discretionary factors in light of decided cases. Questions the influence stakeholder interests can play in the granting of permission by the courts through the focus on the s. 172 duty.

- Gray, A. M., 'The statutory derivative claim: an outmoded superfluousness?' (2012) 33 Co Law 295
  Explores the distinction between derivative claims and unfair prejudice petitions, concluding the derivative claim continues to add value to company law and provides a deterrent to directors considering breaching their duties.

- Griffin, S., 'Shareholder remedies and the no reflective loss principle—problems surrounding the identification of a membership interest' [2010] JBL 461
  Suggests that the unfair prejudice jurisdiction effectively blurs the conceptual boundaries of 'membership interest', bringing together a number of issues including membership interests, personal claims, corporate claims, and reflective losses.

■ Griffin, S., 'Alternative shareholder remedies following corporate mismanagement—which remedy to pursue?' (2010) Co LN 1

A helpful summary of the different options open to shareholders, contrasting their nature and scope, distinguishing between them, and highlighting areas where they overlap.

■ Hannigan, B., 'Drawing boundaries between derivative claims and unfairly prejudicial petitions' [2009] JBL 606

Criticises the failure of some courts to distinguish adequately between derivative and personal claims, in particular when ordering corporate relief in an unfair prejudice petition.

■ Mitchell, C., 'Shareholders' claims for reflective loss' (2004) 120 LQR 457

Examines the justifications and policy reasons for the bar on claims for 'reflective loss', exploring when and why shareholders can claim for loss in share value.

■ Paterson, P., 'A criticism of the contractual approach to unfair prejudice' (2006) 27 Co Law 204

An account of the unfair prejudice remedy including a review of conduct that can be 'unfair', arguing that the modern approach is not properly explained by contractual analysis.

■ Payne, J., 'Section 459 and public companies' (1999) 115 LQR 368

Considers the reasons why unfair prejudice claims are unlikely to be successful in public companies, with particular reference to Re Astec (BSR) plc.

■ Wedderburn, K. W., 'Shareholders' rights and the rule in *Foss v Harbottle*' [1957] CLJ 194, [1958] CLJ 93

This classic article (in two parts) examines the rule in Foss v Harbottle *and its exceptions, linking to the enforceability of the articles of association and focusing on when a minority shareholder can take action.*

Online Resource Centre   www.oxfordtextbooks.co.uk/orc/qanda/

Go online for extra essay and problem questions, a glossary of key terms, online versions of all the answer plans and audio commentary on how selected ones were put together, and a range of podcasts which include advice on exam and coursework technique and advice for other assessment methods.

8

Corporate Liability: Contracts, Torts, and Crimes

ARE YOU READY?

- Principles of corporate liability
- Pre-incorporation contracts
- Contractual capacity, the ultra vires doctrine, ss. 31 and 39
- Authority: actual, usual, and apparent
- Restrictions on authority, the *Turquand* rule and s. 40
- Contracts with connected persons and s. 41
- Tortious and criminal liability
- Corporate manslaughter
- Connections (in particular) with: corporate personality, directors' duties, company management

 ## KEY DEBATES

Debate: how should liability for torts and crimes be attributed to companies?

This is a problem that has long exercised the finest corporate, tort, and criminal law minds. Currently the 'directing mind and will' test appears to live on, despite widespread criticism, and some optimism at a change of focus in *Meridian*. There is something for everyone in this topic with articles ranging from the highly theoretical to the intensely practical, all trying to cope with the application of established legal concepts to the corporate entity.

Debate: corporate manslaughter

Unsurprisingly given the huge public interest in this area, corporate manslaughter has been a particularly fruitful area for law reform and academic discussion. Views range from those advocating more specifically 'corporate' liability, to those insisting that liability should remain based on individual culpability, with many critical opinions of CMCHA 2007.

QUESTION | 1

How effective have the legislature's efforts been at removing the problems associated with pre-incorporation contracts?

CAUTION!

- The question is fairly straightforward and the topic fairly narrow, so you will need a good understanding of the wider and deeper issues to impress the examiner
- Avoid a chronological approach that sets out the pre-reform law and then the current law; instead use your structure effectively to highlight and address the problems

DIAGRAM ANSWER PLAN

Introduction: the problem of pre-incorporation contracts

Validity of a pre-incorporation contract

Who is bound? Considering agents, companies and novation

Avoidance of liability

Areas where statute does not apply

Conclusion: evaluate effectiveness of reform

[1]Use your introduction to define any important terms

Pre-incorporation contracts are contracts purportedly entered into by or on behalf of a company prior to its incorporation.[1] Since a company comes into existence only on incorporation (**Companies Act 2006 (CA 2006), s. 16**), it cannot be party to a contract entered into before that point. The primary concern for the law is to determine the status of and parties to that 'pre-incorporation contract', but there are other connected issues. To evaluate the effectiveness of the legislature's attempts to remove problems in this area[2] it is necessary to compare the position at common law with that under statute (now **CA 2006, s. 51**), looking in particular at the parties to the contract, liability, and ongoing problems in this area.

[2]Refer specifically to the question statement to show your focus, and then set out what you are going to do

At common law there was a degree of confusion surrounding the validity of a pre-incorporation contract. Because the company was non-existent at the time of the contract, there was no doubt that the company itself could not be bound by a pre-incorporation contract, nor could it adopt or ratify such a contract after incorporation (*Natal Land Co & Colonization Ltd v Pauline Colliery and Development Syndicate Ltd* **[1904] AC 120**). But would the contract be void, or treated as a valid contract with the person acting for the non-existent company? This apparently turned on the intentions of the parties, as revealed by the contract (*Phonogram Ltd v Lane* **[1982] QB 938**). In *Kelner v Baxter* **(1866) LR 2CP 174**, the court found the person contracting on behalf of the company personally liable on the agreement. However, *Newborne v Sensolid (GB) Ltd* **[1954] 1 QB 45** held that a contract signed in the name of the unincorporated company (and 'authenticated' by the signature of the 'director'), was purportedly made by the company itself and so was void. The potential injustice in such a distinction was clear, and reform came via the **First Company Law Directive 68/151/EEC (9 March 1968), Article 7**, which became part of UK law in the **European Communities Act 1972, s. 9(2)** (later incorporated into the **Companies Act 1985** and now **CA 2006, s. 51**).[3]

[3]Indicate the legislative history (not least as it gives the background to the arguments in *Phonogram v Lane*), but don't spend too much time reciting the details

Under **s. 51(1)** a person purporting to act on behalf of a company or as agent for it in entering into a contract (prior to incorporation) is personally liable on that contract. The section itself is slightly ambiguous as to whether it has the effect of creating a full contract between the 'agent' and the third party, or simply imposes liability on the 'agent'. In *Braymist Ltd v Wise Finance Co Ltd* **[2002] Ch 273**, the court confirmed that **s. 51** does create a contract between the parties that can be relied on by the 'agent' as well as his being liable. The section thus ensures a valid contract between the third party and the person acting for the unincorporated company, and deals with the discrepancy between *Kelner v Baxter* and *Newborne v Sensolid (GB) Ltd*—all such contracts will be valid, however the contract is signed.[4] The courts have ensured that the section is construed purposively, rejecting arguments designed to narrow its scope in *Phonogram Ltd v Lane* [1982] QB 938. In that case Lane argued, referring back to the original French text of the Directive, that a company must be in the process of being formed for the section to apply. Here, not only was the company not in the process of being formed, it was never actually formed. The court held that the section applied regardless. Neither did the court accept that there must have been some belief that the company was already in existence—the section still applied even where both parties were aware that the company had yet to be created.

Although a binding contract is created with the 'agent', it is clear that **s. 51** does not create what the parties to such a contract probably intend, which is a contract with the company.[5] It does not make the contract automatically binding on the company when (or if) it comes into existence, nor does it provide for a company to adopt or ratify a pre-incorporation contract. This is contrary to the recommendations of the **Report of the Jenkins Committee (Cmnd 1749, 1962)** which recommended a right for companies unilaterally to adopt pre-incorporation contracts. This approach has been taken in many Commonwealth countries and was included in the abortive Companies Bill 1973, but has not been adopted in the UK.

Accordingly, just as under the common law,[6] a company wishing to take up a pre-incorporation contract must go through the process of novation, entering into a new contract with the original contractor on the same terms. This requires the agreement of both parties (so may not be possible), and novation cannot simply be assumed from the fact that both parties acted as if they were bound: *Re Northumberland Avenue Hotel Co* (1886) 33 ChD 16. The **Contracts (Rights of Third Parties) Act 1999** could possibly come to the aid of the company, as it can apply to individuals not in existence at the time of contracting (**s. 1(3)**), but the Act is aimed at contracts where there is an intention to benefit the third party, rather than where the 'third party' is intended to be a party to the contract. Savirimuthu has raised the issue of whether the 'agent' could assign the contract to the company[7] ('Pre-incorporation contracts and the problem of corporate fundamentalism: are promoters proverbially profuse?' (2003) 24 Co Law 196) but this would clearly be less straightforward than ratification.

Although from the third party's perspective the situation is better than the common law, the fairness of binding the 'agent' without providing for the company to take on the contract following incorporation can be questioned. It could be a matter of chance which one of several founding members put their name to a contract, and yet **s. 51** makes that individual personally liable, when he might not be in a position to ensure subsequent novation. It might be argued in response

[8] Think PEA: make the point (exclusion of liability), evidence and explain it (s. 51 and *Phonogram*), and then assess it by considering whether it is of any use in practice

that the person acting for the company was free to exclude liability,[8] as **s. 51** applies 'subject to any agreement to the contrary'. This requires clear and express exclusion of liability, the way in which the contract is entered into (for example) is not sufficient: ***Phonogram Ltd v Lane***. Few individuals acting for a company pre-incorporation will have sufficient legal awareness to protect themselves in this way.

[9] This paragraph is important as it deals with several areas where s. 51 does not apply. This helps you to consider how far s. 51 can help with associated problems

Section 51 has further limitations.[9] Clearly it only applies to pre-incorporation contracts and not more generally to the problem of non-existent or misnamed companies. This limitation has led to some criticism (eg Griffiths, 'Agents without principals: pre-incorporation contracts and section 36C of the Companies Act 1985' (1993) 13 LS 241). The section has been held not to apply where a company trades under a new name before the change is operative: ***Oshkosh B'Gosh Inc v Dan Marbel Inc & Craze*** [1989] BCLC 507—once a company is in existence (even if not using its intended name) **s. 51** cannot operate, which is obviously an issue where companies are purchased 'off the shelf'. Similarly it does not apply where a company had been described by an incorrect name: ***Badgerhill Properties Ltd v Cottrell*** [1991] BCLC 805. It was also held not to apply where a person contracted in the name of a company that had been struck off the register and a new company of the same name was subsequently incorporated to continue the business as there had been no intention to create the new company at the time of the contract: ***Cotronic (UK) Ltd v Dezonie*** [1991] BCLC 721. Furthermore, the common law position still applies to companies registering outside the UK: ***Rover International Ltd v Cannon Films Ltd*** [1989] 1 WLR 912.

To conclude, it has been seen that **s. 51** deals with the primary problem of whether a pre-incorporation contract is binding, protecting the person dealing with the non-existent company, and so the legislature's efforts have been effective to that extent. But it is not a panacea for all problems concerning wrongly named or non-existent companies, and gaps remain where individuals deserve protection. Although creating a binding contract, the section does not provide parties with what they expect, nor does it provide a simple route for companies to adopt a pre-incorporation contract (as in many other countries), leaving companies reliant on the common law process of novation. As Milman has observed ('Company contracts: a review of the current and restated law' (2008) 240 Co LN 1) it is 'inexplicable' that the CA 2006 reforms did not provide a ratification facility to bring the UK in line with other developed systems of corporate law. Furthermore, although it is understandable that the primary concern of the legislature is the third

[10] Bring in your understanding of the origins of the provision and thus its focus

party (unsurprising as the origins of the section lie in the European provisions designed to protect persons dealing with companies[10]), it does not appear fair to leave an unsuspecting 'agent' facing significant personal liabilities. Given the remaining gaps and deficiencies, further legislative reform would be beneficial.

LOOKING FOR EXTRA MARKS?

- Use your further reading to develop your ideas and raise issues and problems
- Show an awareness of reform proposals and the origins of the provision, particularly where this supports or informs the points you are making
- Incorporate your basic knowledge concisely and within your discussion. This shows you are using your knowledge (rather than simply presenting it) and also leaves you maximum space for deeper analysis

QUESTION | 2

Extreem Ltd was incorporated in January by ten friends, to sell party decorations and related items. The 10 friends took equal shareholdings in the company. Three of the friends were appointed to be the officers of the company—Caspar as Managing Director, Feliz as Operations Director, and Rudy as company secretary.

Shortly after incorporation, Caspar ordered a large consignment of party balloons, streamers, and table decorations (for £15,000) from Soiree Ltd on behalf of the company. The following week Feliz ordered two small delivery vans (for £40,000) from a local dealer, Noelle, who is Feliz's mother. (Feliz had told the other directors of Noelle's relationship to him.) In the same week Rudy ordered 200 boxes of drinking glasses (for £6,000). Rudy assured the seller, Kriss, that as company secretary he had the authority to make the purchase, and with this assurance, Kriss went ahead with the contract.

The other shareholders are now getting nervous about the rate of spending in this new company and would like to get out of these contracts.

Advise the shareholders, considering how, if at all, your advice would differ if Extreem Ltd's articles of association contained a clause stating 'All contracts for a value in excess of £3,000 must be approved in advance by the general meeting'.

CAUTION!

- Separate the different contracts and deal with them one at a time, and one stage at a time, to avoid muddling issues
- Contracts questions almost inevitably involve some overlap with directors' duties so keep an eye out for these, while keeping your focus on the validity of the contracts
- There is a lot to cover in this question, so refer back to earlier discussion if the same point arises again rather than repeat yourself

DIAGRAM ANSWER PLAN

Identify the issues	■ Identify the issues: capacity; authority; directors

Relevant law	■ Corporate capacity and the ultra vires doctrine ■ Unrestricted objections: s. 31 ■ Restricted objects: operation of s. 39 ■ Types of authority: actual, usual, apparent ■ Restrictions on authority: *Turquand's rule* ■ Restrictions on authority: s. 40 ■ Connected persons and s. 41 ■ Directors exceeding authority: s. 171(a) and substantial property transactions

Apply the law	■ Apply the relevant law to the facts

Conclude	■ Conclude on each contract

SUGGESTED ANSWER

This question concerns the validity of several contracts—with Soiree, Noelle, and Kriss—entered into on Extreem Ltd's behalf. It raises various issues concerned with corporate capacity and directors' authority, and connected breaches of directors' duties.[1]

[1] Just set out the main areas in your introduction; otherwise you'll cover too much material before you get the chance to apply it to the facts

Soiree Contract

Historically, capacity was a major issue in contractual validity as the ultra vires doctrine made void any contract outside a company's capacity (as determined by the company's objects): ***Ashbury Railway Carriage & Iron Co v Riche* (1875) LR 7 HL 653)**. But under **Companies Act (CA 2006), s. 31**, provided Extreem Ltd's articles do not specifically restrict its objects, its capacity will be unlimited. This is the most likely position.[2] If Extreem Ltd did have restricted objects, the contract appears to be within the scope of a 'party decoration' business in any event. Even if it wasn't, Soiree would be protected by **CA 2006, s. 39** which prevents anyone questioning challenging a contract on the ground of lack of capacity arising from anything in its constitution. Clearly capacity is not a problem for this contract.

[2] As you are not told whether the company has restricted objects or not, you can say what position is most likely, but you need to cover other possibilities as well, albeit concisely

The validity of the contract depends also on the authority of the person acting for the company. There is no evidence that Caspar has actual authority to enter into this contract (and he could not have actual authority if the restriction were in place) but usual authority or apparent authority are also sufficient to bind the company. Usual authority is the authority that is usual for someone in the position of that individual to have. This has been analysed either as a form of implied actual authority (eg Hannigan, *Company Law*, 4th edn, Oxford, 2015), or a form of apparent authority (eg *Mayson, French & Ryan on Company Law*, 32nd edn, Oxford, 2015), but the difference doesn't matter here.[3] A managing director's usual authority is extensive (eg **Hely-Hutchinson v Brayhead Ltd [1967] 3 All ER 98**) and so this contract appears to be within the scope of Caspar's usual authority. Extreem Ltd will be bound by the contract.

[3] A quick nod to the examiner that you have looked into this point

If the restriction was there,[4] the contract should have been approved by the general meeting. But even if approval were not obtained, the contract will be binding on the company. In balancing the interests of the shareholders (seeing the restriction upheld) and the third party (ensuring the contract is binding), both courts and statute have leant firmly in favour of the third party.

[4] Make clear when you are discussing the alternative scenario—you could even use a further sub-heading if you wanted

At common law the *Turquand* rule (*Royal British Bank v Turquand* **(1856) 6 El & Bl 327**) permits the third party to assume all matters of internal management and procedure have been complied with (provided there was no knowledge or suspicion of the irregularity). So provided Soiree was unaware of the irregularity it would be protected. **CA 2006, s. 40** goes even further. Where a person deals with a company in good faith, the power of the directors to bind the company or authorise others to do so, is deemed free of any limitation under the company's constitution: **s. 40(1)**. Soiree is dealing with the company as a party to the transaction (**s. 40(2)(a)**), and under **s. 40(2)(b)** is presumed to be acting in good faith, is not bound to enquire as to any limitations on the powers of directors, and will not be regarded as in bad faith even if it knew the act was outside the limitation. Soiree will therefore be protected by **s. 40**, and the contract will be binding notwithstanding the restriction in the articles. The shareholders have the right to bring proceedings to restrain acts outside the powers of directors (**s. 40(4)**), but this will not help them as the act is completed.[5]

[5] Shows that you know the point of law, and also recognise why it won't help here

By acting without approval Caspar would breach **CA 2006, s. 171(a)**. This requires him to act in accordance with the company's constitution and is not affected by validation of the contract under **s. 40 (s. 40(5))**. The company could therefore claim against Caspar if his breach caused loss. The shareholders could not make the directors bring proceedings as they would need a special resolution to direct the directors (Article 4, Model Articles for Private Companies: **Companies (Model Articles) Regulations 2008, Sch 1**) and they only have 70 per cent of the shares. Neither would they be likely to get permission for a derivative claim as they are majority shareholders. However they could dismiss the directors by ordinary resolution under **CA 2006, s. 168** and appoint new directors. Whether this is advisable would depend on how concerned the shareholders are about the direction of the company, and would not change the fact that the Soiree contract is binding on Extreem Ltd.[6]

[6] This paragraph covers a lot of ground—duties, management, and remedies—but crucially links it all back to the validity of the contract

Noelle Contract

There is no problem with the company's capacity, for the reasons given in relation to Soiree.[7] But there are problems with Feliz's authority, and from his relationship to Noelle.

[7] If the same points arise, it is fine to refer back to previous discussion. But do remember to check that there aren't any different facts to take into account

Feliz seems to have usual authority to enter into this contract. Although the usual authority of an individual director is fairly limited, it expands within the ambit of an executive role. The purchase of vans would arguably come within the remit of an Operations Director, which would put it within the scope of Feliz's usual authority and therefore, prima facie, binding on Extreem Ltd. However, this could be a substantial property transaction[8] within **CA 2006, ss. 190–6**. Noelle is a connected person as Feliz's mother (**CA 2006, ss. 252(2) (a) and 253(2)(e)**) and the transaction is over £5,000, and probably over 10 per cent of the company's asset value. If so, it needed prior approval of the shareholders (**s. 190**), and without this the contract is voidable unless certain exceptions apply (**s. 195(2)**). Feliz's disclosure of Noelle's involvement to the other directors, would prevent a possible breach of **CA 2006, s. 177** but not **s. 190**.

[8] Remember that breach of some obligations can impact on the validity of a transaction

If the restriction in the articles were in place,[9] the contract would be voidable regardless of whether the contract is a substantial property transaction. Although **s. 40** would appear to apply, where a contract's validity depends on **s. 40** but the contract is between the company and a director or connected person, the contract is voidable at the instance of the company (**s. 41(2)**) unless affirmed by the company or another exception in **s. 41(3)** applies. The shareholders should therefore be advised that in these circumstances the company could avoid this contract. Feliz would also be in breach of **s. 171(a)** for acting outside the company's constitution, as for Caspar.

[9] Don't forget to cover the alternative scenario

Kriss Contract

Although the purchase of glasses may be outside the business of party decorations, capacity is not a problem, because of **CA 2006, s. 31** (and **s. 39** if necessary), as discussed for Soiree. Here the primary problem is one of Rudy's authority. Rudy does not appear to have actual authority, and as company secretary his usual authority is quite limited. *Panorama Developments (Guildford) Ltd v Fidelis Furnishing Fabrics Ltd* **[1971] 2 QB 711** accepted a company secretary was not a 'mere clerk' and had authority to deal with the administrative side of the company's affairs but as the contract with

Kriss does not fall within 'administrative' matters, it would not be within the scope of Rudy's usual authority. However the company will still be bound if Rudy was acting within his apparent (or ostensible) authority.

Apparent authority is authority as it appears to others, and requires a representation that the agent had authority, made by someone with actual authority to manage the business, and inducing the third party to enter into the contract (***Freeman & Lockyer v Buckhurst Park Properties (Mangal) Ltd*** [1964] 2 QB 480). As a form of estoppel, apparent authority cannot be relied on if the other party knows (or should have known) of the individual's lack of actual authority, although **s. 40** offers a great deal of protection in this regard. The problem for Kriss is that the representation was by Rudy himself, so apparent authority does not arise and the contract does not bind the company. If there was apparent authority, **s. 40** would allow Kriss to rely on this notwithstanding any restriction in the articles (even if he knew of it) but it cannot operate so as to 'create' authority in these circumstances. Similarly the rule in ***Turquand's Case*** cannot create authority here, as Rudy's lack of authority is not due to some internal irregularity. Accordingly the company is not bound by this contract (although could ratify it if it chose), and Rudy may face a claim by Kriss for breach of warranty of authority.

[10] The conclusion gives you the last chance to check that you have advised explicitly on the validity of each of the contracts

Conclusion[10]

The shareholders should be aware that the Soiree contract is binding on Extreem Ltd, even if the restriction is in place. For the Noelle contract, if the restriction is in place, the contract will be voidable: **s. 41**, and may be voidable even without the restriction if this contract is a substantial property transaction (**ss. 190–6**). Both Caspar and Feliz will have breached their duty to the company under **CA 2006, s. 171(a)**. As Rudy does not have authority at all, the contract with Kriss is not binding on the company, although the shareholders can ratify it if they choose to do so.

LOOKING FOR EXTRA MARKS?

- Recognising links between topics shows your deeper understanding of the subject: here you can bring in relevant points from directors' duties (and even shareholder remedies and company management) at appropriate points, while keeping the focus on the validity of the contracts

- Show you understand how the different statutory provisions operate and connect

- Delve more deeply into the complexities surrounding establishing authority, for example in relation to who can make representations for the company

'**The Companies Act 2006** has finally removed all issues of capacity and authority for anyone entering into a contract with a company.'

Discuss.

CAUTION!

- Remember to consider both capacity and authority issues
- The statement refers to 'all issues' so you need to think about things where the Act has no effect, as well as the more obvious things that the Act addresses explicitly
- With a question like this it is very easy to slip into an overly descriptive approach, so make sure you comment and relate your discussion back to the question regularly

DIAGRAM ANSWER PLAN

Introduction: issues in corporate contracts

⬇

Capacity and ultra vires

⬇

Dealing with ultra vires: s. 31 and s. 39

⬇

Authority: types of authority and restrictions

⬇

Dealing with authority problems: s. 40 and *Turquand's* rule

⬇

Limitations: charitable companies and connected persons

⬇

Conclusion: review the question

A company as a separate legal person can enter contracts in its own right, but does so through the agency of its representatives, particularly the directors. Corporate contracts can cause problems for the law because limitations can be imposed on the company or its agents' ability to enter into contracts, of which the third party may not be aware. Although historically the law appeared keener to protect a company's shareholders by upholding internal limitations, the need to protect third parties dealing with a company has now long been in the ascendant. It will be seen that **Companies Act 2006 (CA 2006)** has gone a very long way in dealing with issues arising in both capacity and authority for someone dealing with a company, but it has not removed absolutely all issues.[1]

Capacity Issues

CA 2006 has almost entirely removed issues of capacity within corporate contracting, with more success than previous reform efforts, although not quite laying 'to rest the corpse of the ultra vires doctrine'[2] (Milman, 'Company contracts: a review of the current and restated law' (2008) 240 Co LN 1). The ultra vires doctrine held that contracts outside a company's objects were void: *Ashbury Railway Carriage & Iron Co v Riche* **(1875) LR 7 HL 653**. Although designed to uphold the constitution (and thus protect shareholders), the doctrine could cause hardship to the company itself as well as to the third party. The effect of the doctrine was mitigated by company draftsmen creating long (and thus essentially meaningless) objects clauses and including 'independent objects' clauses (*Cotman v Brougham* **[1918] AC 514**) and subjective objects clauses (*Bell Houses Ltd v City Wall Properties Ltd* **[1966] 1 QB 207**). Even so, contracts could occasionally fall foul of the doctrine (eg *Re Introductions Ltd* **[1970] Ch 199**). In *Rolled Steel Products (Holdings) Ltd v British Steel Corpn* **[1986] Ch 246**, the courts took a more pragmatic approach to such issues than in *Re Introductions Ltd*, but this could not entirely remove capacity as a potential threat to a corporate contract.[3]

Statutory attempts at reform prior to **CA 2006** (in particular **Companies Act 1989** which amended **Companies Act 1985 (CA 1985)**), went some way towards removing issues related to capacity, but the provisions were not entirely clear, nor were they fully effective. For example[4] **CA 1985, s. 3A**, designed to do away with long objects clauses, simply had the effect of adding an extra clause to already long objects clauses (as predicted by Ferran, 'The reform of the law on corporate capacity and directors' and officers' authority Part 2' (1992) 13 Co Law 177).

[1] Linking to the question and indicating your line of argument helps both to reassure and interest the examiner

[2] Making use of a memorable phrase can add a spark to your work, as well as gaining credit for using your wider reading

[3] This paragraph packs in a lot of information as a compromise between getting straight to CA 2006 (which would be focused but miss the context) and telling the examiner everything about ultra vires (which would show lots of knowledge but not be sufficiently focused)

[4] Rather than spend a lot of time detailing the problems with the earlier provisions, an example suffices

The position is significantly clearer after **CA 2006**, which takes a different approach. Following a recommendation of the Company Law Review (Final Report), companies now have unrestricted capacity unless they specifically restrict their objects (**CA 2006, s. 31**). So most new companies (and existing companies which alter their articles) will have no restriction on their capacity. Where a company does have objects and acts outside them, the contract is saved by **CA 2006, s. 39** (a modified version of **CA 1985, s. 35**), which prevents any person calling the validity of the company's act into question on the ground of lack of capacity by reason of anything in the company's constitution. Accordingly all issues in this area have been removed as far as third parties are concerned (a couple of exceptions will be considered later).[5] Internally a director acting outside restricted objects will remain liable to the company for breach of **CA 2006, s. 171(a)** but this does not affect the contract.

[5] You could instead deal with the exceptions at this point, and then again (referring back) when looking at authority

Authority Issues

A crucial issue for the validity of corporate contracts is the authority of the person acting for the company. The board of directors is given all the powers of the company (Article 3, Model Articles for Private Companies: Companies (Model Articles) Regulations 2008, Sch 1), but companies often act through individual directors (or other agents), rather than through the board. A contract only binds a principal if the agent is acting within the scope of his authority, so whether an individual has authority is very important.

As observed in *First Energy (UK) Ltd v Hungarian International Bank Ltd* **[1993] BCLC 1409**, the court has to strike a balance between two conflicting commercial considerations: (i) a contracting party cannot be expected to know all internal procedures to be sure they are dealing with a fully authorised agent, and (ii) a contracting party cannot simply rely on any person purporting to represent the company. It is the first consideration that statute has been most concerned with.

[6] Recognises that statute is not concerned with all issues of authority

At the basic level of determining authority, statute has had little impact,[6] and normal agency rules governing actual, usual, and apparent authority (as applied in company law cases such as *Freeman & Lockyer v Buckhurst Park Properties (Mangal) Ltd* [1964] 2 QB 480) remain relevant. Accordingly not everyone who purports to be acting for a company will be found to have authority, although in many cases apparent authority will be found either through a direct or indirect representation of authority. Where the nature of the transaction is itself suspicious though, a court is unlikely to find apparent authority (*Re Capitol Films Ltd* **[2010] EWHC 2240 (Ch)**). Statute comes into play to protect a third party where authority appears to be present, but in fact was restricted by some constitutional limitation. This is dealt with by **CA 2006, s. 40**.

Section 40 is a modified version of **CA 1985, s. 35A**, clarifying some aspects of the former provision. This provides that in favour of a person dealing with a company in good faith, the powers of the directors to bind the company or authorise others to do so are deemed free of any constitutional limitation.[7] Dealing with a company is widely defined (**s. 40(2)(a)**), although it won't include 'inside' transactions such as a bonus issue of shares: *EIC Services Ltd v Phipps* [2004] **2 BCLC 589**. 'Good faith' is also generously defined: good faith is presumed, it is not lost simply through knowledge of the limitation, and the third party is under no obligation to make enquiries of any limitations (**s. 40(2)(b)**).

Before statutory reform, those dealing with a company could rely on the rule in *Turquand's case (Royal British Bank v Turquand* **(1856) 6 El & Bl 327)**, but this is limited to matters of internal procedure, and cannot be relied on where an individual has notice of an irregularity (*B. Liggett (Liverpool) Ltd v Barclays Bank Ltd* [1928] **1 KB 48**). **Section 40** is obviously wider as knowledge of an irregularity does not prevent a person being in good faith. Furthermore, the minor redrafting in **CA 2006** is generally thought to have dealt with the few remaining interpretational concerns about **CA 1985, s. 35A** (relating to restrictions on individuals, and inquorate boards).[8] Accordingly while **CA 2006** hasn't dealt with all authority issues, those dealing with the company in good faith (which will be most people) will be protected from constitutional limitations on that authority. Shareholders could seek to restrain an act outside directors' powers (**s. 40(4)**) but this right is rarely, if ever, exercised as shareholders are usually unaware of the issue until after the company is bound. Directors remain liable for breach of duty for exceeding their powers under **s. 171(a)** (**s. 40(5)**).

Limitations on Operation of ss. 39–40

Sections 41–42 cover some specific exceptions to **ss. 39–40**. **Section 42** limits the operation of **ss. 39–40** for charitable companies so they apply only in favour of a person who does not know they are dealing with a charity, or who gives full consideration and doesn't know the act is outside the objects or directors' powers.

Section 41 restricts the protection of **s. 40** when the party to the contract is a director or connected person under **ss. 252–6**. In such cases the contract is voidable (**s. 41(2)**) unless restitution is no longer possible, the company has been indemnified for any losses, rights acquired by a non-party would be affected, or the company affirms the transaction (**s. 41(4)**). The loss of protection under **ss. 39–40** is justified because directors and connected persons will, or should, be aware of any internal restrictions.[9]

[7] There isn't much choice here but to pretty much repeat the words of the section

[8] You could expand on this if you have time and have covered it on your course

[9] This provides a bit of comment to an otherwise rather descriptive part of the essay

Conclusion

For a person entering into a contract with a company (other than charitable companies), **CA 2006** has finally (after decades of reform attempts) removed all issues of capacity. While the director will have breached his duty to the company, this need not concern the other party. **CA 2006** has not quite removed all issues of authority for anyone entering into a contract with a company, but the combination of agency principles and **s. 40** work together to protect most contracting parties. Those who are not protected will be those who should not have assumed the authority of the person acting, and/or who are acting in bad faith, and/or or are a director or connected person. It can be argued that in these cases the company is more deserving of protection than they are.

LOOKING FOR EXTRA MARKS

- Explore the overlap between the *Turquand* rule and apparent authority and the changing focus of the courts in this area
- Consider how far the current position reflects the EU First Company Law Directive from which reform in this area originated, and the problems the legislature has faced in transposing the Directive into the law

QUESTION | 4

'The attribution of liability for torts or crimes to a company has caused great difficulties for the courts and Parliament but the position is gradually becoming a little clearer.'

Discuss.

CAUTION!

- Read the question carefully to pick up on all the points—both torts and crimes, both the courts and Parliament
- Be prepared to comment on the legal position and approaches as well as describing and explaining them
- You need to assess whether, and how, the legal position is getting clearer in order to address the question fully

DIAGRAM ANSWER PLAN

Inroduction: corporate liability for torts and crimes

Attribution through identification

Meridian and its impact

Corporate manslaughter

Conclusion: summary and comment

A SUGGESTED ANSWER

As a legal person a company can be liable for torts and crimes in its own right. However, because a company is not a natural person it must act through others—its directors and agents. It is the acts of these individuals that must be examined to determine what a company did, knew, etc and so attribute liability to a company.

[1] The introduction follows the classic approach of briefly setting the scene for the topic, and then explaining what will be considered

In addressing the statement, this essay will[1] examine how liability attaches to a company, considering the difficult issue of whose acts and states of mind can be attributed to the company and in what circumstances. This will involve consideration of different approaches, particularly the identification doctrine, the *Meridian* principles (*Meridian Global Funds Management Asia Ltd v Securities Commission* **[1995] 2 AC 500**), and statutory developments particularly in the **Corporate Manslaughter and Corporate Homicide Act 2007 (CMCHA 2007)**.

Liability in Tort and Crime

Campbell v Paddington Corporation **[1911] 1 KB 869** established that a company could be liable for its own wrongs, rejecting the argument that tortious acts would be ultra vires the company. Companies could even be liable for crimes requiring mens rea: *R v ICR Haulage Ltd* **[1944] KB 551**; *DPP v Kent & Sussex Contractors Co Ltd* **[1944] KB 146**. Accordingly, a company can in principle be liable for

[2] This makes the point implicitly that a company cannot be treated in all respects as the same as a natural person

any tort or crime, other than where a company cannot commit an element of the wrong (eg bigamy), or cannot be subject to the penalty (murder).[2]

A company can be made liable primarily (ie liable for its own wrong-doing) or vicariously (liable 'as if' it were a wrongdoer). Vicarious liability is relatively straightforward and causes few problems unique to companies[3]—a company (as employer or principal) is liable for the wrongdoing of its employee/agent. It is common in tort liability, and in regulatory offences, eg *Re Supply of Ready Mixed Concrete (No. 2)* [1995] 1 BCLC 613. This does not however create truly corporate liability, and is usually viewed as inappropriate for criminal liability, where some level of blame, or moral culpability, is expected. Primary liability is liability of the company itself, and is not dependent on liability of an individual. Nonetheless corporate primary liability rests on the actions and state of mind of individuals, and attributing these to the company causes some problems for the courts. Further problems arise in deciding whether an individual can be liable as well as the company, and whether the company's claim against a wrongdoer should be barred by the *ex turpi causa non oritur actio* principle, but these issues are outside the scope of this essay.[4]

[3] For a company law course you wouldn't normally be expected to go into detail on vicarious liability; a very brief explanation is sufficient

[4] You can use this technique to let the examiner know that you are aware of other related issues, even though the question doesn't explicitly direct you into them

Identification

The identification doctrine or 'alter ego' approach attributes liability through the company's 'directing mind and will': *Lennard's Carrying Co Ltd v Asiatic Petroleum Co Ltd* [1915] AC 705. The court finds someone, sufficiently high up the corporate hierarchy, who can be identified with the company, in whom the various elements of the wrong can be found. In *R v Andrews-Weatherfall Ltd* [1972] 1 WLR 118 Eveleigh J said that the person (or persons) must have 'the status and authority' which makes their acts the acts of the company. In *HL Bolton (Engineering) Ltd v TJ Graham & Sons Ltd* [1957] 1 QB 159, Lord Denning likened a company to a 'human body', with a controlling 'brain and nerve centre', and 'hands which hold the tools' and follow instructions—only the former (the directors and managers) could be viewed as the 'directing mind and will' of a company. This 'anthropomorphic' attitude was explicitly criticised in *Meridian* as well as by many writers[5] (eg Ferran, 'Corporate attribution and the directing mind and will' (2011) 127 LQR 239).

[5] You need to be aware of Denning's memorable analogy in *HL Bolton*, but it is only right to recognise that it has not been met with universal enthusiasm

Although the identification approach can found corporate liability, it has limitations. One obvious problem lies in identifying the person who is the directing mind and will of a company. Who this is may depend on the wrong in question (*R v ICR Haulage Ltd; HL Bolton (Engineering) Ltd v TJ Graham & Sons Ltd*, although this was doubted in *Tesco Supermarkets Ltd v Nattrass* [1971] 2 All ER 127). Unless a 'directing mind and will' can be identified, a company will avoid liability under this doctrine. In *Tesco Supermarkets Ltd v Nattrass*, a branch manager was held not to be identified with the company and so was 'another person', which allowed the company to avoid liability for misleading pricing.

A connected problem is what to do when the individual elements of the wrong are made out, but are not located within a single individual. This caused particular problems in the area of manslaughter. The courts accepted that a company could in principle be liable for manslaughter (*R v HM Coroners for East Kent, ex p Spooner* (1987) **3 BCC 636**) but this depended on identifying the company with an individual guilty of the crime. The courts rejected the option of aggregating the acts and states of mind of various individuals to found liability. Consequently no corporate liability resulted from the P&O Ferries disaster in Zeebrugge (*R v P&O Ferries (Dover) Ltd* (1991) **93 Cr App Rep 72**) despite the company being 'infected with the disease of sloppiness'[6] from top to bottom (Department of Transport, *MV Herald of Free Enterprise: Report No. 8074* (1987)).

[6] A particularly telling finding that highlights the corporate (and not just individual) failings

Under the identification doctrine, liability becomes harder to establish the larger and more complex a company becomes. Just as in *R v P&O Ferries (Dover) Ltd*, liability could not be established in the Southall rail crash (*A-G's Reference (No. 2 of 1999)* [2000] QB 796). In contrast, corporate liability was established in relation to the Lyme Bay canoeing accident in *R v Kite and OLL Ltd* Independent, **Dec 9, 1994**, where the company was small.

The Meridian Approach

In *Meridian*, the Privy Council appeared to signal a move away from the identification doctrine. Lord Hoffmann identified three types of attribution rules:[7] (i) primary rules of attribution (generally found in the company's constitution), (ii) general rules of attribution that are also applicable outside companies (such as agency and vicarious liability), and (iii) special rules of attribution, which are (exceptionally) fashioned by the courts to deal with laws that exclude attribution through the primary or general rules of attribution. The starting point should be an examination of the purpose or policy of the rule in question, using this to determine whose acts or state of mind should be relevant. The judge explained the approach in *Lennard's Carrying Co Ltd v Asiatic Petroleum Co Ltd* as based on the language and purpose of the provision in question, indicating the 'directing mind and will' test should be viewed as a special rule of attribution based on the particular rule, rather than an all-encompassing approach to liability.

[7] You should be able to explain the three types of attribution rules from *Meridian*

At first sight *Meridian* seemed to make significant inroads into the identification doctrine, and knowledge lower down the corporate hierarchy has been held sufficient for particular charges: *Morris v Bank of India* [2005] EWCA Civ 693, *Meridian*. Nonetheless, the 'directing mind and will' rule still applies in most cases, at least for criminal offences involving mens rea as seen in *A-G's Reference (No. 2 of 1999)* [2000] QB 796, and *R v St Regis Paper Company Ltd*

[2012] 1 Cr App R 14 where the Court of Appeal applied the principle and rejected any alternative special rule of attribution.

Attribution and Corporate Manslaughter

[8] There is a lot of academic writing surrounding CMCHA 2007. Try to bring a little of this in, even in a general essay like this one where you have to be brief. If the question was just on corporate manslaughter you should engage more deeply with a selection of materials

Parliament took a different approach to attribution in **CMCHA 2007**,[8] following public disquiet over the failure to secure manslaughter convictions against large companies. **CMCHA 2007** moves away from identification. Instead it looks at the way in which the company's activities are managed or organised (**s. 1(1)**), allowing the courts to consider the activities and faults of multiple individuals and the corporate culture. The involvement of 'senior management' must still be a substantial element (**s. 1(3)**) which has led to criticism for retaining a significant focus on people rather than on truly 'corporate' liability (eg Price, 'Finding fault in organisations—reconceptualising the role of senior managers in corporate manslaughter' (2015) 35 LS 385). **CMCHA 2007** was used in *R v Cotswold Geotechnical Holdings Ltd* **[2011] EWCA Crim 1337**, finding the company guilty where there was a gross breach of duty through a demonstrably unsafe system of work, but liability would probably have resulted here under the 'directing mind and will' test in any event.

Conclusion

It is apparent that the attribution of criminal and tortious liability to a company causes difficulties for the law, because of the complex interaction of human actors and the company as a separate entity. The courts tend to require an embodiment of the company, and although *Meridian* offers some flexibility, the directing mind and will test still dominates. While Parliament has finally created a uniquely corporate form of liability in **CMCHA 2007**, this is limited to corporate manslaughter, and its impact is questionable. Parliament has also sought to prevent problems in new offences, by legislating specifically to deal

[9] Links back to the words of the question

with corporate liability, such as under the **Bribery Act 2010**. While the courts and Parliament have gradually made some areas of the law clearer,[9] much remains to be done.

LOOKING FOR EXTRA MARKS?

- Show your appreciation of the complications the corporate form can bring to the application of more general principles of tort and crime

- There is a lot of academic work in this area that you can engage with further to add depth and strengthen your analysis

- You could raise connected issues such as individual liability and operation of the *ex turpi causa non oritur actio* principle (see now *Jetivia SA v Bilta (UK) Ltd* [2015] UKSC 23) in this question (if covered by your course) to show your grasp of the bigger picture

TAKING THINGS FURTHER

■ Ferran, E., 'The reform of the law on corporate capacity and directors' and officers' authority: Parts 1 and 2' (1992) 13 Co Law 124 and 177

Critique of the 'technically defective' statutory reform brought in by Companies Act 1989 (in particular CA 1985, ss. 35–35A) aimed at problems of capacity and authority. Useful to compare with the approach of CA 2006 and to understand some of the reasons behind further reform.

■ Ferran, E., 'Corporate attribution and the directing mind and will' (2011) 127 LQR 239

Revisits Meridian, *questioning its long-term impact on attribution in UK law. Also helpful in highlighting the views of other leading writers. (Note: the discussion of* Stone & Rolls Ltd v Moore Stephens *[2009] UKHL 39 should be read in the light of the recent critical view of the case in* Jetivia SA v Bilta (UK) Ltd *[2015] UKSC 23.)*

■ Field, S. and Jones, L., 'Death in the workplace: who pays the price?' (2011) 32 Co Law 166

Provides a summary of the pre- and post-CMCHA 2007 position and looks at sentencing for corporate manslaughter and health and safety offences causing death. See also Field, S. and Jones, L., 'The Corporate Manslaughter and Corporate Homicide Act 2007 and the sentencing guidelines for corporate manslaughter: more bark than bite?'(2015) 36 Co Law 327 for further consideration that challenges a 'somewhat timid prosecutorial policy' and penalties which 'lack bite'.

■ Gobert, J., 'The Corporate Manslaughter and Corporate Homicide Act 2007—thirteen years in the making but was it worth the wait?' (2008) 71 MLR 413

An in-depth critical view of CMCHA 2007. Describes the Act as 'limited in its vision and lacking in imagination', not least for its failure to deal with corporate criminality more generally.

■ Griffiths, A., 'Agents without principals: pre-incorporation contracts and section 36C of the Companies Act 1985' (1993) 13 LS 241

A very useful consideration of pre-incorporation contracts, explaining the background and issues and identifying ongoing problems. Appeals for a more purposive interpretation to deal with the more general problem of non-existent companies, and for inclusion of a ratification procedure. See also Green, N., 'Security of Transaction after Phonogram'(1984) 47 MLR 671 for an earlier consideration of the problems.

■ Hsiao, M. W. H., 'Abandonment of the doctrine of attribution in favour of gross negligence test in the Corporate Manslaughter and Corporate Homicide Act 2007' (2009) 30 Co Law 110

Focuses on the basis of attributing liability on companies, revisiting the 'directing mind and will' test and its limitations, to contrast with the approach of CMCHA 2007.

■ Law Commission, 'Legislating the Criminal Code: Involuntary Manslaughter' (1996) Law Com No. 237. See also Law Commission, 'Criminal liability in regulatory contexts' (2010) Consultation Paper No. 195

■ Milman, D., 'Company contracts: a review of the current and restated law' (2008) 240 Co LN 1

A brief review of the law on corporate contracts and pre-incorporation contracts at the time CA 2006 came into force, summarising the issues and highlighting the problems.

- Omerod, D. and Taylor, R., 'The Corporate Manslaughter and Corporate Homicide Act 2007' (2008) 8 Crim LR 589

  A helpful critique of CMCHA 2007, explaining its origins and approach. While welcoming the Act, raises the question of whether it might prove in practice to be 'little more than a symbolic statement about corporate responsibility'.

- Price, L., 'Finding fault in organisations—reconceptualising the role of senior managers in corporate manslaughter' (2015) 35 Legal Studies 385

  An interesting exploration of whether corporate manslaughter is a truly corporate or organisational crime, assessing in particular the emphasis on involvement of senior management in the offence under CMCHA 2007. Advocates an approach based on senior managers' role in corporate systems of work.

- Savirimuthu, J., 'Pre-incorporation contracts and the problem of corporate fundamentalism: are promoters proverbially profuse?' (2003) 24 Co Law 196

  This article re-evaluates the earlier cases on pre-incorporation contracts and questions their assumptions, and analyses CA 1985, s. 36C (now CA 2006, s. 51)

- Sullivan, G. R., 'The attribution of culpability to limited companies' [1996] CLJ 515

  A classic article examining in depth the principles of corporate criminal liability. Considers Meridian, and the Law Commission proposals for a 'corporate killing' offence (pre-dating CMCHA 2007) arguing that corporate liability cannot be dissociated from the culpability of individuals.

- Talbot, L. E., 'A contextual analysis of the demise of the doctrine of ultra vires in English company law and the rhetoric and reality of enlightened shareholders' (2009) 30 Co Law 323

  Reviews the ultra vires doctrine in the context of protecting shareholders at a time when their role was increasingly inactive. Argues the CA 2006 reform 'expresses the passivity of company members' despite a reform agenda promoting active, involved shareholders.

- Wickins, R. and Ong, C. A., 'Confusion worse confounded: the end of the directing mind theory?' [1997] JBL 524

  Accuses Meridian and other cases of reducing the 'elegant structure' of the directing mind and will test to 'a heap of intellectual rubble'. Particularly useful for a detailed examination of the development and application of the directing mind and will test.

 Online Resource Centre   www.oxfordtextbooks.co.uk/orc/qanda/

Go online for extra essay and problem questions, a glossary of key terms, online versions of all the answer plans and audio commentary on how selected ones were put together, and a range of podcasts which include advice on exam and coursework technique and advice for other assessment methods.

Share Capital **9**

ARE YOU READY?

- Share capital
- Capital maintenance: principle and purpose
- Issue of shares at a discount
- Issue of shares at a premium
- Reduction of capital
- Purchase of company's own shares
- Redemption of shares
- Distributions/dividends
- Financial assistance
- Connections (in particular) with: shares and shareholders; directors' duties; loan capital

 ## KEY DEBATES

Debate: the continuing relevance of the capital maintenance doctrine

Although the capital maintenance doctrine is well established, it has many critics, both of the doctrine itself, and of the way in which the current law upholds the doctrine. The legislative framework is complex and, for many, overly restrictive, but to a great extent driven by European requirements in relation to public companies. For a deeper consideration of the law in this area than offered by most textbooks, see Ferran, E. and Ho, L. C., *Company Law and Corporate Finance* (2nd edn, Oxford, 2014).

'The complex and harsh regulation of the issue of shares in a public company for non-cash consideration is hard to justify, particularly when compared with the position for private companies.'

Discuss.

CAUTION!

- You need to be familiar with the relevant sections of CA 2006 before you start. If you are allowed a statute book in your exam you can use it to check aspects of the law, but you will struggle to find what you need if you haven't got a good understanding to begin with

- Don't limit your consideration to the law on valuation of non-cash consideration, there are other relevant sections to reflect on as well

- Remember to compare the position of public companies with that of private companies

DIAGRAM ANSWER PLAN

Introduction: issue of shares and capital maintenance

Contrasting public and private company regulation

Valuation of non-cash consideration

Other provisions relating to non-cash consideration

Justification for regulation

Conclusion: evaluate statement

Ensuring companies receive full value for the shares they issue (so receiving the capital they claim to have raised) is part of the capital maintenance doctrine[1] (*Trevor v Whitworth* (1887) 12 App Cas 409). Perhaps surprisingly, at common law there was little regulation of the issue of shares for non-cash consideration, and this remains the position for private companies.

[1] Recognise the connection with the capital maintenance principle, but don't spend too much time on this general point

For public companies the regulatory position changed significantly with the implementation in the **Companies Act 1980** of the **Second Company Law Directive 77/91/EEC (13 December 1976)**, with the law now in the **Companies Act 2006 (CA 2006), ss. 580–609**. This imposes many restrictions on public companies in relation to the issue of shares and the consideration received. This essay will examine the current regulation of the issue of shares for non-cash consideration (comparing the position for public and private companies) to consider whether it is complex, harsh, and difficult to justify.[2]

[2] Reassure the examiner that you are focusing on the particular issues raised in the question—it helps to focus your mind too

The Position for Private Companies

A private company may receive money or money's worth (ie non-cash consideration) for its shares, including any premium: **CA 2006, s. 582**. This reflects the common law. Although past consideration for shares is not adequate (*Re Eddystone Marine Insurance Co* [1893] 3 Ch 9), non-cash consideration was accepted in *Re Wragg Ltd* [1897] 1 Ch 796. There the court held that companies could allot shares in return for property and services and, importantly, in the absence of fraud, the value received by the company could not be inquired into. This can be seen in *Salomon v A. Salomon & Co Ltd* [1897] AC 22,[3] where Lord Macnaghten observed the valuation of £39,000 placed on the business (consideration for Salomon's shares) 'represented the sanguine expectations of a fond owner' rather than a realistic valuation, but this had no legal consequence.

[3] This shows that you recall more than just the main legal principle from *Salomon*, and supports the more general point you are making

The problem with this very relaxed approach to valuation of non-cash consideration is that it provides scope to avoid the rule prohibiting issue of shares at a discount to their nominal value. This rule was established in *Ooregum Gold Mining Co of India v Roper* [1892] AC 125 and is now in **CA 2006, s. 580(1)**. Accordingly, despite an apparently strict rule, it is easy for private companies to evade the prohibition on issue at a discount by issuing shares for over-valued non-cash consideration, and so not actually receive the capital they have declared.[4]

[4] The point about issue at a discount is a valid one regardless, but this final sentence shows you are thinking about it within the context of raising capital

Public Companies—Issue for Non-cash Consideration

Shares taken by a subscriber to the memorandum of a public company, and any premium, must be paid up in cash: **CA 2006, s. 584**. Subject to that **s. 582** applies, so public companies (like private companies) may receive money or money's worth (ie non-cash consideration) for their shares. But there are additional and significant hurdles for public companies wanting to issue shares for non-cash consideration, with harsh consequences for breach.[5]

Under **CA 2006, s. 593**, public companies must not allot shares other than for cash unless the consideration has been independently valued, with a copy of the valuer's report given to the company within six months immediately preceding the allotment and a copy given to the allottee (and the registrar of companies, **s. 597**). Very detailed rules relating to the valuation are laid down in **s. 596**, with **ss. 1150–3** setting out the required qualifications and independence of the valuer.[6] While **s. 593** does not apply to mergers or divisions (**s. 595**) or arrangements within **s. 594**, this is because other statutory requirements apply in these cases.

Under **s. 598** even more stringent regulations apply to agreements for transfer of a non-cash asset to a company by a subscriber to the memorandum within the company's initial period (two years from the date of issue of a trading certificate under **s. 761**). If the consideration given by the company for such a transfer is equal in value to one-tenth or more of the company's issued share capital then both independent valuation (**s. 599–600**) and approval of the members (**s. 601**) is required.

If **s. 593** is breached, the company and any officer in default are guilty of an offence and liable to a fine (**s. 607**). The logic of fining the company when the provisions are designed to protect the company and its creditors is not clear. More importantly for the allottee, if he did not receive the valuer's report, or if he did but knew or ought to have known of some contravention of **s. 593** or **s. 596**, then he is liable to pay the company the nominal value of the shares and any premium plus interest: **s. 593(3)**. Furthermore subsequent holders of the shares are jointly and severally liable, subject to exemption for a purchaser for value without notice or someone acquiring the shares from such a person: **s. 605**.

The harshness of the law is somewhat tempered by the power of the court to grant relief from liability (**s. 606(1)**).[7] The court can grant relief (in whole or in part) if it is just and equitable to do so, having regard to the factors in **s. 606(2)** which include any other liabilities the applicant or other persons have in regard to the shares. Unsurprisingly, given that the purpose of **s. 593** is to ensure the company receives its capital, the 'overriding principle' (**s. 606(4)**) is that a company should receive money or money's worth equivalent to the nominal value of the shares plus premium. In *Re Bradford Investments plc (No. 2)* **[1991] BCLC 688** a partnership business was transferred to the company in consideration for 1,059,000 £1 shares, without complying with the regulations, and subsequently, the company claimed £1,059,000 from the transferees. The court refused relief as it was not satisfied the business had any value when it was transferred to the company. In contrast, in *Re Ossory Estates plc* **[1988] BCLC 213** relief was granted as there was clear evidence that the company had received property equal to (and probably exceeding) the value of the shares.

Public Companies—Other Restrictions

[8] Although the valuation of non-cash consideration is the most significant provision for this question, there are other provisions you also need to deal with

The valuation requirements of **s. 593** are not the only restriction on public companies issuing shares other than for cash.[8] Public companies cannot accept any undertaking to work or perform services for the company or for another person as payment for their shares: **s. 585(1)**. Breach means the shareholder is liable to pay the nominal value of the shares and any premium plus interest (**s. 585(2)**), subject to relief: **s. 589** (which is in similar form to **s. 609**). The company and any officer in default commit an offence (**s. 590**).

Public companies must also not allot shares for consideration that is a 'long-term undertaking', that is the undertaking will or may be performed more than five years from allotment: **s. 587(1)**. As for other provisions, the allottee is liable to pay the nominal value and any premium plus interest: **s. 587(2)**, subject to relief under **s.589**, and the company and officers commit an offence (**s. 590**). Under **s. 588**, subsequent holders of any shares issued in breach of these provisions will be jointly and severally liable with the original holder, unless they are a purchaser for value without actual notice of the contravention, or who acquired the shares from such a person (**s. 588(2)**).

Justifications for Regulation

[9] It is essential you deal with this point—it is raised expressly in the question, but even if it wasn't, it is your best chance to show your deeper understanding and analysis on this topic

It has been seen that the regulations are certainly complex, and have potentially harsh consequences. Can they be justified?[9] Arguably the regulations are excessive in imposing complex and costly obligations on a company to support a capital maintenance doctrine that has little value in practice (as creditors rarely rely much on a company's share capital). But the regulations do provide protection against obvious potential abuse and, in so doing, ensure the company receives the capital that it declares it has received. While this capital may subsequently be lost in the course of business, at least investors can be confident that the company has commenced trading with the stated capital. The rules can be seen as contributing to investor confidence in public companies and the markets more generally. That factor does not apply with nearly as much force to private companies, justifying the difference in approach. Even so some aspects of the provisions seem unnecessary (such as the need for a copy of the valuation report to be sent to the allottee) and others illogical (such as making the company—and not just the directors—criminally liable and subject to a fine).

Conclusion

It is hard to disagree with the statement that the regulation of the issue of shares for non-cash consideration in public companies is both complex and harsh. The law regulating the issue of shares in a public company for non-cash consideration, has been described

[10] A particularly memorable quote that helps to make your overall point

as a 'pretty large sledgehammer to crack a fairly small nut'[10] (Sealy and Worthington, *Cases and Materials on Company Law* (10th edn, Oxford, 2013)) and there is a lot of truth in this. Some regulation seems advisable to prevent abuse and uphold investor confidence as the common law position (governing private companies) is notably lax, but the current state of affairs is difficult to justify in its entirety.

LOOKING FOR EXTRA MARKS?

■ Examine the justifications for the regulation more fully to provide a deeper consideration of the merits (or otherwise) of the provisions

■ Bring in some wider reading for additional points or to support or strengthen your arguments

■ Draw clear distinctions between the regulation of public companies and private companies

QUESTION | 2

In May, Kapital plc issued 10,000 £1 shares to Athena in consideration for the transfer of a piece of land to the company. Prior to this the company had instructed the local estate agent to value the land for them (he placed a value of £15,000 on the land) and they notified Athena of this valuation. In a separate arrangement, Kapital plc issued 2,000 £1 shares to Cayenne for £1,000. Cayenne has since given the shares to her daughter, Suva.

In June, Kapital plc was contacted by Dublin, an elderly shareholder who wanted to give his 500 £1 shares back to the company rather than leave them to his children. The directors felt it was unfair to take the shares without payment so the company paid Dublin £500 for the shares.

In July, the directors of Kapital plc learned that a debt of £20,000 owed by Hamilton to the company is unlikely to be paid. They wish to cancel £20,000 of the company's capital to take account of this bad debt.

Advise Kapital plc in respect of all of these matters. How, if at all, would your advice differ if it was a private limited company?

CAUTION!

- This question covers aspects of both raising and maintaining capital
- Check whether the company is private or public as the rules differ. Here the company is a public limited company so advise accordingly, but you are also specifically told to consider if the advice would change if it was a private company so don't forget to do this
- Deal with each scenario separately, rather than discussing capital maintenance in general terms
- There is lots of statutory material to deal with; remember to apply it, don't just copy it out

DIAGRAM ANSWER PLAN

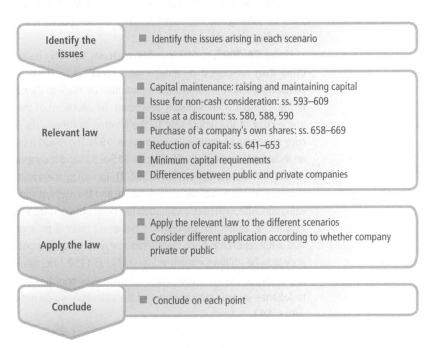

Identify the issues	■ Identify the issues arising in each scenario
Relevant law	■ Capital maintenance: raising and maintaining capital ■ Issue for non-cash consideration: ss. 593–609 ■ Issue at a discount: ss. 580, 588, 590 ■ Purchase of a company's own shares: ss. 658–669 ■ Reduction of capital: ss. 641–653 ■ Minimum capital requirements ■ Differences between public and private companies
Apply the law	■ Apply the relevant law to the different scenarios ■ Consider different application according to whether company private or public
Conclude	■ Conclude on each point

SUGGESTED ANSWER

This question raises issues of law that have their origins in the capital maintenance doctrine. The capital maintenance doctrine requires a company to raise and maintain its share capital (ie not return it to shareholders), on the basis that creditors must rely on the company's assets as the liability of members is limited (*Trevor v Whitworth*

(1887) 12 App Cas 409). Although common law in origin, the current law is mostly statutory and found in the **Companies Act 2006 (CA 2006)** which regulates public companies (such as Kapital plc) much more stringently than private companies.[1] Each scenario will be examined in turn to advise Kapital plc, before considering whether the position would be different if the company was a private company.

Athena

Companies can issue shares for money or money's worth (**CA 2006,**

s. 582). An exception is that shares taken by subscribers to the memorandum of a public company must be paid in cash (**s. 584**), but this is not the case for Athena.[2] Public companies are not however entirely free to issue shares other than for cash, and face various restrictions. The applicable provisions here are **ss. 593–7** which establish detailed rules for valuing non-cash consideration, and it appears that Kapital plc has breached these.

Under **CA 2006, s. 593** a public company can only issue shares other than for cash if an independent valuation report is made in compliance with the statute. The report must be made to the company in the six months immediately preceding the allotment of the shares

and a copy of the report sent to the allottee, ie Athena[3] (**s. 593**). A copy must also be sent to the registrar (**s. 597**). The report must be by an independent valuer (**s. 596(1); ss 1150–53**) and the report must contain the details set out in **s. 596(2)**, including the value of the shares, a description of the consideration, and the method and date of valuation. Although here a valuation has been obtained (and it will be assumed is within the six-month timeframe), there is no suggestion

that a full report has been completed, nor does a 'local estate agent' appear to be an independent valuer within **s. 1150**.[4] Neither is there any evidence the valuation report (if there was one) has been sent to Athena—merely informing her of the valuation would not comply with **s. 593**.

If, as seems to be the case, **s. 593(1)** has been breached, the company, and any officers in default, will commit an offence and be liable for a fine (**s. 607**). Athena will be liable to pay the company the aggregate amount of the nominal value of the shares, the whole of the premium, and interest at the appropriate rate: **s. 593(3)**. Athena could apply to the court for relief from liability under **s. 606** which gives the court discretion to exempt her from liability in whole or in part if it is 'just and equitable' to do so. The court will take into account whether the company has actually received value for the shares (**s. 606(4);**

Re Bradford Investments plc (No. 2) **[1991] BCLC 688).** If the valuation of £15,000 is correct, and Athena's shares are not carrying a significant premium,[5] then it appears the company has received full value and she may well be granted relief (as in **Re Ossory Estates plc [1988] BCLC 213**, where the consideration had already been sold by the company for more than the value of the shares).

Cayenne

In issuing 2,000 shares to Cayenne for only £1,000, Kapital plc has issued the shares at a discount to their nominal value, which is prohibited. The prohibition was established in **Ooregum Gold Mining Co of India v Roper [1892] AC 125** which held that a company could not issue shares at a discount, even though the market price had dropped below the nominal value. The prohibition is now in **CA 2006, s. 580(1)**. As Kapital plc has breached **s. 580(1)**, Cayenne is liable to pay the company the amount of the discount (ie £1,000) with interest (**s. 580(2)**). Furthermore, under **s. 588**, Suva will be jointly and severally liable with Cayenne, as Suva is a subsequent holder of the shares who is not a purchaser for value without notice.[6] Kapital plc and its officers in default have also committed an offence and are liable to a fine (**s. 590**).

[6] Don't forget the subsequent holder of the shares is also potentially liable

Dublin

Trevor v Whitworth established that a company must not purchase its own shares. **CA 2006, s. 638** now prohibits a company from acquiring its own shares' other than in accordance with the statute. Had Kapital plc simply accepted the shares as a gift, this would have been lawful, as acquisition other than for valuable consideration is permitted (**s. 659(1)**). **CA 2006, s. 690(1)** does give companies the power to purchase their own shares, but only by following the complex statutory procedure in **ss. 690–708**.[7] This permits either a market purchase (on a recognised investment exchange) or an off-market purchase (**s. 693**). The former requires an ordinary resolution setting boundaries for the proposed purchase (number of shares, price, time, etc), while the latter requires a special resolution approving the terms of the purchase contract. As a public company the purchase can only be funded out of distributable profits or the proceeds of a fresh issue of shares (**s. 692(2)**). As it appears Kapital plc has not complied with **ss. 690–708**, the purchase is in breach of **s. 658** and so void (**s. 658(2)(b)**). Furthermore the company and any officer in default commit an offence, and are liable to a fine/imprisonment (**s. 658(2)–(3)**).

[7] It can be helpful to find ways of summarising these points, as you don't have space to set them out in detail

Hamilton

The capital maintenance doctrine prohibits the reduction of capital by a company, other than in accordance with the statutory framework (**Trevor v Whitworth**). Under **s. 641(1)(b)** a public company may reduce its capital by special resolution confirmed by the court. A company can reduce its capital in any way, and **s. 641(4)(b)(i)** states a company can cancel any paid-up share capital that is lost or unrepresented by available assets. To obtain the court's confirmation Kapital plc may need to settle a list of creditors (**ss. 645–7**), and the court may also consider whether the reduction is fair as between the members, applying 'broad standards of fairness, reasonableness and equity' (*Scottish Insurance Corp v Wilsons & Clyde Coal Co Ltd* **[1949] AC 462**). Assuming the court confirms the reduction, it takes effect only when the order is registered. If the reduction takes Kapital plc's capital below the authorised minimum of £50,000 (**s. 763**), the company would normally need to be re-registered as a private company[8] using an expedited procedure under **s. 651** before the registrar can register the order.

[8] A minor issue but it does show appreciation of a point that only applies because Kapital is a public company

Differences for Private Limited Company[9]

[9] You could just as effectively deal with the 'what if …' points as you go along (ie after each scenario)

If Kapital was a private company, the issue to Athena would be lawful. Despite the opportunity it provides for avoiding the prohibition on issue at a discount, the courts have declined to question the value placed by a company on non-cash consideration provided it is not dishonest or 'colourable' (*Re Wragg Ltd* **[1897] 1 Ch 796**). So provided there is no evidence of fraud and the consideration is not illusory (*Hong Kong and China Gas Co Ltd v Glen* **[1914] 1 Ch 527**)—and neither appears to be the case here—the issue will be lawful and there will be no legal consequences for Athena, Kapital Ltd, or the directors.

The position with regard to the issue at a discount to Cayenne would be unchanged: the prohibition and consequences apply equally to public and private companies.

The purchase of Dublin's shares would still only be lawful if in accordance with the statute (as the general prohibition on the acquisition of a company's own shares in **s. 658** applies to both public and private companies). As a private company, the purchase would have to be an off-market purchase, but the company would have more freedom in funding the purchase as **s. 692(1ZA)** allows private companies to make payment out of capital up to (the lower of) £15,000 or 5 per cent of the paid-up share capital.

As a private company Kapital Ltd need not go to the time and expense of court confirmation in order to reduce its capital (to reflect the Hamilton bad debt). Under **s. 641(1)(a)** a private company can reduce its capital by special resolution supported by a solvency statement. This must be in accordance with **s. 643** and made no more than 15 days before the resolution (**s. 642**). The resolution, a copy of the solvency statement, and a statement of capital must be sent to the Registrar within 15 days of the resolution.

[10] As the essay concludes on each point as it comes, there isn't much to finish off the essay with—a final comment can help to complete the picture though

Overall, it can be seen[10] that the statutory requirements would be significantly less onerous if Kapital was a private company, but most of the scenarios would still be subject to some regulation.

LOOKING FOR EXTRA MARKS?

- Make sure you know where the provisions on liability can be found; they are not always located within or immediately after the particular section you are looking at

- Even if you want to be really thorough, avoid working through provisions subsection by subsection, as this can look as if you are reading through your statute book rather than applying law you already know. Instead, select particularly pertinent aspects of the provisions to slot in at appropriate points

- Add some brief comment about the justifications behind various provisions, or the difference in approach for public and private companies

QUESTION | 3

'Paid-up capital may be diminished or lost in the course of a company's trading; that is a result which no legislation can prevent; but persons who deal with, and give credit to, a limited company, naturally rely upon the fact that the company is trading with a certain amount of capital already paid, as well as upon the responsibility of its members for the capital remaining at call; and they are entitled to assume that no part of the capital which has been paid into the coffers of the company has been subsequently paid out, except in the legitimate course of its business.'

(Lord Watson, **Trevor v Whitworth** (1887) 12 App Cas 409 at 423)

Critically discuss the extent to which this statement accurately reflects the present law.

CAUTION!

- The statement isn't just about the requirements of the capital maintenance doctrine, but about the justifications behind it. So to discuss this 'critically', you need to assess the value of the capital maintenance principle more generally as well as reviewing the present law relating to capital maintenance

- Best to avoid discussion of the rules of raising capital—it isn't directly covered by the question and you would rapidly run out of time

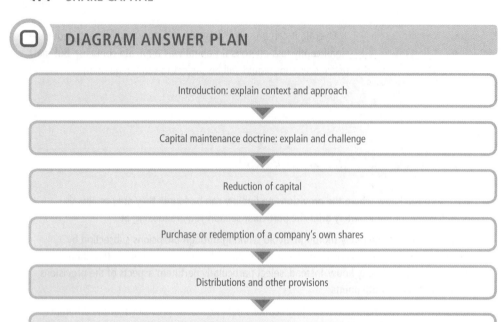

DIAGRAM ANSWER PLAN

> Introduction: explain context and approach

> Capital maintenance doctrine: explain and challenge

> Reduction of capital

> Purchase or redemption of a company's own shares

> Distributions and other provisions

> Conclusion

A SUGGESTED ANSWER

The capital maintenance doctrine requires share capital raised by the company to be 'maintained', meaning it must not be returned to shareholders, rather than kept intact. In order to address the question, the doctrine and its justifications will be examined. Then the circumstances in which the law (currently in **Companies Act 2006 (CA 2006)**) allows capital to be returned to shareholders will be considered to evaluate how far the statement reflects the present law.[1]

[1] Use the introduction to explain what you are going to do, and why it relates to the question

Capital Maintenance

The quote justifies the capital maintenance doctrine by saying that creditors dealing with the company rely on the company's capital. A similar point was made in *Re Exchange Banking Co, Flitcroft's Case* **(1882) 21 ChD 519**: a creditor can only rely on the assets of the business, and gives credit in faith that the capital will be applied only for the purposes of the business and not returned to shareholders. But the justification in the quote can be questioned on several grounds.

At the time of *Trevor v Whitworth* **(1887) 12 App Cas 409** it was common for companies to have shares of high nominal value, issued partly paid. The quote reflects this in referring to members' responsibility for capital remaining at call.[2] Accordingly, there would commonly be a fund (the amount remaining unpaid on the shares) that could be called on from shareholders on the company's insolvency.

[2] This shows you have thought about the content of the quote

But the position now is very different. Most companies have shares of very low nominal value, issued fully paid, meaning there is no un-called capital to reassure creditors. Furthermore, as the quote recognises, the capital that has been raised may have been lost 'in the ordinary course of trading', so the capital on which creditors are allegedly relying may no longer exist. Yet such losses are not the concern of the law, other than through the obscure **CA 2006, s. 656** which requires directors of a public company to call a general meeting following a 'serious loss of capital' (net assets fallen to less than half of called-up share capital). As Ferran points out, capital maintenance rules are not concerned with 'capital adequacy' ('Creditors' interests and "core" company law' (1999) 20 Co Law 314).[3]

[3] Use your further reading to support the points you make

Trevor v Whitworth asserts that creditors rely on the company's share capital when dealing with a company. This assertion is questionable, at least in modern times. Although large creditors will have regard to company accounts, it is the overall financial picture that will influence the decision to trade with the company, rather than the share capital fund as such. Smaller creditors are less likely to have regard to the company's finances, let alone its share capital. In any event, for many companies share capital is a minimal figure (the vast majority of companies have issued share capital of £100 or less)[4]—if this was 're-turned to shareholders' it would make very little difference to creditors.

[4] You could add more detailed statistics, and information on public companies' minimum capital requirements here if you wanted

The assumptions in *Trevor v Whitworth* underlying capital maintenance are thus questionable. Despite this, a great deal of law puts a great deal of effort into upholding the principle. While the present law makes some inroads into the doctrine, companies still usually need to jump through hoops before doing anything that might return capital to shareholders. These circumstances will now be examined.

Reduction of Capital

The capital maintenance doctrine only prohibits reduction of capital other than as permitted by statute. Statute makes provision (**CA 2006, s.641–9**) for a company lawfully to reduce its capital. This can be done in any way (**s. 641(3)**) but in particular a company can (a) extinguish or reduce liability on shares in respect of unpaid capital, (b) cancel paid-up capital that is lost or unrepresented by assets, or (c) repay paid-up capital in excess of the company's wants (**s. 641(4)**). It can be seen that (b) simply restores reality to the share capital figure and causes no (further) damage to creditors' interests, and (c) will not harm creditors as the company has more money than it needs. While (a) potentially removes a valuable fund for creditors, the statutory procedure ensures this will not be done when creditors might be at risk.[5] This procedure allows private companies to reduce capital through a special resolution supported by a solvency statement, indicating the company can pay all its debts (**s. 641(1)(a), ss. 642–4**). The

[5] You need to link your discussion of capital reduction to the principle and justifications of capital maintenance to ensure your essay is not too descriptive

procedure for public companies requires a special resolution and then court confirmation (**s. 641(1)(b), ss. 645–51**), which usually requires the company to settle a list of creditors and ensure fairness between members (*Scottish Insurance Corp v Wilsons & Clyde Coal Co Ltd* **[1949] AC 462**). Accordingly, while capital can be reduced, statute ensures creditors are protected.

Purchase and Redemption of a Company's own Shares

Trevor v Whitworth established that a company could not purchase its own shares. This prohibition is now in **CA 2006, s. 658**: breach is an offence by the company and officers in default. However, the statute does provide a lawful route for a company to purchase its own shares.

To be lawful, a purchase must be in accordance with **ss. 690–708**: either an off-market purchase (requiring a special resolution), or a market purchase (requiring an ordinary resolution establishing various limits for the purchase) and, usually, cancelling the shares after purchase. However, public companies cannot use capital to purchase their shares (they must use distributable profits or the proceeds of a fresh issue of shares made for the purpose (**s. 692**)), so upholding the capital maintenance principle.[6] While private companies may use capital, the risk to creditors is small: private companies can use a small amount of capital (£15,000 maximum, or 5 per cent of the share capital if lower, **s. 692(1ZA)**) but thereafter must use the same funding sources as public companies, or use the complex process (which includes a solvency statement and auditor's report) in order to use a 'permissible capital payment' under **ss. 709–23**. In essence a lawful share repurchase either doesn't use capital, or does so only where risk to creditors is minimised.

[6] Again, indicate the significance of the point you make to the theme of the essay

Companies can also issue redeemable shares[7] under **CA 2006, s. 684**, which would seem to be contrary to the *Trevor v Whitworth* statement. However, even here, the basis of the principle is observed, as the funding of the redemption (**s. 687**) echoes that for a purchase of a company's own shares, thus protecting capital and creditors.

[7] You could add more detail on redeemable shares, but the simple point relating to capital maintenance can be dealt with concisely by referring to previous discussion

Distributions and other Provisions

To ensure companies do not return capital to shareholders through dividends, there are restrictions on when distributions (including dividends) can be made. These can only be out of 'profits available for the purpose', ie 'accumulated realised profits less accumulated realised losses' (**s. 830**). Further restrictions apply to public companies (**s. 831(1)**). Directors authorising an unlawful dividend are liable to repay the distribution to the company (*Bairstow v Queens Moat Houses plc* **[2001] 2 BCLC 531**; breach is non-ratifiable: *Aveling Barford Ltd v Perion* **[1989] BCLC 626**) and members are liable to repay an unlawful distribution if they knew or had reasonable grounds to believe it was paid contrary to the statute.

The courts have also been alert to transactions with shareholders that may be a disguised return of capital.[8] In *Re Halt Garage (1964) Ltd* [1982] 3 All ER 1016, the court overturned payments to shareholders labelled as director remuneration. In *Progress Property Co Ltd v Moorgarth Group Ltd* [2010] UKSC 55, the court highlighted the need to examine the substance of a transaction rather than merely the name given it by directors to ensure capital was not being returned other than through the statutory framework.

Another area of law with its origins in the capital maintenance doctrine (although now with stronger links to preventing market abuse) is financial assistance. **CA 2006, s. 678** prevents a public company from assisting a purchaser of its shares, by, eg paying for the shares, or providing or guaranteeing a loan. While many examples of financial assistance do not diminish the company's capital, there is obviously potential to do so, and the courts have interpreted exceptions very strictly (*Brady v Brady* [1989] AC 755). However since **CA 2006** these rules only apply to public companies, showing the legislature's preference to minimise the impact of the capital maintenance doctrine on private companies at least.

Conclusion

There have been inroads into the capital maintenance principle: companies can reduce their capital, purchase and redeem their own shares, and, if a private company, fund share purchases out of capital and give financial assistance for the purchase of its own shares.[9] But there are still very few opportunities for companies to return capital to shareholders and where it is permissible, statute seeks to ensure there is no sensible risk to creditors. *Trevor v Whitworth* is thus still very much part of our law. The bigger issue is arguably whether the statement is correct in the assumptions and justifications it relies on.[10] As this is questionable, the law may be misplacing its energy in continuing to support the capital maintenance doctrine, and might be better directed at improving protection for creditors on insolvency.

[8] It is easy to concentrate on the statutory provisions and forget about this line of cases

[9] A very concise summary of the second part of the essay

[10] This reminds the examiner that you have questioned the principle, as well as discussing the provisions themselves

---

 LOOKING FOR EXTRA MARKS

- Refer back to the question statement to show you have really understood the points being made, and that you can challenge some of them

- Show you understand why the law has departed from the strict principle on occasion, eg why the law does sometimes allow capital to be reduced, shares purchased, etc

- Explore the various rules and procedures in a bit of depth so you can assess how well they fit either with the capital maintenance principle in an absolute sense, or with the wider justifications behind the principle

Gary is the managing director and major shareholder (holding 5 million shares) of Takeout plc, a property development company. In negotiations to bring Howard, a wealthy businessman, into the company, Gary agreed on behalf of Takeout plc to acquire a property with planning permission for commercial development from Howard for £3m. (The property was recently valued at £1.5m.) Howard then obtained an unsecured loan of £2m from Eastern Bank and purchased 50 per cent of Gary's shareholding in Takeout plc for £5m. Howard joined the board of Takeout plc, and shortly after, Takeout plc created a floating charge over its property portfolio to secure Howard's loan from Eastern Bank.

Advise on the legality of the transactions entered into by Takeout plc and the rights and liabilities of Gary, Howard, and the Bank.

CAUTION!

- Work through the financial assistance provisions step by step in order to cover all the points and draw clear conclusions

- Remember that although CA 2006 changed the law by removing private companies from the ambit of the financial assistance provisions, pre-2006 case law is still relevant on many points

- Follow the instructions: advise on the consequences for the transaction and the various parties involved in it

DIAGRAM ANSWER PLAN

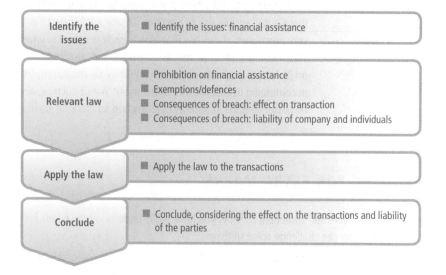

Identify the issues
- Identify the issues: financial assistance

Relevant law
- Prohibition on financial assistance
- Exemptions/defences
- Consequences of breach: effect on transaction
- Consequences of breach: liability of company and individuals

Apply the law
- Apply the law to the transactions

Conclude
- Conclude, considering the effect on the transactions and liability of the parties

This problem raises the question of whether Takeout plc has been guilty of the offence of providing financial assistance for the acquisition of its own shares under **Companies Act 2006 (CA 2006), ss. 677–83**. Although **CA 2006** abolished financial assistance for private companies, it remains applicable to public companies (and private companies in a group with public companies), meaning Takeout plc is subject to the prohibition. As well as potentially offending the capital maintenance doctrine, financial assistance is prohibited because it gives companies scope to manipulate their share price and/or allow new controllers to engage in asset-stripping to the detriment of existing shareholders and creditors.[1]

[1] While in a problem question you should focus on application of the law to the facts, there is usually the opportunity to show a little bit of your more general knowledge

There are two situations here which could constitute financial assistance: the purchase of the commercial property from Howard for £3m and the creation of a floating charge to secure Howard's loan of £2m. The transactions will be considered to see if they amount to financial assistance, together with any potential exceptions to the offence, and the liability of the parties discussed.[2]

[2] Even in a problem question it can be helpful to set out your approach in your introduction, but it is less important than in an essay

CA 2006, s. 678 prohibits a public company (or its subsidiary, other than a foreign subsidiary: **Arab Bank plc v Mercantile Holdings Ltd [1994] 2 All ER 74**) from giving financial assistance to any person for the purpose of the acquisition of its shares. This is prohibited whether given directly or indirectly, and whether given before or at the same time as the share acquisition (contemporaneous financial assistance), or after the acquisition takes place (subsequent financial assistance): **s. 678**.

According to **British and Commonwealth Holdings plc v Barclays Bank plc [1996] 1 WLR 1** the provision 'requires that there should be assistance or help for the purpose of acquiring shares and that that assistance should be financial' (Aldous J). Financial assistance is not defined as such in **CA 2006** but **s. 677** states[3] that it includes financial assistance given by way of a guarantee, security, or indemnity: **s. 677(1)(b)(i)**. This would cover the creation of the floating charge, which is indirect subsequent financial assistance, enabling Eastern Bank to enforce the change against Takeout plc's assets in the event of Howard defaulting on the loan.

[3] It is tempting to view s. 677 as a definition provision, but it isn't and the examiner will be pleased to see you recognise this

Under **s. 677(1)(d)(i)** financial assistance also includes any other financial assistance given by the company where the net assets of the company are reduced to a material extent by the giving of the assistance (or where the company has no net assets). This would cover the purchase of Howard's property as[4] the purchase price significantly exceeds the value of the property acquired. For example in **Belmont Finance Corpn Ltd v Williams Furniture Ltd [1979] Ch 250**

[4] Remember to apply the law explicitly to the facts—just setting out the relevant law isn't enough in itself

directors of the defendant company, with the connivance of some of the directors of the claimant, sold its property at a substantial over-value. The four directors then used the money to purchase all the is-sued shares in the plaintiff company. The Court of Appeal held that the transaction was illegal financial assistance and a breach of what is now **CA 2006, s. 678(1)**. While the courts have indicated that they will view potential financial assistance pragmatically and look at the overall commercial realities of a situation (***Charterhouse Investment Trust Ltd v Tempest Diesels Ltd* [1986] BCLC 1;*Anglo Petroleum Ltd v TFB Mortgages* [2008] 1 BCLC 185**), the timing and detail of this purchase suggests it is very much part of a deliberate scheme to assist financially in the purchase of Takeout plc's shares, rather than a genuine commercial arrangement. It therefore seems likely that the purchase of the commercial property from Howard was contempora-neous financial assistance.

Prima facie then, Takeout plc has been involved in two examples of unlawful financial assistance. However both offences are subject to the purpose exceptions under **CA 2006, s. 678(2) and(4)**.[5] The first of these (**ss. 678(2)(a) and 678(4)(a)**) permits a company to give financial assistance if its principal purpose in giving the assistance is not to give it for the purpose of any such acquisition (in the case of contemporaneous financial assistance) or to reduce or discharge any liability incurred (in the case of subsequent financial assistance) and the assistance is given in good faith in the interests of the company. The second purpose exception (**ss. 678(2)(b) and 678(4)(b)**) permits a company to give financial assistance if the giving of the assistance (or the reduction or discharge of liability) is only an incidental part of some larger purpose of the company and the assistance is given in good faith in the interests of the company.

Although clearly designed to ensure genuine commercial transac-tions were outside the ambit of the prohibition, the scope of the pur-pose exceptions were severely restricted by ***Brady v Brady* [1989] AC 755.** In this case the House of Lords rejected the decision of the lower courts that the financial assistance fell within the purpose ex-ceptions, despite being given as part of a major company reorgani-sation to resolve intractable conflict between the two controlling parties and so avoid the company's likely liquidation.[6] The House of Lords distinguished between a purpose and the reason why a pur-pose is formed and held that a 'larger purpose' must be something more than the reason why the transaction was entered into. This deci-sion has rendered the purpose exceptions of 'little, if any, practical value' (Mercouris, 'The prohibition on financial assistance: the case for a commercially pragmatic interpretation' (2014) 35 Co Law 321),[7] although the exception was held to have been satisfied in ***Re Uniq plc* [2011] EWHC 749** (on very different facts to the present case).

[5] The two purpose exceptions are both contained within subsections (2) and (4), rather than one in each, so make sure you know where to find them before you are in the exam

[6] As it is such a significant case it is helpful to give some case facts, but you should still be concise and focus on the points that relate to the issue at hand

[7] You could make the point about the problem with *Brady* without specific support, but it is good to show your further reading if you can

Applying the cases and the reasoning in **Brady v Brady** it is highly unlikely that Takeout plc could argue that the financial assistance is to achieve the larger purpose of bringing Howard and his expertise into the company, even if this were in the interests of the company. Neither is the financial assistance incidental to some larger purpose of the company, which requires there to be some 'larger overall corporate purpose' in which the assistance is merely incidental (**Brady v Brady**).

There are other exceptions to the prohibition on financial assistance, for example when in relation to a reduction of capital or purchase of shares undertaken in accordance with the statutory schemes (**s. 681**) but these do not apply to Takeout plc's case. Neither do the exemptions for money-lending companies or employee share schemes apply (**s. 682**). Accordingly it seems highly probable that Takeout plc will be found to have breached the prohibition on financial assistance.

Breach of the financial assistance provisions is a criminal offence by the company and every officer of the company who is in default: **CA 2006, s. 680(1)**. The company would be liable to a fine and any officer liable to a fine and/or imprisonment: **s. 680(2)**. Although the statute does not make provision for the civil consequences of the breach, the courts have held that any unlawful financial assistance is unenforceable by either party,[8] meaning that the floating charge granted to Eastern Bank will be illegal and unenforceable against the company by the bank: **Heald v O'Connor** [1971] 1 WLR 497. However, the courts are willing to sever any illegal element from the rest of a transaction where possible (**Carney v Herbert** [1985] 1 All ER 438), so the rest of the arrangement should remain valid.

Gary, as a director of Takeout plc, will be in breach of his duty to the company[9] by authorising the giving of financial assistance (**Re In a Flap Envelope Co Ltd** [2004] 1 BCLC 64) and liable to account to the company for any losses caused. He may have breached multiple duties in causing the company to purchase Howard's property and giving security for Howard's loan (for example using his powers for an improper purpose under **CA 2006, s. 171(b)**, or not acting in good faith to promote the success of the company under **s. 172**). Howard too, in authorising the giving of security after being appointed a director, will be in breach of his duties as a director, including a potential conflict of interest. In addition, if Howard received payment for his property knowing that the transaction was improper and an abuse of Gary's fiduciary duties, he could also be liable as a constructive trustee to account to Takeout plc: **Belmont Finance Corpn Ltd v Williams Furniture Ltd** (No. 2) [1980] 1 All ER 393; **Royal Brunei Airlines Sdn Bhd v Tan Kok Ming** [1995] 2 AC 378. It is also possible for the company to sue Gary and Howard for damages for conspiracy, despite the company being a party to the transaction:

[8] Remember to think about the civil consequences of breach, as well as criminal liability

[9] Directors' duties will inevitably be relevant, but don't get too distracted and provide too much detail—the focus of the question is financial assistance rather than duties per se

Belmont Finance Corpn Ltd v Williams Furniture Ltd **[1979] Ch 250**. Should Takeout plc get into financial difficulties there is also the possibility that the purchase of Howard's property could be challengeable under **Insolvency Act 1986** (as a transaction at an undervalue: **s. 238**) while causing a company to give financial assistance is evidence of unfitness under **Company Directors Disqualification Act 1986, s. 6**: *Re Continental Assurance Co of London plc* **[1997] 1 BCLC 48**.

LOOKING FOR EXTRA MARKS?

- Explore the purpose exception in more depth and examine some of the criticism surrounding *Brady v Brady*

- Examine the reasons behind the financial assistance prohibition and assess whether those justifications are present in the case at hand

- Show your awareness of how directors' duties are relevant to financial assistance, but be careful not to spend too much time on this element of the question

TAKING THINGS FURTHER

- Armour, J., 'Share capital and creditor protection: efficient rules for a modern company law' (2000) 63 MLR 355

  Questions whether the rules on capital raising and maintenance fulfil the stated aim of creditor protection, through the prism of economic analysis. Concludes that while such rules could enhance efficiency, the form of existing regulation is not justified by such principles.

- Daehnert, A., 'The minimum capital requirement—an anachronism under conservation: Parts 1 and 2' (2009) 30 Co Law 3 and 34

  Discusses the value of a minimum capital requirement and its link to limited liability and creditor protection, with particular reference to the position in Germany.

- Ferran, E., 'Creditors' interests and "core" company law' (1999) 20 Co Law 314

  An exploration of the role of debt finance in the corporate capital structure, and the impact and value of the capital maintenance rules to creditors and more generally.

- Ferran, E., 'Corporate transactions and financial assistance: shifting policy perceptions but static law' [2004] CLJ 225

  A critical account of the financial assistance provisions pre-CA 2006. Many of the comments and criticisms are still relevant to the current law.

- Mercouris, S., 'The prohibition on financial assistance: the case for a commercially pragmatic interpretation' (2014) 35 Co Law 321

  Considers the policy arguments behind financial assistance and examines recent case authorities. Argues that the financial assistance prohibition fails to offer adequate protection while also putting legitimate commercial transactions at risk.

■ Micheler, E., 'Disguised returns of capital—an arm's length approach' [2010] CLJ 151

An interesting article considering when payments to shareholders may be viewed as a disguised return of capital, and examining the relationship with the doctrines of capital maintenance, ultra vires, and abuse of corporate power.

Online Resource Centre

www.oxfordtextbooks.co.uk/orc/qanda/

Go online for extra essay and problem questions, a glossary of key terms, online versions of all the answer plans and audio commentary on how selected ones were put together, and a range of podcasts which include advice on exam and coursework technique and advice for other assessment methods.

10 Loan Capital

ARE YOU READY?

- Corporate borrowing
- Fixed charges
- Floating charges
- Registration of charges
- Priority of charges on insolvency
- Vulnerability of floating charge on insolvency
- Connections (in particular) with: share capital; directors' duties; corporate insolvency

KEY DEBATES

Debate: distinguishing between fixed and floating charges

The efforts of creditors to gain the advantages of fixed charges in situations where floating charges might be thought more appropriate (in particular in relation to charges over book debts) led to some much criticised cases and academic dispute. The distinction between fixed and floating charges is now tolerably clear, but grey areas remain. Keep in mind when reading academic commentary whether it pre- or post-dates the decisions in *Re Brumark* (Privy Council), and *Re Spectrum* (House of Lords). See also more generally Ferran, E. and Ho, L. C., *Principles of Corporate Finance Law* (2nd edn, Oxford, 2014).

Debate: reforming the company charge registration system

Reform of the registration system had been long anticipated, but the eventual changes (in 2013) were not particularly extensive. In this area the Law Commission papers are helpful in explaining problems and alternative solutions, but you should weigh up the much more ambitious proposals against the final cautious reform.

QUESTION | 1

'A specific charge, I think, is one that without more fastens on ascertained and definite property or property capable of being ascertained and defined; a floating charge, on the other hand, is ambulatory and shifting in its nature, hovering over and so to speak floating with the property which it is intended to affect until some event occurs or some act is done which causes it to settle and fasten on the subject of the charge ...' Lord Macnaghten, *Illingworth v Houldsworth* **[1904] AC 355**

Critically assess the characteristics of fixed and floating charges, and how the law distinguishes between them.

CAUTION!

- Remember to address both parts of the instruction—it is easy to forget to deal with 'how' the law distinguishes them ie the process, not just the distinguishing features
- As part of your critical assessment, make sure you identify why it has become so important to distinguish between fixed and floating charges—in particular the attempts to create fixed charges over fluctuating assets

DIAGRAM ANSWER PLAN

Introduction: companies, security, and fixed and floating charges

Fixed charges: features and benefits

Floating charges: features, benefits, and drawbacks

Distinguishing between fixed and floating charges: the courts' approach

Charges over book debts/receivables

Conclusion: review of distinguishing features and approach

A company may grant security to a creditor by creating fixed (or specific) or floating charges over its assets, whereas sole traders and partnerships (other than LLPs) cannot create floating charges. The two types of charge do not offer equal security to creditors in the event of a company's insolvent liquidation and this makes it particularly important to be able to distinguish between the two types of charge.[1] This essay will explore the characteristics of both forms of charge, highlighting their distinguishing features, and will explain the approach adopted by the courts in distinguishing between them.

> [1] This shows you know why the distinction matters

Fixed Charges

Fixed charges are legal or equitable charges created by the company over specific, identified assets. However the quote's focus on the nature of the charged asset[2] is slightly misplaced, as the critical feature of a fixed charge (and the element distinguishing it from a floating charge) is that the company cannot deal with or dispose of the charged asset without the chargeholder's consent, rather than the type of asset as such. Accordingly while a fixed charge is generally created over property such as land, fixed plant, and machinery, with care fixed charges can also be created over less permanent assets.

> [2] Although the question itself doesn't ask specifically about the quote, your answer should still reflect on the issues raised by the quote

A fixed charge gives the holder priority over other creditors[3] on the company's insolvency—a creditor with a fixed charge can realise his debt from the charged asset. Unlike floating charges, assets subject to a fixed charge are not vulnerable to meeting the costs of the liquidation or paying preferential creditors, and no part of such assets are taken for the benefit of unsecured creditors. Furthermore a fixed charge does not risk invalidation under **Insolvency Act 1986 (IA 1986), s. 245** if created in the period prior to the commencement of winding up. Other provisions such as **IA 1986, s. 239** (preferences) may operate to remove the benefit of the security for the creditor but these are harder to establish than **s. 245**. Unsurprisingly, creditors will seek to create a fixed charge rather than a floating charge where possible, in order to achieve these advantages.

> [3] This paragraph is important as it sets out why fixed charges tend to be preferred to floating charges and so backs up the brief comment in the introduction

Floating Charges

The floating charge is 'an equitable charge on the assets for the time being of a going concern' (***Governments Stock and Other Securities Investment Co Ltd v Manila Railway Co Ltd* [1897] AC 81**) and was first recognised by the courts in ***Re Panama, New Zealand and Australian Royal Mail Co* (1870) 5 Ch App 318**. Three characteristics were identified by Romer LJ in ***Re Yorkshire Woolcombers Association Ltd* [1903] 2 Ch 284 (*Yorkshire Woolcombers*)**:[4] (i) it is a charge on a class of assets of a company

> [4] You don't need to remember the precise words, but you should be able to summarise these three characteristics

present and future; (ii) the class is one which, in the ordinary course of business of the company, changes from time to time; and (iii) until some future step is taken (and the charge 'crystallises'), the company can carry on its business using the assets as if uncharged. It is the final characteristic, the company's ability to use the assets in the ordinary course of business, rather than the class of assets, that is the essential characteristic distinguishing a floating charge from a fixed charge.

Crystallisation is when the charge ceases to float over the body of assets covered by the charge and attach to those assets comprising that class at that time. The crystallising event will usually be a formal act of the chargeholder (such as appointing an administrator or giving notice) but it need not be directly triggered by the chargeholder (eg the commencement of winding up, or the company ceasing to be a 'going concern' (*Re Woodroffes (Musical Instruments) Ltd* [1985] **3 WLR 543**)). Charges may even use an automatic crystallisation clause (*Re Brightlife Ltd* [1987] **Ch 200**). However, floating chargeholders cannot claim that by crystallisation they gain the benefit of being a fixed chargeholder on winding up. **IA 1986, s. 251** provides that charges created as floating charges rank as such and so do not change position in the priority order of creditors even if crystallising before commencement of winding up or administration.

[5] This paragraph sets out some of the benefits of a floating charge, but then goes on to give some more detail on its drawbacks, filling out the detail of the points raised earlier

A floating charge is a flexible device[5] that enables creditors to take security over the entire undertaking of a company, but leaves the company free to deal with its assets in the ordinary course of business (*Agnew v IRC; Re Brumark Investments Ltd* [2001] **2 AC 710** (*Brumark*)). The holder of a 'qualifying' floating charge also has the right to appoint an administrator over the company (**IA 1986, Sch B1**). However it has significant drawbacks compared with a fixed charge. Assets subject to a floating charge may be used to pay the expenses of the liquidation and to pay preferential debts where the company's free assets (those not subject to any charge) are insufficient to meet those claims (**IA 1986, s. 176ZA and s. 175(2)**). Furthermore part of the recoveries will usually be available to unsecured creditors as the 'prescribed part' under **IA 1986, s. 176A**. In addition, floating charges created other than for new consideration will be invalid if created during a relevant time (one or two years prior to the commencement of the winding up) (**IA 1986, s. 245**).

Distinguishing between Fixed and Floating Charges

It is for the court to determine whether a charge is a fixed or a floating charge, irrespective of how the parties have described the charge: *Re Armagh Shoes Ltd* [1984] **BCLC 405**. In *Brumark*,

[6] It is important to deal with the process for determination as well as the distinguishing features

the Privy Council held that determination is a two-stage process.[6] The court must first identify the rights the parties intended to create (looking at the rights rather than the label attached to the charge by the parties) and then decide, as a matter of law, whether those rights create a fixed or floating charge. The **Brumark** approach was accepted by the House of Lords in **Re Cosslett Contractors Ltd [2002] 1 BCLC 77**.

In deciding whether a charge is fixed or floating, it is clear that the third **Yorkshire Woolcombers** characteristic—the ability to deal with the assets charged in the ordinary course of trading—is more important than the others. In **Re Spectrum Plus Ltd [2005] 2 AC 680 (Spectrum)**, Lord Scott said this was 'the essential feature of the floating charge, the characteristic that distinguishes it from a fixed charge'. Other characteristics are thus not determinative. However, the nature of the asset charged may well be indicative, with Lord Scott in **Spectrum** connecting the company's ability to remove assets from the security, with the circulating character of assets typically subject to a floating charge.

The **Brumark** approach, focusing on the rights and obligations actually given, guards against the mislabelling of charges, but does not necessarily mean attempts to create fixed charges in novel situations are bound to fail. A particular area of difficulty for the courts was whether fixed charges could be created over book debts (or receivables)[7]—a valuable asset that by its nature is constantly changing and over which a company usually needs to retain some control.

In **Siebe Gorman & Co Ltd v Barclays Bank Ltd [1979] 2 Lloyd's Rep 142 (Siebe Gorman)**, the court upheld a fixed charge over book debts: the terms of the charge required debts to be credited to a specific bank account and restricted the company's rights to dispose of those monies. As it was not always possible for a chargeholder to restrict a company's rights in this way, a 'hybrid' charge (a fixed charge over book debts while outstanding and a floating charge over the proceeds) was created in **Re New Bullas Trading Ltd [1993] BCC 251**. However this was heavily criticised[8] and held in **Brumark** to have been wrongly decided. In **Spectrum**, the House of Lords unanimously overruled both **Siebe Gorman** and **Re New Bullas Trading Ltd**.

Post-**Brumark** and **Spectrum**, it is not impossible to create a fixed charge over book debts, but only if the assets are permanently appropriated to the payment of the debt—the chargeholder must have control of the proceeds. Although some dealings in the charged property are not necessarily fatal to the existence of a fixed charge (eg **Arthur D Little Ltd (In Administration) v Ableco Finance LLC [2003] Ch 217**), in practice it is now very difficult to create a fixed charge over book debts as the chargeholder will need to require and control an account into which proceeds are paid.

Conclusion

Fixed and floating charges have different characteristics but the key distinguishing feature is the extent to which the company retains the

[7] You will need to consider the book debts saga, but concentrate on the current law

[8] If you had time you could consider some of the criticisms here

ability to deal with the charged asset. The nature of the asset charged is not determinative but it is significant (as the quote indicates)[9] and may strongly influence the level of control retained by the company. The courts' approach to distinguishing between fixed and floating charges looks at the true picture of what has been created, rather than that presented by the draftsman. This ensures that creditors do not gain the benefit of a fixed charge in situations when in truth they have created a floating charge.

[9] Linking back to the quote at the end shows that you have understood the significance of the point it raises

LOOKING FOR EXTRA MARKS?

- Engage with some of the (many) critical pieces relating to fixed charges over book debts and academic views of the various cases in this saga
- Consider some of the practical elements of corporate lending, and whether changes (such as *Brumark*, and the 'prescribed part') have impacted on lending practices
- Develop the examination of floating charges by exploring differing academic views about the nature of the charge and its proprietary status prior to crystallisation

QUESTION | 2

'The reforms to the registration of charges introduced into the **Companies Act 2006** by the **Companies Act 2006 (Amendment of Part 25) Regulations 2013** were extremely limited and not worth the wait.' **Discuss.**

CAUTION!

- You will need to have an appreciation of both the pre- and post-2013 law to answer this question well, as you will need to explain how the new provisions have changed the law, and where the law remains unchanged
- If you structure your answer by first discussing the original law, and then the new law, your answer is likely to be quite descriptive. Instead, identify important features of the registration system and assess the changes within these areas

DIAGRAM ANSWER PLAN

```
┌─────────────────────────────────────────────────┐
│            Purpose of registration              │
└─────────────────────────────────────────────────┘
                      ▼
┌─────────────────────────────────────────────────┐
│            Identifying relevant law             │
└─────────────────────────────────────────────────┘
                      ▼
┌─────────────────────────────────────────────────┐
│              Registrable charges                │
└─────────────────────────────────────────────────┘
                      ▼
┌─────────────────────────────────────────────────┐
│        Registration: the system and process     │
└─────────────────────────────────────────────────┘
                      ▼
┌─────────────────────────────────────────────────┐
│          Effect of failure to register          │
└─────────────────────────────────────────────────┘
                      ▼
┌─────────────────────────────────────────────────┐
│        Other issues, including amendment         │
└─────────────────────────────────────────────────┘
                      ▼
┌─────────────────────────────────────────────────┐
│      Conclusion: summarise impact of reforms     │
└─────────────────────────────────────────────────┘
```

SUGGESTED ANSWER

[1] Explain the context of the question at the start

The registration system enables those dealing with a company to check for charges over a company's assets:[1] in *Re Welsh Irish Ferries Ltd* [1985] BCLC 327, Nourse J said the object of registration is to warn 'unsuspecting creditors' that the company has charged its assets. A failure to register may also affect the priority of lenders in the event of a company's insolvency. Registration is thus of significance to companies and those dealing with them. This essay will explain the system of registration for company charges as created by **Companies Act 2006 (Amendment of Part 25) Regulations 2013 (SI 2013/600) (2013 Regulations)**, assessing the changes and their significance.

After several abortive reform attempts, the registration system in **Companies Act 2006 (CA 2006), Part 25** was largely unchanged from **Companies Act 1985** and based on a system from 1901. However, **CA 2006, s. 894** empowered the Secretary of State to make regulations altering **Part 25** and, following consultations, the **2013 Regulations** came into force on 6 April 2013.[2] This replaces **CA 2006, Part 25, Chapter 1** (governing companies registered in England, Wales, and Northern Ireland) and **Chapter 2** (governing

[2] As the question focuses on the reform (and not just the system) it is helpful to indicate how and when the reform came into being. You could also provide a bit more detail on the 'abortive reform attempts' if you had time.

companies registered in Scotland) with **Chapter A1** applying to all parts of the UK. **Chapter A1** only applies to charges created on or after 6 April 2013; for charges created before then the old law applies.

Registrable Charges

One of the most significant changes introduced by the **2013 Regulations** is the type of charges that are registrable. Before 2013, **CA 2006, s. 860**[3] provided a list of registrable charges in nine categories (including charges on land and on book debts). Only if a charge fell within one of these categories was it registrable. Since the effect of non-registration of a registrable charge is that the charge is void against the liquidator, administrator, or any creditor, it could be essential to prove that an unregistered charge was not registrable if it were to be enforceable. This made the categories critical and could provide an additional incentive to draft charges as fixed rather than floating charges,[4] as all floating charges were registrable, but not all fixed charges were (eg a charge on shares: *Arthur D Little Ltd (In Administration) v Ableco Finance LLC* [2003] Ch 217).

Chapter A1 does not provide a list of registrable charges; instead, all charges are registrable unless specifically excluded in **s. 859A(6)**: (a) a charge in favour of a landlord on a cash deposit given as a security in connection with the lease of land; (b) a charge created by a member of Lloyd's to secure its Lloyd's underwriting obligations; and (c) a charge specifically excluded by another Act. During consultation, consideration was given to excluding charges arising by operation of law, but these were not included in **s. 859A(6)** and so such charges (eg a vendor's lien: *London and Cheshire Insurance Co Ltd v Laplagrene Property Co Ltd* [1971] Ch 499) are now registrable.

Registration

Registration can be by the company or a person interested: it is usually by the chargeholder as they have more to lose in the event of a failure to register.[5] Under **s. 859D** the company or interested person sends a certified copy of the charge instrument to the registrar, together with a 'statement of particulars': the registrar is then under a duty to register that charge (**s. 859A**). This is an improvement on the old system[6] that required delivery of more detailed 'prescribed particulars' together with the original charge instrument, with the registrar then having to check the particulars against the instrument before returning the original instrument of charge. The new system allocates a unique reference code to each charge, displayed on the charge certificate, which should allow easier tracking of charges by those searching the register. In a distinct improvement on the former, paper-based system, charges and statements of particulars

[3] Don't worry if you don't know the previous section numbers: you are unlikely to be able to remember them all and most statute books will show only the new law

[4] A small extra point that links effectively into a connected topic

[5] A comment like this shows a level of understanding beyond the simple knowledge that chargeholders can register the charge

[6] Explicitly compare the two systems, indicating where there are changes, in order to address the question

(and statements of full or partial satisfaction) can now be filed electronically.

As under the previous provisions, the charge and particulars are to be delivered to the registrar within 21 days from the day after the day the charge is created, **CA 2006, s. 859(4)**. (The new provisions, **s. 859E**, provide a table identifying the date of creation of the charge depending on its type and the date of delivery.) The system thus continues the risk of the 21-day 'invisibility period' during which anyone searching the register would not be aware of all existing charges, demonstrating some limits to the 2013 reforms. It therefore remains important to check with the company for any further charges that have yet to be registered.

It is possible to apply for an extension to the time for delivery by virtue of **s. 859F(3)**, echoing the previous system in the former **s. 873**. This allows the court (on application of the company or person interested) to extend the period for delivery if satisfied the failure to deliver the documents was 'accidental or due to inadvertence or to some other sufficient cause', or is 'not of a nature to prejudice the position of creditors or shareholders of the company', or that it is just and equitable to grant relief. The courts have generally been willing to extend the period for registration, provided that rights acquired in the meantime are not prejudiced, although the courts may refuse to extend the period after a long delay: *Re Teleomatic Ltd* **[1994] 1 BCLC 90**.

Failure to Register

A failure to register results in the charge being void against the company's liquidator, administrator, or any creditor (**s. 859H**). This position is unchanged[7] (formerly in **s. 874**). This does not affect the validity of the debt itself which remains payable (*Re Monolithic Building Company* **[1915] 1 Ch 643**), but will rank as an unsecured debt on a company's liquidation. *Re Cosslett (Contractors) Ltd* **[2002] 1 BCLC 77** made clear that the charge is not void against the company while it is not in administration or winding up. When a charge becomes void, the money secured by the charge becomes immediately payable (**s. 859H(4)**, formerly **s. 874(3)**). Other than the statutory invalidity, registration does not determine priorities between charges. Priorities remain governed by common law, but notice is important, and registration will amount to constructive notice of the existence of the charge, if not all of its terms (Graham, 'Registration of Company Charges' [2014] JBL 175 considers constructive notice would apply only to the terms disclosed in the registered particulars).[8]

There is no longer a duty on the company to register a charge. The former **s. 860** stated the company 'must' deliver the documents to the registrar; and a failure to register was a criminal offence

[7] It is equally important to show where there have not been changes

[8] Examiners like to see you have engaged with further reading, so bring in some additional comment or observation if you can

by the company and every officer in default. The new **s. 859A** is phrased in terms of the obligation being on the registrar to register the charge once the documents are filed within the delivery period. Of course, as an unregistered charge is invalid against the liquidator etc, in practice the company/lender will be commercially obliged to register in any event, but the **2013 Regulations** have removed the criminal sanction.[9]

Other Issues

One complaint of the old system was that variations in a registered charge could only be made by effectively registering anew. Under **s. 859O**, where a charge is amended by adding a negative pledge clause (restricting creation of charges ranking ahead or equal to the charge) or varying the ranking of the charge in relation to any other charge, either the company or the person with the benefit of the charge can register the amendment.

Before 6 April 2013 companies had to keep their own register of charges (which was open to inspection) (**CA 2006, s. 876**) but this requirement has been abolished. Companies do need to keep copies of instruments creating or amending charges (**s. 859P**) which will be open to inspection (**s. 859Q**) so the impact of this change is limited.

The **2013 Regulations** have not made changes in respect of the effect of the certificate of registration. Accordingly, the certificate remains conclusive evidence that documents were delivered to the registrar before the end of the delivery period (as extended): **s. 859I(7)**. This applies even if the certificate is demonstrably inaccurate, as in *Re Mechanisations (Eaglescliffe) Ltd* [1966] **Ch 20**, where the amount secured was incorrectly stated, and *Re CL Nye Ltd* [1971] **Ch 442** where the date of creation of the charge was wrong.

Conclusion

Reform to the company charge registration system was much delayed and limited. Those favouring a different system such as the US-style 'notice filing' system (eg Company Law Review ('Modern Company Law for a Competitive Economy' Final Report and Graham [2014] JBL 175)) may well feel it was not 'worth the wait'.[10] Nonetheless, the changes at least reduce confusion over what charges are registrable, introduce a UK-wide system, remove the unnecessary criminal penalty for failure to register, and allow electronic filing. Furthermore, by taking a fairly cautious approach to reform in such a commercially important area, users can adapt to the changes without significant difficulty.

LOOKING FOR EXTRA MARKS

- Show an appreciation of the reform proposals and explore the reasons why a less ambitious route was ultimately preferred
- Consider why the changes were thought necessary: this provides an additional point of analysis of the provisions and their significance
- Engage with the academic material on this topic and/or contrast the UK system with other registration systems

QUESTION | 3

Francis is the controlling shareholder and managing director of two companies, Gato Ltd and Canis Ltd.

Gato Ltd suffered a financial crisis in 2014 and it was agreed in January 2015 that Canis Ltd would pay off its outstanding debts and advance a further £50,000 on the security of a floating charge on Gato Ltd's assets. Canis Ltd settled the debts and advanced the money to Gato Ltd in March 2015, although the debenture containing the charge was not actually executed until July 2015. The charge was registered within 21 days of its creation.

Gato Ltd had a major supplier, Lapin plc, which in September 2015 refused to make further deliveries to Gato Ltd on credit since it was already owed £40,000 for previous deliveries. Following talks between the directors of Gato Ltd and Lapin plc, Lapin plc agreed to continue to supply Gato Ltd on condition that Gato Ltd created in its favour a fixed charge over its freehold premises to cover the existing debt of £40,000. The charge was created in October 2015 and registered within 21 days.

Gato Ltd went into creditors' voluntary liquidation in March 2016.

Advise the liquidator of Gato Ltd on the validity of the charges created in favour of Canis Ltd and Lapin plc.

CAUTION!

- Although at first sight this looks like a question on corporate insolvency, it expressly asks you to advise on the validity of the charges, rather than more generally on insolvency or liability matters. Make sure you focus your answer accordingly
- Nonetheless, there is a lot of overlap between company charges and corporate insolvency. Here you need to be aware in particular of the possibility of a liquidator invalidating a charge under IA 1986, either using s. 245 (floating charges only) or s. 239
- Don't forget to draw conclusions after explaining the relevant law

DIAGRAM ANSWER PLAN

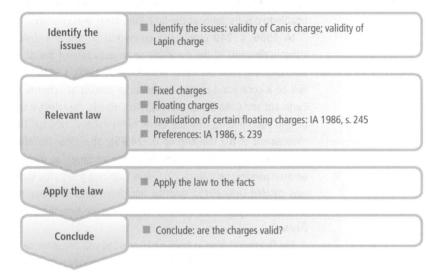

| Identify the issues | ■ Identify the issues: validity of Canis charge; validity of Lapin charge |

| Relevant law | ■ Fixed charges
■ Floating charges
■ Invalidation of certain floating charges: IA 1986, s. 245
■ Preferences: IA 1986, s. 239 |

| Apply the law | ■ Apply the law to the facts |

| Conclude | ■ Conclude: are the charges valid? |

SUGGESTED ANSWER

¹Indicate that you know why the issue matters

It is important for the liquidator of Gato Ltd to consider the validity of the charges, as this will determine whether Canis Ltd and Lapin Ltd are secured creditors (benefiting from priority over unsecured creditors in winding up) or unsecured creditors.[1] A charge may be invalidated on liquidation either because it has not been registered, or because a liquidator successfully challenges it under provisions of the **Insolvency Act 1986 (IA 1986)**. In this case both charges (in favour of Canis Ltd and Lapin plc) have been registered within 21 days of creation, so will not be void for non-registration by virtue of **Companies Act 2006, s. 859H**.[2] The validity of the charges therefore turns on the application of **IA 1986, s. 245** (which relates to floating charges only) and **IA 1986, s. 239** (which relates to preferences, which can include the creation of a charge, whether fixed or floating).

²This just confirms to the examiner that you realise why the mention of 21 days in the question is significant

Charge in Favour of Canis Ltd

The charge created in favour of Canis Ltd is a floating charge and therefore vulnerable to challenge by the liquidator under **IA 1986, s. 245**. This provides that floating charges created at a 'relevant time' are invalid, except to the extent that they are created for new consideration.

The relevant time is 12 months ending with the onset of insolvency (**s. 245(3)(b)**), provided that the company was unable to pay its debts within **IA 1986, s. 123** (or became unable to pay its debts as a consequence of the transaction) (**s. 245(4)**). However if the floating charge is given to a connected person this period is extended to two years (**s. 245(3)(a)**) and there is no need to show the company was unable to pay its debts at the time the charge was created.

IA 1986, s. 249 provides a connected person is a director (or shadow director) of the company or an associate of the director or the company, with associate defined in **IA 1986, s. 435**. Canis Ltd will be a connected person as the same person has control of both Canis Ltd and Gato Ltd (**s. 435(6)**). Accordingly, the relevant time will be two years ending with the 'onset of insolvency', which is the commencement of the winding up (**s. 245(5)**). It is clear therefore that the creation of the charge was at a relevant time,[3] as the company entered winding up (March 2016) less than two years after the charge was created (July 2015), and the liquidator does not have to show that Gato Ltd was unable to pay its debts at the time the charge was created.

[3] Think IRAC within each individual point: the issue (relevant time) has been identified, and the rule/law explained. The various elements of this have been applied to the facts, allowing the conclusion to be reached here

The floating charge in favour of Canis Ltd will therefore be invalid, except to the extent of the value of any (i) money paid or goods or services supplied to the company, (ii) discharge or reduction of any debt of the company, and (iii) interest payable, provided as consideration for and at the same time as, or after, the creation of the charge (**s. 245(2)**). Clearly in this case the money paid and the discharge of the debts by Canis Ltd were consideration for the charge, but were they paid 'at the same time or after the charge was created'?[4] They were paid after the agreement to give the charge, but before the charge was actually executed.

[4] It can sometimes be helpful to set out the issue as a question; not least as it reminds you that you've got to answer it

In *Re F & E Stanton Ltd* [1929] 1 Ch 180, applying an earlier equivalent section, a floating charge was held to be valid when the company had resolved to create the charge prior to the loan being advanced, even though the charge was not actually created until after all the money had been received. However, a much stricter approach was taken in relation to **IA 1986, s. 245** in *Re Shoe Lace Ltd; Power v Sharp Investments Ltd* [1994] 1 BCLC 111 (*Shoe Lace*) where the Court of Appeal declined to follow the earlier authority.

In *Shoe Lace*, the court considered the ordinary words used in **s. 245** and concluded that no monies paid prior to the creation of the charge could be taken into account, unless the interval between payment and creation of the charge was minimal (the example of a 'coffee break' was given by Sir Christopher Slade). Accordingly, although in *Shoe Lace*, loans had been made between April and early July in consideration of the proposed creation of a debenture, they could not be said to have been made at the same time as the creation of the charge, which was finally executed in late July. The reason for any delay was immaterial and the floating charge was invalid.

[5] Connecting discussion of the authority with your conclusion in this way makes it abundantly clear that you are actively applying the authority

Applying *Shoe Lace*,[5] it is clear that the liquidator can avoid Canis Ltd's floating charge under **s. 245(2)** as the charge was created only after the payment had been received by Gato Ltd. This means that Canis Ltd is no longer a secured creditor of Gato Ltd and the charged property is released for the benefit of unsecured creditors. Canis Ltd will be an unsecured creditor[6] and will have to claim alongside the other unsecured creditors.

[6] Show that you've thought about the consequence of invalidating the charge

Charge in Favour of Lapin plc

IA 1986, s. 245 will not apply in relation to the charge in favour of Lapin plc, even though the charge was created to secure an existing debt, as it is a fixed rather than floating charge. However the charge is potentially vulnerable as a preference under **IA 1986, s. 239**, which would open up a range of possible orders under **s. 241**, including the release of security.

A preference is where the company (at a relevant time) does something that puts a creditor (or guarantor or surety) in a better position that he would have been in in the event of the company's insolvent liquidation. Giving Lapin plc a fixed charge makes it a secured rather than unsecured creditor and so puts it in a much better position as it would be significantly higher up the creditor priority order on liquidation.[7]

[7] It is common for students to forget to identify explicitly what the 'preference' consists of

The relevant time for preferences is two years (for connected persons) and six months (for non-connected persons) ending with the onset of insolvency: **s. 240(1)(a)–(b)**, provided that the company was unable to pay its debts (within **IA 1986, s. 123**) at the time of the preference (whether or not the person is connected). Here Lapin plc does not seem to be a connected person,[8] so the relevant time is six months, ending with start of winding up. The charge will therefore fall within the relevant time, provided that the liquidator can show Gato Ltd was unable to pay its debts when the charge was created in October 2015.

[8] As there is nothing in the facts to suggest a connected person, you can assume there is no connection; there is no need to cover both possibilities in your answer

However the problem for the liquidator is that he must show that Gato Ltd in deciding to give the charge was influenced by a desire to prefer Lapin plc: **IA 1986, s. 239(5)**. This is presumed for connected persons (**s. 239(6)**) but as Lapin plc is not a connected person, the onus remains on the liquidator to prove the requisite 'desire'. In *Re MC Bacon Ltd* **[1990] BCLC 324 (*MC Bacon*)**, the desire to prefer was interpreted as being a subjective concept requiring that the company 'positively wished' to improve the creditor's position. Accordingly, in *MC Bacon* the court held there was no desire to prefer, because the company granted charges to its bank only because it was concerned that the bank would otherwise call in its debts and stop the company trading. Similarly in *Re Fairway Magazines Ltd* **[1992] BCC 924** the court held that the company's payment to its bank was motivated by commercial considerations and not by a desire to improve the bank's position. Accordingly creditor pressure operates as an effective defence to a preference, a position which has

[9] There is less scope for academic comment in a problem question than an essay, but you can still recognise particular issues as you go through the problem points

understandably been criticised as encouraging undesirable behaviour in creditors (eg Finch, V., Corporate Insolvency Law, 2nd edn, 2009),[9] but remains the law.

For Gato Ltd, the decision to give Lapin plc the fixed charge is clearly motivated by the desire to ensure further deliveries from their major supplier, rather than to improve Lapin plc's position. Even if Gato Ltd was fully aware that Lapin plc's position would be improved as a consequence of the action, this is not sufficient: *MC Bacon* makes clear that desire is distinct from intention, and a company is not to be taken as desiring all the consequences of its actions. The liquidator would thus have great difficulty in establishing the requisite desire to improve Lapin plc's position.

[10] As the individual issues have been concluded on fully within the answer, all that is needed in the conclusion is a final brief summary

Conclusion[10]

The floating charge in favour of Canis Ltd will be invalid under **IA 1986, s. 245** as created at a relevant time and after the payments made by Canis Ltd. The fixed charge in favour of Lapin plc is not worth challenging however. Although it was created at a relevant time and puts Lapin plc in a better position than it would have been in, it was created as a result of pressure from the chargeholder which negatives the desire to prefer required by **IA 1986, s. 239(5)**. Lapin plc's fixed charge will thus remain valid.

LOOKING FOR EXTRA MARKS?

- Make sure you deal with all elements of the relevant provisions: remember the relevant time and defences, as well as the key concepts
- Recognise and explore criticisms of the provisions, particularly where these are relevant to the issues arising in the question
- Examine the key cases on both provisions and don't forget to then apply them to the facts of the problem

TAKING THINGS FURTHER

- Atherton, S. and Mokal, R., 'Charges over chattels: issues in the fixed/floating jurisprudence' (2005) 26 Co Law 10
  Examines the features of fixed and floating charges, including the nature of the asset charged, and the degree of control over the charged asset. Also considers the process for distinguishing between types of charge and the relevance of post-contract conduct in this regard.
- Capper, D., 'Fixed charges over book debts—the future after *Brumark*' (2003) 24 Co Law 325
  Provides a brief examination of the floating charge's place in secured lending, including a review of various academic articles, before critiquing Brumark *itself and identifying particular areas of interest or concern.*

■ Graham, P., 'Registration of company charges' [2014] JBL 175

A useful article considering the 2013 reforms to the company charge registration system. Explores the historical background, the problems in the previous system, the changes made, and areas where reform has not been followed through.

■ Law Commission, 'Company security interests' (2005) Law Com No 296, Cm 6654

■ McCormack, G., 'The Law Commission Consultative Report on company security interests: an irreverent riposte' (2005) 68 MLR 286

Considers and critically discusses the Law Commission report in depth, including exploring doubts about whether wholesale change in this area is desirable.

■ Pennington, R., 'Recent developments in the law and practice relating to the creation of security for companies' indebtedness' (2009) 30 Co Law 163

A thoughtful consideration of a range of issues relating to fixed and floating charges.

■ Smart, P., 'Fixed or floating? *Siebe Gorman post-Brumark*' (2004) 25 Co Law 331

Some useful consideration of the Brumark *approach, but bear in mind that the article was written before the House of Lords decision in* Spectrum.

■ Wild, L., '*Spectrum* and *Leyland DAF*: the spectre of new claims' (2006) 27 Co Law 151

An article focusing on the potential consequence of major legal developments on past insolvency distributions (note that the outcome of Leyland DAF *was subsequently reversed by statute).*

Online Resource Centre   www.oxfordtextbooks.co.uk/orc/qanda/

Go online for extra essay and problem questions, a glossary of key terms, online versions of all the answer plans and audio commentary on how selected ones were put together, and a range of podcasts which include advice on exam and coursework technique and advice for other assessment methods.

11 Corporate Insolvency

ARE YOU READY?

- Corporate rescue, particularly administration and CVAs
- Winding up—petitions and 'inability to pay debts'
- Assets available for distribution to creditors
- The distribution hierarchy
- *Pari passu*
- Dispositions of property after the commencement of winding up
- Transactions at an undervalue
- Preferences
- Vulnerable floating charges
- Wrongful and fraudulent trading
- Disqualification of directors
- Connections with (in particular): corporate personality; directors; directors' duties; loan capital

KEY DEBATES

Debate: Corporate rescue and pre-pack administrations

An important recent development in corporate rescue has been pre-packaged administrations ('pre-packs'). These now make up a large proportion of administrations (which themselves make up a very large proportion of formal rescue procedures), but concerns about pre-packs have been expressed by a range of academics, practitioners, creditors, and politicians. Various modifications to practice have been proposed, including those of the government-commissioned Graham Review in 2014.

▶

Debate: Liability of directors on insolvent liquidation

How far should those who managed a company in insolvent liquidation bear personal responsibility for creditor losses? This obviously overlaps with fundamental concepts of separate corporate personality and limited liability. The law must tread a fine line between protecting creditors from irresponsible management, and avoiding discouraging entrepreneurship and responsible risk-taking. Some argue the risk of wrongful trading and disqualification can have a stifling effect, encouraging premature liquidation, while others see the statutory framework as an inadequate and ineffective response to directorial inadequacies.

QUESTION | 1

Midas plc is a successful publisher with several bestselling authors. Unfortunately problems (not of Midas plc's making) with printing facilities in India, where their books are produced, meant that the full autumn production was lost. The company was unable to find alternative printers and so lost significant sales over the lucrative Christmas period. The company has found it difficult to continue to meet its salary bills and rental for its UK warehouse.

Midas plc granted a floating charge over its undertaking to Gold Bank several years ago. At present it is unable to meet the interest payments on the bank loan. Once the immediate production problems are over, there is every expectation that the business should return to its normal profitable state.

Advise Midas plc and Gold Bank of the legal options available to resolve the problems.

CAUTION!

- As the question states that a return to profitability is likely, you should be considering alternative solutions to liquidation, focusing on CVAs and administration, rather than winding up itself

- Tailor your response according to the emphasis of your own course: it is more likely that you will be expected to show an outline knowledge of the rescue procedures and an appreciation of their different merits, rather than detailed knowledge of the legal processes and procedures relating to CVAs and administrations

DIAGRAM ANSWER PLAN

Identify the issues	■ Identify the problem ■ Identify the options available
Relevant law	■ Insolvency and the role of corporate rescue ■ Company Voluntary Arrangements ■ Administration ■ Pre-packaged administrations
Apply the law	■ Apply the law to the facts ■ Consider advantages and disadvantages of different options in the circumstances
Conclude	■ Conclude, advising on the best option in the circumstances

SUGGESTED ANSWER

Midas plc's financial difficulties appear too serious for informal agreements with creditors or management changes to make a difference. With Midas unable to pay its creditors, it risks being wound up under the **Insolvency Act 1986 (IA 1986), s. 122(1)(f)** if a creditor brings a winding up petition, despite the underlying strength of its business.

[1] This links an appreciation of the problems of insolvent liquidations with the purpose of corporate rescue

The impact of a corporate collapse can be significant, causing a 'ripple effect' of insolvencies amongst suppliers and customers, and wider financial and social harm. Accordingly the framework of 'corporate rescue' aims to maintain viable businesses[1] through offering alternatives to liquidation. As Finch has observed, modern insolvency law has seen 'a discernible move from pathology to preventative medicine' ('Corporate rescue: who is interested?' [2012] JBL 190)

There appear to be two main legal options here: a company voluntary arrangement (CVA) or administration. Administrative receivership is unlikely to be an option in this case, as Gold Bank's floating charge was almost certainly created after 15 September 2003[2] (the availability of administrative receivership was hugely reduced by **Enterprise Act 2002 (EA 2002)**). Other legal options, such as a Scheme of Arrangement under **Companies Act 2006, ss. 895–901**, are possible, but would be more complex and do not offer any obvious advantages in these circumstances. Accordingly, this answer

[2] Although you are not given the date of the floating charge, it is safe to make this assumption as no examiner will expect you to interpret 'several years ago' as stretching back to 2003

will focus on CVAs and administration. Both were introduced in **IA 1986** following the Cork Report (Report of the Insolvency Law Review Committee, 'Insolvency Law and Practice' (Cmnd 8558, 1982), which aimed to build a corporate rescue culture, and have been further enhanced by reforms in **EA 2002**.

CVA

A CVA (under **IA 1986, Part 1**) is, at first sight, a good option for a company such as Midas plc with a strong business but (hopefully) temporary financial difficulties. It would allow Midas plc to enter into a binding agreement with its creditors where they agree to delay or otherwise change the terms of payment (a scheme of arrangement), or to receive a smaller sum in full satisfaction of their debt (a composition of debt).[3]

> [3] This concisely establishes the essence of a CVA

To pursue a CVA the directors of Midas plc would make a proposal providing for a nominee (who will become the supervisor if the CVA is agreed, and must be a qualified insolvency practitioner) and explaining why a CVA is desirable. The nominee makes a report to the court and, if the report indicates that the CVA is desirable, will call meetings of the members and the creditors. The CVA will be effective (and binds all creditors with notice of and entitled to vote at the meeting) if approved by a 75 per cent majority of creditors (by value) and a simple majority of members (**IA 1986, s. 4**). There is no need for court approval, although the CVA can be challenged under **IA 1986, s. 6** if it unfairly prejudices the interests of a creditor, member, or contributory (eg *Mourant Trustees v Sixty UK Ltd* **[2011] BCLC 383**) or there is some material irregularity in relation to the meeting (eg *HMRC v Portsmouth FC* **[2010] EWHC 2013 (Ch)**). A successful CVA would mean Midas plc could continue to exist in its current form with its directors remaining in post.[4]

> [4] You could comment on the attraction of such an outcome for the directors, particularly when compared with other insolvency procedures

A major drawback to a CVA under **IA 1986, Part 1** is that it does not provide a moratorium during the pre-agreement period, so nothing stops a creditor from taking precipitate action against Midas plc (including bringing a winding up petition) before a CVA is approved. This obviously reduces the chances of successfully approving a CVA. A new-style CVA with a moratorium under **IA 1986, Sch A1** is only available to small private companies so is not available to Midas plc (and has not proved very popular in practice in any event). If Midas plc wanted to pursue a CVA with the benefit of a moratorium, it could do so under the 'wrapper' of an administration,[5] but this would obviously add to the costs of the rescue process.

> [5] Structurally this leads in nicely to the next point

Administration

Administrations (under **IA 1986, Sch B1**) have proved much more popular than CVAs in practice. Administrations were intended to reflect the best elements of administrative receivership (an outside expert brought in to run the company to maximise value) but acting for creditors collectively rather than for the chargeholder alone. Their use was further encouraged by reforms in **EA 2002**.

An administrator must be a qualified insolvency practitioner. He can be appointed by the court (under an administration order), or (following **EA 2002**) out-of-court by the holder of a qualifying floating charge or by the company or its directors. As a qualifying floating charge holder (ie with a charge over the whole, or substantially the whole, of a company's undertaking, **IA 1986, Sch B1, para 14**) Gold Bank could appoint an administrator out of court, or Midas plc's directors could do so, by filing notice of intention to appoint an administrator with the court, followed by notice of appointment. An interim moratorium takes effect when notice of intention is filed and becomes permanent (for the duration of the administration) when the appointment takes effect.

Once appointed the administrator sets out proposals for achieving the purpose of the administration—one of the three objectives of administration (**IA 1986, Sch B1, para 3**), namely (a) rescuing the company as a going concern, (b) achieving a better result for the company's creditors than on a winding up, or (c) realising property to make a distribution to one or more secured or preferential creditors. Objective (a) should be pursued unless the administrator thinks it is not reasonably practicable to achieve that aim or objective (b) would achieve a better result for the company's creditors as a whole. Objective (c) can only be pursued if neither of the first two objectives is reasonably practicable and it would not unnecessarily harm the interests of creditors as a whole.

[6] Having established the aims of administration, this paragraph now applies those aims to the case at hand

The administrator would therefore have to consider whether Midas plc itself can be rescued[6] (which may involve seeking a CVA within the administration), or whether there are other options, including selling off Midas plc's business (rescuing the business, but not the company itself) to maximise returns for creditors. The proposals should be sent to the registrar, creditors, and members and the administrator should call a creditors' meeting to consider whether to accept or reject the proposal (or accept a modified version, if the administrator approves)—a simple majority by value is sufficient. The administrator then takes over the management of the company, carrying out his functions with a view to achieving the administration objectives (and must apply to terminate the administration if he believes the purpose cannot be achieved).

Pre-pack Administration

[7] Pre-packs are a very topical issue in corporate insolvency so it is sensible to consider them explicitly, as well as administration more generally

If the business of Midas plc is going to have to be sold, the directors and Gold Bank may wish to pursue a pre-packaged administration (a 'pre-pack').[7] These are increasingly popular, making up around 50 per cent of administrations. The sale of the business is arranged prior to the administration following discussion between the directors, the proposed administrator, and the proposed purchaser (often a vehicle controlled by the directors—'phoenix' pre-packs), and usually the main creditor, here Gold Bank.[8] The sale is completed immediately after the company enters administration, without consultation with other creditors.

Pre-packs have been widely criticised for avoiding the statutory process (as there is no proposal and no creditors' meeting) and for lack of scrutiny and independence. Although the courts have recognised the criticisms (*Re Kayley Vending* [2011] 1 BCLC 114; *Re Hellas Telecommunications* [2010] BCC 295), they have accepted the validity of pre-packs (*Re Transbus International* [2004] 1 WLR 2654; *DKLL Solicitors v HMRC* [2008] 1 BCLC 112). Pre-packs can maximise value for creditors by allowing a quick sale avoiding negative publicity to the most likely buyer, but creditors can feel overlooked. Some protection is offered through Statement of Insolvency Practice 16 (SIP 16) which requires an administrator to, inter alia, provide information to creditors. SIP 16 was updated recently to reflect the Graham Report proposals, including the new 'pre-pack pool' designed to provide an independent opinion on proposed pre-pack sales.[9] In practice, provided the requirements of SIP 16 are substantially complied with, a pre-pack sale is unlikely to be successfully challenged in the courts (*Re Halliwells LLP* [2011] 1 BCLC 345).

Conclusion

Midas plc or Gold Bank should appoint an administrator over the company.[10] While a CVA is more likely to result in the rescue of Midas plc itself by allowing the breathing space necessary for the company to survive, if a CVA is desirable, pursuing this within administration should increase the prospects of success. Alternatively the administrator could sell off the viable business, with the administrator distributing the purchase money within the administration (dissolution following under **IA 1986, Sch B1, para 84** without need for intervening liquidation). This would provide a swift resolution to the financial difficulty while ensuring the business can continue free of its current financial burden. If this is considered to be the best option then a pre-pack administration should be considered but the insolvency practitioner will need to balance the benefits and drawbacks of a quick sale.

---

[8] A quick reference to the characters in the question reassures the examiner that you are still focusing on the facts

[9] Show your awareness of recent developments in the area

[10] Giving clear advice is always welcomed, so don't hold back even if you are worried the examiner might come to a different conclusion

---

 LOOKING FOR EXTRA MARKS?

- Use some of the many critical academic articles and empirical research papers (particularly relating to pre-packs) to enhance and support the points you make
- You could make reference to real life examples of corporate collapses or rescues, or insolvency statistics, to highlight the use of particular provisions
- Show an awareness of ongoing debates and reforms in this area

QUESTION | 2

Critically assess the circumstances in which a creditor can bring a petition to wind up a company and the possible reasons why such a petition might be rejected.

CAUTION!

- Balance your essay carefully: if you spend too long looking at the grounds for a petition you may run out of time before adequately dealing with rejection/dismissal of a petition

- Focus on the main issues (cash flow test, balance sheet test, disputed debts, cross-claims) but don't forget to at least mention other points such as statutory demands and improper purpose.

DIAGRAM ANSWER PLAN

> Introduction: creditor petitions and deemed inability to pay debts

> Statutory demands and failed execution of judgment: s. 123(1)(a)-(b)

> Cash flow test: s. 123(1)(e)

> Balance sheet test: s. 123(2)

> Disputed debts and cross-claims

> Other grounds for rejection: settlement, improper purpose, creditor wishes

> Conclusion: linking the two elements of the question

SUGGESTED ANSWER

[1] This introduction briefly establishes the groundwork for the discussion, so that the bulk of the essay can get straight into the detail

Creditors may petition for the compulsory winding up of a company under the **Insolvency Act 1986 (IA 1986), s. 122(1)(f)** on the ground that it is unable to pay its debts. **IA 1986, s. 123** deems a company to be unable to pay its debts in four circumstances: (i) failure to pay a statutory demand for £750 or more (**s. 123(1)(a)**); (ii) failed execution of judgment (**s. 123(1)(b)**); (iii) inability to pay debts as they fall due (**s. 123(1)(e)**), and (iv) assets less than liabilities (**s. 123(2)**).[1] This essay will examine those tests to assess the circumstances in which a creditor may bring a winding up petition, and then consider the various reasons why a creditor petition may be rejected.

Statutory Demand and Failed Execution of Judgment

The tests in **IA 1986, s. 123(1)(a)–(b)** are very specific. The statutory demand under **s. 123(1)(a)** requires a creditor to serve a written demand for payment (for a due debt that is currently payable: *JSF Finance v Akma Solutions* **[2001] 2 BCLC 307**) at the company's registered office. If after three weeks the company has failed to pay the debt (which must be at least the statutory minimum of £750) or to secure or compound for it to the creditor's satisfaction, it is presumed unable to pay its debts. For a creditor the downside to this test is the element of delay.[2]

The second option, under **IA 1986, s. 123(1)(b)** is where a creditor has a judgment or court order against the company, has tried to enforce this through the court but has not been paid. This requires the petitioner to have gone through the process of obtaining judgment and attempting execution and so is unattractive to most creditors. Because of the downsides to the two specific tests, many creditors prefer to use the general tests under **IA 1986, s. 123(1)(e) and (2)**.

Cash Flow Test

The test under **s. 123(1)(e)**—that a company is unable to pay its debts as they fall due—is known as the cash flow test.[3] A company's failure to pay an undisputed debt is in itself evidence that a company cannot pay its debts as they fall due and so can found a creditor's petition. This was seen in *Taylor's Industrial Flooring Ltd v M & H Plant Hire (Manchester) Ltd* **[1990] BCLC 216** where the Court of Appeal rejected a claim that such a process was abusive. A company can be wound up on this basis even if it has a surplus of assets over liabilities, as made clear in *Cornhill Insurance v Improvement Services* **[1986] BCLC 26**. Crucially, the petition must relate to an undisputed debt: disputed debts will be considered later.[4]

Under this head the court is entitled to consider debts that will fall due in the 'reasonably near' future. Quite how far the court will look depends on the nature of the business: *Re Cheyne Finance Ltd* **[2008] 1 BCLC 741** and *BNY Corporate Trustee Services Ltd v Eurosail-UK plc* **[2013] UKSC 28**.[5]

Balance Sheet Test

Section 123(2) looks at whether the value of the company's assets is less than the amount of its liabilities, including contingent and prospective liabilities—the balance sheet test.[6] This is usually fairly

---

[2] Even a brief comment indicates that you are not simply setting out the law, but thinking about its significance

[3] The cash flow test is all about whether a company can actually pay its debts as demanded, regardless of whether it has an excess of assets over liabilities

[4] You could happily deal with disputed debts at this point, but as the essay splits quite neatly into 'grounds for petition' and 'reasons for rejection', it makes a bit more sense to leave this until later

[5] If you had time you could add some more detail about these cases and judgments

[6] The balance sheet test means that a company can be deemed 'unable to pay its debts' even if it is paying its debts as they fall due, provided its liabilities exceed its assets

straightforward to apply, but in cases of marginal solvency the valuation of assets and liabilities can become critical. The risk with this test is that even a company with few financial difficulties and a healthy outlook could be technically 'balance sheet insolvent' at some points in its life, particularly when it starts out.

In *BNY Corporate Trustee Services Ltd v Eurosail-UK*, the Supreme Court stated the test simply required the court to make a judgment as to whether the company cannot reasonably be expected to meet its liabilities, bearing in mind that the more distant those liabilities, the harder it will be to establish this. The Supreme Court rejected the view of Neuberger LJ in the Court of Appeal that it required a demonstration that a company had reached the point of no return (or 'the end of the road').

Disputed Debts

In order for a creditor to petition, the debt relied on under **IA 1986, s. 123(1)(e)** must be undisputed. Two reasons have been given for this:[7] first, someone whose debt is justifiably disputed is not in a position to present a petition as he is not established as a creditor (*Mann v Goldstein* [1968] 1 WLR 1091) and, secondly, the winding up jurisdiction is not intended for the resolution of disputes between parties (*Re Selectmove Ltd* [1995] 1 WLR 474).

For the petition to be rejected, it is necessary for the company to establish that there is a genuine and bona fide dispute, that the company honestly believes this to be the case and there are reasonable or substantial grounds for this belief. The court should not conduct a lengthy or elaborate hearing on this matter: *Tallington Lakes Ltd v Ancasta International Boat Sales Ltd* [2012] EWCA Civ 1712. If this is established it has been stated that the dismissal of the petition is not discretionary but compulsory: *Re Bayoil SA* [1999] 1 WLR 147. Nonetheless the court has allowed a petition to proceed even with a bona fide dispute as to the amount of the debt if the company clearly owes money to the petitioner in excess of the statutory minimum: *Re Tweeds Garages Ltd* [1962] 1 Ch 406. Furthermore, *Re GBI Investments* [2010] 2 BCLC 624 indicated a petition might also, exceptionally, be allowed to proceed notwithstanding a dispute as to the debt if injustice would otherwise result. This would seem to be contrary to the first reason given for rejecting disputed debts (unless the petitioner is a creditor, he has no standing to petition),[8] but is perhaps justified when winding up is viewed as a discretionary and collective creditor remedy.

Cross-claims

Even where a debt is due and not disputed, a petition may be dismissed where the company has a 'genuine and serious' (*Re Bayoil SA*) cross-claim against the petitioner that exceeds the company's debt to the petitioner. This allows the court to dismiss the petition (it remains

[7] It is helpful to give these reasons: not only does it show you understand the justification for the courts' approach, it also gives you a focus for later comment

[8] Think PEA: having made the point (about petitions based on disputed debts occasionally being allowed to proceed) and evidenced it, it can be assessed by commenting on whether the reasoning is valid or not

a matter for the court's discretion) even if the company had been in a position to litigate their claim but had chosen not to (*Montgomery v Wanda Modes Ltd* [2002] **1 BCLC 289**, doubting *Re Bayoil SA* on this point). This approach recognises that even if the petitioner is nominally a creditor, it would normally be unjust to wind up a company in such circumstances, particularly as set-off is compulsory once the company is wound up (**Insolvency Rules 1986 (IR 1986), r. 4.90**).[9]

[9] This takes the opportunity to link a point connected to creditor claims, to a question ostensibly only about petitions

Other Grounds for Rejecting a Petition

If the debt that is the subject of the petition has been paid by the time of the hearing then the petition will be rejected—the petitioner is no longer a creditor. However, the court has the ability to substitute another creditor to the petition in certain circumstances (**IR 1986, r. 4.19**), and so the petition may continue regardless of payment of the initial petition debt.

Another important reason for rejecting a petition is where it is brought for an improper purpose. The courts have held that a petitioner must not act in order to obtain some private advantage or for some ulterior motive. For example in *Re Leigh Estates Ltd* [1994] **BCC 292** the court rejected a petition brought against a company in administration where the petitioner brought the petition to put themselves in a stronger position—winding up is a collective remedy and petitions should be brought for the benefit of creditors generally. However, *Mann v Goldstein* made clear that the mere fact that a petitioner has acted with 'personal hostility' or hope of some indirect advantage is not in itself an abuse of process.

Finally, the court may reject a petition where the creditors disagree as to whether the company should be wound up. For example in *Re ABC Coupler & Engineering Ltd* [1961] **1 WLR 243** a petition was rejected where other creditors opposed the making of a winding up order and the court found they were reasonable in wanting the company to continue as there were good prospects of payment in due course. While the views of the majority of creditors will be highly influential, the court may still choose to make a winding up order (*Re P & J MacRae Ltd* [1961] **1 WLR 229**); it remains a matter for the court's discretion.

Conclusion[10]

[10] As the essay question itself did not provide much of a 'handle' for a thesis, the conclusion creates a link between the two halves of the question to show further understanding of the points raised throughout the essay

The circumstances in which a creditor may bring a petition and the grounds for rejecting a petition are connected in several ways, particularly through the notion of disputed debts. While statute gives creditors the ability to petition to wind up a company, a creditor must also be careful not to abuse the process, and ultimately winding up remains in the court's discretion. A creditor's ability to petition must be balanced against the need to act fairly to the company and respect the collective nature of the winding up jurisdiction.

LOOKING FOR EXTRA MARKS?

■ Comment on the significance of the points you make, and link between them, to avoid the answer being too descriptive

■ Recognise where cases have taken different approaches, and try to reflect the most recent authorities

■ Use your wider understanding of insolvency and liquidation to add depth to the discussion

QUESTION | 3

A winding up order was made on 30 April 2015 against Hebejebe Ltd, following a creditor's petition which was presented to the court on 8 April 2015. Lara has been appointed liquidator. The creditors of Hebejebe Ltd include:

i. Wizzerd Bank, which is owed £250,000 and has a fixed charge (duly registered) over Hebejebe Ltd's freehold premises. Hebejebe Ltd's premises have been valued at £200,000

ii. Pocus Finance plc which provided an initial £10,000 loan to Hebejebe Ltd on 2 April 2014, and then a further loan of £5,000 on 20 April 2014. Hebejebe Ltd granted Pocus Finance plc a floating charge (which was duly registered) to secure the full £15,000 on 20 April 2014

iii. Hebejebe Ltd's senior employees who received no pay during the company's last three months of trading

iv. HM Revenue and Customs which is owed £30,000 in respect of unpaid PAYE and national insurance payments

v. Abracadabra, a trade creditor, who is owed £2,000. Abracadabra had been owed £3,000 but Hebejebe Ltd paid off £1,000 of this debt on 12 April 2015 as Abracadabra refused to continue to supply essential raw materials until the debt was reduced. Hebejebe Ltd would have had to cease trading immediately had these materials not been supplied.

Advise Lara on how the company's assets should be distributed to the creditors in light of the information above. Lara has incurred costs and expenses of £10,000.

CAUTION!

■ Make sure you understand the creditor priority list and where different claimants fit within this. You need to be able to identify all the claimants and the nature of their claim and slot them into place

■ Keep an eye on any dates in insolvency questions—they can be crucial to whether some provisions apply or not

■ Watch out for any surrounding issues as it is easy for questions like this to add in any number of other insolvency topics

DIAGRAM ANSWER PLAN

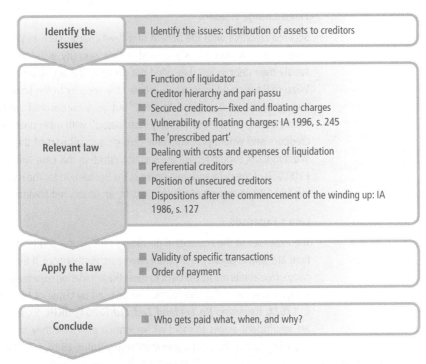

Identify the issues	■ Identify the issues: distribution of assets to creditors
Relevant law	■ Function of liquidator ■ Creditor hierarchy and pari passu ■ Secured creditors—fixed and floating charges ■ Vulnerability of floating charges: IA 1996, s. 245 ■ The 'prescribed part' ■ Dealing with costs and expenses of liquidation ■ Preferential creditors ■ Position of unsecured creditors ■ Dispositions after the commencement of the winding up: IA 1986, s. 127
Apply the law	■ Validity of specific transactions ■ Order of payment
Conclude	■ Who gets paid what, when, and why?

SUGGESTED ANSWER

As liquidator, Lara's function is 'to secure that the assets are got in, realised and distributed to the company's creditors and, if there is a surplus, to the persons entitled to it' (**Insolvency Act 1986 (IA 1986), s. 143(1)**). Accordingly, having gathered in all the assets belonging to the company (which may be swelled by claims in respect of, eg preferences (**IA 1986, s. 239**), transactions at an undervalue (**IA 1986, s. 239**), or wrongful trading (**IA 1986, s. 214**)), she must distribute the assets according to a strict order of priority. Creditors must submit a proof of debt in order to claim in the liquidation, and it will be assumed that all have done so.[1]

The basic order for priority of payment is as follows,[2] although it will be seen shortly that the situation is more complex than at first appears:

- Secured creditors with a fixed charge
- Expenses of liquidation
- Preferential creditors
- Secured creditors with a floating charge
- Unsecured/ordinary creditors
- Deferred creditors
- Members

[1] Most courses would not expect you to know the rules of proof of debt, so it is fine to make this assumption

[2] It isn't usually good practice to set out a list or bullet points in an essay, but this helps to establish both the basic principles and the framework of your essay

The various claims in the question will be considered in the order they might be expected to appear in this list.

Fixed Charge Holders

Secured creditors with the benefit of a fixed charge, such as Wizzerd Bank, are in a strong position, and if their security is sufficient to satisfy their debt in full they need not prove in the liquidation at all. Wizzerd Bank could choose to surrender the security to the liquidator and prove as an unsecured creditor,[3] but as an unsecured creditor Wizzerd Bank would rank rateably ('*pari passu*') with other unsecured creditors and would probably only recover a small part of the debt. Wizzerd Bank should realise the security, which in this case will cover £200,000 of the debt and then prove in the liquidation for the remaining £50,000, in respect of which it will be an unsecured creditor.

[3] In more unusual cases a secured creditor might choose to give up the security, for example if there were other prior secured creditors—then they might be better off claiming as an unsecured creditor and sharing in the prescribed part. That is not the case here

Lara's Expenses

The expenses of the liquidation (including Lara's costs and remuneration) are paid in priority to all other payments. Furthermore, if the company's free assets are insufficient to meet the liquidation expenses then assets subject to a floating charge can be used by virtue of **IA 1986, s. 176ZA** (reversing *Re Leyland Daf Ltd* [2004] **UKHL 9**). If there are insufficient assets to meet all liquidation expenses they are paid according to the order set out in **Insolvency Rules 1986, r. 4.218.**[4]

[4] Don't waste your time setting this priority order out unless you have covered it on your course and there is something in the question to indicate that all the costs/expenses might not be met

Preferential Creditors

Preferential debts are those debts that statute provides are paid in priority to other debts, other than the expenses of winding up (**IA 1986, s. 175**) and are found in **IA 1986, Sch 6**. The main preferential debts are unpaid employee remuneration relating to the four months prior to the liquidation (to a maximum of £800 per employee), accrued holiday pay, and loans used specifically for paying employee remuneration. Accordingly the unpaid senior employees can claim as preferential creditors but only for £800 each—if they are owed more they will need to claim for this as unsecured creditors. Unpaid PAYE and national insurance are no longer preferential debts after the **Enterprise Act 2002** which reduced the category of preferential debts in order to benefit unsecured creditors. HM Revenue and Customs will, therefore, not be a preferential creditor.[5]

[5] A common mistake is to assume that HM Revenue and Customs is still a preferential creditor

If the company's free assets are insufficient to pay the preferential debts, then property subject to a floating charge can be used (**s. 175(2)**). Should there be insufficient assets to meet all the preferential debts in full, then preferential creditors are paid rateably (*pari passu*).

Floating Charge Holders

Pocus Finance claims to have a floating charge securing £15,000. However, a floating charge created at a relevant time is only valid to the extent it is created in consideration for money paid or goods or services supplied 'at the same time as, or after, the creation of the charge' (**IA 1986, s. 245**). Here the first £10,000 of the debt was provided before the creation of the charge and so would be invalid (*Re Shoe Lace Ltd; Power v Sharp* [1994] 1 BCLC 111).

The relevant time for a person who is not connected with the company (**IA 1986, s. 249** and **s. 435**) is 12 months ending with the onset of insolvency (**s. 245(3)**), provided the company is unable to pay its debts within the meaning of **IA 1986, s. 123**. In a compulsory liquidation the 'onset of insolvency' is the date of presentation of the petition, so this charge has been created just within the 12-month period, but Lara would need to check whether the company was unable to pay its debts at that time. If so then the floating charge is likely to be valid only in relation to the £5,000, leaving Pocus Finance to claim as an unsecured creditor for the remaining £10,000. If Hebejebe Ltd was able to pay its debts as at 20 April 2014 then it would not be a relevant time and the floating charge will be valid for the full £15,000.[6] Although providing security for an existing debt (as here) can also amount to a preference under **IA 1986, s. 239**, Lara cannot use **s. 239** as the charge was created outside the relevant time of six months.

As has been seen, even where Pocus Finance has the benefit of a floating charge, it may lose some of the benefit of that security if the company's free assets are insufficient to meet the liquidation expenses and preferential debts. In addition, following the **Enterprise Act 2002**, a 'prescribed part' of the realisations of assets subject to a floating charge is reserved for unsecured creditors unless disapplied (in exceptional circumstances) by the liquidator or the court (**IA 1986, s. 176A**). The prescribed part is 50 per cent of net property under £10,000 and 20 per cent over this, to a maximum of £600,000.

Unsecured Creditors

Unsecured creditors share *pari passu* in the remaining assets of the company[7] and the prescribed part, although secured creditors with a shortfall (here Wizzerd Bank and Pocus Finance) cannot share in the prescribed part (*Re Airbase Ltd* [2008] EWHC 124).

Abracadabra is also an unsecured creditor, but her position is complicated by the company's payment of £1,000 after presentation of the petition.[8] Dispositions of the company's property after commencement of the winding up (ie the presentation of the petition: **IA 1986, s. 129**) are void under **IA 1986, s. 127** unless validated by the court. Disposition is defined widely (*Re J. Leslie Engineering* [1976] 1 WLR 292) and so prima facie Lara can recover the £1,000 from Abracadabra, and Abracadabra would have to prove as an unsecured creditor for the full £3,000.

However, the court is likely to be willing to validate the payment retrospectively. In *Re Gray's Inn Construction* [1980] 1 WLR 711 the court indicated that a payment made in good faith in the ordinary

[6] As sufficient facts aren't given in the question, the two alternative outcomes are given. You could assume that the company could (or couldn't) pay its debts at that time, and conclude accordingly—but you need to state expressly that you've made that assumption

[7] Always try to get a reference to *pari passu* into an insolvency distribution question. In an essay you could be asked to consider the notion in more depth

[8] It is essential to keep an eye on the dates (and remember how the commencement of the winding up is backdated), or you'll miss this point

course of business, where the parties were unaware of the petition and there was no intention to prefer the creditor, is likely to be validated. These factors seem to apply to Abracadabra and this conclusion is supported by *Denney v John Hudson* **[1992] BCLC 901**[9] where a good faith payment of a debt to a fuel supplier in order to ensure continued trading was validated.

[9] Remember to apply the law to the case at hand, and support your conclusion with case authority where you can

Conclusion

It appears that Wizzerd Bank can realise its security to recover £20,000 but will need to claim the outstanding £50,000 as an unsecured creditor. Lara's costs and expenses including her remuneration will be paid first out of the free assets of the company, and out of the floating charge realisations if necessary. Next come the preferential creditors, including the senior employees to a maximum of £800 each but not including HM Revenue and Customs. Pocus Finance's floating charge could be entirely valid (if the company was able to pay its debts as at the date of the charge) or may be valid only for the 'new debt' of £5,000. To the extent that the debt is not secured by the charge, Pocus Finance will have to claim as an unsecured creditor. So far as the charge is valid, property subject to it will have the prescribed part set aside for distribution amongst the unsecured creditors (other than Wizzerd Bank and Pocus Finance). Abracadabra faces having to return the £1,000 to Lara as a void disposition, but could apply to the court for validation and has quite a strong case. Depending on the outcome of that validation application, Abracadabra will claim either £2,000 or £3,000 as an unsecured creditor.

Having paid the expenses of the liquidation, the preferential debts and the claim of any valid floating charge holder, Lara must distribute the remaining assets of the company *pari passu* amongst the unsecured creditors. If there were any assets remaining (which is improbable in an insolvent liquidation), she should then pay any deferred debts (which include interest on proved debts: **IA 1986, s. 189**) and pay any surplus to members. Once the winding up is complete Lara should apply to have Hebejebe Ltd dissolved (**IA 1986, s. 205**).[10]

[10] Having summarised the main points from the essay (slotting everything into the payment hierarchy) it is time to finish off the question (and the company)

LOOKING FOR EXTRA MARKS

- A clear conclusion (or a separate summary prior to a shorter conclusion) is particularly valuable in a question like this as it shows you can fit all the elements together and links back to your starting list

- Reflect on more practical matters, such as how employees can make claims under the Redundancy Payments Scheme, or when the prescribed part might be disapplied

- Recognise where you don't have quite enough evidence to conclude, and offer alternative conclusions if appropriate (eg whether the floating charge was created within a relevant time)

'On the liquidation of a company, all of the assets belonging to the company at the commencement of the liquidation are available for the creditors.'

Discuss.

CAUTION!

- At first sight this appears quite an innocuous question, but working out what assets belong to the company and what assets are available to creditors (and what is the 'commencement of the liquidation') requires you to cover a lot of ground

- Matters included in this question, such as transaction avoidance, disclaimer, and disposition of property, more commonly appear in problem questions, but you need to be able to deal with them in essays too

DIAGRAM ANSWER PLAN

Introduction: context of question and commencement of winding up

▼

Assets unavailable for distribution: including trusts, retention of title, security, set off, disclaimer

▼

Swelling the assets: including post-petition dispositions of property, transactions at undervalue, preferences

▼

Conclusion: summary and comment

SUGGESTED ANSWER

The liquidator's function includes distributing the company's assets to its creditors (**Insolvency Act 1986 (IA 1986), s. 143(1)**) but identifying what assets are available for distribution is sometimes difficult. Some assets that at first sight appear to belong to the company are not in fact available to the general creditors. Conversely, the asset pool may be swollen by the liquidator recovering assets previously disposed of.[1]

The commencement of the liquidation may be backdated by statute, which can be important in identifying what assets are available. The

[1] Identify the two halves of the essay—reduction of available assets, and swelling of available assets

commencement of a voluntary winding up is the date of the passing of the resolution to wind up (**IA 1986, s. 86**), while the commencement of a compulsory winding up is the date of the presentation of the petition (**IA 1986, s. 129(2)**) except where the company is already in voluntary winding up: **s. 129(1)**.

Assets Unavailable for Distribution

Assets that do not pass to the liquidator include property held as trustee for another. In *Re Kayford Ltd* **[1975] 1 All ER 604**, customer deposits paid into a special account pending delivery of goods were held on trust and so had to be returned to the customers (see also *Barclays Bank v Quistclose Investments Ltd* **[1970] AC 567**).[2]

In addition, property in the company's possession under a contract containing a valid reservation of title or '*Romalpa*' clause (*Aluminium Industrie Vaassen v Romalpa Aluminium* **[1976] 1 WLR 676**) does not pass if the goods remain identifiable and removable (*Hendy Lennox v Grahame Puttick* **[1984] 1 WLR 485**). The contract may also validly include an 'all-monies' clause, reserving title until all outstanding debts between the parties have been met (*Clough Mill v Martin* **[1985] BCLC 64**).

Often many of a company's valuable assets are subject to a fixed charge. These can be realised by the chargeholder to meet their own debt without involvement of the liquidator, so will not be available for distribution to other creditors.[3] While assets subject to a floating charge also offer the benefit of security to the chargeholder, not only are these charges vulnerable to challenge by the liquidator under **IA 1986, s. 245** unless given for fresh consideration, but a significant part of the realisations of these assets will usually be available for distribution to unsecured creditors through the prescribed part (**IA 1986, s. 176A**). Accordingly while assets subject to a fixed charge will not be available to general creditors (unless the charge can be challenged as a preference under **IA 1986, s. 239**, for example), assets subject to a floating charge may be at least partially available to the company's general creditors.

A company's assets include debts owing to it, and a liquidator will normally seek to recover any money owing to the company. But not all sums due are recoverable by the liquidator. If an individual both owes money to the company and is owed money by the company, these sums must be set off (**Insolvency Rules 1986, r. 4.90**) and only the balance can be claimed by the liquidator (or proved in the liquidation).

More positively for general creditors, liquidators may wish to reject onerous property belonging to the company. Liquidators have a right of disclaimer in respect of unprofitable contracts, property that is unsaleable or not readily saleable, or property giving rise to liability to pay money or perform any other onerous act: **IA 1986, s. 178**.

[2] You could explore how the *Quistclose* trust enables a lender to reclaim a loan given for a frustrated purpose in full, rather than claiming *pari passu* with other unsecured creditors

[3] Security is the prime reason why so few of the company's assets are available for the general body of creditors

Disclaimer terminates the rights, interests, and liabilities of the company and victims of disclaimer must prove as creditors.

Swelling the Assets

[4] This sentence provides a structural link between the two parts of the essay

While not all assets apparently belonging to the company are available to the liquidator, several statutory provisions allow the liquidator to recover previously disposed of property.[4]

Under **IA 1986, s. 127** dispositions of the company's property after commencement of the winding up are void unless validated by the court. This allows the liquidator to recover property disposed of

[5] This is the main reason why the backdating of the commencement of the winding up can be so important (it also pushes back the relevant times for IA 1986, ss. 239–45)

after presentation of the winding up petition,[5] unless the court validates the disposition. The court will normally approve bona fide payments in the ordinary course of business where the parties were unaware of the petition and the payment does not seek to prefer the creditor: *Re Gray's Inn Construction Ltd* **[1980] 1 WLR 711**, but it remains a matter for the court's discretion.

Liquidators may also avoid transactions at an undervalue occurring within a relevant time: **s. 238**. The relevant time is two years prior to commencement of the winding up provided the company at the time was unable to pay its debts (within **s. 123**, presumed for transactions with connected persons): **s. 240(2)**. A company enters into a transaction at an undervalue if it makes a gift, receives no consideration, or receives consideration significantly less than the value of the consideration supplied by the company (**IA 1986, s. 238(4)**). The last of these requires the balancing of consideration received and given and the liquidator must usually establish the value of any consideration (*Phillips v Brewin Dolphin* **[2001] 1 WLR 143**). The transaction will not be avoided if the company entered into the transaction in good faith with reasonable grounds for believing it would benefit the company: **s. 238(5)**, but this defence must be established by the person relying on it (*Re Barton Manufacturing Ltd* **[1999] 1 BCLC 740**).

Liquidators can also challenge preferences under **IA 1986, s. 239**—where the company does something within the relevant time that puts creditors (or guarantors or sureties) into a better position in the event of the company's insolvent liquidation than they would otherwise have been. The relevant time is two years for connected persons and six months for outsiders (**s. 240(1)(a)–(b)**), and the company must have been unable to pay its debts. Preferences are only voidable where the company was motivated by a desire to prefer the individual (**s. 239(5)**), which requires a positive wish to improve their position (*Re MC Bacon Ltd* **[1990] BCLC 324**) but this desire to prefer is presumed for connected persons: **s. 239(6)**.

[6] This is crucial to link to the focus of the essay ie the assets available to creditors

In respect of transactions at an undervalue and preferences, the court may make a variety of orders, including a retransfer of property, repayment to the liquidator, or revival of guarantees: **s. 241**.[6]

Third parties who are bona fide purchasers for value are protected: **s. 241(2)** and **(2A)**. Proceeds of a successful claim are held for the unsecured creditors: *Re Yagerphone Ltd* **[1935] 1 Ch 392**.

As mentioned earlier, liquidators can use **IA 1986, s. 245** to invalidate floating charges created other than in relation to money paid, goods or services supplied, or discharge or reduction of the company's debts at the same time or after creation of the charge. The relevant time for creation is one year for non-connected persons provided the company was unable to pay its debts: **s. 245(4)**. For connected persons, the period is two years and is not conditional upon the company being unable to pay its debts. The effect of **s. 245** can be seen In *Re Shoe Lace Ltd* **[1994] 1 BCLC 111**, where a charge executed in July, relating to loans made between April and early July, was invalidated. Banks operating a current account have some protection from **s. 245**. *Re Yeovil Glove Co Ltd* **[1965] Ch 148** held (thanks to the rule in *Clayton's Case* **(1816) 1 Mer 572**, whereby credits to a current account discharge debts in the order in which they were incurred) the honouring of cheques after the creation of a charge were new advances even when the overdraft remained virtually unchanged. When **s. 245** does apply, assets otherwise subject to security are instead available for distribution to general creditors.[7]

Liquidators may also apply to set aside extortionate credit transactions within the three years prior to the making of the winding up order: **IA 1986, s. 244**. The court has a range of possible orders including setting aside or varying the transaction, refunding sums paid by the company, and surrendering security.

Liquidators (and victims) can also challenge transactions defrauding creditors made at any time—transactions at an undervalue made with the aim of putting assets beyond the reach of a creditor or otherwise prejudicing their interests: **IA 1986, s. 423(3)**. Possible court orders are similar to those in **s. 241**: **s. 425**.[8]

Conclusion

A company's assets at the commencement of liquidation may be much smaller than might first appear because of security interests, and devices such as trusts and retention of title clauses. This is balanced to some extent by the ability of liquidators to seek to recover assets disposed of both before and after presentation of the winding up petition. In addition the liquidator may be able to claim contributions from company directors, for example by using misfeasance proceedings (**s. 212**) or fraudulent or wrongful trading (**ss. 213–14**) to further swell the assets available for creditors. The ability to assign a liquidator's statutory rights of action (**IA 1986, s. 246ZD**, introduced by **Small Business, Enterprise and Employment Act 2015**) may make at least some financial recovery more likely,[9] to the benefit of creditors.

LOOKING FOR EXTRA MARKS?

■ Keep your focus on the question, and be careful not to spend too much time on the detail of the provisions without linking back to the question of asset reduction or asset swelling

■ Explore which of a liquidator's claims relate to property of a company existing at the time of liquidation, and which claims are subsequently acquired, and the difference this makes to which creditors primarily benefit from the recovery. See eg *Re Oasis Merchandising* [1995] 2 BCLC 493

■ Recognise the changes made in this area by SBEEA 2015

QUESTION | 5

Joe, and his wife Chelsey, are the shareholders and directors of Stamford Ltd, a company that owns and manages several health spas. The day-to-day running of the business is undertaken by Joe, and although Chelsey undertakes clerical and administrative tasks, she leaves management decisions to Joe and simply signs documents as and when directed by him to do so. The company pays them each an annual salary of £45,000.

Stamford Ltd was incorporated in 2008 and was profitable initially, but was hit heavily by the economic downturn and began making losses from early 2011. Although the losses were apparent from the company's financial documents, Joe continued to believe that the problems were temporary and Chelsey was happy to believe him. In 2013 one of the company's spas was forced to close and no buyer could be found for the property, although Joe continued to include the property at full value in the company's accounts. Pressure from unpaid creditors continued through 2013 and 2014, but Joe continually assured Chelsey that the problem was simply a short-term cash flow issue that would be resolved as the economy improved, which Joe believed would be very soon. In the meantime Joe only paid those creditors who actively demanded payment, while creditors who did not demand payment were left unpaid. The business continued to decline and in March 2015 a winding up order was made against Stamford Ltd. Luigi has been appointed liquidator.

Advise Luigi in relation to both wrongful trading and disqualification proceedings against Joe and Chelsey.

CAUTION!

■ You must consider both wrongful trading and disqualification: deal with wrongful trading first, and then go on to consider how the facts might relate to disqualification

■ Make sure you explain the law and then apply each element to the facts of the question. Don't be tempted simply to recite the problem facts—show explicitly how they are relevant

■ As the question expressly instructs you to consider particular areas of law, keep your focus on these rather than considering other provisions

DIAGRAM ANSWER PLAN

| Identify the issues | ■ Identify the issues: wrongful trading and disqualification |

| Relevant law | ■ Wrongful trading: IA 1986, s. 214
 ■ Consequences of breach of s. 214
 ■ Disqualification (wrongful trading): CDDA 1986, s. 10
 ■ Disqualification (unfitness): CDDA 1986, s. 6
 ■ Position of directors and liquidator |

| Apply the law | ■ Apply to the facts |

| Conclude | ■ Conclude, evaluating strength of case |

SUGGESTED ANSWER

Luigi seeks advice regarding wrongful trading proceedings (**Insolvency Act 1986 (IA 1986), s. 214**) and disqualification (**Company Directors Disqualification Act 1986 (CDDA 1986)**). This answer will accordingly address each in turn but will not address other possible avenues such as misfeasance (**IA 1986, s. 212**) or fraudulent trading (**s. 213**).[1]

[1] This demonstrates that you know there are other possibilities for a liquidator to consider, but that you are following instructions in not dealing with them

Wrongful Trading

Wrongful trading proceedings would be brought by Luigi, as the liquidator. A director of a company in insolvent liquidation is liable for wrongful trading if, prior to the commencement of winding up, he knew or should have realised that there was no reasonable prospect of the company avoiding insolvent liquidation (**s. 214(2)**) unless he took every step to minimise loss to creditors (**s. 214(3)**). Stamford Ltd is in insolvent liquidation and Joe and Chelsey are directors of the company[2] so both are potentially liable.

[2] You are told in the question that they are directors, so you don't need to spend time considering de jure, de facto, and shadow directors

The issue is thus whether Joe and/or Chelsey knew or ought to have known, before liquidation commenced, that the company could not reasonably avoid insolvent liquidation. The facts they knew, or should have known, and the conclusions they should have reached are those known or reached by a 'reasonably diligent person' with (a) the general knowledge, skill, and experience of someone carrying out the functions of that director (including the functions that should have been carried out but weren't: **s. 214(5)**) and (b) the general knowledge, skill, and experience that the director has (**s. 214(4)**). Thus, part (a) imposes a minimum objective standard (**Re DKG Contractors Ltd [1990] BCC 903**) varying according to the type of company and role, while (b) is subjective, imposing additional expectations on someone with greater skills than expected of someone in that position. Joe and Chelsey do not appear to have any specific skills, etc so their knowledge will be assessed on the basis of the minimum objective standard expected of directors in their roles in a company of the size and type of Stamford Ltd. In **Re Produce Marketing Consortium Ltd [1989] BCLC 520** (**Produce Marketing**), the court took account of information the directors should have had, even though they did not actually have it because of their own failures to draw up accounts. So reliance on inaccurate accounts will not protect Joe and Chelsey, nor will Joe's continuing belief that problems were temporary.[3] In **Re Rod Gunner Organisation Ltd [2004] 2 BCLC 110**, the directors hung on to hopes of refinancing, but these hopes were unrealistic— similarly Joe's hopes do not seem to be based on facts. Chelsey, as a director, should have been aware of the financial position and not simply accepted Joe's reassurances.

Although the company started making losses in 2011, making losses does not make insolvent liquidation inevitable—even knowledge of insolvency is not sufficient in itself (**Re Hawkes Hill Publishing Ltd [2007] BCC 937**)—but by 2013 as losses continued, the property could not be sold and creditor pressure mounted, the directors should have realised liquidation was inevitable. In **Re Brian D Pierson Ltd [1999] BCC 26**, a husband and wife were both liable where they refused to face facts and made only superficial judgments as to the company's financial state—this is similar to Joe and Chelsey's position.

Directors can avoid liability if they took 'every step' they ought to have taken to minimise loss to creditors (**IA 1986, s. 214(3)**), assessed using the **s. 214(4)** dual objective/subjective standard. The onus is on the director to establish such a defence: **Brooks v Armstrong [2015] EWHC 2289 (Ch)**. **Re Brian D Pierson Ltd** indicates directors should show specific steps to preserve or realise assets for creditors—Joe and Chelsey have taken no such steps. Chelsey might claim in relying on Joe she acted 'honestly, reasonably and ought fairly to be excused' and so should be relieved from liability under **Companies Act 2006, s. 1127** but even if a court thought her behaviour reasonable, **Produce Marketing** concluded that **s. 1127** does not apply to wrongful trading.[4]

If Joe and Chelsey were found liable for wrongful trading the court can order them to make such contribution to the company's assets

[3] See how the relevant case facts are indicated (which also identifies the issue) and then expressly applied to the problem facts; the same technique is used in the next sentence. This is in essence a condensed version of IRAC.

[4] Not an essential point but the examiner will be pleased to see you recognise it, while still relating it to the facts of the question

as it thinks proper (**s. 214(1)**). The measure of liability is compensatory—the amount the company's assets were depleted by the director's actions (**Produce Marketing**)—ie the losses incurred after Joe and Chelsey should have realised the company was unlikely to avoid insolvent liquidation. Accordingly, provided Joe and Chelsey have sufficient private resources to meet the claim[5] Luigi should seriously consider bringing proceedings against them.

[5] This is a practical observation—there would be no point in bringing proceedings if the directors don't have the money to meet the claim—and shows you are thinking about the situation

Disqualification

The primary purpose of **CDDA 1986** is to protect the public from those who are unfit to be directors (**Re Sevenoaks Stationers (Retail) Ltd [1991] Ch 164 (Sevenoaks)**).[6] A disqualification order prohibits that person, for a period of time, from being a director, receiver, or taking part in the promotion, formation, or management of a company or acting as an insolvency practitioner.

[6] A basic introductory point: it can be useful to set the scene but don't get distracted into a more general discussion of disqualification

If Luigi successfully brings wrongful trading proceedings against Joe and Chelsey, the court can disqualify the directors under **CDDA 1986, s. 10**.[7] However, the more common ground for disqualification is 'unfitness' where a company has gone into insolvent liquidation (**s. 6**). Under **s. 7A** Luigi has an obligation to make a report on the conduct of the directors to the Secretary of State, who then decides whether to bring proceedings under **s. 6**.

[7] This is a commonly overlooked point

In assessing unfitness **CDDA 1986, s. 12C** directs the court to **Sch 1**. This is a non-exhaustive list of factors for consideration. The **Small Business, Enterprise and Employment Act 2015 (SBEEA 2015)** replaced the former list[8] with fewer, more general concepts, such as breach of duty, material contravention of obligations, and responsibility for the causes of insolvency. The courts have held that unfitness does not require deliberate wrongdoing or dishonesty: negligence (or even marked incompetence) can amount to unfitness (**Sevenoaks**).

[8] The SBEEA 2015 made a number of significant changes to CDDA 1986

A common ground for disqualification is trading at creditors' risk. This is similar to wrongful trading, although it is not necessary to establish breach of **IA 1986, s. 214**. By continuing to trade and building up further debts when there is little prospect of creditors being paid, a director is unfit: **Re Living Images Ltd [1996] 1 BCLC 348**. A policy of paying only pressing creditors, as in this case, is clear evidence of unfitness (**Sevenoaks**). While paying directors' salaries is not in itself unfitness, this may be unfit if it is more than the company can afford (**Secretary of State v Van Hengel [1995] 1 BCLC 545**).

Chelsey's failings lie in inactivity which can amount to unfitness. Directors can delegate but cannot abrogate their responsibilities or allow themselves to be dominated by a board member (**Re Westmid Packing Services Ltd [1998] 2 All ER 124**). **Re Barings plc (No. 5) [2000] 1 BCLC 523** makes clear that each individual director has inescapable minimum obligations and Chelsey seems to have failed to meet these.

If unfitness under **s. 6** is established—there seems to be evidence of unfitness for both—the court must make a disqualification order of at least two years (maximum 15 years). *Sevenoaks* established three brackets: 2–5 years for relatively not very serious cases, 6–10 years for serious cases not meriting the top bracket, and 11–15 years for particularly serious cases. Here Chelsey's behaviour would put her in the lower end of the bottom bracket, while Joe's behaviour warrants a higher tariff, although still not a particularly serious case.[9] While the period may be reduced by mitigating factors (including the age and health of the director and his/her general conduct before and after the liquidation), there are no particular mitigating factors mentioned in this case.

Until recently there was no direct financial penalty for unfit directors, unless they acted in breach of a disqualification order and so incurred personal liability for the debts of the company in which they were acting whilst disqualified: **CDDA, s. 15.** However **CDDA s. 15A** (introduced by **SBEEA 2015**), would allow the Secretary of State to apply for a compensation order[10] against Joe and Chelsey, if disqualified, requiring them to pay an amount for the benefit of a specified creditor, creditors, or class of creditor, or contribute to the assets of Stamford Ltd (**s. 15B**).

Conclusion

Luigi has a good case against Joe and Chelsey for wrongful trading in continuing to trade for over a year after they should have realised there was no reasonable prospect of the company avoiding insolvent liquidation, and if successful the creditors will benefit from the recovery of losses made after that point. If wrongful trading proceedings succeed then the directors could be disqualified under **CDDA 1986, s. 10.** In any event Luigi must make a report with regard to their conduct, and the case under **s. 6** against Joe and Chelsey appears strong. The directors may wish to offer a 'disqualification undertaking' (**CDDA 1986, s. 1A; s. 7(2A)**) to avoid the cost of proceedings; the undertaking operates just like a disqualification order. If subject to a disqualification order or undertaking, the court may make a compensation order against them (or they could give a compensation undertaking: **s. 15A(2)**).

[9] Even without extensive knowledge of likely disqualification periods, you can still have a go at applying the facts to the *Sevenoaks* brackets based on the kind of behaviour you've seen in other cases. Of course the period of disqualification is not up to Luigi, and you could make that point.

[10] Another important recent development

LOOKING FOR EXTRA MARKS?

- Explain and assess the relevant changes made in this area by SBEEA 2015
- Explore some of the facts of the key cases to highlight similarities or differences with the facts of the problem question
- Consider the factors that may encourage or discourage Luigi from taking action against the directors for wrongful trading, such as funding, and the possibility of assigning this right of action

TAKING THINGS FURTHER

- Astle, T., 'Pack up your troubles: addressing the negative image of pre-packs' (2015) 28 Insolv Int 72

  A concise review of the main criticisms of pre-packs and the recommendations of the Graham Review.

- Finch, V., 'Corporate rescue: who is interested?' [2012] JBL 190

  An examination of corporate rescue processes, focusing in particular on whose interests are and should be the focus on these processes.

- Frieze, S., 'The company in financial difficulties: the alternatives' (2008) 21 Insolv Int 124

  A brief consideration of options open to a company approaching insolvency.

- Hicks, A., 'Director disqualification: can it deliver?' [2001] JBL 433

  Based on some empirical studies, this article considers how effective the CDDA 1986 is in removing 'rogue' directors and protecting creditors. Suggestions for reform and alternative approaches are also discussed.

- Kastrinou, A., 'An analysis of the pre-pack technique and recent developments in the area' (2008) 29 Co Law 259

  Explores the practice and legality of pre-pack administrations.

- Keay, A., 'Disputing debts relied on by petitioning creditors seeking winding up orders' (2001) 22 Co Law 40

  A helpful examination of the law on disputed debts and cross-claims.

- Keay, A., 'Wrongful trading: problems and proposals' (2014) 65 NILQ 63

  Considers the principal difficulties facing liquidators in bringing wrongful trading claims and makes proposals for reform.

- McCormack, G., 'Swelling corporate assets: changing what is on the menu?' (2006) 6 JCLS 39

  A wide-ranging examination of the transaction avoidance provisions.

- Milman, D., 'Personal liability and disqualification of company directors: something old, something new' (1992) 43 NILQ 1

  Explores the trend towards imposing personal liability on directors of collapsed companies, examining the circumstances in which this might arise. Bear in mind that there has been some significant case law and statutory development since this article, but many of the points it makes remain valid.

- Williams, R., 'Disqualifying directors: a remedy worse than the disease' (2007) 7 J Corp Law Studies 213

  A critical view of the merits of the director disqualification regime, arguing that it fails to meet its stated aims.

- Williams, R., 'What can we expect to gain from reforming the insolvent trading remedy?' (2015) 78 MLR 55

  Argues that even when reformed the wrongful trading provision will fail to bring significant recoveries for creditors as it has inherent limitations. Includes a helpful account of the origins, objectives, and use of the remedy.

Online Resource Centre www.oxfordtextbooks.co.uk/orc/qanda/

Go online for extra essay and problem questions, a glossary of key terms, online versions of all the answer plans and audio commentary on how selected ones were put together, and a range of podcasts which include advice on exam and coursework technique and advice for other assessment methods.

12 Mixed Topic Questions

ARE YOU READY?

Lots of topics in company law interlink so there is plenty of scope for mixed questions in company law exams. (You'll already have noticed some overlapping of topics in some questions in previous chapters.) While mixed topic questions are often problem questions, essay questions can also require you to stretch over two (or more) topics. Some examiners make more use of mixed questions than others so check your own course to see whether there is any particular approach to setting mixed questions—look at past papers, attend revision sessions, ask your tutor what the practice is (they may or may not tell you). Just about any topics in company law can be connected in a question, but be particularly aware of any connections your lecturer explicitly highlights in class. Some common connections are:

- Directors' duties and shareholder remedies
- Corporate personality and insolvency
- Articles of association, shareholders, and shareholder remedies
- Directors' duties and insolvency
- Share capital and loan capital; loan capital and insolvency
- Corporate contracts and pre-incorporation contracts; contracts and directors' duties
- Corporate personality and corporate liability

 QUESTION | **1**

In October 2015 Stella decided to turn her hobby of craft-making into two businesses. She planned to incorporate two companies, Beadie Ltd (through which she would run a jewellery making business) and Craftie Ltd (which would run craft-making courses). Accordingly, on 3 November 2015 Stella entered into a contract with Alexis for a large supply of glass beads for making jewellery. She

▶

signed the contract 'Stella, director, Beadie Ltd' and put her initials beneath it. On the same day she entered into a contract with Indira for fabrics for her craft courses, signing the contract 'Craftie Ltd'.

The following week Stella decided she would run both businesses through a single company to save on registration costs and so incorporated Craftie Ltd, with Stella as sole shareholder (holding one £1 share) and director. Craftie Ltd's certificate of incorporation is dated 15 November 2015. On 20 November 2015 Stella purchased £1,000 worth of office supplies (in the name of Craftie Ltd) from Paperco plc.

It is now clear that Stella has sold all the jewellery she had made at a loss and has failed to get any customers for the craft-making courses. All the stock and supplies have been used and Craftie Ltd has no assets of any value. Alexis is owed £500 for the beads, Indira is owed £800 for the fabrics, and Paperco is owed £1,000.

Advise Alexis, Indira, and Paperco.

CAUTION!

- Focus on what the individuals want to achieve, and think of the routes by which this might be possible. Start with the facts, and use these to direct you to the right areas of law, rather than searching specifically for particular topics

- Remember that personal liability is not just about piercing the veil of incorporation. Think about the other ways in which personal liability might attach to a shareholder or director, particularly when a company is insolvent

- If dates are given, they are probably there for a reason, so considering their significance might give you a clue as to the relevant topic

DIAGRAM ANSWER PLAN

[1] Identify what the individuals want to achieve, and why, to show the examiner you understand the basic premise of the question

As Craftie Ltd has no assets, Alexis, Indira and Paperco will be looking to establish personal liability on the part of Stella.[1] At first sight this is not easy: *Salomon v A. Salomon & Co Ltd* **[1897] AC 22** (*'Salomon'*) shows a company is a separate legal person from its shareholders (and directors); even in a 'one-man company' (like Craftie Ltd), the individual behind the corporate veil is not normally liable for the company's obligations.

However, the positions of Alexis and Indira, and of Paperco are distinct because the contracts with Alexis and Indira were entered into prior to incorporation, while Paperco's contract was entered into after Craftie Ltd was incorporated. It will be necessary to consider the law on pre-incorporation contracts for Alexis and Indira, and to consider more generally the liability of those behind the corporate veil in relation to Paperco.

[2] You could deal with these two contracts separately, to ensure you deal with their different features

Alexis and Indira[2]

A company comes into existence on incorporation (**Companies Act 2006 (CA 2006), s. 16**), the date of its certificate of incorporation. This is 15 November for Craftie Ltd, while Beadie Ltd was never actually formed. Accordingly, on 3 November when the contracts were entered into, the companies did not exist and could not be bound.

Liability under a pre-incorporation contract is now governed by **CA 2006, s. 51**. This makes the person purporting to act for a company (or as agent for it) before it is formed, personally liable on the contract.

[3] This shows a bit of further analysis about what is happening, and links implicitly to the wider context of the question

Although it might be tempting to view **s. 51** as piercing the veil of incorporation by imposing liability for 'the company's contract' on someone behind the veil, this isn't so, as the company was never itself liable. At most the veil is glanced behind to check the date of incorporation,[3] like checking an individual's birthdate.

Section 51 makes Stella personally liable on both contracts; it is irrelevant how they were signed. At common law the form of signature could be crucial: in *Kelner v Baxter* **(1866) LR 2CP 174** (*Kelner*) where the contract was signed by the promoter on behalf of the company, the promoter was bound, but in *Newborne v Sensolid (GB) Ltd* **[1954] 1 QB 45** (*Newborne*) where the contract was signed purportedly by the company (authenticated by the individual) the contract was void (as with a non-existent principal).

[4] Always try to link the law to the facts of the question

This would have led to different results for Alexis (akin to *Kelner*) and Indira (akin to *Newborne*)[4] but **s. 51** removes the distinction: Stella is bound by both the contracts, notwithstanding the difference in signature. Although **s. 51** allows an individual to exclude personal liability, this must be explicit, and signing in the company's name (as in Indira's contract) is not sufficient to exclude liability: *Phonogram Ltd v Lane* [1982] QB 938 (*Phonogram*).

[5] If dealing with the two contracts within the same part of the essay as here, make sure you expressly recognise (and deal with) their different features

Another difference between Alexis and Indira's contracts is that while Craftie Ltd was subsequently incorporated, Beadie Ltd was not in fact formed.[5] But this does not prevent **s. 51** operating. In *Phonogram*, the court held the section applied wherever a company was in contemplation of formation, it didn't matter that the company was never actually incorporated.

Alexis and Indira can therefore be advised that Stella is personally liable on the contracts with them. Stella could have avoided liability by expressly excluding personal liability in the contract (**s. 51**; *Phonogram*) but it is highly unlikely she has done so. She could also avoid liability if the contracts had been novated after Craftie Ltd's formation, although simple adoption or ratification of the contract by the company would not be effective (*Natal Land Co & Colonization Ltd v Pauline Colliery and Development Syndicate Ltd* [1904] **AC 120**). However novation requires the company to make a new contract on the terms of the old one; simply acting in the belief the old contract is binding is not sufficient (*Re Northumberland Avenue Hotel Co* (1886) **33 ChD 16**). Novation does not appear to have happened here; Stella remains personally liable on both contracts.

Paperco

Paperco's contract was entered into after incorporation of Craftie Ltd. The contract appears valid (as director, Stella had authority to enter into it on the company's behalf); the problem is that Craftie Ltd does not have the resources to meet its obligations.

[6] It is tempting to provide a lot of information about *Salomon* and the veil of incorporation more generally but this would be very descriptive; make sure you concentrate on points that are really relevant to the problem question

The starting point is *Salomon*: as the company is a separate legal person, Stella is not personally liable for debts incurred by the company.[6] However there are exceptions: the court may pierce the veil of incorporation, or Stella could be personally liable through other legal routes or statutory provisions.

Unfortunately for Paperco, the jurisdiction to pierce the veil of incorporation, to make Stella liable for Craftie's debt, is now very limited. In *Prest v Petrodel Resources Ltd* [2013] **UKSC 34**, the Supreme Court held it could be used only as a last resort (when no other remedy was available) and only where the corporate form had been used to evade or frustrate an existing legal right or remedy.

[7] This passage deals with the fundamental points concisely; if you had time you could expand this a bit more and provide additional authority

That is clearly not the case here; there is no 'relevant impropriety' to trigger the jurisdiction. Stella was using the company legitimately to run her business, not evade existing liabilities: choosing the corporate form in order to avoid personal liability is not impropriety, but a legitimate reason for incorporation (*Salomon*; *Adams v Cape Industries plc* [1990] **Ch 433**).[7]

Liability could fall on Stella ('lifting the veil' in a wide sense) if Craftie Ltd were acting as her agent—Stella would therefore be liable as principal. But that argument is highly unlikely to succeed; it failed in *Salomon* and very few cases have found agency on the facts (eg *Smith, Stone & Knight v Birmingham Corpn* **[1939] 4 All ER 116**). More recent cases indicate clear evidence of an agency relationship will be needed (*Adams v Cape Industries plc; Yukong Line Ltd of Korea v Rendsburg Investments Corpn of Liberia (No. 2)* **[1998] 1 WLR 294**). It is highly improbable an agency relationship would be found here. Other ways in which the courts have effectively avoided the veil, for example through imposing direct liability on an individual through tort law, do not apply here.[8]

[8]This shows you understand there are other ways around the veil, but without wasting time

Relevant statutory provisions that might impose personal liability on Stella are triggered by the company going into liquidation and Paperco, as a creditor owed more than £750, could present a winding up petition under **Insolvency Act 1986 (IA 1986), s. 122(1)(f)**.[9] The liquidator can seek a contribution to the company's assets from Stella under **IA 1986, ss. 213–4** for fraudulent or wrongful trading. Fraudulent trading (**s. 213**) seems unlikely as there is no suggestion of intent to defraud creditors or a fraudulent purpose. Wrongful trading (**s. 214**) is where a director continues to trade beyond the point s/he should have concluded there was no reasonable prospect of the company avoiding insolvent liquidation. Arguably Stella should have realised at an earlier stage (it is not clear how long she has been making losses and failing to fill her courses) that failure was inevitable. If found liable the measure is compensatory, ie the losses arising after the point of 'no return': (*Re Produce Marketing Consortium Ltd* **[1989] BCLC 520**). This would swell the company's assets and make it more likely Paperco could recoup some of its loss.

[9]A minor point, but one that shows the examiner your knowledge and understanding stretches beyond the key topics raised in the question

As director, Stella may have breached her duties to the company, eg the duty of care, skill, and diligence, **CA 2006, s. 174**, although more facts would be needed to conclude on this. If in breach, the liquidator can recover using the misfeasance procedure under **IA 1986, s. 212**. A creditor such as Paperco can also apply under **s. 212**. The liquidator could also make use of other insolvency provisions, such as transactions at an undervalue (**IA 1986, s. 238**) if there were evidence of disposal of Craftie Ltd's assets, but the current facts do not indicate this.

A problem with **IA 1986, s. 214** (and most other relevant **IA 1986** provisions including in practice, **s. 212** as creditors rarely have the information to start proceedings), is action is taken by the liquidator. This depends on having sufficient assets in the liquidation to meet expenses and creditors may be reluctant to fund quite speculative proceedings.[10] A further possibility (which is not in the hands of the liquidator) is disqualification for unfitness under the **Company Directors Disqualification Act 1986 (CDDA 1986), s. 6** as if Stella

[10]Show you recognise practical as well as legal difficulties in bringing claims

is disqualified the Secretary of State may now seek a contribution order from her (**CDDA 1986, s. 15A**), which could benefit Paperco. However disqualification proceedings against Stella are not inevitable, would take some time to conclude, and might not result in a compensation order.

Conclusion

The position of Alexis and Indira is strong. **CA 2006, s. 51** operates to protect them by making the contracts enforceable against Stella personally. The position is very different for Paperco: the courts are reluctant to pierce or lift the veil of incorporation, and its only hope is for some recovery from Stella through the insolvency process if and when the company is wound up—but this is both uncertain and quite unlikely to result in full recovery.

LOOKING FOR EXTRA MARKS?

■ Make sure you concentrate on the relevant areas of law rather than discussing the veil of incorporation more generally

■ Don't just explain the possible routes; evaluate their chances of success. As part of this, recognise more practical issues, such as the likelihood of action actually being taken

■ Consider more generally the issue of creditors, risk, and limited liability, linking the discussion to the facts of the problem

QUESTION | 2

'Despite the contractual effect of the articles of association, minority shareholders are greatly in need of the additional remedies provided for them by statute.'

Discuss.

CAUTION!

■ Mixed essay questions can be tricky as you need to balance the topics appropriately, and draw the connections between them, so plan your essay carefully before starting to write

■ Don't be tempted to provide a standard consideration of the articles of association in answer to this question; it is clear that a more wide-ranging response is required

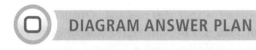

DIAGRAM ANSWER PLAN

Introduction: minority shareholders and majority rule

▼

The contractual effect of the articles

▼

Alteration of the articles and protection from alteration

▼

Enforcement of the articles and personal rights

▼

Derivative claims

▼

Unfair prejudice

▼

Conclusion: finding a balance

SUGGESTED ANSWER

A company is an association of members, operating on the principle of majority rule. This doesn't mean a minority shareholder should have no rights, only that these must be considered within the wider framework of an effective corporate structure, taking into account the courts' reluctance to get involved in internal affairs (***Carlen v Drury*** **(1812) 35 ER 63**). The law attempts to balance the interests of the company, the majority, and the minority, but this can be complicated.

This essay will first explain[1] the contractual nature of the articles of association and explore the extent to which this 'contract' provides secure and enforceable rights, to assess whether minority shareholders need further assistance. Secondly, the essay will examine the statutory remedies available to minority shareholders, considering how these improve a minority shareholder's position. The essay will conclude that[2] although the statutory remedies are of undoubted value, the position of a minority shareholder remains a vulnerable one.

The Articles as a Contract

By virtue of **Companies Act 2006 (CA 2006), s. 33**, the articles (the internal rules of the company) bind the company and members as if

[1] With a question like this, it is important to set out what you will be discussing and, in particular, how it relates to the question. This also helps to balance the context-setting first paragraph to reassure the examiner you haven't lost sight of the question itself

[2] It isn't necessary to indicate your conclusion from the start, but it can be quite effective if you know where you are heading

³ Link the discussion of the articles to the particular issues raised in the question

terms of a contract. It might be thought therefore that placing rights within the articles provides a minority shareholder with all the protection of contract law.³

However, standard contractual remedies, including mistake, misrepresentation, and undue influence do not apply (***Bratton Seymour Service Co Ltd v Oxborough* [1992] BCLC 693**). Furthermore, unlike a standard contract, articles are alterable by special resolution (**CA 2006, s. 21**), so are subject to removal or alteration by the majority.

⁴ The passage on alteration, variation, and entrenchment has to deal with a lot of points very concisely; be strict with yourself and don't get caught up in detailed discussion

Alteration must be bona fide in the interests of the company as a whole⁴ (***Allen v Gold Reefs of West Africa Ltd* [1900] 1 Ch 656**) but alterations are rarely challenged successfully. If the right is a class right (defined in ***Cumbrian Newspapers Group Ltd v Cumberland & Westmorland Herald Newspaper & Printing Co Ltd* [1986] BCLC 286**) then variation requires the consent of the majority of the class: **CA 2006, s. 630**. However the courts have interpreted 'variation' narrowly (***White v Bristol Aeroplane Co Ltd* [1953] Ch 65**), reducing the protection offered by statute. Significant protection from alteration is possible through entrenchment under **CA 2006, s. 22**, but of course a shareholder would need to be sufficiently aware to insist on this.

Importantly, articles are not necessarily enforceable as of right, as might have been expected from their contractual nature. Only 'insider' rights (ie rights relating to a member's capacity as a member) can be enforced, while 'outsider' rights (rights relating to another capacity) are not directly enforceable: ***Hickman v Kent or Romney Marsh Sheep-Breeders' Association* [1915] 1 Ch 881**. However, outsider rights may be indirectly enforced through a member suing qua member (***Quin & Axtens Ltd v Salmon* [1909] AC 442**; Wedderburn, 'Shareholder rights and the rule in *Foss v Harbottle*' [1957] CLJ 194), or through a contract extrinsic to the articles (***Re New British Iron Co***

⁵ If you had time you could expand this discussion a bit

[1898] 1 Ch 324). There remain fundamental questions about which articles are directly enforceable, by whom, and in what circumstances, despite determined academic attempts to reconcile the cases⁵ (summarised by Drury, 'The relative nature of the shareholder's right to enforce the company contract' [1986] CLJ 219).

⁶ This is an important link between the two key elements of the question—the articles and shareholder remedies

Enforcement of the articles is particularly complex because of the courts' desire not to undermine the rule in ***Foss v Harbottle* (1843) 2 Hare 461**.⁶ This consists of two principles: the 'proper claimant' principle, preventing members bringing action in respect of wrongs done to the company; and the 'majority rule' principle, preventing action about internal matters that can be regularised by the majority.

The proper claimant principle does not prevent a shareholder bringing a personal claim relating to his personal rights, rather than rights of the company. However, as previously discussed, not all rights contained in the articles can be enforced directly by a shareholder. Members' claims in relation to matters of internal management of the company may fall foul of the majority rule principle. Quite what amounts to a directly enforceable personal right remains uncertain: the cases are inconsistent, and the opportunity to clarify the position in **CA 2006** was not taken. While a shareholder has a personal right to have his vote recorded in accordance with the articles (*Pender v Lushington* (1877) 6 Ch D 70), in *MacDougall v Gardiner* (1875) 1 Ch D 13 the court held a failure to call a poll in accordance with the articles was a matter of internal management. Sometimes courts will prevent a company from acting contrary to the articles (eg *Quin & Axtens Ltd v Salmon*); sometimes not (eg *Irvine v Union Bank of Australia* (1877) 2 App Cas 366). A shareholder may bring a personal claim to restrain an illegal or ultra vires act of the company (*Simpson v Westminster Palace Hotel Co* (1860) 8 HL Cas 712) but this is clearly of very limited scope.

[7]This paragraph highlights the relevance of the points made, and links forward to the next point. It reduces the risk of the answer appearing to be two separate essays

It can be seen that despite the articles being of a 'contractual nature', this does not provide a minority shareholder with secure, absolute, and enforceable rights. Even if the terms of the articles were unalterable and fully enforceable by a shareholder, a shareholder might still suffer from wrongdoing or oppression, as actions of the directors or majority could be within the terms of the articles but still harmful.[7]

Statutory Remedies

The true exception to the rule in *Foss v Harbottle* is a derivative claim, originally a common law remedy based on 'fraud on the minority', but now in **CA 2006, ss. 260–4**. This allows a shareholder to bring proceedings in relation to the company's cause of action relating to a breach of duty by a director (**s. 260(3)**), recognising directors are unlikely to commence action against themselves. However, strict boundaries are placed on claims to ensure the company is protected from undue interference from shareholders. This means minority shareholders can find it very difficult to bring derivative claims, as a range of factors (**s. 263**) must be considered by the court before granting permission to continue the claim. With a risk of costs (unless an indemnity is granted by the court) and any eventual recovery benefiting the company rather than the shareholder directly, derivative claims are unsurprisingly uncommon. Attempts to outflank the rule in *Foss v Harbottle* by alleging 'personal' loss through a diminution in the value of shares because of wrongdoing, have been rejected as merely 'reflective' of the company's loss: *Johnson v Gore Wood and Co* [2002] 2 AC 1.

Given the difficulties shareholders have in enforcing the articles, or pursuing a derivative claim, the statutory 'unfair prejudice' remedy

[8]There isn't time to look at s. 122(1)(g) in any depth, and it is clearly much less relevant to the issues in the question, so this simply indicates it has been considered

(**CA 2006, s. 994**) has become very important. (Shareholders could also seek to wind up the company on the just and equitable ground (**Insolvency Act 1986, s. 122(1)(g)**) in some cases but its restricted scope and fatal consequences for the company rarely make it the best option for a minority shareholder.)[8]

Under **s. 994** a member may petition the court where the conduct of the company's affairs has been unfairly prejudicial to his interests as a member. This is wide enough to encompass non-compliance with the articles, ignoring or removing a shareholder's rights, and wrong-doing that harms the company as well as the individual.[9] 'Interests as a member' is interpreted generously, and not limited to strictly 'membership rights': *Gamlestaden Fastigheter AB v Baltic Partners Ltd* **[2007] 4 All ER 164**.

[9] Bring together the complaints considered in the earlier paragraphs, to show how s. 994 is relevant and so of assistance to a minority shareholder

Nonetheless, although it is a wide remedy it is not 'unbounded' (*Re Tobian Properties Ltd* **[2012] EWCA Civ 998**). Complaints must relate to the conduct of the company's affairs, which is interpreted widely but would not cover, for example, arrangements between members for the sale of shares: *Re Leeds United Holdings plc* **[1996] 2 BCLC 545**. More significantly the conduct must be 'unfair' as well as prejudicial. In *O'Neill v Phillips* **[1999] 1 WLR 1092** the House of Lords held this does not encompass all failures to meet a shareholder's 'legitimate expectations', but requires some breach of the terms on which the association was formed or continued, other than a 'trivial' breach, or use of legal powers in a manner contrary to equity, normally requiring the company to be a quasi-partnership (per *Ebrahimi v Westbourne Galleries Ltd* **[1973] AC 360**). Not all shareholder complaints will therefore fall within **s. 994**.

[10] In a mixed topic essay question it is particularly important that your conclusion brings together the different topics to show how they interrelate

Conclusion[10]

The articles have contractual effect but this does not mean a shareholder can enforce terms of the articles exactly as if they were contractual terms. A shareholder is a member of an association, where individual rights cannot be absolute and majority rule normally prevails, which can lead to complexity and result in harsh or apparently inconsistent outcomes. Because of the vulnerability of minority shareholders to oppression or wrongdoing, it is right that statute provides some additional remedies, but equally important that these are not so wide as to undermine fundamental principles underlying company law. By restricting access to derivative claims and providing limits to the notion of 'unfair prejudice', the law maintains a balance between individual rights, majority rule, and the separation of powers.

LOOKING FOR EXTRA MARKS?

- Make sure you spread your time sensibly across the various elements within the question, rather than going too deeply into one part only: it is by dealing with all the elements and making the connections that you will get the most marks here

- Recognise the link between enforcement of the articles, personal rights, and the rule in *Foss v Harbottle*, engaging with the academic discussion if you have time

■ Pack in your knowledge by making more peripheral, basic, or supporting points in passing, rather than setting them out in detail

Jaime is a shareholder in Winterfell Ltd, which has three directors, Arya, Sansa, and Ramsay. Although Arya, Sansa, and Ramsay run the business on a day-to-day basis, it is well known that they refer all major issues to Tyrion for a final decision. Tyrion was managing director of Winterfell Ltd for many years but resigned in 2014 following a local scandal.

Jaime has recently learned that Arya and Tyrion have set up a new business, developing a product Jaime knows the designer originally offered to Winterfell Ltd. Jaime believes this business would have been highly profitable for Winterfell Ltd, and therefore financially beneficial to him. Jaime owns 50 of Winterfell Ltd's 500 issued shares, 25 of which were allotted to him in return for his help updating Winterfell Ltd's computer systems. The board has recently demanded that Jaime either pay for or forfeit those shares, which Jaime suspects is because he had asked questions about Arya and Tyrion's new business.

Advise Jaime.

CAUTION!

■ Duties and shareholder remedies are a common combination so be prepared to deal with both in a question but always check the question instruction to see if you are advising the company, a shareholder, or some other party, so you can direct your discussion accordingly

■ Think about how the issues in a problem interrelate when planning your answer; sometimes it is more efficient to deal with issues in a different order to how they appear in the question

DIAGRAM ANSWER PLAN

Identify the issues	■ Identify the various issues
Relevant law	■ Issue of shares for non-cash consideration ■ Forfeiture of shares ■ Proper purposes doctrine ■ De facto and shadow directors ■ Duties owed by shadow directors ■ No conflict/no profit rule ■ The corporate opportunity doctrine ■ Rule in *Foss v Horbottle* ■ Derivative claims ■ Unfair prejudice
Apply the law	■ Apply the law to the various scenarios
Conclude	■ Conclude on each point

A **SUGGESTED ANSWER**

¹Indicate that you've spotted there is more than one topic in this question

This question raises several connected issues concerning directors' duties, shareholder remedies, and issue of shares.¹ After examining the share issue and threat of forfeiture, the answer will discuss Arya and Tyrion's situation and consider what action Jaime could take.

Jaime's Shares

A private company can issue shares for non-cash consideration (**Companies Act 2006 (CA 2006), s. 582(1)**), without need for formal valuation (unlike public companies: **s. 593**). The courts will not question the value of consideration received (***Re Wragg Ltd* [1897] 1 Ch 796**), provided it is not clearly illusory (***Hong Kong and China Gas Co Ltd v Glen* [1914] 1 Ch 527**). Accordingly Jaime's services can be valid consideration for the shares, which would indicate no further liability on his part.

²If the facts are ambiguous, that is almost certainly deliberate

However, the facts are not entirely clear² whether the services were intended as consideration for shares, or the shares were subsequently given to Jaime as a thank you for his help. If the latter then the consideration would be past, and so invalid: ***Re Eddystone Marine Insurance Co* [1893] 3 Ch 9**, meaning Jaime would remain liable to pay for those shares, and potentially at risk of forfeiture.

[3] Most examiners would not expect you to know this; it is fine simply to state you are assuming the company has power to forfeit in its articles

To forfeit unpaid shares the company would need the power to do this in its articles (it is not within the current private company model articles: **Companies (Model Articles) Regulations 2008 Sch 1**).[3] Exercising a power to forfeit shares does not breach the prohibition on a company acquiring its own shares (**CA 2006, s. 658**): **s. 659(2)(c)**.[4] However, if the directors sought to exercise the power here, it could be challenged for breaching their duty to exercise powers only for the purposes for which they are conferred: **s. 171(b)**. Here the

[4] Not an essential point, but if you can show off connected knowledge concisely, then take the opportunity

primary motivation of the directors seems to be to stifle discussion of their activities, rather than to secure payment for the company. If the 'substantial' purpose for which a power is exercised is not within the proper boundaries of the power, its exercise is void: ***Howard Smith Ltd v Ampol Petroleum Ltd* [1974] AC 821**; ***Eclairs Group Ltd v JKX Oil plc* [2015] UKSC 71**. This is so even if the directors genuinely believed their action would benefit the company: ***Lee Panavision Ltd v Lee Lighting Ltd* [1992] BCLC 22**. However, as directors' duties are owed to the company (**CA 2006, s. 170(1)**) Jaime may have difficulty remedying breaches—this will be considered later.

Arya and Tyrion

Arya is a de jure director, as are Sansa and Ramsay, and therefore undoubtedly owes duties to the company. Tyrion is not formally appointed director but may be a de facto or shadow director[5] (and these concepts may overlap: ***Re Paycheck Services Ltd* [2010] 1 WLR 2793**). It is unlikely that Tyrion is a de facto director: this is someone assuming the status and functions of a director (***Re Kaytech International plc* [1999] BCC 390**). However, on the facts he may well be a shadow director: someone in accordance with whose directions or instructions the directors are accustomed to act (**CA 2006, s. 251**). Tyrion's involvement does not need to be hidden for him to be a shadow director, nor need he be followed on every matter (***Secretary of State for Trade and Industry v Deverell* [2001] Ch 340**). Although the extent to which shadow directors are subject to directors' duties remains unsettled, following ***Vivendi SA v Richards* [2013] EWHC 3006 (Ch)** and **CA 2006, s. 170(5)** (as amended by **Small Business, Enterprise and Employment Act 2015**), it is highly probable Tyrion will be found to owe the same duties to Winterfell Ltd as the de jure directors.[6]

[5] If you are told individuals are directors you can assume they are properly appointed (don't speculate further). If not then consider the possibility of de facto or shadow directorship

[6] Remember to consider whether shadow directors owe duties to the company

By taking up the product offered to Winterfell Ltd, it seems likely Arya and Tyrion are in breach of **CA 2006, s. 175**: a director must not allow a conflict between his interest and his duty. This applies in particular to the exploitation of any property, information, or opportunity: **s. 175(2)**. Pre-2006 cases remain relevant to the interpretation and application of the statutory duty (**s. 170(4)**).[7] They show a generally strict approach to the duty, with liability even if the company

[7] This section avoids a historical account of the duty by starting with the statutory formulation, and then explaining why earlier cases are relevant, before considering those cases

was unable to take up the opportunity itself (*Regal (Hastings) Ltd v Gulliver* [1942] 1 All ER 378; *Industrial Development Consultants Ltd v Cooley* [1972] 1 WLR 443).

Sometimes directors have been permitted to take on opportunities, if rejected by the company in good faith (*Peso Silver Mines Ltd v Cropper* [1966] SCR 673) while other cases impose liability only when there was a 'maturing business opportunity' (*Canadian Aero Service Ltd v O'Malley* (1973) 40 DLR (3d) 371; *Island Export Finance Ltd v Umunna* [1986] BCLC 460). However, on the facts the opportunity appears to have been 'live' and the directors still in post, (and recent cases indicate a strict approach: *O'Donnell v Shanahan* [2009] 2 BCLC 666), making it more likely than not that Arya and Tyrion would be in breach. As far as the facts reveal, the conflict has not been authorised by the other directors, but if it had been there is no breach (**s. 175(4)**). Authorisation is clearly a possibility as the directors' actions indicate they do not want Arya and Tyrion's actions challenged. If the directors did authorise Arya and Tyrion's actions, but this was patently not in the interests of the company, then all the directors might be in breach of both **s. 171(b)** and **s. 172** (duty to promote the success of the company).

What Can Jaime Do?

The general duties of directors are owed to the company (**s. 170(1)**) and the rule in *Foss v Harbottle* (1843) 2 Ha 461 means shareholders cannot usually bring proceedings on the company's behalf. However derivative claims (now in statutory form: **CA 2006, ss. 260–4**) are an exception to this rule. Jaime has the basis of a derivative claim as this is a cause of action vested in the company (**s. 260(1)(a)**), relating to a breach of duty by a director (**s. 260(3)**), and would be seeking relief for the company (**s. 260(1)(b)**).

Under **s. 261** Jaime would have to apply to court for permission to continue a derivative claim, first showing a prima facie case (**s. 261(2)**). Permission will be refused if a person subject to the **s. 172** duty (often called 'the hypothetical director') would not seek to continue the claim, or if the breach has been authorised or ratified by the company (**s. 263(2)**). Assuming this stage is passed (as seems likely), the court then must consider various factors in the exercise of its discretion. Key amongst these factors are the good faith of the claimant (ie Jaime), the importance the hypothetical director would attach to continuing the claim, and whether Jaime would have a claim in his own right (**s. 263(3)**).[8] The court should take particular account of the views of any independent shareholders (**s. 263(4)**). Accordingly it would be necessary to consider the circumstances surrounding Jaime's concerns to evaluate whether permission is likely

[8] You are unlikely to have time to set out all the factors and consider each in turn (at least not in a question like this), but the examiner will want to see that you have some knowledge of them

to be granted. If permission is given Jaime is likely to be granted an indemnity against his costs (***Wallersteiner v Moir (No. 2)* [1975] 1 QB 373**), and if successful the benefit will accrue to the company, not him personally.

An alternative to a derivative claim would be for Jaime to petition on the ground that the conduct of the company's affairs has been unfairly prejudicial to his interests as a member (**CA 2006, s. 994**). Given the apparent breach(es) of duty and hostile attitude of the directors, there seem to be grounds for establishing both unfairness and prejudice (***Re Saul D Harrison & Sons plc* [1995] 1 BCLC 14; *O'Neill v Phillips* [1999] 1 WLR 1092**). If Jaime were to succeed, the court has a wide discretion as to the order it makes (**s. 996**), but by far the most common order is for the purchase of the petitioner's shares. Accordingly, assuming Jaime wants to remain in the company, this remedy may not be as attractive as pursuing a derivative claim.[9]

[9] This implicitly justifies dealing with the remedy only briefly

Conclusion

It seems probable that Jaime has no liability to pay for his shares, and so there is no risk of forfeiture. Even if Jaime was liable to pay for the shares, and the articles contained a power of forfeiture in these circumstances, any exercise of that power might well be void because of breach of **CA 2006, s. 171(b)**. Tyrion appears to be a shadow director, and it is probable he therefore owes duties to Winterfell Ltd. In taking up the opportunity offered to Winterfell Ltd, it seems likely that both Arya and Tyrion have breached their duty to the company under **s. 175**, and there could be further connected breaches of other duties (eg **s. 172**) as more than one duty can apply at one time (**s. 179**).[10] To remedy this Jaime would have to bring a derivative claim under **s. 260**, and appears to have reasonable prospects of success. Alternatively, if Jaime sought a personal rather than corporate remedy, he could consider a petition for unfair prejudice under **s. 994**.

[10] This takes the opportunity to make a minor additional point that was not included earlier on

LOOKING FOR EXTRA MARKS?

- Explore the requirements of the relevant shareholder remedies in more depth, including the relationship between the different remedies

- Indicate where facts are not clear or where more facts are necessary and why this matters for a particular issue. If you need to take alternative paths (or make a sensible assumption based on the available facts), then do so, explaining what you are doing and why

Q

QUESTION | 4

Beacho Ltd, a provider of health supplements, is in financial difficulty and is currently not able to meet its debts in full each month, although it is managing to keep trading for the moment, relying to a great extent on the forbearance of its creditors. The company has three directors, Sandy, Ceecee, and Lilo. Angelo (Ceecee's husband) also attends all board meetings and generally helps out in running the business, and calls himself director when dealing with customers. Together, Sandy, Ceecee, Lilo, and Angelo have concluded that the company should continue trading as they believe that there is a chance that they will manage to pull the company through its current difficulties and so this course of action will be the best for the company's shareholders.

Advise the directors whether this course of action risks breaching their duties to the company, and whether there would be any consequences for them should the company ultimately be placed into insolvent liquidation.

CAUTION!

- This question requires you to explore both directors' duties when the company is a going concern, and directors' liability on insolvency. Make sure you are confident on both topics, and the overlap between them
- Don't forget to consider who 'the directors' are in this scenario

DIAGRAM ANSWER PLAN

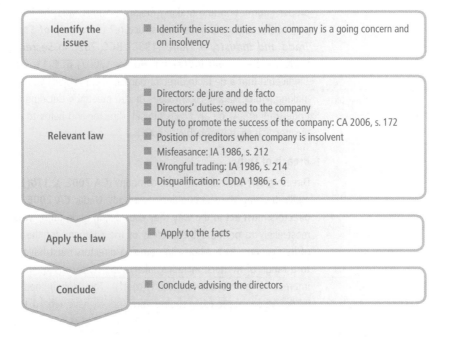

| Identify the issues | ■ Identify the issues: duties when company is a going concern and on insolvency |

| Relevant law | ■ Directors: de jure and de facto
■ Directors' duties: owed to the company
■ Duty to promote the success of the company: CA 2006, s. 172
■ Position of creditors when company is insolvent
■ Misfeasance: IA 1986, s. 212
■ Wrongful trading: IA 1986, s. 214
■ Disqualification: CDDA 1986, s. 6 |

| Apply the law | ■ Apply to the facts |

| Conclude | ■ Conclude, advising the directors |

The directors face a common dilemma: whether to keep going hoping Beacho Ltd will pull through, or admit defeat. We are told they have chosen to continue trading. If successful this would benefit shareholders (who will not lose their investment, and may get dividends later), employees (who keep their jobs), and creditors (who will eventually receive payment). But if unsuccessful, further debt will have been incurred by the time Beacho Ltd fails—additional creditor losses.[1]

[1] Starting the essay in this way shows that you understand the significance of the decision the directors are making, and also sets the scene for the later discussion on s. 172 and wrongful trading

The essay will first assess whether Angelo (as well as Sandy, Ceecee, and Lilo) is a director, and then advise whether their decision risks breaching their duties to the company (particularly **Companies Act 2006 (CA 2006), s. 172**) and the consequences for them should Beacho Ltd go into insolvent liquidation.

Directors

[2] There is too much else to pack into this question to spend time also explaining shadow directors, or to delve further into why the law imposes obligations on de facto or shadow directors

Sandy, Ceecee, and Lilo are de jure directors of Beacho Ltd. Angelo may be a de facto director. If so he would also owe duties to the company and be subject to post-liquidation consequences such as wrongful trading and disqualification.[2]

Re Hydrodam (Corby) Ltd **[1994] BCC 161 ('*Hydrodam*')** held a de facto director assumes to act as director and is held out as such by the company. Later cases, notably *Re Kaytech International plc* **[1999] BCC 390**, emphasised all relevant factors should be considered; the *Hydrodam* points are not determinative. Relevant factors include holding out and using the title of director, but also access to proper information and making major decisions: was the individual part of the corporate governing structure? (*Secretary of State for Trade and Industry v Tjolle* **[1998] BCC 282**). In *Secretary of State for Trade and Industry v Hollier* **[2007] BCC 11**, Etherton J indicated that a de facto director participates in collective decision-making, which Angelo clearly does (board meetings, deciding to continue trading). As he also calls himself director and helps to run the business,[3] it seems probable Angelo is a de facto director.

[3] Identify the relevant problem facts and link these to the authorities

Breach of Duty

Directors owe their duties to the company (**CA 2006, s. 170(1)**), normally meaning the shareholders as a body. Under **CA 2006, s. 172** directors must act in the way they consider, in good faith, 'would be most likely to promote the success of the company for the benefit of its members as a whole'. In doing so directors must have regard to a range of matters, including likely long-term consequences and interests of employees (**s. 172(1)(a)–(f)**). This 'enlightened shareholder value' approach[4] requires directors to have regard to other

[4] Show you know the basis for s. 172, albeit only in passing

stakeholder interests in order to achieve corporate success for the benefit of members.

'Creditors' do not appear in **s. 172(1)(a)–(f)** as a separate category. In any event **s. 172** does not impose duties directly owed to stakeholders. This might indicate the directors' actions do not risk breach of duty, as continuing to trade would benefit shareholders.[5] However **s. 172** is subject to any 'rule of law requiring directors, in certain circumstances, to consider or act in the interests of creditors of the company' (**s. 172(3)**). This relates to an important common law qualification (and to wrongful trading (**Insolvency Act 1986 (IA 1986), s. 214**), considered later).

In *West Mercia Safetywear Ltd v Dodd* [1988] BCLC 250, the court adopted the approach of *Kinsela v Russell Kinsela Pty Ltd* [1986] 4 NSWR 722: while shareholders could be regarded 'as' the company while the company is solvent, 'where a company is insolvent the interests of the creditors intrude'. Once a company is insolvent, creditors rather than shareholders have everything to lose or gain from directors' decision-making. Directors do not owe duties to individual creditors (*Yukong Line Ltd v Rendsburg Investments Corp* [1998] 1 WLR 294), but creditors are now the residual claimants whose interests the directors should consider.[6]

Accordingly, as Beacho Ltd is insolvent (unable to pay its debts), the directors should be considering the position of creditors rather than shareholders in deciding whether to continue. They could still conclude it is right to continue trading, but that would depend on how realistic the 'chance' of success is. Although acting in good faith, by not considering creditor interests at all, the directors are prima facie in breach of **s. 172**. Where directors have not considered the issue at all the courts have looked at whether an 'intelligent and honest' director could reasonably have believed the action to benefit the company: *Extrasure Travel Insurances Ltd v Scattergood* [2003] 1 BCLC 598.[7] That would depend on Beacho Ltd's financial position and prospects.

The directors could also be in breach of their duty of care, skill, and diligence: **CA 2006 s. 174** which is measured objectively in relation to a reasonably diligent director, with additional expectations on directors with particular knowledge, skill, or experience. Completely failing to consider the interests of creditors when the company is insolvent would seem to breach this duty (*Madoff Securities International Ltd v Raven* [2013] EWHC 3147).

The directors are unlikely at present to face any threat of action in respect of breaches of duty—there is little risk of a derivative claim in these circumstances. However the position changes if the company subsequently fails.[8]

---

[5] Link the discussion to the issue at hand

[6] If you had time you could expand this consideration and reflect on the Company Law Review's decision not to bring creditor interests explicitly into s. 172(1)

[7] How the courts should assess breach when directors have failed to consider the question at all is interesting: see further Teele Langford & Ramsay 'Directors' duties to act in the interests of the company—subjective or objective?' [2015] JBL 173

[8] This recognises the practical point about enforcement while also linking to the next section

Insolvent Liquidation—Consequences for Directors

If directors breach their duties and Beacho Ltd goes into insolvent liquidation, the liquidator (or creditor or contributory) can take action using the misfeasance procedure: **Insolvency Act 1986 (IA 1986), s. 212.** This does not create new rights or obligations, it just provides a summary procedure (**Bentinck v Fenn (1887) 12 App Cas 652**; **Cohen v Selby [2001] 1 BCLC 176**). Any defences the directors had would remain available, as would relief under **CA 2006, s. 1157**: **Re DKG Contractors Ltd [1990] BCC 903**.

Probably more significant is the potential for the liquidator to bring wrongful trading proceedings against them: **IA 1986, s. 214.** Section 214 is designed to ensure directors stop trading when a company is inexorably moving towards insolvent liquidation, the circumstance Beacho Ltd may be in.[9] A director can be ordered to contribute to the company's assets if the company continues to trade beyond the point he 'knew or ought to have concluded' (evaluated using the dual objective/subjective test in (**s. 214(4)**) that there was 'no reasonable prospect' of the company avoiding insolvent liquidation). Given the directors are already relying on the forbearance of creditors, if the financial position is not improving it seems likely they ought to conclude insolvent liquidation is all but inevitable. Realistic prospects of a change in fortune would change the position, but a blind hope of improvement is not enough (**Roberts v Frohlich [2011] 2 BCLC 625**). Directors are not liable if they 'took every step with a view to minimising potential loss' to creditors that they 'ought to have taken' (**s. 214(3)**), but relying on 'a chance' of recovery would not meet that test. On the (limited) given facts, there is a serious risk of wrongful trading by the directors. Contribution 'as the court thinks proper' (**s. 214(1)**) is a compensatory measure, the amount by which the company's assets were further depleted by the wrongful trading (**Re Produce Marketing Consortium Ltd [1989] BCLC 520**).

The directors could potentially face liability for fraudulent trading under **IA 1986, s. 213**, but the facts do not indicate intent to defraud creditors, which requires 'actual dishonesty' (**Re Patrick and Lyon Ltd [1933] Ch 786**). While fraudulent trading includes incurring debts in the knowledge they cannot be repaid (**Re William C Leitch Bros [1932] 2 Ch 71**), this is more than suggested here.

Another important consequence of the directors' continuation of trading is potential disqualification for 2–15 years under the **Company Directors Disqualification Act 1986 (CDDA 1986), s. 6** as unfit to be concerned in the management of a company. (They could also face disqualification if liable for wrongful trading: **CDDA 1986, s. 10**.) Although mere errors of judgment do not amount to unfitness (**Re Lo-Line Electric Motors Ltd [1988] Ch 447**), trading at risk of creditors is a very common factor in disqualification. This

[9] Show you understand what wrongful trading is all about and so why it is relevant to the problem

means accumulating further debt when there is no realistic prospect of repayment, often relying on the forbearance of creditors, as here: *Re Sevenoaks Stationers (Retail) Ltd* **[1991] Ch 164.** Trading whilst insolvent is not unfit in itself[10] (*Secretary of State for Trade and Industry v Taylor* **[1997] 1 WLR 407**), provided directors have properly taken the view the company has a sound future. Much therefore depends on the decision to continue trading, and whether this is objectively reasonable.

[10]It is important to recognise that 'trading at creditors' risk' is not satisfied just because the company continues trading whilst insolvent

Conclusion

The directors of Beacho Ltd (including Angelo, as a de facto director) are at risk of breaching their duties to the company (particularly **CA 2006, s. 172**) if they continue to trade, unless they carefully consider the position of creditors. With only a chance of the company surviving, then unless this chance is realistic and substantial, the directors should be considering liquidation or a rescue process such as administration. If they continue to trade and Beacho Ltd does enter into insolvent liquidation, there are real risks they would face personal liability under **IA 1986, s. 214**, and/or disqualification for unfitness under **CDDA 1986, s. 6**.

LOOKING FOR EXTRA MARKS

■ Engage with and critique the academic work relating to when duties are owed to creditors

■ Explore the connections between directors' duties and liability on insolvency, not just through the misfeasance procedure, but through the development of both sets of obligations

■ Use your time carefully to ensure you cover both halves of the question in sufficient depth

Online Resource Centre   http://www.oxfordtextbooks.co.uk/orc/qanda/

Go online for extra essay and problem questions, a glossary of key terms, online versions of all the answer plans and audio commentary on how selected ones were put together, and a range of podcasts which include advice on exam and coursework technique and advice for other assessment methods.

Skills for Success in Coursework Assessments

Some company law courses are assessed by exam only, but many will include at least some element of coursework. Coursework is simply an assessment, other than an exam, where the mark counts towards the final course grade. Preparing coursework shares some features with writing exam answers—the importance of relevance, structure, and answering the question, for example—but there are differences too.

Why Coursework?

To understand how to do well in coursework it is worth thinking about why it has been included as one of your company law assessments. First, it provides a different way to demonstrate knowledge and skills, recognising different people excel in different forms of assessment. Secondly, it provides more than one chance to gain some marks, providing some cushion against the risk of having an 'off day' on exam day.

But the most important reason for assessing by coursework is to test slightly different skills and abilities than an exam: research skills, engaging in extended argument, presentational and referencing skills, communication, and so on. Remembering that a coursework assessment is designed to test slightly different skills (or to test skills and abilities in different ways) can be helpful when thinking about what you should be aiming to demonstrate in your coursework. It should also remind you that simply producing what you would produce in an exam is unlikely to achieve great marks.

Types of Coursework

In company law coursework can take a variety of forms, depending on the inventiveness (or particular interests or habits) of the question-setter, and the learning outcomes of your course. The most common form is an essay, often of extended length. Question-setters like essays as they give the opportunity to explore a particular issue or issues in more depth. Almost as popular are problem questions, usually involving several different points and rather grey areas of law, to test your ability to identify issues and apply the law.

But company law coursework can encompass a wide range of other tasks. For example, advising a body (such as a government department) on a particular area of law, perhaps including suggestions for reform. Or drafting a briefing document for a law firm or business, preparing slides or a script for a presentation, or creating a poster for a research conference. Other exercises might be more ongoing or reflective, requiring you perhaps to engage with online discussion, contribute to a blog, or engage with topical news stories, and perhaps reflect on your learning journey as part of this. Most coursework will be individual, but you may be asked to prepare work in a pair or small group and this of course brings with it a whole range of different issues connected with team-working. While the advice that follows is primarily directed to traditional forms of coursework, such as essays and problem questions, much is equally applicable to other forms of coursework.

Things to Consider in Coursework

Assessment/marking criteria: Check the assessment or marking criteria that apply to your work—these may be generic to your university or department, or specific to your course or the assessment itself. If you don't know what they are, then ask. Keep the criteria in mind when preparing and reviewing your coursework as these are the things you will be tested against.

Identifying issues in company law: Coursework exercises may cover a range of issues, or make connections between topics, or require you to explore a topic that hasn't been covered in depth in lectures. Don't assume you know what the question is about: think, think, and think some more, and ensure you cover the points you need to. If your lecturer has highlighted particular links, personal research interests, or topical subjects during the course then it is worth considering whether any of these are relevant. To make an obvious, but necessary, point, make sure that your answer responds to the question asked, rather than discusses a topic that you wanted to write about instead.

Research: You are expected to undertake your own research into the topic(s) covered in the assessment—whatever form it takes. Any reading list you've been provided with is a great starting place. But do explore more widely—textbooks will have further reading suggestions at the end of chapters or within footnotes, and one article may well refer to another that could be worth following up. Take the opportunity to engage more deeply with the primary material too—markers love to see you've actually read a case and are not just repeating points from a textbook. Research properly (remember: Google is not a legal research tool!) and use appropriate and respected sources (eg academic journals and reform papers, not wikipedia and online student essays).

Planning your work: Start work early—if you leave things to the last minute you won't have time to think about the question, develop your ideas, and do your research. Think carefully about the structure of your work, this is a crucial step in creating a thoughtful, analytical argument, and addressing the question. Write a plan, initially in skeleton form, adding more detail as your research and ideas start to flow—modify it as necessary. With a plan in place it is usually helpful to start writing quite early, as this helps to trigger fresh ideas and highlight structural problems. But you must be willing to rewrite (or even scrap) these early efforts: your ideas will change as you write, and you need to be flexible in adapting your work.

Length: Coursework is often of a longer length than can be produced in an exam, giving you the chance to show you can maintain and develop an argument. Alternatively you may be set a short piece of coursework that can be just as challenging (if not more so) as you need to pack your brilliance into a very limited space. Use the set length of the work as an indication of the depth and breadth of the material you need to cover but remember that just because you've got more words to play with, you still need to be as precise and concise as you possibly can. Don't waste words on waffle. It hardly needs saying but do abide by any word limit you are set, many institutions impose extremely strict and severe penalties for breaching these.

Presentation: You will have much longer to prepare your coursework than you have to write an exam answer, and the marker will therefore expect to see a clearly and professionally presented piece of work. Check whether there are any particular presentational rules that you need to follow: ignoring these will, at best, annoy the marker, and at worst you may be penalised. Your work should be clearly and neatly presented, using an appropriate font and type size. Include a bibliography unless instructed not to. As part of your professional presentation, make sure your work is written clearly, with a high degree of accuracy, no ambiguity, and only sensible abbreviations.

Referencing and bibliography: Sources must be referenced properly (normally in footnotes), using a consistent format, and following any requirements (or preferences) of your department. This is both a matter of good legal practice (and may well be part of your assessment/marking criteria) and essential to avoid plagiarism. As company law is generally taught later in your legal studies, markers will expect referencing to be of a high standard—both in what you reference and how you reference. If you are not given a specific style to follow, then use OSCOLA (Oxford University Standard for the Citation of Legal Authorities). Don't leave referencing to the last minute, keep good records as you go along. Your bibliography should be prepared sensibly (OSCOLA is helpful here too), ideally with separate sections for different types of sources, and then arranged alphabetically by author surname. A bibliography should include all the material used in the preparation of your coursework, not just sources specifically referenced.

Be critical: As you prepare and write your work, challenge ideas and arguments to develop your analysis and identify other points of view. Try to avoid casual or broad statements that aren't strictly accurate. Read your work with a critical eye, and make sure you have really expressed every point as clearly as you can, remembering that the marker can't see what is in your head, s/he can only mark what is on the paper.

Checklist

- Have I addressed the question that was set, considering all the issues?
- Have I assessed, applied, and analysed the law and not simply described it?
- Have I given authority for all points of law, and referenced all uses of material, including quotes, paraphrasing, explanations, opinions, views, and ideas?
- Are my references complete, accurate, and in proper form?
- Is the work the correct length?
- Have I expressed myself clearly, precisely, concisely, and unambiguously? Have I checked for typographical errors?
- Have I reviewed my work against the assessment/marking criteria that apply to this assessment and evaluated its strengths and weaknesses?

Index

A

Account of profits 83, 91–2
Accounts 17, 113, 115, 191
Administration 201–4, 205, 245
Administrative receivership 202–4
Agents 19, 21, 144–5, 148–57, 229–30
Allotment of shares 58–9, 77, 166–7, 236–7
Annual accounts and reports 17
Articles of association 60, 240
  agents, authority of 154
  allotment of shares 58
  contract, articles as a 29, 34–8, 40–1, 44, 53, 55,
    121, 231–6
  directors 76, 102–4, 115
  enforcement 35–6, 40–1, 233, 235
  implied terms 35, 36, 37
  Model Articles 15, 38–40, 45, 76, 102–4, 154
  outsider rights/insider rights 35–7, 40
  proper purposes rule 76
  registration 15, 46
  shareholders 34–6, 40–1, 44, 48, 53, 102–4, 111,
    232–4
  voting rights 38, 40–1, 64–5
  see also Articles of association, alteration of
Articles of association, alteration of 29–35, 38–44,
  67
  'bona fide' test 32–3, 34, 37, 66, 233
  bonuses, payment of 38, 41–2
  contracting out 31
  directors, remuneration of 41
  entrenchment 31–2, 34, 37, 233
  outsider rights/insider rights 41, 233
  restrictions 31, 32–3
  retrospective or prospective effect 41–2
  share capital, alteration of 38–9, 42–3
  veto rights, enforceability of 38, 40–1, 42–3
  weighted voting rights 31–2, 33, 42–3
Attribution of liability 142, 156–60
Audit committees 106, 113
Auditors, role of 110–11, 113–14

B

Bearer shares 52
'Bona Fide' test
  allotment of shares 58
  articles, alteration of 32–3, 34, 37, 66, 233
  directors, duties of 72, 76, 81, 239, 242–3
  see also Good faith
Bonus shares 58–9
Bonuses, payment of 38, 41–2
Business names 16–17

C

Capacity 148–56
Capital see Capital maintenance doctrine; Share
  capital
Capital maintenance doctrine 163, 164–77
  distributions and other provisions 176–7
  forfeiture of unpaid shares 237–8, 240
  justifications for doctrine 173–5
  private companies 153, 164–9, 237–8
  public companies 163, 164–76
  purchase of own shares 171–2, 176–7, 179, 238
  reduction of capital 175–7, 179, 181
  share issues for non-cash consideration 164–8, 170–1
Care, skill and diligence, director's duty of
  reasonable 82, 84–8, 97, 127, 220–1, 230, 243
Charge registration system, reform of 184, 189–94
  constructive notice 192
  criminal offences 192–3
  electronic filing 192–3
  failure to register 190–3
  unregistered charges 191, 193
Charges see Charge registration system, reform
  of; Fixed and floating charges
Charities 117, 155–6, 171–2
Class rights 32, 42, 46, 50–2, 58–68
Codes see UK Corporate Governance Code
Company voluntary administration (CVA) 201–3, 205
Compensation orders 8, 223, 231

Comply or explain principle 101, 105, 107–9, 111–12

Conflicts of interest 71, 76, 87–92, 238–9

account of profits 83, 91–2

codification 83, 89

competing directorships, holding 82

declarations of interests in transactions 91–2

direct/indirect interests 91, 117

financial assistance for purchase of own shares 181

good faith 90, 239

opportunities, taking on 89–91, 239

substantial property transactions 88–9, 91–2

transactions with the company 88–9, 91–2

Constitution of the company 29–49, 76

memoranda of association 15, 31, 35

shareholder agreements 43–8

see also **Articles of association**

Continuing responsibilities 17, 79–82

Contracts

articles of association as a contract 29, 34–8, 40–1, 44, 53, 55, 121, 231–6

partnership agreements 6–7

service, contracts of 41, 108, 111, 115

shareholder agreements 33, 43–7

validity of contracts and contractual liability 147–56, 229–30

see also **Pre-incorporation contracts**

Cork Report 203

Corporate governance 100–1, 105–14

auditors, role of 110–11, 113–14

board of directors, balance on 101, 107

codes of practice 101, 105–11

deregulation 101

directors 95–6, 101, 107, 111, 114–18, 242

management of companies 104–5

remuneration 114–16

self-regulation 101, 105–10

separation of ownership and control 110–11

shareholders, role of 110–14

soft law 101, 105–10

see also **UK Corporate Governance Code**

Corporate insolvency *see* **Insolvency**

Corporate liability 142–62

attribution of liability 142, 156–60

corporate manslaughter 157, 159–60

Corporate Manslaughter and Corporate Homicide Act 2006 157, 160

criminal liability 142, 156–60

directing mind and will 142, 158–9, 160

directors 12–13, 147–8, 155–7

identification doctrine/'alter ego' approach 157, 158–9

Meridian principles 157, 159–60

personal liability 144–5, 229–30

pre-incorporation contracts 143–7

senior management 160

separate legal personality 229

tortious liability 142, 156–60

validity of contracts and contractual liability 147–56, 229–30

Corporate personality 4–28, 123, 201, 227, 229

Costs 125, 132, 240

Coursework assessment skills 246–8

Creation of companies *see* **Formation/incorporation of companies**

Creditors' interests

capital maintenance doctrine 169–70, 172, 174–7

directors 12, 70–1, 73–4, 220–3, 230, 241–5

distribution 211–19

financial assistance for purchase of own shares 179

fixed/floating charges 184, 186–92, 216

preference shares 59–62, 64, 197–8

preferential creditors 186, 212–14

pre-pack administration 200, 205

priority 61, 186–7, 211–13

secured creditors 61, 195–7, 212

shareholders 53, 59–62, 64

unsecured creditors 74, 197, 212–14

veil of incorporation, lifting/piercing the 5

winding up 61, 73–4, 195–7, 201–23, 230, 241–5

wrongful trading 220

Criminal offences *see also* **Fraud**

capital maintenance doctrine 167

charge registration system, reform of 192–3

corporate liability 142, 156–60

fines or imprisonment 181

purchase of own shares 176, 180–1

share issues for non-cash consideration 166, 167, 170–1

D

Davies Report 107

Deadlock 103, 133, 138–9

Debentures 194, 196

Derivative actions

contractual liability 149–50

directors, duties of 74, 83, 239–40, 243

Foss v Harbottle 83, 239

permission 239–40

Directors
age 107
agents 148, 154
allotment of shares 58–9, 77
articles of association 40–1, 64, 66–7, 102–4, 154
board of directors, balance on 101, 106–7
'bona fide' test 72, 76, 81, 239, 242–3
breach of duty 79–87, 91–2, 96–7, 148, 238–9,
    242–3, 245
    minority shareholder remedies 121–41
    ratification/authorisation 129–30, 176, 239
business reviews, requirement for 74
care, skill and diligence, duty of reasonable 82,
    84–8, 97, 127, 220–1, 230, 243
chair 101, 106, 108
chief executive officer and chair, separation of roles
    of 106, 108
codification 72, 76–8, 83, 84, 88
continuing duties 79, 82
contracts of service 41, 108, 111, 115
contributions 12, 218, 221–2, 246–7
corporate governance 95–6, 101, 104, 106–8, 111,
    114, 242
corporate liability 12–13, 147–8, 155–7
de facto directors 92–3, 94–7, 238, 242, 245
de jure directors 93–7, 238, 242
default powers 103
delegation 86
derivative actions 74, 83, 239–40, 243
director, definition of 95–6
diversity 101, 107
duties 70–99, 220–3, 230, 236–45
enlightened shareholder value (ESV) 71, 73, 81, 242–3
entrenching provisions 104, 111–12, 115
fiduciary duties 74, 80, 82, 89, 96
general duties 76, 80, 84, 96–7
good faith 72, 74, 77–8, 81
independence of NEDs 107–8
management of companies 76–7, 100, 101–5
minority shareholder remedies 121–41
non-executive directors (NEDs) 101, 106, 107–8, 113–18
objective/subjective test 81–3, 86–7, 221
personal liability 12–13, 223, 227, 243–6
proper purposes rule 75–9
qualifications 107
ratification/authorisation of breach 76, 239
removal of directors 83, 103–4, 111, 135–7
shadow directors 92–7, 103, 238, 240
shareholders 70–4, 101–5, 121–41, 242–3

stakeholders 70–4, 75, 111, 243
statements of duties 121
statutory duties 84–8
substantial property transactions 88–9, 91–2
whom, duties owed to 70–1
winding up/insolvency 116, 201, 218, 227, 241, 243–5
wrongful trading 85–7, 88, 96, 103, 220–3, 244–5
see also **Conflicts of interest; Directors,**
    disqualification of
Directors, disqualification of 86–8, 95
compensation orders 8, 223, 231
contribution orders 231
de facto directors 242
delegation 222–3
duration 223, 244–5
financial assistance for purchase of own
    shares 182
fraudulent trading 220
mitigation 223
negligence 222
remuneration 116
undertakings 223
unfitness 102–3, 132, 182, 222–3, 230–1, 244–5
winding up 116, 219–22, 223
wrongful trading 103, 222, 223, 244–5
Disclaimers of onerous property 215, 216–17
Disclosure 91, 115
see also **Publicity**
Disqualification *see* **Directors, disqualification of**
Distributions
capital maintenance doctrine 176–7
public companies 176–7
swelling the assets 217–19
unavailable assets 216–17
winding up 210–19
see also **Dividends**
Dividends
'bona fide' test 66
minority shareholder remedies 135–6
preference shares 52, 54, 60–1, 64, 67–8
repayment 176
unfair prejudice petitions 137–8

E

Electronic filing 15, 192–3
Employees
directors, duties of 73
employee share schemes 59

Employees (*Cont.*)
 employment-ownership 52
 remuneration, priority in winding up of 212, 214
Entity maximisation and sustainability model 75
EU law 144–6, 156, 163, 165
Exam skills 1–3
Extortionate credit transactions 218

F

Fiduciary duties 17, 74, 80, 82, 89, 96
**Financial assistance for purchase of own
  shares** 178–82
Financial Reporting Code (FRC) 106–7, 108
Fixed and floating charges
 book debts 188
 connected persons 196–7
 creditors 184, 186–92, 216
 crystallisation of floating charges 187, 189
 distinguishing between fixed and floating charges 184–9
 financial assistance for purchase of own shares 179,
   181
 floating charge, definition of 186–7
 hybrid charges 188
 insolvency 201–2, 204
 loan capital 184–9
 partnerships and sole traders 8, 186
 priority 186–7, 195–8, 210, 212–14
 validity 194–8
 winding up 186–7, 194–8, 216
Floating charges *see* **Fixed and floating charges**
Formation/incorporation of companies
 advantages and disadvantages 9–13, 102
 dates of incorporation 228
 limited liability 9–13
 names 13–14, 16–17
 officers, statements of proposed 15
 personal liability 229
 promoters 17, 18, 128–9
 registration 13–18, 228–9, 231
 shelf companies 15–16, 18, 146
 statements of capital and initial shareholdings 15
 see also **Pre-incorporation contracts**
Forms of business enterprise 4–9, 11, 13
Foss v Harbottle, **rule in**
 derivative actions 83, 123, 126, 234, 239
 majority rule principle 123, 125, 232–5
 minority shareholder remedies 121, 127–8, 233–4

 personal claims 121, 127–8
 proper claimant principle 123, 233–4
 unfair prejudice petitions 129–30
Fraud
 directors, duties of 86
 fraudulent trading 12, 218, 220, 230, 244
 minority, fraud on the 123–4, 128, 234
 veil of incorporation, lifting/piercing the 12, 20–1,
   23–5

G

Gender 101, 107
Good faith
 derivative actions 124–5, 129
 directors, duties of 72, 74, 77–8, 81, 90, 149, 155–6,
   239
 financial assistance for purchase of own shares 180–1
 winding up 213–14, 217
 see also **'Bona Fide' test**
Graham Review 200, 205
Guarantee, companies limited by 7

H

Hampel Committee 106
Holding out 94, 242

I

Identification doctrine/'alter ego' approach 157,
   158–9
Incorporation *see* **Formation/incorporation of
  companies**
Insolvency 200–25
 administration 201–4, 205, 245
 administrative receivership 202–4
 capital maintenance doctrine 174
 charge registration system, reform of 190
 company voluntary administration (CVA) 201–3, 205
 corporate rescue 200–3, 204, 245
 creditors, interests of 73–4, 243
 directors 116, 201, 227, 241, 243, 245
 floating charges 201–2, 204
 insolvency practitioners 204
 limited liability 12
 moratoriums 204
 pre-pack administration 200, 204–5

winding up 201–2, 204
see also **Winding up**
Institutional investors 107, 108, 110, 112

J

Jenkins Committee 145

K

Kay Committee 107

L

Liability see **Corporate liability**
Lifting/piercing the veil of incorporation see **Veil of incorporation, lifting/piercing the**
Limited liability 4–5, 7–13, 227
Liquidation see **Winding up**
Listed companies 108–12, 116
Loan capital 8, 11, 184–99

M

Majority rule principle 123, 125, 232–5
Management of companies 76–7, 100–5
Manslaughter see **Corporate manslaughter**
Memoranda of association 15, 31, 35
Mere facades 19–20
Minority shareholder remedies 121–41
    abuse of majority power 32–3
    articles of association 32–3, 121, 231–4
    breach of duty 121–41, 176, 239
    care, skill, and diligence, duty of 127
    corporate and personal wrongs, difference
        between 121
    decision-making 102
    directors 121–41
    discrimination between minority and majority
        shareholders 32–3
    Foss v Harbottle 47, 121, 123, 125, 127–8, 232–5
    fraud on the minority 123–4, 128
    offer to purchase shares 131–2, 134, 135–6, 139
    private companies 130
    public companies 126–30
    reflective loss, personal claims for 121, 128, 234
    shareholder agreements 47
    ultra vires or illegal activities 234

unfair prejudice petitions 33, 122, 129–38, 234–5, 240
    winding up 122, 129, 132, 138–9, 234
Misfeasance procedure 12, 97, 218, 220, 230, 244–5
Myners Report 112

N

Names of companies 13–14, 16–17
    business names 16–17
    'limited' or 'Ltd', use of 16
    prohibited names 16–17
    publicity requirements 17
    similar names 17
Negative pledge clauses 193
Negligence 12–13, 128, 222
Nomination committees 106, 108
Nominees 72, 203
Non-executive directors (NED) 101, 114–18
Novation 145–6, 229

O

Objects clauses 153–4
Offer to purchase shares 131–2, 134, 135–6, 138–9
One-person companies 19, 51, 228

P

Partnerships 6–8, 10, 13, 130, 132–3, 137–8, 186, 235
Personal liability 7–8
    corporate liability 144–5, 229–30
    directors 12–13, 223, 227, 243–6
    forms of business enterprise 5–9, 13
    insolvency 201, 227, 245
    limited liability 12–13, 227
    pre-incorporation contracts 17, 144–5, 228–30, 231
    veil of incorporation, lifting/piercing the 227–8, 231
    wrongful trading 230
Piercing the veil of incorporation see **Veil of
    incorporation, lifting/piercing the**
Pre-emption rights 55–6, 58–9
Pre-pack administration 200, 204–5
Preference shares 52, 54, 59–67, 197–8
Pre-incorporation contracts 16–17, 18, 228–9
    personal liability 17, 228–30, 231
    promoters 17, 18
    ratification/adoption 229
    signatures 228–9

Pre-incorporation contracts (*Cont.*)
   veil of incorporation, lifting/piercing
      the 228–9, 231
Pre-pack administration 200, 205
Priority
   charge registration system, reform of 190, 192
   creditors 61, 186–7, 211–13
   employee remuneration 212, 214
   expenses 212–14, 230
   fixed and floating charges 186, 194–8, 210, 212–14
   HM Revenue and Customs, debts owed to 210, 212
   preference shares 52, 60–1, 63
   preferential creditors 212–14
   winding up 61, 63, 187, 210–14
Private companies 7–9
   capital maintenance doctrine 153, 164–9, 172, 237–8
   limited liability 7–8
   minority shareholder remedies 130
   publicity 8–9
   purchase of own shares 172, 178–9
   re-registration as a public company 7, 172
   small companies 4, 8–9
Promoters 17, 18, 128–9
Proper claimant principle 123, 233–4
Proper purposes rule 58, 75–9
Public companies
   capital maintenance doctrine 163, 164–76
   corporate governance 105–11
   directors and shareholders, balance of power
      between 104–5
   distributions 176–7
   EU law 163
   listed companies 108–12, 116
   minority shareholder remedies 126–30
   purchase of own shares 171–2, 176, 178–82, 238
   re-registration as private companies 7, 172
   share issues for non-cash consideration 164–8, 170–1
Publicity requirements 8–9, 17, 46, 108, 112, 193
Purchase of own shares 171–2, 176–82, 238

R

Registration
   charges, registration of 184, 189–94
   fees 15–16, 17
   formation/incorporation of companies 13–18,
      228–9, 231
   officers, statements of proposed 15

re-registration as private companies 7, 172
shareholder agreements 45–6
statements of capital and initial shareholdings 15
Remuneration of directors 36, 114–18
   corporate governance 106, 108, 114–16
   distributions 177
   loss of office, shareholder approval of payments
      for 115
   non-executive directors 114–18
   remuneration committees 108, 116–17
Reservation of title 216, 218

S

Schemes of arrangement 202–3
Separate legal personality 4–28, 123, 201, 227, 229
Separation of ownership and control 104–5, 110–11
Share capital 8, 32, 52–4, 163–83, 233
   articles, alteration of 38–9, 42–3
   consolidation 39, 42–3
   financial assistance for purchase of own
      shares 178–82
   limited liability 10–11
   public companies and capital maintenance
      doctrine 163, 164–73, 237–8
   raising capital 5–9, 169–70
   reduction in capital 171–2, 175–7
   shareholder agreements 45
   see also **Capital maintenance doctrine**
Shareholders 50–4
   agreements 33, 43–8
   articles of association 34–6, 40–1, 53, 102, 104, 111
   corporate governance 104, 110–14
   creditors 53, 59–62, 64, 74, 243
   decision-making 102
   default powers 103
   directors 70–4, 100, 101–5, 111, 115, 242–3
   engagement 111–13, 115–16
   enlightened shareholder value (ESV) 71, 73, 81,
      242–3
   institutional investors 107, 108, 110, 112
   management of companies 100, 101–5
   personal liability 227
   primacy of shareholders 70–4, 114
   public companies 104–5, 111–12
   remedies 46–8, 68, 236–7
   stakeholders 70–4
   variation of rights 65

voting rights 31–3, 42–3, 54, 62–8, 104, 111–12, 124
see also **Minority shareholder remedies**
Shares 50–8
  allotment of shares 58–9, 77, 166–7, 236–7
  class rights 32, 42, 46, 50–2, 58–68
  discount, shares issued at a 171–2
  estoppel by share certificate 55–7
  forged transfers 55–7
  issues of shares for non-cash consideration 164–8,
    170–1
  nature of a share 50, 51–5
  nominal value 52, 53, 64
  offer to purchase shares 131–2, 134, 135–6, 138–9
  ordinary shares 52, 58–67, 68
  partly paid shares 174
  personal property, as 52–3
  pre-emption rights 55–6, 58–9
  preference shares 52, 54, 59–68, 197–8
  share purchase orders 68, 138, 240
  transfers 53, 55–7
  unfair prejudice petitions 139
  valuation 135, 139
  see also **Dividends; Share capital; Shareholders**
Shares, companies limited by 7
Shelf companies 15–16, 18, 146
Small companies 4, 8–11, 13, 44, 113, 203
Sole traders 6, 8, 10, 186
Stakeholders 66, 70–5, 105, 242–3
Stewardship Code (FRC) 107, 108, 112
Substantial property transactions 77–8, 88–9,
  91–2, 151

Tortious liability 19, 21, 142, 156–60
  see also **Negligence**
Trusts 26, 181–2, 216, 218
***Turquand's* case, rule in (internal management
  rule)** 149, 151, 155

UK Corporate Governance Code 104–12
  audit committees 106
  Cadbury Code 106–7, 116
  Combined Code 106–7
  comply or explain principle 101, 105, 107–9, 111
  Financial Reporting Code (FRC) 106–7, 108

Greenbury Code 106
non-executive directors 106, 107–8
public companies 105–11, 116
remuneration committees 106, 108
Ultra vires 148, 153, 157, 234
Unanimous consent rule (*Duomatic* principle) 44,
  48
Undervalue, transactions at an 182, 215, 217–18,
  230
Unfair prejudice
  company voluntary administration (CVA) 203
  derivative actions 122, 125, 234
  dividends, failure to pay 137–8
  Foss v Harbottle 129–30
  legitimate expectations 133, 235
  minority and majority shareholders, discrimination
    between 33
  minority shareholder remedies 122, 129–38, 234–5,
    240
  offer to purchase shares 131–2, 134, 138–9
  pre-emption rights 59
  preference shares 63, 67–8
  quasi-partnerships 130, 132–3, 137–8, 235
  share purchase orders 68, 138, 240
  shareholder agreements 47
  unfairness, scope of 122, 132–4, 137
  winding up 138–9
  separation, rights on 23–4

Veil of incorporation, lifting/piercing the 18–26
  commercial certainty/strict approach 5, 18–19,
    21–2, 25–6
  concealment principle 21, 24–5
  contractual liability 229–30
  fraud and evasion, statute must not be used
    for 20–1, 23–5
  interventionist and proactive approach 5
  lifting and piercing, distinction between 19
  limited liability 5, 10–12
  matrimonial proceedings, dishonourable conduct
    in 20–1, 23–5
  mere facades concealing the true facts 19–20
  permissive approach 18, 19, 20–2
  personal liability 227–8, 231
  pre-incorporation contracts 228–9, 231
  Salomon principle 5, 19, 21, 23, 229–30

Veil of incorporation, lifting/piercing the (*Cont.*)
 separate corporate personality 19, 21–4
 single economic unit 19, 20
Veto rights 38, 40–1, 42–3, 64, 66–8
Vicarious liability 158
Voting rights 31–3, 42–3, 54, 62–8, 104, 111–12, 124

W

Walker Report 106, 112, 117
Winding up 52, 201–2, 204, 206–19
 balance sheet test 207–8
 cash flow test 207
 commencement of liquidation 215–18
 compulsory winding up 206–7, 213, 216
 creditors 61, 73–4, 195–7, 201–23, 230, 241–5
 cross-claims 208–9
 directors 116, 218–22, 223, 242, 244
 disclaimers of onerous property 215, 216–17
 disputed debts 208
 distribution 210–19
 execution of judgments, failed 207
 fixed charges and floating charges 186–7, 216
 good faith, payments made in 213–14, 217
 grounds 206–9

improper purpose, petitions brought for an 206, 209
 inability to pay debts 195–6, 206–7, 213
 just and equitable grounds 122, 129, 132, 138–9, 209, 234
 minority shareholder petitions 122, 129, 132, 138–9, 234
 petitions 202–19
 preferences, challenging 67, 197–8, 216–18
 priority 61, 63, 187, 210–14, 230
 rejection/dismissal of petitions 206, 209
 shares 52, 61, 63
 statutory demands 206–7
 undervalue, transactions at an 215, 217–18, 230
 undisputed debts 207
 unfair prejudice petitions 138–9
 unsecured creditors 212–14, 216
 voluntary winding up 63, 216
 wrongful trading 8, 12, 218–22, 223, 244
Wrongful trading
 directors, liability of 85–7, 88, 96, 103, 220–3, 244–5
 minimise loss, steps taken to 220–1
 personal liability 230
 veil of incorporation, lifting/piercing the 12
 winding up 8, 12, 218–22, 223, 244